Structural Transformation in South Africa

Structural Transformation in South Africa

The Challenges of Inclusive Industrial Development in a Middle-Income Country

Edited by
ANTONIO ANDREONI, PAMELA MONDLIWA,
SIMON ROBERTS, AND FIONA TREGENNA

OXFORD
UNIVERSITY PRESS

Great Clarendon Street, Oxford, OX2 6DP,
United Kingdom

Oxford University Press is a department of the University of Oxford.
It furthers the University's objective of excellence in research, scholarship,
and education by publishing worldwide. Oxford is a registered trade mark of
Oxford University Press in the UK and in certain other countries

Published in the United States of America by Oxford University Press
198 Madison Avenue, New York, NY 10016, United States of America

British Library Cataloguing in Publication Data

Data available

Library of Congress Control Number: 2021937979

ISBN 978-0-19-289431-1

DOI: 10.1093/oso/9780192894311.001.0001

Printed and bound by
CPI Group (UK) Ltd, Croydon, CR0 4YY

Links to third party websites are provided by Oxford in good faith and
for information only. Oxford disclaims any responsibility for the materials
contained in any third party website referenced in this work.

Preface

Taking South Africa as an important case study of the challenges of structural transformation, this volume offers a new micro-meso level framework and evidence linking country-specific and global dynamics of change, with a focus on the current challenges and opportunities faced by middle-income countries. Detailed analyses of industry groupings and interests in South Africa reveal the complex set of interlocking country-specific factors underlying the patterns of structural transformation over three decades—from the 1990s and the first democratic election in 1994, up to 2019. The book also shows how new global drivers of change—digital industrialization, global value-chain (GVC) consolidation, and sustainability management—are reshaping structural transformation dynamics across middle-income countries like South Africa. While these new drivers of change are disrupting existing industries and interests in some areas, in others they are reinforcing existing trends and configurations of power.

By structural transformation, we refer to changes in the structure of the economy towards activities with the scope for sustained high growth in productivity, in particular through cumulative improvements. This has a strong sectoral dimension, and specifically recognizes the central importance of industrialization to a path of sustained economic growth and catching-up. We draw attention not just to the need for change in the broad sectoral composition of the economy, but also to the heterogeneity within, and linkages between, sectors. Developments such as the 'industrialization of freshness', digitalization and technological upgrading, and the changing nature of value-chain linkages between activities all point to the need for a sophisticated and nuanced approach to sub-sectors and to the diversity of activities within sectors.

Structural transformation is being recognized internationally as critical for economic development. It figures prominently on the international development agenda—such as the Sustainable Development Goals (SDGs)—and national policy debates, especially among low- and middle-income countries. This recognition is linked to a growing field of academic literature which advances the debates on industrialization and industrial policy. Some of these contributions have also started to link structural transformation to the major global drivers of change, including climate change, digitalization, and the new terms of trade and production along GVCs.

A structural transformation approach understands the relationships between economic structure and performance in dynamic terms, taking into account sector- and country-specific conditions, as well as the institutional and political economy factors that underpin the processes of structural change (or lack thereof).

South Africa offers an important case study of a middle-income country which has emphasized the importance of structural transformation, in particular through its industrial policies. Black economic empowerment policies and competition law have also been important initiatives adopted by the South African government, as it seeks to drive the structural transformation of the country and address the entrenched industrial structure and its concentration. The outcomes, however, have been mixed, as the analyses in the book suggest.

A number of chapters in the volume draw on research undertaken under the auspices of the Industrial Development Think Tank (IDTT), based at the University of Johannesburg.[1] The IDTT is a collaboration between the Department of Trade, Industry, and Competition (DTIC),[2] the Centre for Competition, Regulation, and Economic Development (CCRED) (which also houses the IDTT), and the DST/ NRF South African Research Chair in Industrial Development (SARChI Industrial Development).

The book contributes to the new literature on structural transformation and the understanding of the challenges it presents in the South African context in three main ways.

First, the book aims to engage the academic literature by developing a micro-meso level analysis of the specific processes and interdependencies underlying countries' structural transformation. This micro-structural perspective is original in its framing of structural transformation in detailed analyses of industry groupings and ecosystems, including the interests, sources of economic power, and governance. It then links these micro-meso dynamics to the global forces driving economic, institutional, and social change.

Second, the book applies this framework to South Africa. The structural transformation trajectory of South Africa presents a unique country case, given its industrial structure, concentration, and highly internationalized economy, as well as the objective of black economic empowerment. It is also an important case because of the country's economic and political role on the African continent. The South Africa case offers a prism through which to investigate what structural transformation means for middle-income countries today, in light of the rapid global changes in technologies, competition, and industrial organization.

Third, building on and expanding the analysis of the case of South Africa, the book links country-specific and global dynamics, with a focus on the new challenges and opportunities faced by middle-income countries. In particular, the book engages with three major global drivers of change: digital industrialization,

---

[1] Background working papers to those chapters are available at https://www.competition.org.za/idtt/.
[2] Formerly the Department of Trade and Industry ('the DTI').

GVC integration and consolidation, and environmental and other sustainability challenges. The book analyses the ways in which both the domestic and global drivers of structural transformation shape—and, in some cases, are shaped by—a country's political settlement and its evolution. By focusing on the political economy of structural transformation, the book disentangles the specific dynamics underlying the South African experience. In so doing, it brings to light the broader challenges faced by similar countries in achieving structural transformation via industrial policies.

Chapter 1, 'Framing Structural Transformation in South Africa and Beyond', locates the case of South Africa in the wider context of structural transformation in middle-income and other developing countries. In this chapter, Antonio Andreoni, Pamela Mondliwa, Simon Roberts, and Fiona Tregenna set out a specific analytical perspective on structural transformation. They argue that structural transformation is a complex, long-term historical process entailing both structural change in the sectoral composition of an economy, as well as broader societal changes in the productive organizations, institutions, and political economy of a country. With a focus on South Africa as a middle-income country, the chapter advances a holistic and integrated perspective on the nature and dynamics of structural transformation and highlights a specific set of interlocking critical factors and dimensions. These are: the processes of learning and productive capabilities development and accumulation; technological changes—digitalization, specifically—and their relationship with sustainability; power dynamics along GVCs and their relation to inequality; and finally, the political economy of development and the role of the state. Over the course of its democratic history, since 1994, South Africa has not undergone sustained and thoroughgoing structural transformation. Despite some areas of partial success, there has been premature deindustrialization, lack of sufficient development of the local production system alongside weak integration into GVCs, and persistent cross-cutting challenges of inclusiveness and sustainability. The authors suggest that the holistic and integrated framework developed here can help in developing a policy approach to devising feasible and effective packages of industrial policies for structural transformation.

In Chapter 2, 'Structural Change in South Africa: A Historical Sectoral Perspective', Nimrod Zalk traces how policies and institutions flowing from the post-apartheid political settlement gave rise to a range of rents and rent-like transfers, which have not been adequately invested to advance structural transformation. Rather, corporate and industrial restructuring has been associated with a 'high-profit low-investment' economy and deindustrialization. Low investment, job losses, and limited black participation in the 'commanding heights' of the economy from the mid-1990s spurred the political impetus for a stronger role for the state in the 2000s. The chapter argues that the formal introduction of industrial policy in 2007 has had some successes and has helped to avert even deeper deindustrialization. However, it has been undermined by unsupportive macroeconomic policies and a weak articulation between policies to advance black ownership and structural transformation. Rising corruption and mal-administration have further undermined structural transformation. A striking pattern of low investment and large-scale job losses in tradable sectors is evident. Manufacturing has exhibited limited structural transformation, showing a con-tinued primacy of capital-intensive chemicals and metals and unsatisfactory growth of diversified manufacturing sectors. Zalk reflects on the implications of South Africa's structural transformation experience for other middle-income developing countries. These implications include the need to elevate industrial policy and structural transformation as an economy-wide imperative rather than a 'microeconomic' one, and recognize that the failure to structurally transform can fuel the conditions for unproductive rent-seeking and corruption to flourish.

Chapters 3 to 7 analyse structural transformation in South Africa through industry case studies. Chapter 3, 'Metals, Machinery, and Mining Equipment Industries in South Africa: The Relationship between Power, Governance, and Technological Capabilities', by Antonio Andreoni, Lauralyn Kaziboni, and Simon Roberts focuses on the metals, machinery, and mining equipment industries, which have been at the heart of South Africa's industrial ecosystem. Their central position is associated with the long-term importance of mining, and with which there are extensive demand- and supply-side linkages. This chapter reviews key turning points in the development and restructuring of these value chains in post-apartheid South Africa, from 1994 to 2019. The overall record is of a basic steel industry that has performed better in terms of value added relative to the more diversified downstream industries, despite government industrial policy targeting more labour-intensive downstream industries. The downstream machinery and equipment industry struggled to compete with imports in the 2000s and 2010s and only partially engaged with digitalization. In explaining these developments, the authors critically examine the grand bargains struck by the state, with the main company producing basic steel and the use of procure-ment as a demand-side industrial policy. The chapter also provides micro-level evidence of the evolving relationships between mining houses; engineering, pro-curement, and construction management services companies; and input suppliers along the value chain. Overall, it is argued that the relatively poor performance of this industry grouping in South Africa has been due to power asymmetries along the value chains, upstream concentration, high levels of fragmentation in the domestic ecosystem, the lack of key institutional ingredients, and poor policy design. Lessons for resource-endowed middle-income countries are discussed, and policy challenges for upgrading and diversification are presented.

Next, the plastic industry is discussed in Chapter 4, 'Leveraging Linkages for Developing Plastic Products: An Assessment of Backward Input Linkages from Polymers and Forward Output Linkages to the Automotive Industry', by Jason Bell,

Lorenza Monaco, and Pamela Mondliwa. The chapter considers the role of linkages, lead firm strategies, industrial policies, and value-chain governance in the performance of the South African plastic products industry. The chapter assesses the extent to which the linkages of the plastic products sub-sector backwards with the polymers industry, and forwards to plastic automotive components, have influenced the performance of the industry. The forward linkages to the automotive industry are assessed through a comparative assessment of technological capability accumulation in South Africa with its relatively more successful upper-middle-income counterpart, Thailand. The analysis shows that vertical integration and horizontal collaborations through clusters, as well as the different roles played by multinational corporations and the state, have exerted a stronger influence on the accumulation of capabilities in Thailand, compared with South Africa. The assessment of backward linkages to polymers shows how the linkage development in South Africa has been undermined by market power in the upstream polymers industry. This is coupled with a failure of industrial policy to support diversified industries such as plastic products, including through addressing the challenges related to input prices and supporting the accumulation of capabilities.

Chapter 5, 'Government Policy in Multinational-Dominated Global Value Chains: Structural Transformation within the South African Automotive Industry', by Justin Barnes, Anthony Black, and Lorenza Monaco focuses on the automotive industry. Through a series of government plans, undeniable success has been achieved, especially in terms of its export orientation. The industry uses efficient technologies and is integrated into global markets. However, major structural weaknesses exist. Export growth has not been accompanied by increasing local content, investment has been modest, and employment creation insignificant. Vehicle and component imports into the domestic market are high and the industry runs significant trade deficits. Most core technologies are imported, including advanced power trains and electronics. This chapter considers the structural impediments to the sector's development, as well as issues related to ownership and power relations between the state and multinational firms. Analysing the potential for further localization and the deepening of the supply chain, the chapter considers global technology developments, domestic productive capabilities, and power dynamics in the GVC. The chapter argues that state–business bargaining dynamics have negatively affected this potential. While efforts to deepen the supply chain would allow for more sustainable growth, the achievement of such goals is impossible without concerted commitment from all stakeholders.

In Chapter 6, 'The Industrialization of Freshness and Structural Transformation in South African Fruit Exports', Christopher Cramer and Shingie Chisoro-Dube provide a new perspective on the agricultural value chain. Economists have historically tended to identify industrial processes and technological sophistication with manufacturing, and not with agriculture. This chapter illustrates the substantial scope to apply sophisticated technologies and industrial processes necessary to shift resources out of low-productivity activities into higher-productivity activities, i.e. to generate 'structural change', in the production of 'fresh' agricultural export production. Leveraging the concept of the 'industrialization of freshness', this chapter uses evidence from South Africa's fresh-fruit industry to show how advances in technology have been a key mechanism through which structural transformation towards high-value fruit has occurred in the industry. Cramer and Chisoro-Dube also show how building capabilities to harness technological changes is necessary for increased market access through enabling producers to keep up with escalating quality standards; to comply with the many—and complex—sanitary and phytosanitary requirements; and to adapt to climate change. However, despite evidence of dynamism in fruit production, effective structural transformation in the South African fruit industry has been limited by widespread underinvestment in infrastructure—ports, rural internet capacity, water infrastructure, and technical capacity.

Chapter 7, 'Sustainability and Green Capital Accumulation: Lessons from the South African Wine Value Chain', highlights how sustainability and green capital accumulation go hand in hand. Stefano Ponte argues that these operate on the back of a structural logic that allows the extraction of value from producers as they attempt to improve their environmental performance. The case study of the wine industry in South Africa is, at a superficial level, a success story of economic and environmental upgrading and of improved international competitiveness. However, Ponte analyses how the growing concentration of the wine industry globally has come together with increased bargaining power by retailers and international merchants, which is leading to a cascade of squeezed margins upstream all the way to grape and wine suppliers. This chapter shows that: (1) sustainability is used opportunistically by global 'lead firms' for marketing, reputational enhancement, and risk management purposes; (2) South African value-chain actors and institutions have invested heavily in portraying the industry and individual companies as caring for the environment; and (3) major economic and environmental upgrading processes in the South African wine value chain have taken place, but have not led to positive economic outcomes for most domestic players. Collectively, these lessons suggest a combined process of capital accumulation by lead firms, coupled with a process of supplier squeeze.

The chapters that follow turn to a number of cross-cutting social, institutional, and power dynamics that underpin structural transformation. These are central to the South African experience, but are also relevant to understanding the challenges of structural transformation in other middle-income countries. Chapter 8, 'Structural Transformation, Economic Power, and Inequality in South Africa', examines how economic power, understood as control over accumulation, has influenced the poor progress of structural transformation in South Africa.

Sumayya Goga and Pamela Mondliwa argue that this, in turn, has impacted on inequality through income and wealth effects. The chapter asserts that the failure to diversify and develop downstream capabilities in manufacturing in South Africa reflects, among other things, the entrenched advantages of incumbent upstream firms, as well as the lack of a policy agenda for transformation that incorporates a recognition of the economic power of these upstream firms. The inability to change the patterns of accumulation underlies the persistent inequality in income and wealth. The chapter involves an analysis of interests in the South African economy within key industry groupings (specifically the metals and plastics value chains), and how these interests have set agendas and shaped policy and regulation to set the rules of the game for the benefit of upstream firms. Goga and Mondliwa's analysis shows that economic structure is a source of economic power, and that the relative strength of the upstream industries means that their interests are better served than those of diversified downstream industries.

In Chapter 9, 'Black Economic Empowerment, Barriers to Entry, and Economic Transformation in South Africa', Thando Vilakazi and Teboho Bosiu discuss the key issue of black economic empowerment in relation to structural transformation. One of the main challenges of South Africa's democratic project has been supporting the effective participation of the previously excluded black majority in the economy. The broad-based black economic empowerment (BBBEE) policy, as the primary tool employed to drive racial transformation, is assessed and found to have had a limited impact, although there has been some progress. The chapter considers the link between structural transformation and black economic empowerment in three key parts. First, relevant literature is drawn on to build the argument that inclusion matters for structural transformation. Second, is an examination of the factors that have underpinned the challenges with the implementation of BBBEE to open up the economy for broader participation, including its limited focus on key barriers to entry, and the implications for structural transformation in South Africa. Third, the chapter presents a case study based on a survey of applicants under the government's 'black industrialists scheme' as a critical evolution from, and alternative to, the approach followed with BBBEE, as it is able to contribute to both racial and structural transformation of the economy. The chapter concludes with a reflection on the roles of black economic empowerment and the black industrialists scheme, barriers to entry, and structural transformation of the economy.

Chapter 10, 'Profitability without Investment: How Financialization Undermines Structural Transformation in South Africa', takes up the issue of finance. Antonio Andreoni, Nishal Robb, and Sophie van Huellen argue that sustained investment in productive capabilities and fixed-capital formation is a key driver of inclusive and sustainable structural transformation. Both historically and compared to other middle-income countries, South Africa has performed poorly in terms of sustaining domestic-productive investments. This failing has coexisted with the development of a stock market with the second-highest level of capitalization over GDP in the world, and high levels of profitability across several economic sectors. This chapter provides new evidence on the specific ways in which the financialization of non-financial corporations in South Africa has resulted in low investment performances, focusing on two large, publicly listed corporations operating across different economic sectors between 2000 and 2019. The analysis shows that despite sector heterogeneities, (1) corporations have increasingly financed operations, capital expenditure, and distributions to shareholders with debt; (2) the US dollar-denominated share of this debt has grown rapidly, exposing corporations to increased exchange and interest rate risk; and (3) distributions to shareholders, driven by dividends rather than share repurchases, have risen markedly. The authors attribute these financialization dynamics to the distribution of power in the domestic political economy and the subordinate nature of South Africa's integration with global finance. Driving financialization, these two mutually reinforcing factors have undermined the translation of profits into domestic investment, reducing its capacity to drive structural transformation.

Chapter 11, 'The Middle-Income Trap and Premature Deindustrialization in South Africa', by Antonio Andreoni and Fiona Tregenna takes an international comparative perspective on structural change in South Africa. South Africa has been experiencing premature deindustrialization and poor growth over an extended period of time. Premature deindustrialization is among the key factors locking many middle-income countries in a trap of stagnant growth and thwarting their catching-up with advanced economies. Premature deindustrialization shrinks middle-income countries' opportunities for technological development, and also their capacity to add value in GVCs, which reduces their scope for the sustained increases in productivity required for catching up. Andreoni and Tregenna analyse key structural factors contributing to a 'middle-income technology trap'. Throughout the chapter, reference is made to the divergent experiences of three middle-income comparator countries to South Africa: Brazil, China, and Malaysia. Building on this framework, the chapter presents new econometric evidence of premature deindustrialization in South Africa through an international comparative lens. By studying the relationship between countries' GDP per capita and their shares of manufacturing in total employment, the authors identify the level of GDP per capita and share of manufacturing in total employment associated with the 'turning point' at which the share of manufacturing levels off and begins to decline. The chapter groups countries into four categories based on their (de)industrialization dynamics, and identifies possible premature deindustrializers, among which South Africa is found. South Africa's lack of structural transformation helps to explain its failure to escape the middle-income technology trap.

The issues of technological upgrading, and specifically digitalization, are taken up in Chapter 12, 'Digitalization, Industrialization, and Skills Development: Opportunities and Challenges for Middle-Income Countries', by Antonio Andreoni, Justin Barnes, Anthony Black, and Timothy Sturgeon. The world economy is undergoing a period of structural and technological transformation, driven by the increasing digitalization of economic and social life. Digitalization is being experienced differentially across the globe, reflecting the different opportunities it offers as well as the particular challenges countries face in digitalizing their economic systems. This chapter looks at the opportunities and challenges of digital industrialization through the lens of the South African case. In South Africa, digitalization is occurring in an economy that has prematurely deindustrialized, where the digital capability gap in terms of digital infrastructures and skills is wide, and where organizations need significant investments to retrofit their existing systems. Despite this, South Africa has islands of excellence in which firms are embracing the opportunities provided by digitalization to achieve greater efficiency, process innovation, and supply-chain integration. These examples point to what is possible, while at the same time revealing gaps and shortcomings. The potential and shortcomings are evident both across firms (in terms of their investment rates), within GVCs (domestic firms, engagement with multinationals), and across public institutions and industrial policies. The development of digital skills in cross-cutting fields such as data science and software engineering, as well as transversal technologies in complementary services, are identified as particularly important. The chapter concludes with a discussion of the policy implications for South Africa and beyond.

In Chapter 13, 'Global Value Chains, "In-Out-In" Industrialization, and the Global Patterns of Sectoral Value Addition', Antonio Andreoni, Keun Lee, and Sofia Torreggiani focus on the role of GVCs in structural transformation. Since the emergence and diffusion of regional and GVCs, production-chain development has always played a key role in shaping countries' structural transformation. Over the years, the geographical breadth, length, and depth of these chains has changed significantly. Building on the catching-up experience of South Korea and China, this chapter investigates the conditions and processes under which today's catching-up economies can benefit from integrating into GVCs. The chapter empirically documents how successful catching-up has been associated with an 'in-out-in' industrialization process of GVC integration: where countries first 'couple' by entering GVCs in low value-added segments, then 'decouple' by building domestic supply chains and upgrading existing local capabilities, and finally 'recouple' by performing high value-addition activities in GVCs. The authors also assess the extent to which middle-income countries like South Africa have managed to increase their sectoral value addition in this global production settlement over the last two decades. The chapter finds that today's middle-income countries have experienced different fortunes at the country and sectoral level when it comes to increasing domestic value addition. The chapter concludes, reflecting on possible future scenarios arising in the post-Covid-19 international context and the emergence of potential new industrialization models.

The last two chapters of the book engage with the political economy of structural transformation and advance a new industrial policy framework and agenda for South Africa. Chapter 14, 'The Political Economy of Structural Transformation: Political Settlements and Industrial Policy in South Africa', examines the evolution of the political settlement in South Africa. Pamela Mondliwa and Simon Roberts argue that this is critical for understanding its structural transformation path as well as for the reconfiguration of industrial policy. The success or failure of countries to drive structural change is understood in terms of the extent to which the political settlement, or governing coalition of interests, supports the growth of diversified industrial activities with higher levels of productivity. The chapter analyses why and how, despite the developmental agenda of the ruling African National Congress (ANC), South Africa has failed to achieve its production transformation. According to Mondliwa and Roberts, the political settlement forged around South Africa's transition from apartheid to democracy has created the conditions for a corporate restructuring of the economy characterized by high profitability, despite low investments. This has involved power entrenchment in large incumbent organizations and coalitions of rentieristic interests, which have undermined necessary industrial policy enforcement. Persistently high unemployment and inequality have fuelled dissatisfaction and contestation over the core objectives of a more developmentalist state. Industrial policies have also been undermined by the fragmentation of the state, leading to misaligned policies.

Finally, Chapter 15, 'Towards a New Industrial Policy for Structural Transformation', by Antonio Andreoni, Pamela Mondliwa, Simon Roberts, and Fiona Tregenna analyses some central challenges and policy implications relating to structural transformation in South Africa and in middle-income countries more broadly. The South African case provides important insights into the challenges facing middle-income countries as they attempt to build productive capabilities to drive their structural transformation. Despite South Africa having opened up and integrated with the global economy, liberalizing trade and financial markets, it has remained stuck in relatively lower-productivity activities with weak diversification of exports. There continues to be a strong path dependency where markets are structured and shaped by previous investment decisions, state interventions, and entrenched rentieristic interests. The authors identify five important lessons. First, premature deindustrialization needs to be arrested and reversed, including the growth and upgrading of the manufacturing sector. Second, the technological changes underway with the digitalization of economic activities mean that developing an industrial ecosystem of firms with effective links to public institutions is critical. Third, inclusive industrialization depends on achieving structural change and dismantling barriers to entry to allow a new system of accumulation to emerge. Fourth, structural transformation depends on a country's political settlement, specifically whether coalitions of interests that support the organization of industries for long-term investment in capabilities hold sway. Fifth, purposive and coordinated industrial policies are central to achieving these goals and improving the country's productivity and competitiveness. These are applied to identify key considerations for industrial strategy in South Africa, including confronting concentration and the urgent implications of the climate crisis, to 'build back better' from the Covid-19 pandemic.

We hope that this volume will make an important contribution to research and policy debates on structural transformation, in South Africa, and in middle-income countries and developing countries more widely.

Antonio Andreoni, Pamela Mondliwa, Simon Roberts, and Fiona Tregenna

Acknowledgements

In addition to the authors, a number of people have contributed to this volume. We would like to thank our Commissioning Editor at Oxford University Press, Adam Swallow, for his support and guidance of the project. A number of the chapters draw on research undertaken under the auspices of the Industrial Development Think Tank (IDTT). We are very grateful for the generous financial support from the Department of Trade, Industry, and Competition (DTIC) to the IDTT, to the IDTT Steering Committee that oversaw that research, to the researchers who contributed to the working papers on which some of the chapters drew, and to all those who commented on the research in various IDTT workshops and events. The University of Johannesburg provided valuable support in hosting the IDTT and the Centre for Competition, Regulation, and Economic Development (CCRED) and the South African Research Chair (SARChI) in Industrial Development provided the institutional home for the IDTT at the university. We are indebted to Catherine Garson for her superb editing of all the chapters, as well as for her indispensable role in supporting the management of the book project. Lastly, we would like to thank all the reviewers who provided detailed and helpful peer reviews of the draft chapters; these reviews contributed substantially to improving the quality of the chapters.

Contents

List of Figures   xxi
List of Contributors   xxiii
Endorsements   xxvii

1. Framing Structural Transformation in South Africa and Beyond   1
   Antonio Andreoni, Pamela Mondliwa, Simon Roberts,
   and Fiona Tregenna

2. Structural Change in South Africa: A Historical Sectoral Perspective   28
   Nimrod Zalk

3. Metals, Machinery, and Mining Equipment Industries in
   South Africa: The Relationship between Power, Governance,
   and Technological Capabilities   53
   Antonio Andreoni, Lauralyn Kaziboni, and Simon Roberts

4. Leveraging Plastics Linkages for Diversification: An Assessment
   of Backward Linkages from Polymers and Forward Linkages to
   the Automotive Industry   78
   Jason Bell, Lorenza Monaco, and Pamela Mondliwa

5. Government Policy in Multinational-Dominated Global Value
   Chains: Structural Transformation within the South African
   Automotive Industry   100
   Justin Barnes, Anthony Black, and Lorenza Monaco

6. The Industrialization of Freshness and Structural Transformation
   in South African Fruit Exports   120
   Christopher Cramer and Shingie Chisoro-Dube

7. Sustainability and Green Capital Accumulation: Lessons from
   the South African Wine Value Chain   143
   Stefano Ponte

8. Structural Transformation, Economic Power, and Inequality
   in South Africa   165
   Sumayya Goga and Pamela Mondliwa

9. Black Economic Empowerment, Barriers to Entry, and Economic
   Transformation in South Africa   189
   Thando Vilakazi and Teboho Bosiu

10. Profitability without Investment: How Financialization
    Undermines Structural Transformation in South Africa   213
    Antonio Andreoni, Nishal Robb, and Sophie van Huellen

11. The Middle-Income Trap and Premature Deindustrialization in
    South Africa   237
    Antonio Andreoni and Fiona Tregenna

12. Digitalization, Industrialization, and Skills Development:
    Opportunities and Challenges for Middle-Income Countries   261
    *Antonio Andreoni, Justin Barnes, Anthony Black,
    and Timothy Sturgeon*

13. Global Value Chains, 'In-Out-In' Industrialization, and the
    Global Patterns of Sectoral Value Addition   286
    Antonio Andreoni, Keun Lee, and Sofia Torreggiani

14. The Political Economy of Structural Transformation: Political
    Settlements and Industrial Policy in South Africa   312
    Pamela Mondliwa and Simon Roberts

15. Towards a New Industrial Policy for Structural Transformation   337
    *Antonio Andreoni, Pamela Mondliwa, Simon Roberts,
    and Fiona Tregenna*

Index   363

List of Figures

1.1 Manufacturing value added, changes in selected sub-sectors   8

1.2 Merchandise export shares   13

1.3 South Africa's export basket, 2018   15

3.1 Metals to machinery and equipment value chain   55

3.2 Metals, machinery, and equipment trade balances, nominal US$ millions   59

3.3 Machinery and equipment imports of selected SADC countries from South Africa versus the rest of the world, in US$ billions   60

4.1 The petrochemical value chain   83

4.2 Turning point in the performance of the plastic products industry   94

5.1 Value addition breakdown of global and South African automotive supply chains   113

6.1 Value of fruit exports from South Africa and competitors, 2001–2018   126

6.2 Volume of avocado exports from South Africa and competitors   126

6.3 Volume of berries exports from South Africa and competitors   127

6.4 Volume of exports from South Africa and competitors: clementines and mandarins   128

6.5 Volume of exports from South Africa and competitors: lemons and limes   128

6.6 South Africa's fruit export markets: 2001 and 2018   129

10.1 Fixed capital formation and stock market capitalization   222

10.2 Profitability and dividend payments   223

10.3 Composition of distributions to shareholders, 2000–9 vs. 2010–19   229

10.4 Sources and uses of funds in Sasol and Shoprite (2000–19)   229

11.1 South Africa and comparator countries: % of US GDP per capita 1960–2019   241

11.2 Domestic value-added content of South African exports by major manufacturing sub-sectors   243

11.3 Capturing high-value niches and the need for multiple sets of complementary capabilities   244

11.4 Estimated relationship between GDP per capita and manufacturing share of employment, 2015   249

11.5 Characterization of international trends in deindustrialization   250

12.1 Data flow across key transversal technologies in the digital economy   264

12.2 Digital industrial policy for South Africa   282

13.1 Backward participation in manufacturing GVCs by macro-regions, 1995–2011   295

13.2 Backward participation in manufacturing GVCs, South Africa, and selected emerging and transition economies, 1995–2011   297

13.3 The 'in-again' phase in South Korea: backward integration in medium-high-tech sectoral value chains   299

13.4 The 'out' phase in China: backward integration in medium-high-tech sectoral value chains   300

13.5 Backward participation in manufacturing GVCs: South Africa and other middle-income countries   303

14.1 Trade and the real effective exchange rate   318

14.2 Portfolio and FDI inflows, outflows, and JSE capitalization   319

List of Contributors

Editors

Antonio Andreoni is Associate Professor of Industrial Economics at University College London (UCL) and Head of Research at the UCL Institute for Innovation and Public Purpose. He is also Visiting Associate Professor in the Fourth Industrial Revolution, at the South African Research Chair in Industrial Development, University of Johannesburg and Research Associate at SOAS University of London. He has researched and published extensively on issues of production, technology and innovation dynamics; structural change, global value chains and industrial development; financialisation and corruption; governance and industrial policy. He also consults to international organizations such as UNIDO, UNCTAD, UNDP, ILO, UN ECA, World Bank, and OECD. Antonio holds a PhD from the University of Cambridge and is an Editor of *The European Journal of Development Research*.

Pamela Mondliwa is a Senior Managing Consultant at Berkeley Research Group (BRG) and Research Associate at the Centre for Competition, Regulation, and Economic Development (CCRED), University of Johannesburg. Pamela has worked across consulting, academia, and policy. She has researched and published on issues related to competition, industrial development, industrial policy, economic regulation, and inequality in Southern Africa. Pamela was previously a Senior Researcher at CCRED, where she led the research on industrial development and an Economist at the Competition Commission of South Africa. Pamela obtained an MCom in Economics from the University of Johannesburg.

Simon Roberts is Professor of Economics at the University of Johannesburg, where he founded CCRED, and also Visiting Professor at the Institute for Innovation and Public Purpose at University College London (UCL). He has researched and published extensively on issues of industrial development, trade, regional value chains, competition, and economic regulation in Southern and East Africa. Simon was chief economist at the Competition Commission South Africa, an economics director at the UK's Competition and Markets Authority and has provided advice on competition issues to authorities in many African countries and to international organizations.

Fiona Tregenna holds the DSI/NRF South African Research Chair (SARChI) in Industrial Development and is a Professor of Economics at the University of Johannesburg. She has a PhD in Economics from the University of Cambridge. She has received various awards and grants for her research, and has led major research projects. Fiona is a part-time Member of the Competition Tribunal where she adjudicates competition (antitrust) cases, and serves on a number of high-level boards, advisory panels, and councils, including the Presidential Economic Advisory Council. She consults to various research institutes and international organizations such as UNIDO, UNCTAD, and the ILO. Her primary research interest is in issues of structural change, industrial development, deindustrialization, and industrial policy.

Contributors

Justin Barnes is Executive Director of the Toyota Wessels Institute for Manufacturing Studies and an Associate Professor at the Gordan Institute of Business Science, University of Pretoria. He is a recognized international manufacturing expert and has worked on industrial policies in over thirty countries. He has advised the South African government on various industrial policies, most notably in the automotive sector.

Jason Bell is a Researcher at CCRED where he writes on topics related to industrial policy, political economy, economic power, and global and regional value chains. He has published in peer-reviewed journals such as *Development Southern Africa*, book chapters, as well as doing work for the World Bank.

Anthony Black is Professor in the School of Economics at the University of Cape Town and Director of Policy Research in International Services and Manufacturing (PRISM). He is a development economist whose main fields of expertise are industrial development, foreign investment, and trade. He has been a leading advisor to the government on South Africa's programme to develop its automotive industry.

Teboho Bosiu is a Researcher at CCRED. He has worked extensively on value chains, covering sectors such as agroprocessing, chemicals, poultry, and fertilizer. His work also looks at the role of development finance on South Africa's industrialization and black economic empowerment (BEE). He has published several working papers, a book chapter, and a journal article.

Christopher Cramer is Professor of the Political Economy of Development at SOAS University of London. He has made important contributions on various aspects of development in Africa.

Shingie Chisoro-Dube is a Researcher at CCRED. She has worked on issues of industrial development, regional value chains, and competition in agriculture and agro-processing in Southern and East Africa. She has published in the *Development Southern Africa Journal* and co-authored book chapters in the *HSRC Press*.

Sumayya Goga is a Senior Researcher at CCRED, where she leads research on structural transformation and inequality. She has published in various journals, including the *Journal of African Economies* and the *South African Journal of Economics.*

Lauralyn Kaziboni is a consultant at DNA Economics, research associate at CCRED, University of Johannesburg. Her research focuses on investigating issues in value chain analysis, regional integration, and sustainable development. She holds an MCom in Development Economics from the University of Johannesburg.

Keun Lee is Professor of Economics at Seoul National University, and Editor of *Research Policy*. He is a leading thinker in the economics of catching up and has widely researched and published on middle-income countries. He was awarded the Schumpeter Prize in 2014.

Lorenza Monaco is a Researcher for the International Research Network on the Automobile Industry (GERPISA) at the ENS Paris Saclay and a Senior Research Associate at the South African Research Chair (SARChI) in Industrial Development, University of Johannesburg.

She holds a PhD from SOAS, University of London. Her research focuses on industrial development & policy, on the auto industry and on employment issues in emerging economies.

Stefano Ponte is Professor of International Political Economy at Copenhagen Business School, and the Director of the Centre for Business and Development Studies. He is also a Distinguished Visiting Professor at the University of Johannesburg. His research focuses on transnational economic and environmental governance in Africa and the Global South.

Nishal Robb is a research working at CCRED, University of Johannesburg. He completed his MSc in the Economics Department at SOAS University of London. He works on education, labour-intensive manufacturing, illicit financial flows, industrial policy, and financialization.

Timothy Sturgeon is a Senior Research Affiliate at the Industrial Performance Center at MIT. His research focuses on the process of global integration, with an emphasis on offshoring and outsourcing practices in the electronics, automotive, and services industries. He works actively with policymakers in international development agencies, industrialized countries, and developing countries on effective policy responses to global integration.

Sofia Torreggiani is a PhD Candidate in Development Economics at SOAS University of London. Her research focuses on international trade, global production networks and industrial development, with special reference to the issues faced by emerging countries.

Sophie van Huellen is Lecturer in Economics at SOAS University of London. She has researched and published extensively on financial markets, commodity and food prices, and international economics with a focus on sub-Saharan Africa and West Africa in particular.

Thando Vilakazi is Executive Director at CCRED. He leads research on regional integration, barriers to entry, competition and inclusive growth, and industrial development. He holds a PhD from the University of Johannesburg.

Nimrod Zalk is Industrial Development Policy and Strategy Advisor at the South African Department of Trade and Industry, and has been centrally involved in industrial policy for many years. He holds a PhD from SOAS University of London.

Endorsements

This volume offers highly original perspectives on structural transformation in South Africa. It provides sophisticated analyses of productive transformation at the sectoral level, based on profound understanding of national political economy and global technological trends. It is a unique contribution to industrial policy making in middle-income countries.

—Ha-Joon Chang, Reader, University of Cambridge

Can industrial policy achieve structural transformation in a developing country in the 21st century? This fascinating volume identifies new and emerging constraints in the context of South Africa, including GVCs, automation, digitalisation and much else—and provides a positive agenda for economic policy in the new context. A must-read for policy makers and researchers on development.

—Jayati Ghosh, Professor of Economics, University of Massachusetts, Amherst

The policy challenges facing middle-income countries have, for far too long, been neglected by the development community, squeezed out by an undue focus on countries where extreme poverty is the norm and a misguided faith in attracting more foreign investment as a guarantee to catching up. Drawing on the South African experience, this volume is a timely contribution to filling the gap. Blending heterodox economic analysis with selected sectoral case studies, the different chapters examine the damaging legacy of the Washington Consensus on the South African economy and make a clear and convincing case for putting industrial policy back at the centre of development strategy, not only to correct past failures but to manage the new challenges arising from an increasingly digitalized, monopolized and environmentally fragile world. While the South African economy takes centre stage in the volume, the analysis and policy recommendations speak to a wider audience across the developing world. A valuable read.

—Richard Kozul-Wright, Director of the Globalisation and Development Strategies Division, United Nations Conference on Trade and Development (UNCTAD)

This book is a reminder of the unfinished business of building economies that can deliver shared prosperity. This is especially so for South Africa, a middle-income country that has faced economic stagnation in the decade following the Great Recession. In its earlier years, post-apartheid South Africa scored significant achievements in extending basic services to the majority of the population and reversing the poor macroeconomic metrics inherited from the apartheid regime. But to deliver sustained and inclusive growth, the fundamental structure of the economy must be tackled. The deep research presented in this book provides decision-makers across various sectors of society with the material to think deeply about how the South African economy creates value and the nature of its integration in a rapidly evolving global economy.

—Trudi Makhaya, Economic Advisor to the President of South Africa,
President Cyril Ramaphosa

As we navigate an increasingly uncertain terrain, this book offers a comprehensive and insightful look into the challenges South Africa faces in the quest for greater inclusive industrial development. The inclusion of industry experts alongside in-depth investigations by academics provides a realistic analysis of the current landscape with future prospects for transformation. This is an important and powerful contribution to steering debates away from rhetoric towards reality.

—Tshilidzi Marwala, Vice Chancellor and Principal of
the University of Johannesburg

A highly original and coherent volume blending theories of developmental and entrepreneurial state, with impeccably researched deep dives into the South African economy and society. A timely mine of new evidence to design policies and shape markets towards inclusive and sustainable development.

—Mariana Mazzucato, Professor, UCL Institute for Innovation
and Public Purpose

'Structural Transformation in South Africa is a timely and distinct book for researchers and policymakers who are interested in structural transformation of developing and emerging economies. Diverse leading scholars present deep analysis anchored in rich development concepts with a practical application to South Africa and linking to the challenges of middle-income countries and global dynamics. South Africa presents a particularly riveting case as one of the most advanced economies in Africa, with a large confluence of factors shaping its industrial policy. The book's emphasis on new industrial policy geared to structural transformation within the context of global drivers that shape it, and the extensive use of rich empirical data add to its significance.'

—Arkebe Oqubay, Minister and Special Advisor to the
Prime Minister of Ethiopia

This volume makes a critical contribution to improving our understanding of industrial development and structural change in developing countries. Through in-depth analyses of key industries and policy issues in South Africa, it develops a coherent, ambitious and well-grounded agenda for rethinking industrial policy in South Africa and other middle-income countries.

—Imraan Valodia, Professor and Dean, University
of Witwatersrand, South Africa

1

Framing Structural Transformation in South Africa and Beyond

*Antonio Andreoni, Pamela Mondliwa,
Simon Roberts, and Fiona Tregenna*

1.1 Introduction

Over the course of its democratic history, since 1994, South Africa has struggled to sustain an adequate process of structural transformation, to move from sectors of low to high productivity and complexity, and to upgrade to higher value-added activities within sectors. The structural transformation that has occurred has been discontinuous and uneven. Ongoing premature deindustrialization has negatively affected the long-term performance and potential of the economy. Despite some areas of relative success, overall growth and upgrading in industries have been constrained by low levels of investments. Firms have struggled to build their productive capabilities, diversify their production activities, and develop their domestic supply chains. Given this weakening industrial base, the engagements with global value chains (GVCs) and the emerging technologies of the so-called fourth industrial revolution have been limited, and have generally not delivered the desired outcomes. The imperatives of greater inclusion and environmental sustainability are additional and major cross-cutting challenges within the overall challenge of structural transformation.

Structural transformation is a complex, long-term historical process entailing both structural change in the sectoral composition of an economy and broader societal changes in the productive organizations, institutions, and political economy of a country. Industrial development and structural transformation are intimately linked as the industry-led productive transformation of the economy has been recognized as a critical driver of inclusive and sustainable structural transformation (UNIDO, 2020). Causality runs in both directions, as industrialization both drives and is sustained by broader social, institutional, and political economy changes. And these changes are crucial for delivering sustainable and inclusive outcomes along countries' development journeys.

Structural transformation—industrialization in particular—figures prominently on the international development agenda; for instance, inclusive and sustainable

Antonio Andreoni, Pamela Mondliwa, Simon Roberts, and Fiona Tregenna, *Framing Structural Transformation in South Africa and Beyond* In: *Structural Transformation in South Africa: The Challenges of Inclusive Industrial Development in a Middle-Income Country.* Edited by: Antonio Andreoni, Pamela Mondliwa, Simon Roberts, and Fiona Tregenna, Oxford University Press. © Oxford University Press 2021. DOI: 10.1093/oso/9780192894311.003.0001

industrialization features in the United Nations Sustainable Development Goals (SDGs, 2015–30). The shift from the Millennium Development Goals (MDGs, 2000–15) to the SDGs marks an important turn in the development discourse, which has reintroduced a more holistic notion of 'development as structural transformation', beyond the more limited focus on 'development as poverty reduction' (Andreoni and Chang, 2017). This paradigmatic shift was pushed by the transformational experience of successful late industrializers such as South Korea, as well as the contribution to poverty reduction of China, in particular, as the largest late industrializer.

As a whole, this book examines South Africa as an important case study of the range of challenges that structural transformation presents, as well as locating South Africa's experience in an international context. Detailed analyses of industry groupings and interests in the country reveal the complex set of interlocking country-specific factors which have hampered structural transformation over several decades, but also the emerging productive areas and opportunities for structural transformation. Links between country-specific and global dynamics of change are identified, with a focus on the challenges and opportunities faced by middle-income countries.

In this chapter, a specific analytical perspective on the nature and dynamics of structural transformation is advanced, and a set of interlocking critical factors and dimensions is identified. Framing the contributions that follow in the subsequent chapters of the book, the chapter first engages in a discussion of emerging perspectives on structural transformation. Next is an evaluation of the extent to which South Africa has succeeded or failed in structural transformation, with a focus on particular aspects of industrial performance. This is followed by an exposition of the holistic framework and each of its dimensions, and their relevance in each of the chapters.

1.2 Structural Transformation: Emerging Perspectives

Despite the resurgence of interest in structural transformation, contributions have focused mainly on the impact of changes in the sectoral composition of the economy on increases in cumulative productivity and growth performances. Thus, studies have chiefly focused on a specific set of issues, including: structural change and productivity dynamics within and across sectors (Rodrik, 2008 and 2014; McMillan et al., 2014); the role of endowment structures in the 'new structural economics' and the 'growth identification and facilitation' approach (Lin, 2011; Lin and Monga, 2011; Lin and Wang, 2020); and the macroeconomic link between structural change and economic growth (Ocampo et al., 2009). Some studies have attempted to move one step further in explaining factors driving structural change. These have mainly focused on different trade-based analyses of diversification in the so-called 'product space' (see for example Hausmann and Rodrik, 2003; Hausmann et al., 2007; Hidalgo and Hausmann, 2009).

Structural transformation is, however, a much more complex process which entails both the recomposition of the economy at the sectoral level *and* broader societal changes in the productive organizations, institutions, and political economy of a country. From this perspective, only by analysing these context-specific micro-dynamics of change and their relationship with the evolving international context can the major factors responsible for structural transformation (or the lack of it) be fully understood. Embracing this complexity, the holistic framework advanced in this volume focuses on four dimensions of structural transformation: learning processes and capabilities development, technological change, economic and power relationships along value chains, and broader political economy dynamics.

These dimensions have been identified starting from the recognition of structural transformation as a historical process in which global and local power dynamics constantly shape the economic structure, as it moves along more or less productive pathways. The relationships between economic actors along value chains and the emergence of different institutional and social configurations are therefore an intrinsic part of structural change. They are both drivers and outcomes of structural transformation. Through these processes, effective employment creation in formal industrial sectors, and the diversification of the economy with a more diffused distribution of organizational power, are key to changing the social and political economy dynamics. These, in turn, reinforce transformation in the economy.

Sector-specificity and the evolving nature of sectors matter too, in that different sectors have different characteristics that are relevant for growth. Several classical contributions (Prebisch, 1950; Hirschman, 1958; Kaldor, 1966) in particular, have regarded the manufacturing sector as having features that accord it a special role as an engine of growth. These include dynamic increasing returns to scale; a high propensity for learning-by-doing; greater scope for technological and organizational capabilities development; tradability and hence importance for balance of payments; strong growth-pulling intersectoral (especially backward) linkages; and its importance as the locale for economy-wide technological progress (Tregenna, 2009 and 2013). However, major technological and organizational changes—digitalization and the vertical disintegration of industries into GVCs— have led to a shift in the 'terrain of the industrial' (Andreoni, 2020). As a result, new activities at the interfaces of agriculture, manufacturing, and services have increasingly shown some of the traditional properties associated with manufacturing that are critical for structural transformation. Indeed, the application of manufacturing technologies and organizational practices, including the digitalization of production, has meant a blurring of sectoral boundaries, complex evolving industry organizations, and new business models (Cramer and Tregenna, 2020). This includes the growing importance of knowledge-intensive and production-related business services such as design and post-sale services (i.e. servicification), as well as the changing nature of the industrialization of agricultural production.

The state plays a key role in driving and steering this broader economic change (Chang and Rowthorn, 1995; Andreoni and Chang, 2019). Governments and public institutions create new markets and unlock structural coordination problems such as interdependent investments in productive assets and direct demand expansion. Governments also play a moderating role in contested claims on the redistribution of this created value among productive organizations, groups, and segments of the society and polity. Finally, by implementing industrial policies, governments allocate rents among different constituencies, thus shaping the incentive structure of the economy; and by implementing regulatory policies, they address competition and the concentration of power in markets.

Contributions in the fields of institutional economics and the political economy of industrial policy have stressed the political nature of institutions and recognition that the state is a key player in constructing and shaping the institution of the market. The literature on the political economy of development and governance, and the political economy of industrial policy, has expanded significantly over the last decade in particular.[1]

Some of these contributions have also started to link structural transformation to the major global drivers of change, including climate change, digitalization, and the changing terms of trade and production along GVCs. Specifically, going back to the original roots of the GVC research agenda and its relationship with dependency theory (Evans, 1979; Gereffi, 2018), there has been an increasing recognition of the pervasive and multidimensional role of organized power in the economy, in the local and global context, as well as at the interfaces along value chains (Dallas et al., 2019).

Countries that have attained middle-income status, like South Africa, face a number of challenges—in particular, linking up into GVCs while linking back into their domestic economies, and keeping pace with technological change (Andreoni and Tregenna, 2020). These, and developing countries more generally, are looking at industrialization and industrial policy as ways of addressing these challenges, escaping premature deindustrialization, and changing the structural

---

[1] On the political economy of development and governance leading examples are Chang, 2011; Khan, 2018; Pritchet et al., 2018; and on political economy of industrial policy: Amsden, 1989; Wade, 1990; Chang, 1994; Rodrik, 2004; Stiglitz and Lin, 2013; Mazzucato, 2013; Lee, 2013; Noman and Stiglitz, 2016; Chang and Andreoni, 2020; Oqubay et al., 2020.

and institutional configurations of their economies towards higher-productivity activities. Indeed, structural transformation and industrial policy are returning to the forefront of national policy debates.

The South African case demonstrates the importance of an in-depth industry understanding of productive capabilities and confronting the issues about how to generate sustained industrial and technological upgrading. Middle-income countries are also looking at turning the inclusiveness and sustainability challenges into opportunities for broader societal and environmental transformation. The aspirations of a rising middle class and the broadening of the economic base have the potential to change the political economy of these countries and the functioning of their institutions.

1.3 Structural Transformation in Middle-Income Countries: The Case of South Africa

1.3.1 South Africa's Performance Compared to Other Middle-Income Economies

South Africa offers an important case study of a middle-income country which has, at least in recent years, emphasized the importance of industrial policy in driving structural transformation. This is formally recognized in the National Industrial Policy Framework (2007) and a series of Industrial Policy Action Plans (IPAPs).[2] Black economic empowerment (BEE) policies and competition law have also been important initiatives adopted by the South African government, as they seek to address the entrenched industrial structure and its concentration, as well as its racialized character.

While there have been positive developments in specific sectors, overall, the industrial structure changed relatively little between 1994 and 2019. Fixed investment has remained low, and the economy has exhibited features of premature deindustrialization—instead of the hoped-for broad-based growth that would reverse the legacy of apartheid policies that had focused the economy on a narrow industry and mining base. At the same time, following the liberalization of trade and capital flows in the 1990s, the South African economy has become more open and internationalized. This has been evident in, among other factors, the magnitude of capital flows and the patterns of ownership on the Johannesburg Stock Exchange (JSE). The stock market has expanded to such an extent that the market capitalization in 2019 was equivalent to more than three times the size of

---

[2] See Chapter 2 for an overview of industrial policy in South Africa.

Table 1.1 Economic performance of South Africa and other middle-income countries

	Brazil	Malaysia	South Africa	Thailand	Turkey	Middle-Income	Upper-Middle Income
GDP (US$ billion), 2019	2,347	399	430	453	1,251	30,557	24,302
GDP growth, 1994–2019	2.3%	5.0%	2.6%	3.4%	4.7%	5.0%	5.0%
GDP per capita, 2019 (US$)	11,122	12,478	7,346	6,503	14,999	5,297	8,510
Industry value-added growth, 1994–2019	1.2%	4.0%	1.3%	3.1%	5.4%	5.2%	5.2%
Manufacturing, value-added growth, 1994–2019	0.4%	5.3%	2.0%	3.6%	5.3%		
Manufacturing value added (% of GDP), 2019	9.4%	21.5%	11.8%	25.3%	19.0%	18.8%	19.8%
Manufacturing exports (% of merchandise exports), 2018	36.1%	69.5%	46.6%	77.5%	80.9%	65.8%	68.4%
Growth of exports of goods and services, 1994–2019	4.5%	4.7%	2.8%	5.7%	7.3%		
High-tech exports (as % of manuf. exports), 2018	13.0%	52.8%	5.6%	23.3%	2.3%	22.3%	23.5%
Average gross fixed capital formation (% of GDP), 1994–2018	18.5%	26.7%	18.3%	26.6%	25.6%	27.6%	28.1%
Market capitalization of listed domestic companies (as % GDP), 2019	64.5%	110.8%	300.6%	104.7%	24.5%	60.2%	60.2%

Note: Growth rates are all calculated as compound annual average growth rates from data in 2010 constant US$. The gaps in the table are indicators that the World Bank does not calculate for MIC and upper-middle income groups.

Source: World Bank, World Development Indicators.

gross domestic product (GDP) (Table 1.1) even while investment rates in fixed capital stock in the economy remained poor.

South Africa's poor performance overall is evident when compared to its peer group of upper-middle income countries (Table 1.1).[3] While overall, in upper-middle income countries (and the broader MIC group), industry value added led GDP growth over the period 1994–2019, in South Africa, industry growth lagged. South Africa has not been alone in this; for example, Brazil has recorded a similar pattern with industry—and manufacturing as a sub-set of industry—growing slower than GDP. Average investment rates have also been very poor in both countries. South Africa and Brazil have both had a relatively low share of manufactured exports (less than 50 per cent) in total merchandise exports and a very low share of high-tech exports within these manufactured exports—less than 10 per cent in South Africa, compared with Thailand's 23.3 per cent and Malaysia's 52.8 per cent, for example.

The middle-income countries group (as defined by the World Bank, in 2018) comprised highly heterogenous economies accounting together for 75 per cent of the world's population, and as much as 62 per cent of the world's poor. Indeed, this group includes countries which managed to graduate to higher classifications within the broader MIC group in the 2000s, such as Malaysia and Thailand, as well as recent entrants to the middle-income grouping, like Tanzania.

China is a very important country in the middle-income and upper middle-income groupings. When China is excluded from the data, South Africa's performance is not as far from the averages for the country groupings. Excluding China, middle-income countries recorded average GDP growth over the period of 3.7 per cent and industry growth of 3.2 per cent, while upper middle-income countries recorded rates of 3.1 per cent and 2.6 per cent, still notably better than South Africa's average growth rates of 2.6 per cent and 1.3 per cent. The challenges South Africa has faced with poor industrial performance, low levels of investment, and a lack of diversification and weak exports of more sophisticated products is at the lower end, but reflects a number of other countries.

1.3.2 Trends within Manufacturing: A Failure to Diversify

A deeper look into the value-added performance of disaggregated manufacturing sub-sectors reveals the overall stronger performance of upstream resource-based sub-sectors led by coke and refined petroleum products, with basic chemicals and basic iron and steel also performing strongly (Figure 1.1; and see Chapter 2 for a

---

[3] These countries were selected because they show similar levels of per capita GDP to South Africa in the 1990s and 2000s, are medium-sized in terms of population, and have pursued industrialization strategies.

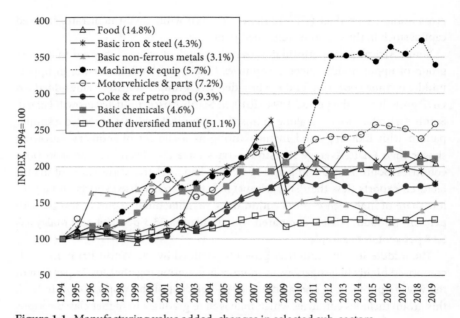

Figure 1.1 Manufacturing value added, changes in selected sub-sectors

Notes: 'Other Diversified Manufacturing' is inclusive of all other manufactured products not separated out in the chart.

Figures in parentheses reflect the shares in manufacturing value added in 2019.

Source: Quantec, authors' calculations.

more detailed analysis of trends).[4] The resource-based sub-sectors, including basic non-ferrous metals (mainly aluminium), grew especially strongly to 2008, reflecting the impact of the global commodities boom. There was also strong growth in value added in machinery and equipment (analysed in Chapter 3) and food products in this period on the back of local demand. The motor vehicle sub-sector stands out as growing value added over the twenty-five years as a result of sustained support through the Motor Industry Development Programme (MIDP, 1995–2012) and the Automotive Production and Development Programme (APDP, 2013–20). However, local content per vehicle declined in the latter period and there are big questions about the strength of local linkages to components (see Chapter 5).

Over the period as a whole, the other diversified manufacturing activities in aggregate (which accounted for more than 50 per cent of total manufacturing

---

[4] The data considered for sub-sector performance are from Quantec. It is important to note that the Quantec data are not official statistics. They have been compiled including data from Statistics South Africa, with some computations by Quantec. This should be borne in mind, and conclusions relating to the details of any short-run changes should be avoided.

value added in 2019) have performed poorly.[5] There has essentially been a regression since the mid-1990s, away from more diversified and sophisticated manufacturing activities. The continued importance of minerals, basic metals, and isolated islands of other products, including those in motor vehicles, machinery, and fruit, is evident in the map of the product space of South Africa's exports in 2018 (Figure 1.3 below).

There have also been important differences between the resource-based sectors, especially from 2009 onwards—reflecting in part the extent to which they are vulnerable to international price volatility and local energy prices. Sasol,[6] which has dominated the value added in the coke and refined petroleum products sub-sector, has benefited from being vertically integrated back into coal and has obtained natural gas from Mozambique at very low prices (Mondliwa and Roberts, 2017). Sasol has also accounted for the majority of value added in the basic chemicals sub-sector.[7] The division of value added between the refineries and basic chemicals sub-sectors has thus been, to a significant extent, influenced by Sasol's internal transfer-pricing decisions between its refinery and chemicals businesses. Both basic iron and steel and non-ferrous metals have faced the challenges of volatile international prices in terms of inputs and outputs, although basic iron and steel is better integrated back into its key inputs.

As South Africa is a small open economy, a key question for industrial policy has been how to manage the impact of large price swings on the local economy, including support for downstream sectors such as fabricated metal products and plastic products (reported separately in Table 1.2), which have performed very poorly and have seen increased import penetration (see also Chapters 3 and 4). The extensive trade liberalization and international integration from the 1990s increased imports and exports, with imports being more than one-third of domestic demand for total manufactured goods in 2019 (Table 1.2). However, some resource-based sub-sectors such as basic chemicals and basic iron and steel had lower imports in 2019 than in 1994. The effect of the motor industry policies reflected increased exports and lower imports.

Looking at employment data, an absolute decline in employment for manufacturing as a whole is evident, as well as for the other diversified manufacturing grouping (Table 1.2). There have been average increases of more than 1 per cent per annum in only three of the selected sectors—in coke and refined petroleum products (which is highly capital-intensive and employs very few people), as well

---

[5] Note that not this does not mean that all segments within the other diversified category in Figure 1.1 have performed equally poorly with, for example, consumer goods such as soaps and cosmetics growing local production in line with local demand.

[6] Sasol is a former state-owned firm that is the largest producer of basic chemicals and one of two synthetic fuel producers.

[7] Basic chemicals include fertilizer and polymer chemicals, which obtain their feedstock from refinery by-products and co-products.

as plastic products and machinery and equipment, each of which are key sub-sectors where diversified capabilities could have been built on more (Table 1.2). The decline in employment for the other diversified manufacturing sub-sectors in Table 1.2, which accounted for more than 45 per cent of all manufacturing jobs in 2019, is emblematic of the failure of the economy to transform. In motor vehicles, while there has been good performance in terms of value added and trade, the failure to deepen and diversify local linkages is reflected in no net employment creation in the sub-sector (Chapter 5).

The relationship between manufacturing and services is important for under-standing the development of industrial capabilities where design, engineering, and IT services tend to be highly productive and tradable, and can play a key role as a growth driver (McMillan et al., 2014). Notwithstanding the challenges of dis-aggregating services, in South Africa at an aggregate level, communication, and finance and insurance services have recorded particularly high growth in value added—above 4 per cent per annum (Table 1.3). However, this has not been accompanied by strong employment growth in these sub-sectors. Employment growth has occurred in business services, which includes large numbers of jobs in areas such as outsourced cleaning and security services, as well as in wholesale and retail trade (Tregenna, 2010). In general, the growth of services exports has also been biased towards traditional rather than advanced services (Bhorat et al., 2017). While there has been employment creation in low-wage, low-productivity sub-sectors, the question is why this has not been accompanied by the growth of the more sophisticated services (and higher-skilled employment within them) required for building advanced industrial capabilities and aggregate economic growth. (This is explored further in Chapter 12.)

To assess patterns of continuity and change in the set of productive capabilities in more detail, disaggregated trade data have been assessed, first as shares in total merchandise exports, and then in the more granular main export products dis-cussed in the following sub-section.[8] The clear failure to substantially diversify is evident in South Africa's merchandise exports over time. Perhaps the most strik-ing feature is the lack of any major change in South Africa's export profile over two decades, following some change in the 1990s with the growth of auto exports. Minerals and resource-based industries continued to account for a high propor-tion of merchandise exports, close to 60 per cent in 2019 (Figure 1.2).[9] Along with growing exports of motor vehicles, machinery and equipment are also not-able, growing in importance in the first decade after 1994. All other exports have remained with a share of around 25 per cent.

---

[8] The focus here is on merchandise trade. While there are also clearly important services exports, such as tourism, these are not well recorded.

[9] This includes minerals resource-based industries of wood, paper and pulp, basic chemicals, and basic metals in Figure 1.2.

Table 1.2 Manufacturing performance: selected sectors

	Total employment			Value added			GFCF, as % value added	Export, as % output		Import, as % domestic demand	
	Growth	Share of total		Growth	Share of total		Average				
	1994–2019	1994	2019	1994–2019	1994	2019	1994–2019	1994	2019	1994	2019
Coke and refined petroleum products	1.6%	1.1%	1.8%	5.0%	4.4%	9.3%	33%	33%	27%	6%	29%
Basic chemicals	0.3%	1.5%	1.8%	3.0%	3.5%	4.6%	56%	20%	46%	58%	37%
Plastics products	1.2%	2.6%	3.9%	1.5%	3.2%	3.0%	18%	3%	17%	11%	34%
Basic iron and steel	–3.3%	5.4%	2.6%	2.3%	3.8%	4.3%	38%	66%	36%	23%	13%
Basic non-ferrous metals	–2.1%	1.8%	1.2%	1.7%	3.2%	3.1%	38%	32%	39%	18%	33%
Metal products excluding machinery	–0.2%	8.1%	8.6%	1.0%	6.9%	5.6%	10%	5%	14%	16%	32%
Machinery and equipment	1.2%	6.3%	9.6%	2.3%	5.2%	5.7%	10%	13%	46%	77%	92%
Motor vehicles, parts and accessories	–0.4%	7.0%	7.1%	3.9%	4.4%	7.2%	17%	10%	49%	50%	46%
Food	0.1%	15.2%	17.5%	2.9%	11.4%	14.8%	25%	8%	11%	11%	13%
Other diversified Manufacturing	–0.9%	51.1%	45.8%	0.9%	54.0%	42.5%	22%				
Total manufacturing	–0.5%	100%	100%	1.9%	100%	100%	23%	14%	26%	26%	35%

Notes: Employment figures include formal and informal employment. Growth rates are all calculated as compound annual average growth rates.

Source: Quantec, authors' calculations.

Table 1.3 Services sector performance

	Total employment			Value added		
	Growth	Share of total		Growth	Share of total	
	(1994–2019)	1994	2019	(1994–2019)	1994	2019
Wholesale and retail trade	3.0%	22.1%	26.6%	3.0%	19.7%	20.4%
Catering and accomm. services	1.5%	5.6%	4.6%	3.2%	1.6%	1.1%
Transport and storage	4.6%	3.0%	5.3%	1.6%	9.7%	9.3%
Communication	−0.5%	2.0%	1.0%	2.9%	1.5%	4.3%
Finance and insurance	1.1%	4.6%	3.4%	7.6%	7.2%	10.1%
Business services	3.5%	15.1%	20.2%	4.5%	18.8%	21.6%
Government, community, and personal services	1.4%	47.7%	38.9%	3.6%	41.6%	33.1%
Total services	3.0%	100.0%	100.0%	3.0%	100%	100%

Notes: Employment figures include formal and informal employment. Growth rates are all calculated as compound annual average growth rates.
Source: Quantec, authors' calculations.

There have been two competing explanations for South Africa's trade performance. First and in line with the analysis above is that the country's approach to trade liberalization reinforced the static comparative advantage in minerals, commodities, and other resource-based manufactures, and exports of diversified manufactured goods have underperformed (Fine and Rustomjee, 1996; Roberts, 2008; Black and Roberts, 2009; Black and Hasson, 2016; Driver, 2019). Second is that there has been a positive relationship between trade liberalization and export performance of manufactured and particularly non-commodity goods (Edwards and Lawrence, 2006 and 2008).

Important differences between these two explanations are due to the grouping of industries. Edwards and Lawrence (2006 and 2008) classify industries into commodity and non-commodity manufacturing, finding that non-commodity manufactured exports showed strong growth in the 1990–2000 period, which they attribute to a positive response to trade liberalization. However, this export growth is largely due to the auto industry (both motor vehicle and components exports) and the target of extensive industrial policy as well as ongoing tariff protection. The components include catalytic converters, an auto component categorized under machinery and equipment, as well as seat leather (classified under leather products) (Roberts, 2008; Black and Roberts, 2009; and Chapter 5).

There are at least three other classifications which have been commonly used in industrial competitiveness and diversification studies. These are: Pavitt's classification (Pavitt, 1984); the OECD classification based on R&D intensity introduced in 1994 (for a review see Galindo-Rueda and Verger, 2016); and, the widely

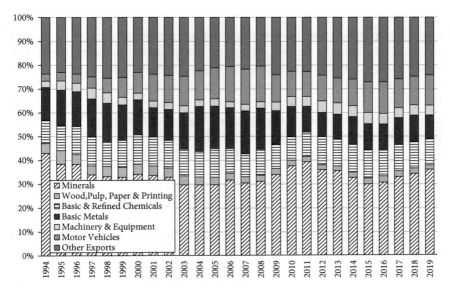

Figure 1.2 Merchandise export shares

Note: Minerals and resource-based exports include minerals; wood, pulp, and paper; basic and refined chemicals; and basic metals (in order from the bottom to the black in the middle of figure).

Source: Quantec, authors' calculations.

used Lall classification (Lall, 2000; see also UNIDO, 2010 for a discussion of the ways in which this classification evolved). As Sanjaya Lall notes (2000: 341) '[j]udgment is inevitably involved in assigning products to categories'. For example, Lall's classification excludes basic chemicals and basic metals (including steel) from resource-based manufactures and rather includes them in medium-technology exports. In South Africa, these industries are closely linked to mineral and resources inputs and, as such, it is clearly more appropriate to group them with resource-based industry. Furthermore, over long periods of time the nature of activities in categories changes and with that their value and technology content (Andreoni, 2020). In this book, the analysis involves in-depth industry studies which take into account the evolving value chain and structure of the sectors.

The South African experience illustrates that diversification, in terms of altering patterns of comparative advantage, is not a simple outcome of trade liberalization. Rather, there is an important role for industrial policy to play in countering path dependency (Amsden 1989 and 2001; Chang and Andreoni, 2020). Instead of growing diversified industries, as many of its middle-income peers have done, South Africa has in fact prematurely deindustrialized (Tregenna, 2016a and 2016b; and Chapter 11). The reasons for this are a core consideration of this book.

The poor overall investment rates (evident from the international comparisons above) are an important factor, even while the commodities boom, infrastructure spending, and credit-driven local demand stimulated higher investment rates in the 2000s, which peaked in 2008 at 30 per cent of value added. These rates of investment have not been sustained and, within manufacturing, have remained heavily skewed towards the capital-intensive industries of coke and refineries, and basic chemicals. The investments in the basic chemicals and refined petroleum products sectors have been essentially driven by Sasol, whose capital expenditure has generally constituted the majority of investments (Chapter 4). High rates of investment were recorded by the basic metals sectors in the 1990s, which under-pinned their growth in output at the time. There has not been any significant sus-tained growth in investment in downstream and diversified manufacturing.

1.3.3 Lack of Diversification in South African Exports

South Africa's failure to diversify is evident in both the fact that traditional resource-based sectors are mainly responsible for industry output growth in the economy, and that higher levels of investment in the manufacturing sector have continued in these sectors rather than shifting to diversified manufacturing activ-ities. Diversification—or the lack of it—can be illustrated in greater detail in the so-called 'product-space' analysis. South Africa was among the first countries to use an early version of this product-space analysis to show its structural trans-formation challenges (Hausmann and Rodrik, 2006).

South Africa's product space did not change substantially between the mid-1990s and 2018 (Bell et al., 2018). It has continued to be dominated by low-complexity products, and there has been a failure to form clusters around more advanced manufactured products. As Figure 1.3 shows, exports of minerals, stone and glass, vegetable and foodstuffs, metal products, and chemical products made up most of the export basket (relatively larger dots). Many of the linkages between various products have not been exploited. Instead, the more important export products appear as isolated points. For example, cars are evident, but not auto components (apart from catalytic converters which are classified under centri-fuges) and there are mining equipment exports, but not a broader clustering of machinery and equipment, which has characterized countries such as Malaysia and Thailand.

It is important to note that a country's export basket (represented in the product space above) attempts to capture the degree of diversification (or spread) of products as well as the clustering in certain types of products (which reflect characteristics including the degree of technology complexity). These can be understood as an outcome of its unique historical processes of accumulation of productive capabil-ities, the extent of structural change, and production transformation.

In the South African case, openness to global trade has amplified major differ-ences and contrasts within the economy and society more than it has driven diversification. Firms in advanced niches have been operating side by side with

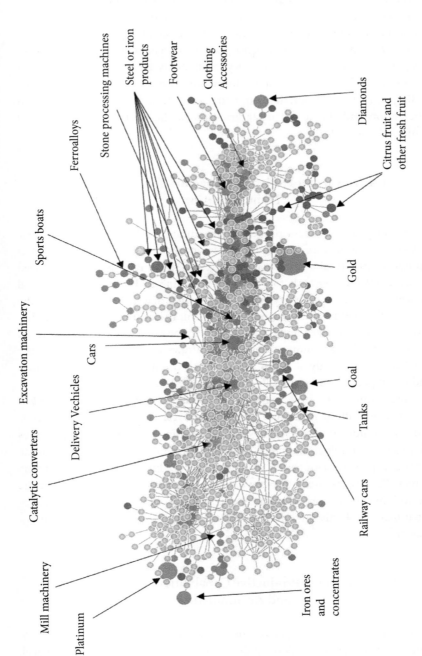

Figure 1.3 South Africa's export basket, 2018

Note: The light grey circles are effectively empty for South Africa, representing product categories in relation to each other based on what countries around the world tend to export, but in which South Africa does not have significant exports.

Source: Atlas of Economic Complexity.

firms with export competitiveness based on historical state support and favourable access to resources, while improvements in living standards for some have coexisted with persistently high levels of unemployment and inequality. Similarly, the expansion of the financial sector has not gone hand in hand with an expansion of productive investments; on the contrary, profitability has been associated with rents capture and weak fixed capital formation (see Chapters 2 and 10). The unfolding of these contradictions and structural tensions has led to political fragmentation and the recent destabilization of the post-apartheid political settlement (Chapter 2).

1.4 Towards a Holistic Framework for Structural Transformation

A number of path-dependent processes, structural interdependencies, and tensions form part of the mix of complex and intertwined factors that have acted as constraints to structural transformation in South Africa. Responding to the need for a more holistic approach to both understanding and advancing structural transformation, this section presents a framework that can be applied in the analysis of the nature and dynamics of structural transformation in middle-income countries more generally. The chapters in the book explore these issues in different ways. The concluding chapter then draws together insights from the comprehensive case study of South Africa, which could help to inform priorities for industrial policy in other middle-income countries.

A holistic framework for structural transformation needs to engage with key micro-structural dimensions and meet several related challenges. The four dimensions embodied in this framework are: learning processes and capabilities development; technological change, and digitalization in particular; economic linkages and power relationships along GVCs; and, broader political economy dynamics. Each is discussed in more detail below. While the dimensions of the framework may be addressed in the chapters at a more implicit level, the chapters that focus explicitly on a particular dimension are mentioned at the end of each section.

1.4.1 Learning, Productive Capabilities Development, and Accumulation

From a micro-structural perspective, production transformation is about learning and selective attempts to develop different types of productive, technological, organizational, and innovative capabilities (Penrose, 1959; Lall, 2001; Teece, 2006; Andreoni, 2014; Chang and Andreoni, 2020; Roberts, 2020a). Firms' capabilities are a combination of the individual and collective competencies that are needed to perform and organize interdependent productive tasks as well as to adapt and undertake improvements across different technological and organizational functions. Capable agents and functioning organizations can only operate if they are matched by investments in production capacity to attain appropriate scale and scope. The capabilities needed to generate, absorb, and manage technological and organizational change and those needed to seize new opportunities—i.e. dynamic capabilities—differ substantially from those needed to operate existing production systems.

Developing and accumulating capabilities in activities in which firms are not yet competitive requires effort to learn to use new technologies and acquire new tacit knowledge. This can be expensive and time-consuming; the returns from these investments are not guaranteed, and they also depend on spillovers and linkages from other firms (Lall and Teubal, 1998; Lall, 1992; Khan, 2009; Andreoni, 2019; Whitfield et al., 2020). There is not comprehensive knowledge of alternative production techniques, and thus finding suitable technology at the right price involves cost and risk (Nelson and Winter, 1982; Lall and Pietrobelli, 2005). As a result, private firms tend to underinvest in the related activities required to accumulate capabilities. The learning element of technologies is important for adapting the technology to different scales, new input and skill conditions, and different product demands. The challenge of ensuring high levels of effort by the firm in the process of learning-by-doing is the biggest constraint to absorbing new technologies. This is where the important role of the state comes into play (Khan, 2009).

These considerations indicate that sub-sectors are internally highly heterogenous as the factors operate and differ at the level of individual firms and clusters within sub-sectors. This is borne out in the micro-industrial development, firm-focused, evolutionary, and related bodies of literature (Penrose, 1959; Andreoni, 2014; Rosenberg, 1982; Amsden, 1989 and 2001; Dosi et al., 2000; Lall, 2001; Teece, 2006; Andreoni and Chang, 2017; Avenyo et al., 2021). Owing in part to data limitations, aggregated quantitative analyses do not account for important differences, and in some cases provide misleading insights about the process of structural transformation. For example, as shown by recent contributions (Dosi et al., 2020; Tregenna and Andreoni, 2020), the traditional patterns of deindustrialization are highly heterogenous across manufacturing sub-sectors, or different sectoral groupings defined by technological or other organizational features (Pavitt, 1984's and Lall, 2000's taxonomies). Thus, it is important to go beyond both the broad sub-sectoral analysis and the recognition of the continuing importance of manufacturing, and to start taking account of the more complex dynamics within and between firms.

This makes the case for in-depth industry study, as reflected in Chapters 3 to 7. Together, these chapters cover developments in metals and mining machinery, manufacture of plastic products, the auto industry, evolving competitiveness in fresh fruit production, and the wine industry. The role of the financial sector in

South Africa in the context of weak investment in more sophisticated and diversi-fied economic activities is considered in Chapter 10.

1.4.2 Technological Change and Digitalization in Light of Sustainability Challenges

Structural transformation perspectives need to take account of the rapid pace of technological change within and beyond the manufacturing sector, and more broadly the rise of cross-sectoral challenges and the need for cross-sectoral solu-tions. Sectoral boundaries are also increasingly redefined by new technologies. The terrain of the industrial has been shifting—contracting and expanding—to give space to both servicification and agricultural industrialization (Andreoni, 2020; Cramer and Tregenna, 2020).

Technological change is of course not new. But the development of wide-scale digital applications is accelerating the pace of technological change exponentially. Further, this change is systemic, pervasive, and includes an integration between the digital, physical, and biological domains in ways thus far not seen. These developments have been characterized under the broad rubric of the 'fourth industrial revolution'. Clearly, the accelerating pace and impact of technological change need to be factored into current thinking and policy prescriptions around structural transformation. They also call for more 'ecosystem'-oriented frameworks (Andreoni, 2018) that are capable of taking into account both sector value-chain specific dynamics and cross-sectoral technological dynamics.

Structural transformation perspectives often have not engaged sufficiently with the relationship between industrialization and climate change, and the need to reduce carbon dioxide (CO_2) emissions in particular. Climate change impacts dif-ferent groups and sectors differently, but it is one of the most striking cross-sectoral challenges of the time. Industrial production has been identified as a key source of emissions, with evidence of an inverted-U relationship between indus-trialization and emissions (see, for example, Barca and Bridge (2015); Avenyo and Tregenna (2021)). This suggests a possible tension between the dual imperatives of industrializing and mitigating climate change. This tension is particularly stark for late industrializers, since early industrializers were not constrained by the need to simultaneously reduce emissions. In recent years, there has been a grow-ing body of literature and policy discourse exploring a green industrialization path that is compatible with mitigating climate change, and green industrial pol-icy (see, for instance, Rodrik (2014); Fischer (2016); Altenburg and Rodrik (2017); Andreoni and Chang, (2017); Pollin (2020)).[10]

---

[10] See also Chapter 7 in this volume, which explores issues of sustainability and inequality in the context of the South African wine value chain.

In addition to the industry-focused chapters which consider both the legacy impacts of resource-based industrialization as well as the impact of sustainability standards (such as in wine), the challenges of the middle-income technology trap are considered in detail in Chapter 11, and digitalization is addressed in Chapter 12.

1.4.3 Global Value Chains and Power Dynamics

The structural transformation of developing economies is taking place in the context of the globalization of production, where decisions on the geographical location of production are largely determined by lead firms in GVCs. Understanding upgrading opportunities from participating in GVCs requires engagement with strategies of multinational corporations (MNCs) including those related to outsourcing, offshoring, and reshoring. Though participation in GVCs presents opportunities for upgrading through international linkages, learning by exporting and FDI spillovers such as access to technological knowledge and generating learning and innovation activities, this process is not automatic (Gereffi et al., 2005). The gains from participating in a GVC are dependent on power asymmetries or the governance structures which determine where and by whom value is created and captured (Gereffi and Lee, 2012) and how this enhances or hinders capability upgrading.

The skewed power relations within GVCs often imply that the bulk of the value is captured by lead firms that can leverage a combination of direct and diffuse forms of power transmissions (Dallas et al., 2019). The distribution of value added in GVCs is often illustrated by means of the 'smile' curve (Durand and Milberg, 2020). In this curve, developing economies tend to participate in the fabrication levels that are subject to intense international competition, and thus have limited possibilities to capture value. This has been further heightened by the disproportionate distribution of value capture to intangible assets (held by lead firms) rather than physical assets (held by suppliers). With increasing levels of competition in the supply levels, lead firms also have reduced incentives to support upgrading of local firms. The state has an important role to play in tipping the calculus of the lead firms in one direction instead of the other. Norms of fair and reasonable market relationships need to incorporate the balance through regulation and building multi-stakeholder consensus on the importance of shared longer-term investments (Goga et al., 2020; Mondliwa et al., 2021). This involves collective and institutional power relations (Dallas et al., 2019).

Though governance and power in value chains has primarily been studied in relation to GVCs, it is important to note that some of the observed dynamics particularly relating to value distribution and capture are also present in domestic value chains (Mondliwa et al., 2020). For example, the competitive dynamics and outcomes in one level of the value chain can impact the development of whole sectors through vertical linkages, which can promote or undermine structural transformation (Lee et al., 2018; Goga et al., 2020).

The influence of power dynamics in industries and the implications for inequality is assessed in the South African case in Chapter 8, and the record on BEE initiatives is analysed in Chapter 9. Chapter 13 looks specifically at industry challenges in linking into GVCs while linking back to develop stronger local production capabilities.

1.4.4 Political Economy and the Role of the State

The micro-structuralist approach advanced here places emphasis on the role of the state in supporting processes of structural transformation. This is because successful structural transformation requires a proactive industrial policy that steers and supports learning, productive capabilities, and technological change; regulates power dynamics and rewards value creation and innovation; and manages conflicting claims, while disciplining unproductive rent-seeking (Andreoni and Chang, 2019; Chang and Andreoni, 2020; Roberts, 2020b). Contributions on the political economy of structural transformation have also emphasized how states' capabilities to manage rents, including monitoring and disciplining rent recipients to ensure productive investment for growth, are in turn influenced by the distribution of power within a society—its broader political settlement (Gray, 2018; Khan, 2018).

The political economy of structural transformation is therefore about not only understanding how the state can drive and give directionality to the process of structural transformation, but also how the state is formed and shaped by emerging interests, conflicting claims, and changes in the distribution of organized power. The analysis of this dialectic process linking structural transformation to state formation is critical in assessing the effectiveness of industrial policy. Research on successful catching-up experiences has shown how state embeddedness is critical in designing effective industrial policy and organizing coalitions of interests around specific structural transformation targets (Chang and Rowthorn, 1995; Evans, 1995; Weiss and Hobson, 1995). However, it has also noted cases in which unproductive interests have captured the state and limited its capacity to drive change through industrial policies (Khan and Jomo, 2000).

Within this perspective, industrial policy is not simply an exercise in addressing market failures, or other types of systemic failures. Instead, industrial policy is the main policy process through which the state sets the terms of the social contract underpinning structural transformation (Andreoni and Chang, 2019). Seen through these lenses, industrial policy and all the related policies shaping capabilities development, technological change, and value distribution within and across productive organizations are central to the study of structural transformation.

The way in which the state uses industrial policy in combination or in contraposition to other policies, such as competition policy, is also central. In fact, from this political economy perspective, the lack of policy coordination is both the result of limited government capabilities, and the fragmentation of interests and power distribution across the economy. The study of the state—its internal configuration and capabilities, as well as its underpinning political settlement—is therefore a key dimension in understanding and driving structural transformation.

The political economy of industrial development cuts across all the chapters and these issues are specifically drawn together in Chapter 14.

1.5 Concluding Remarks

This chapter, and this volume as a whole, draws on the longstanding literature from a broad structuralist perspective on the importance of structural transformation for economic development and catch-up (Blankenburg et al., 2008). For middle-income countries, this is particularly important for avoiding or escaping a middle-income trap, and is a key precondition to sustaining broader structural transformation. This points to the ongoing importance of industrialization, and indeed of reindustrialization where premature deindustrialization has already taken place.

With a focus on the South African economy, the ideas put forward in this chapter advocate for the development of a more holistic approach to structural transformation that is focused on key micro-structural dynamics of change, four of which are highlighted in the chapter: (1) learning, productive capabilities development and accumulation; (2) technical change, digitalization, and sustainability; (3) GVCs and power dynamics; and (4) political economy and the role of the state. These are addressed in the chapters that follow through in-depth studies of key industries in South Africa, which may also make reference to the international context. Other studies address cross-cutting issues, such as BEE, inequality, financialization, and sustainability, and how they pertain to industrial development.

Recognizing the importance of structural transformation underscores the key role of industrial policy, since structural transformation is not something that unfolds automatically (see also Chapter 15). Appropriate state-led interventions are needed to unlock and shape a viable industrialization path that countries can pursue. For industrial policy to successfully advance structural transformation, it needs to be well coordinated with other relevant policy domains. For instance, supportive macroeconomic policy is required to ensure adequate domestic demand, access to finance, and a competitive exchange rate for manufacturing exports. Similarly, there is a need for coordination with competition policy, trade policy, innovation and technology policy, and so on. In these regards, the case of South Africa provides salient lessons, as are drawn out in subsequent chapters.

Industrial policy is critical in enhancing countries' collective capabilities, through transforming sectoral silos into ecosystems of productive organizations and effective institutions. This will enable the digitalization dividend to be harnessed and the sustainability challenge turned into an opportunity for development. The management of rents within markets and along value chains, as well as new forms of rents arising from new digital platforms, is critical, including in opening up economies and unlocking opportunities for more distributed organizational power, beyond conservative and rentieristic positions.

References

Altenburg, T. and D. Rodrik (2017). 'Green industrial policy: accelerating structural change towards wealthy green economies.' In T. Altenburg and C. Assmann (eds), *Green Industrial Policy: Concepts, Policies, Country Experiences*, 2–20. Geneva and Bonn: UN Environment; German Development Institute/Deutsches Institut für Entwicklungspolitik (DIE).

Amsden, A. (1989). *Asia's Next Giant*. New York: Oxford University Press.

Amsden, A. (2001). *The Rise of "The Rest": Challenges to the West From Late-Industrializing Economies*. New York: Oxford University Press.

Andreoni, A. (2014). 'Structural learning: embedding discoveries and the dynamics of production.' *Structural Change and Economic Dynamics* 29: 58–74.

Andreoni, A. (2018). 'The architecture and dynamics of industrial ecosystems.' *Cambridge Journal of Economics* 42: 1613–42.

Andreoni, A. (2019). 'A generalized linkage approach to local production systems development in the era of global value chains, with special reference to Africa.' In R. Kanbur, A. Noman, and J. Stiglitz (eds), *Quality of Growth in Africa*, 264–94. Columbia University Press, New York.

Andreoni, A. (2020). 'Technical change, the shifting "terrain of the industrial", and digital industrial policy.' In A. Oqubay, C. Cramer, H.-J. Chang, and R. Kozul-Wright (eds), *The Oxford Handbook of Industrial Policy*, 369–93. Oxford: Oxford University Press.

Andreoni, A. and H.-J. Chang (2017). 'Bringing production transformation and jobs creation back to development.' *Cambridge Journal of Regions, Economy and Society* 10(1): 173–87.

Andreoni, A. and H.-J. Chang (2019). 'The political economy of industrial policy: structural interdependencies, policy alignment and conflict management.' *Structural Change and Economic Dynamics* 48: 136–50.

Andreoni, A. and F. Tregenna (2020). 'Escaping the middle-income technology trap: A comparative analysis of industrial policies in China, Brazil and South Africa.' *Structural Change and Economic Dynamics* 54: 324–40.

Avenyo, E. and F. Tregenna (2021). 'The effects of technology intensity in manufacturing on CO_2 emissions: evidence from developing countries.' ERSA Working Paper 846.

Avenyo, E., F. Tregenna, and E. Kraemer-Mbula (2021). 'Do productive capabilities affect export performance? Evidence from African firms.' *European Journal of Development Research* 33: 304–29.

Barca, S. and G. Bridge (2015). 'Industrialisation and environmental change.' In T. Perreault, G. Bridge, and J. A. McCarthy (eds), *The Routledge Handbook of Political Ecology*, 366–77. Oxon: Routledge.

Bell, J., S. Goga, P. Mondliwa, and S. Roberts (2018). 'Structural transformation in South Africa: Moving towards a smart, open economy for all.' CCRED Working paper No. 9/2018.

Bhorat, H., M. Oosthuizen, K. Lilenstein, and F. Steenkamp (2017). 'Firm-level determinants of earnings in the formal sector of the South African labour market.' WIDER Working Paper 2017/25. Helsinki: UNU-WIDER.

Black, A. and H. Hasson (2016). 'Capital-intensive industrialisation, comparative advantage and industrial policy.' In A. Black (ed.), *Towards Employment Intensive Growth in South Africa*. Cape Town: University of Cape Town Press.

Black, A. and S. Roberts (2009). 'The evolution and impact of industrial and competition policies.' In J. Aron, B. Kahn, and G. Kingdon (eds), *South African Economy Policy under Democracy*, 211–43. Oxford: Oxford University Press.

Blankenburg, S., G. Palma, and F. Tregenna (2008). 'Structuralism.' In L. Blume and S. Durlauf (eds), *The New Palgrave: A Dictionary of Economics* (2nd edn), 69–74. Basingstoke: Palgrave Macmillan.

Chang, H.-J. (1994). *The Political Economy of Industrial Policy*. Basingstoke: Macmillan.

Chang, H.-J. (2011). 'Industrial policy: can we go beyond an unproductive confrontation?' In J. Lin and B. Pleskovic (eds), *2010 Annual World Bank Conference on Development Economics Global: Lessons from East Asia and the Global Financial Crisis*, 83–109. Washington, DC: World Bank.

Chang, H.-J. and A. Andreoni (2020). 'Industrial policy in the 21st century.' *Development and Change* 51(2): 324–51.

Chang, H.-J. and R. Rowthorn (1995). *The Role of the State in Economic Change*. Oxford: Clarendon Press.

Cramer, C. and F. Tregenna (2020). 'Heterodox approaches to industrial policy and the implications for industrial hubs.' In J. Y. Lin and A. Oqubay (eds), *The Oxford Handbook of Industrial Hubs and Economic Development*, 40–63. Oxford: Oxford University Press.

Dallas, M. P., S. Ponte, and T. J. Sturgeon (2019). 'Power in global value chains.' *Review of International Political Economy* 26(4): 666–94.

Dosi, G., R. R. Nelson, and S. Winter (2020). *The Nature and Dynamics of Organizational Capabilities*. Oxford: Oxford University Press.

Dosi, G., F. Riccio, and M. E. Virgillito (2020). 'Varieties of deindustrialization and patterns of diversification: why microchips are not potato chips.' No. 2020/11. Laboratory of Economics and Management (LEM), Sant'Anna School of Advanced Studies, Pisa.

Driver, C. (2019). 'Trade liberalization and South African manufacturing: looking back with data.' WIDER Working Paper 2019/30. Helsinki: UNU-WIDER.

Durand, C. and W. Milberg (2020). 'Intellectual monopoly in global value chains.' *Review of International Political Economy* 27(2): 404–29.

Edwards, L. and R. Lawrence (2006). 'South African trade policy matters: trade performance and trade policy.' CID Working Paper No. 135. Cambridge, MA: Harvard University.

Edwards, L. and R. Lawrence (2008). 'South African trade policy matters: trade performance and trade policy.' *Economics of Transition* 16(4): 585–608.

Evans, P. (1979). *Dependent Development*. Princeton: Princeton University Press.

Evans, P. (1995). *Embedded Autonomy: States and Industrial Transformation*. Princeton: Princeton University Press.

Fine, B. and Z. Rustomjee (1996). *The Political Economy of South Africa: From Minerals-Energy Complex to Industrialisation*. London: Hurst.

Fischer, C. (2016). 'Environmental protection for sale: strategic green industrial policy and climate finance.' *Environmental and Resource Economics* 66(3): 553–75.

Galindo-Rueda, F. and F. Verger (2016). 'OECD taxonomy of economic activities based on R&D intensity.' OECD Science, Technology and Industry Working Papers, 2016/04. Paris: OECD Publishing, DOI:10.1787/5jlv73sqqp8r-en.

Gereffi, G. (2018). *Global Value Chains and Development: Redefining the Contours of 21st Century Capitalism*. Cambridge: Cambridge University Press.

Gereffi, G., J. Humphreym, and T. Sturgeon (2005). 'The governance of global value chains.' *Review of International Political Economy* 12(1): 78–104.

Gereffi, G. and J. Lee (2012). 'Why the world suddenly cares about global supply chains.' *Journal of Supply Chain Management* 48(3): 24–32.

Goga, S., P. Mondliwa, and S. Roberts (2020). 'Economic power and regulation: the political economy of metals, machinery and equipment industries in South Africa.' In E. Webster, D. Francis, and I. Valodia (eds), *Inequality Studies from the Global South*, 75–98. London: Routledge.

Gray, H. (2018). *Turbulence and Order in Economic Development: Institutions and Economic Transformation in Tanzania and Vietnam*. Oxford: Oxford University Press.

Hausmann, R., J. Hwang, and D. Rodrik (2007). 'What you export matters.' *Journal of Economic Growth* 12(1): 1–25.

Hausmann, R. and D. Rodrik (2003). 'Economic development as self-discovery.' *Journal of Development Economics* 72: 603–33.

Hausmann, R. and D. Rodrik (2006). 'Doomed to choose: Industrial policy as predicament.' John F. Kennedy School of Government, Mimeo.

Hidalgo, C. A. and R. Hausmann (2009). 'The building blocks of economic complexity.' *Proceedings of the National Academy of Sciences* 106(26): 10570–5.

Hirschman, A. (1958). *The Strategy of Economic Development*. New Haven: Yale University Press.

Kaldor, N. (1966). *Causes of the Slow Rate of Economic Growth of the United Kingdom: An Inaugural Lecture*. Cambridge: Cambridge University Press.

Khan, M. (2009). 'Learning, technology acquisition and governance challenges in developing countries.' Research Paper Series on Governance for Growth. School of Oriental and African Studies. London: University of London, http://eprints.soas. ac.uk/9967/1/Learning_and_Technology_Acquisition_internet.pdf.

Khan, M. H. (2018). 'Introduction: political settlements and the analysis of institutions.' *African Affairs* 117(469): 636–55.

Khan, M. and K. S. Jomo, eds (2000). *Rents, Rent-Seeking and Economic Development: Theory and Evidence in Asia*. Cambridge: Cambridge University Press.

Lall, S. (1992). 'Technological capabilities and industrialization.' *World Development* 20(2): 165–86.

Lall, S. (2000). 'The technological structure and performance of developing country manufactured exports, 1985–98.' *Oxford Development Studies* 28(3): 337–69.

Lall, S. (2001). *Competitiveness, Technology and Skills*. Cheltenham: Edward Elgar.

Lall, S. and C. Pietrobelli (2005). 'National technology systems in sub-Saharan Africa.' *International Journal of Technology and Globalisation* 1(3–4): 311–42.

Lall, S. and M. Teubal (1998). '"Market-stimulating" technology policies in developing countries: a framework with examples from East Asia.' *World Development* 26(8): 1369–85.

Lee, K. (2013). *Schumpeterian Analysis of Economic Catch-Up: Knowledge, Path-Creation, and the Middle-Income Trap*. London: Cambridge University Press.

Lee, K., M. Szapiro, and Z. Mao (2018). 'From global value chains (GVC) to innovation systems for local value chains and knowledge creation.' *The European Journal of Development Research* 30(3): 424–41.

Lin, J. (2011). *New Structural Economics*. Washington, DC: World Bank.

Lin, J. Y. and C. Monga (2011). 'Growth identification and facilitation: the role of the state in the dynamics of structural change (January 1, 2011).' World Bank Policy Research Working Paper No. 5313.

Lin, J. Y. and Yan Wang (2020). 'Seventy years of economic development: a review from the angle of new structural economics (July–August 2020).' *China & World Economy* 28(4): 26–50.

Mazzucato, M. (2013). *The Entrepreneurial State: Debunking Public vs. Private Sector Myths*. London: Anthem Press.

McMillan, M., D. Rodrik, and I. Verduzco-Gallo (2014). 'Globalization, structural change and productivity growth with an update on Africa.' *World Development* 63: 11–32.

Mondliwa, P., S. Goga, and S. Roberts (2021). 'Competition, productive capabilities and structural transformation in South Africa.' *European Journal of Development Research* 33: 253–74.

Mondliwa, P. and S. Roberts (2017). 'Economic benefits of Mozambique gas for Sasol and the South African government.' University of Johannesburg Working Paper 23/2017. Johannesburg: Centre for Competition, Regulation and Economic Development.

Mondliwa, P., S. Roberts, and S. Ponte (2020). 'Competition and power in global value chains.' *Competition and Change*. DOI:10.1177/1024529420975154

Nelson, R. and S. Winter (1982). *An Evolutionary Theory of Economic Change.* Cambridge, MA: Belknap Press of Harvard University.

Noman, A. and J. Stiglitz, eds (2016). *Efficiency, Finance and Varieties of Industrial Policy.* New York: Columbia University Press.

Ocampo, J. A., C. Rada, and L. Taylor (2009). *Growth and Policy in Developing Countries.* New York: Columbia University Press.

Oqubay, A., C. Cramer, H.-J. Chang, and R. Kozul-Wright (2020). *The Oxford Handbook of Industrial Policy.* Oxford: Oxford University Press.

Pavitt, K. (1984). 'Sectoral patterns of technical change: towards a taxonomy and a theory.' *Research Policy* 13(6): 343–73.

Penrose, E. (1959 [1995]). *The Theory of the Growth of the Firm.* Oxford: Oxford University Press.

Pollin, R. (2020). 'An industrial policy framework to advance a global green new deal.' In H.-J. Chang, C. Cramer, R. Kozul-Wright, and A. Oqubay (eds), *The Oxford Handbook of Industrial Policy*, 394–428. Oxford: Oxford University Press.

Prebisch, R. (1950). 'The economic development of Latin America and its principal problems.' Economic Bulletin for Latin America, No. 7. New York: United Nations Department of Economic Affairs.

Pritchet, L., K. Sen, and E. Werker (2018). *Deals and Development.* Oxford: Oxford University Press.

Roberts, S. (2008). 'Patterns of industrial performance in South Africa in the first decade of democracy: the continued influence of minerals-based activities.' *Transformation: Critical Perspectives on Southern Africa* 65(1): 4–35.

Roberts, S. (2020a). 'Enterprises and industrial policy: firm-based perspectives.' In H.-J. Chang, C. Cramer, R. Kozul-Wright, and A. Oqubuy (eds), *The Oxford Handbook of Industrial Policy*, 150–77. Oxford: Oxford University Press.

Roberts, S. (2020b). 'Assessing the record of competition law enforcement in opening up the economy.' In T. Vilakazi, S. Goga, and S. Roberts (eds), *Opening the South African Economy: Barriers to Entry and Competition*, 179–98. Cape Town: HSRC Press.

Rodrik, D. (2004). 'Industrial policy for the twenty-first century.' https://ssrn.com/abstract=617,544 or DOI:10.2139/ssrn.617544.

Rodrik, D. (2008). 'Normalizing industrial policy.' Commission on Growth and Development, Working Paper No. 3. Washington, DC: World Bank.

Rodrik, D. (2014). 'Green industrial policy.' *Oxford Review of Economic Policy* 30(3): 469–91.

Rosenberg, N. (1982). *Inside the Black Box: Technology and Economics*. Cambridge: Cambridge University Press.

Stiglitz, J. and J. Y. Lin, eds (2013). *The Industrial Policy Revolution I*. Basingstoke: Palgrave Macmillan.

Teece, D. J. (2006). 'Reflections on "profiting from innovation".' *Research Policy* 35(8): 1131–46.

Tregenna, F. (2009). 'Characterising deindustrialisation: an analysis of changes in manufacturing employment and output internationally.' *Cambridge Journal of Economics* 33(3): 433–66.

Tregenna, F. (2010). 'How significant is the intersectoral outsourcing of employment in South Africa?' *Industrial and Corporate Change* 19(5): 1427–57.

Tregenna, F. (2013). 'Deindustrialisation and reindustrialisation.' In A. Szirmai, W. Naudé, and L. Alcorta (eds), *Pathways to Industrialization in the 21st Century: New Challenges and Emerging Paradigms*, 76–101. Oxford: Oxford University Press.

Tregenna, F. (2016a). 'Deindustrialisation and premature deindustrialisation.' In J. Ghosh, R. Kattel, and E. Reinert (eds), *Handbook of Alternative Theories of Economic Development*, 710–28. Cheltenham: Edward Elgar.

Tregenna, F. (2016b). 'Deindustrialisation: an issue for both developed and developing countries.' In J. Weiss and M. Tribe (eds), *Handbook on Industry and Development*, 97–115. Abingdon: Routledge.

Tregenna, F. and A. Andreoni (2020). 'Deindustrialisation reconsidered: structural shifts and sectoral heterogeneity.' Working Paper Series (IIPP WP 2020–06). UCL Institute for Innovation and Public Purpose, https://www.ucl.ac.uk/bartlett/public-purpose/wp2020-06.

UNIDO (2010). 'Industrial statistics: guidelines and methodology.' Vienna: UNIDO, https://www.unido.org/sites/default/files/2012–07/Industrial%20Statistics%20-%20 Guidelines%20and%20Methdology_0.pdf.

UNIDO (2020). 'Industrialization as the driver of sustained prosperity.' Vienna: UNIDO, https://www.unido.org/industrialization-driver-sustained-prosperity.

Wade, R. (1990). *Governing the Market*. Princeton: Princeton University Press.

Weiss, L. and J. M. Hobson (1995). *States and Economic Development: A Comparative Historical Analysis*. Cambridge: Polity Press.

Whitfield, L., C. Staritz, A. T. Melese, and S. Azizi (2020). 'Technological capabilities, upgrading, and value capture in global value chains: local apparel and floriculture firms in sub-Saharan Africa.' *Economic Geography* 96(3): 195–218.

2

Structural Change in South Africa

A Historical Sectoral Perspective

Nimrod Zalk

2.1 Introduction

Structural transformation is central to economic development through mobilizing fixed investment and shifting people to industries with increasing returns, and the associated institutional learning to acquire industrial capabilities that are becoming ever more sophisticated. Manufacturing has historically been the primary site of increasing returns, hence industrialization's centrality in structural transformation (Kaldor, 1967; Thirlwall, 1983; Amsden, 2003; Rodrik, 2012; Szirmai et al., 2013). It involves not only the development of capabilities at the firm and sectoral level, but supportive economy-wide policies and institutions that span the macroeconomic and financial arena, and infrastructure and skills (Thirlwall, 2002; Ocampo et al., 2009).

Successful structural transformation involves profound changes to economic structure, requiring corresponding institutional development (Gerschenkron, 1962). This is an iterative process with economic and political–institutional structures being shaped over time by the interactions between them (Hirschman, 1971). The interplay between the two can be understood through a country's evolving political settlement that reflects the accommodations forged among powerful political and economic actors around the generation and distribution of rents (Khan and Blankenburg, 2009). Political settlements thus often reflect 'elite bargains' struck between powerful economic and political elites (Di John and Putzel, 2009; and Chapter 14). Various rents and rent-like transfers, rather than being aberrations, are pervasive in capitalist development. These include rents derived from market dominance, natural resources, transfers from real economy to financial sector actors, conditional industrial policies to promote the acquisition of industrial capabilities, and state licensing and procurement instruments. Furthermore, various 'rent-like' transfers to social constituencies are frequently deployed to secure political support and maintain political stability (Khan and Jomo, 2000; Storm, 2018).

Nimrod Zalk, *Structural Change in South Africa: A Historical Sectoral Perspective* In: *Structural Transformation in South Africa: The Challenges of Inclusive Industrial Development in a Middle-Income Country.* Edited by: Antonio Andreoni, Pamela Mondliwa, Simon Roberts, and Fiona Tregenna, Oxford University Press. © Oxford University Press 2021.
DOI: 10.1093/oso/9780192894311.003.0002

What is thus important is the form rents take, the political economy effects of the processes—often highly contested—through which they arise, and whether or not they are used to finance productive investment in sectors with increasing returns. In neoclassical terms, various forms of rents, including returns earned by firms in excess of total costs (including financing costs), are generally considered wasteful (Tollison, 1982). In contrast, in the classical economic tradition profits, regardless of whether they exceed costs, are the primary source for financing capital accumulation (Thirlwall, 2002).

Across developing regions, internally generated revenues and reinvested profits are the primary source of funding for firm-level investment (UNCTAD, 2016). A virtuous 'profit-investment nexus'—where firms make profitable investments, funded through retained earnings, which underpin further investment—is thus especially important for industrial growth in these regions. This positive feedback mechanism was central to East Asia's rapid industrialization, with the state intervening to accelerate productive capital accumulation (Akyüz and Gore, 1996). High levels of fixed investment which build industrial capabilities in sectors that provide increasing returns lead to rising productivity, enhancing export competitiveness and alleviating the balance-of-payments constraint to growth (Thirlwall, 2002).

Thus, three empirical regularities characterize developing countries that have achieved rapid catch-up with advanced economies: first, a high share of fixed investment in gross domestic product (GDP); second, a high share of manufacturing in GDP; and third, substantial increases in the level and sophistication of their exports (Hausmann et al., 2005; World Bank, 2008). As reflected in Chapter 1 (Table 1.1) South Africa has performed disappointingly relative to peer middle-income developing countries (MIDCs) against all three measures.

Section 2.2 of this chapter reviews the patterns of post-apartheid fixed investment, profitability, value added, and employment. It highlights inadequate investment in diversified industries, low profitability, a declining share of tradable sectors in value added, and dramatic declines in employment. This reflects deindustrialization, as discussed further in Chapter 11. Fixed investment has been particularly low in manufacturing and agriculture, with investment in the capital-intensive mining industry growing slightly more than the economy-wide average.

Section 2.3 considers the links between the economic performance and key phases of post-apartheid economic policy, including industrial policy. It traces how orthodox policies and institutions arising from the post-apartheid political settlement accelerated deindustrialization through corporate and industrial restructuring that enabled high corporate profits in some areas of the economy, but not the virtuous profit–investment nexus in the tradable sectors which are needed to drive sustained growth. It argues that the formal introduction of industrial policy reflected a significant policy shift, with some important successes and helped avert even deeper deindustrialization. However, it has been undermined by unsupportive macroeconomic policies and state-owned corporations (SOCs), and the weak articulation between policies to advance black ownership and structural transformation. Rising corruption and maladministration has further undermined structural transformation, particularly through a deteriorating national electricity system.

Section 2.4 concludes that the post-apartheid economy has undergone substantial structural change but limited structural transformation, with some implications for other MIDCs.

2.2 Low Levels of Productive Investment, Declining Manufacturing Profitability, and Limited Structural Transformation

There have been substantial shifts in the corporate and industrial structure of the post-apartheid economy flowing from the political settlement forged during the transition from apartheid to democracy.

2.2.1 High Corporate Profitability, Low Fixed Investment, and the Shift to Low-Tradability Sectors

At the core of changes in the corporate and industrial structure has been the shifting orientation and investment decisions of the country's largest financial and non-financial firms, many of which are listed (Bosiu et al., 2017b). The unbundling of apartheid-era conglomerates and subsequent corporate reconsolidation along more narrowly defined sectoral lines has sustained and often deepened concentration, enabling a small number of large firms to cement their domination of most sectors (Buthelezi et al., 2019).

Concentration and associated market dominance often go hand in hand with high corporate profitability. High returns of listed firms in the 2000s, which had increased substantially from the 1990s, have been widely observed by the International Monetary Fund (IMF) (2011, 2014, and 2016) and World Bank (2011). Similarly, UNCTAD (2016) calculates that South African listed firms have recorded among the highest levels of profitability on MIDC stock markets in the period 1995–2014, with the banking sector particularly profitable. However, South Africa's financial system aggregates far lower levels of savings and fixed investment than peer MIDCs (Bell et al., 2018; and Chapter 1). Fixed investment has been particularly low in two major tradable sectors—agriculture and manufacturing (see Table 2.2)— with profoundly negative consequences for growth, employment, and exports. This is despite tremendous growth in the size of stock market. The market capitalization

Table 2.1 Net markup by broad sector %, 1994–2019

	Average 1994–9	Average 2000–4	Average 2005–9	Average 2010–14	Average 2015–19	Average 1994–2019
Agriculture, forestry, fishing	40.5%	34.8%	36.0%	28.2%	25.9%	33.3%
Mining, and quarrying	17.1%	29.6%	39.0%	35.6%	24.7%	28.8%
Manufacturing	12.3%	11.0%	8.6%	3.4%	3.9%	8.0%
Heavy-industry	11.6%	12.8%	9.8%	0.6%	–1.0%	7.0%
Diversified manufacturing	12.6%	9.9%	7.8%	5.0%	6.9%	8.6%
Electricity, gas, and water	14.6%	15.1%	12.1%	41.2%	37.1%	23.7%
Construction	14.6%	13.4%	19.9%	20.0%	18.0%	17.1%
Wholesale and retail trade	37.7%	38.1%	39.7%	46.3%	44.0%	41.1%
Catering and accommodation	11.8%	11.3%	13.7%	21.6%	19.6%	15.5%
Transport and storage	28.7%	24.6%	41.0%	35.1%	29.9%	31.7%
Communication	48.9%	50.3%	52.7%	35.8%	23.9%	42.6%
Finance and insurance	28.4%	31.6%	39.5%	37.3%	25.6%	32.3%
Business services	40.4%	34.5%	36.9%	33.2%	28.5%	34.9%
Community, social, personal	21.2%	18.9%	21.3%	23.9%	20.8%	21.2%

Notes: Net markup is an industry's net operating surplus as a percentage of the sum of its intermediate inputs, wages, and capital depreciation (Quantec, n.d.). It factors in capital intensity, to an extent, as more capital-intensive industries are likely to have higher levels of depreciation. Heavy-industry comprises: Paper; coke, petroleum and nuclear fuel; basic chemicals; other chemicals; other non-metal minerals; basic iron and steel and non-ferrous metal sectors. Diversified manufacturing sectors comprise all other manufacturing industries.

It is important to note that the Quantec data are not official statistics. They have been compiled using data from Statistics South Africa, with some computations by Quantec, and this should be borne in mind.

Source: Quantec.

Table 2.2 Gross fixed capital formation, gross value added, and employment, 1994–2019

	Gross fixed capital formation		Gross value added		Employment	
	2019 Share	CAGR 1994–2019	2019 Share	CAGR 1994–2019	2019 Share	CAGR 1994–2019
Agriculture, forestry, and fishing	2.7%	0.6%	2.1%	1.2%	7.1%	−0.9%
Mining and quarrying	11.3%	4.7%	8.3%	−0.4%	3.1%	−0.9%
Manufacturing	14.3%	2.3%	13.2%	1.8%	9.3%	−0.5%
Heavy-industry	7.4%	2.6%	3.9%	2.5%	1.9%	−0.7%
Paper and paper products	0.8%	2.1%	0.5%	1.7%	0.2%	1.0%
Cake, petroleum products, and nuclear fuel	1.6%	4.0%	1.0%	4.9%	0.2%	1.5%
Basic chemicals	1.3%	2.4%	0.5%	2.7%	0.2%	0.3%
Other chemical products	0.5%	1.9%	0.8%	3.3%	0.5%	3.2%
Other non-metal mineral products	1.1%	1.8%	0.4%	−0.2%	0.5%	−2.3%
Basic iron and steel products, casting of metal	1.1%	2.8%	0.4%	2.3%	0.2%	−3.2%
Non-ferrous metal products	0.9%	2.8%	0.3%	1.6%	0.1%	−2.0%
Diversified manufacturing	6.8%	1.9%	9.3%	1.5%	7.4%	−0.4%
Food, beverages, and tobacco	3.1%	1.7%	3.7%	1.4%	1.9%	−0.1%
Metal products	0.3%	1.6%	0.7%	1.0%	0.8%	−0.2%
Machinery and equipment	0.4%	2.8%	0.8%	2.2%	0.9%	1.2%
Motor vehicles, parts and accessories	0.6%	2.3%	0.9%	3.8%	0.7%	−0.4%
Other diversified manufacturing	2.5%	1.9%	3.2%	1.1%	3.1%	−0.9%
Electricity, gas, and water	11.1%	6.1%	3.8%	0.7%	0.4%	1.0%
Construction	1.9%	7.0%	3.8%	3.8%	5.8%	2.0%
Wholesale and retail trade	6.3%	5.3%	14.3%	3.1%	19.8%	2.9%
Catering and accommodation services	0.8%	2.0%	0.9%	1.5%	3.4%	1.4%

Transport and storage	16.3%	6.7%	7.9%	2.8%	3.9%	4.5%
Communication	1.6%	11.5%	1.8%	7.3%	0.7%	−0.4%
Finance and insurance	3.9%	2.8%	6.4%	4.2%	2.5%	1.0%
Business services	12.9%	2.3%	13.3%	3.4%	15.0%	3.4%
General government	15.2%	4.3%	18.2%	1.9%	12.9%	1.6%
Community, social, and personal services	1.7%	5.9%	5.9%	2.6%	16.0%	1.2%
All sectors	100.0%	4.0%	100.0%	2.3%	100.0%	1.4%

Note: Growth rates of Gross Fixed Capital Formation and Gross Value Added have been calculated from constant 2010 price series; the shares of sub-sectors in economy totals for GFCF and GVA are calculated from current price data for 2019.

Source: Quantec RSA Standardised Industry Indicator Database.

of South Africa's fifty largest listed firms, excluding cross-listed firms operating predominantly outside South Africa, was equivalent to 162 per cent of GDP in 2017 (Bosiu et al., 2017b), more than double the upper-MIDC average of 60 per cent of GDP.

Relative sectoral profitability is a major factor accounting for patterns and changes in fixed investment. Sectors with the highest average profitability from 1994 to 2019, as measured by net industry markup, were limited tradability service sectors, notably communication (43 per cent); wholesale and retail (41 per cent); business services (35 per cent); finance and insurance, and transport and storage (both 32 per cent); as well as agriculture (33 per cent) (Table 2.1). By contrast, average post-apartheid manufacturing profitability was 8 per cent in 2015 and had fallen to 4 per cent in 2019. Heavy-industry profitability was slightly higher than diversified manufacturing during the commodity boom of the 2000s but fell sharply thereafter. Yet a sizeable and influential literature asserts that South African manufacturing commands high markups, particularly Aghion et al. (2008), Faulkner et al. (2013), and Fedderke et al. (2007 and 2018). This is routinely cited by multilateral institutions and in South Africa's overarching economic strategy: its National Development Plan. Far more plausible than the hypothesis that manufacturing exhibits 'excessive profitability' is Rodrik's (2008: 669) assessment of 'the decline in the relative profitability of manufacturing in the 1990s as the most important contributor to the lack of vitality in that sector'.

Within a context of lacklustre overall investment described in Chapter 1, compound annual growth (CAGR) in gross fixed capital formation (GFCF) increased most in the communication (11.5 per cent), construction (7.0 per cent), transport and storage (6.7 per cent), and community, social, and personal services (5.9 per cent) sectors (Table 2.2). The 6.1 per cent increase in electricity GFCF is overstated in that it includes massive cost overruns of two new coal-fired plants incurred by state-owned Eskom amid corruption and maladministration (Watermeyer and Phillips, 2020), as well as private investment in renewable energy projects.

By contrast, a striking pattern of low investment in agriculture and manufac-turing is evident (Table 2.2). Agriculture GFCF grew marginally between 1994 and 2019 (with a CAGR of just 0.6 per cent) and manufacturing by only 2.3 per cent, while mining grew by 4.7 per cent. Within manufacturing, the heavy-industry grouping recorded GFCF growth of 2.6 per cent and diversified manufacturing 1.9 per cent. Agricultural investment has been curtailed by low public investment (particularly in water infrastructure, and research and development), slow progress by the Department of Agriculture in negotiating access to fast-growing East Asian markets for horticultural products, and land-tenure uncertainties from unresolved contestation over land reform (Cramer and Sender, 2015). Low agricultural investment has prevailed in parallel with relatively high profitability, as corporate consolidation following the liberalization of the sector in the 1990s enabled a small number of large agroprocessing producers to dominate the sector (Bell et al., 2018). Higher mining investment has been constrained pre-dominantly by protracted contention over levels of black ownership in the sector (Jonas, 2019).

As with investment, value added has grown most in the generally more profit-able service sectors with limited tradability, notably communication (7.3 per cent), finance and insurance (4.2 per cent), construction (3.8 per cent), business services (3.4 per cent), and wholesale and retail (3.1 per cent). Lacklustre growth in all three major tradable sectors has prevailed, well below the economy-wide average of 2.3 per cent, namely: agriculture (1.2 per cent), mining (−0.4 per cent), and manufacturing (1.8 per cent). The capital-intensive heavy industries (2.5 per cent) grew faster than diversified manufacturing (1.5 per cent) sectors.

Large-scale job losses have been recorded in all three major tradable sectors, albeit reflective of significant shifts within these sectors. Between 1994 and 2019, over one-fifth of the workforce was lost in both mining (−23 per cent) and agri-culture (−21 per cent), while manufacturing employment fell by 12 per cent. However, an under-recognized process influencing recorded manufacturing employment has been extensive outsourcing starting in the 1990s. Between 1997 and 2007, an estimated 300,000 workers, such as security guards and cleaners, were statistically 'transferred' to business services while they continued to work (under different employers) in manufacturing (Tregenna, 2010). This implies that job losses in manufacturing may not have been as extensive as reflected in official employment statistics. However, changes in employment survey methodology make it difficult to estimate the precise impact of outsourcing over the 1994–2019 period (Kerr and Wittenberg, 2019).

Mining job losses have been mainly due to the long-term decline in labour-intensive gold mining, which has not been offset by growth in other minerals such as platinum (Ritchken, 2018). Agricultural job losses have taken place in field crops and livestock, while, as elaborated in Chapter 6, horticulture has repre-sented a welcome site of employment and export growth (Chisoro-Dube et al., 2018; Zalk, 2019).

2.2.2 Intra-manufacturing Patterns: Limited Diversification and the Continued Dominance of Heavy Industry

As manufacturing's overall share in GFCF fell to 14 per cent in 2019 in line with the sector's share in the economy, above-average GFCF growth has been recorded in coke and petroleum (4.0 per cent), and in basic iron and steel, non-ferrous metal products, and machinery and equipment (which each grew GFCF at average annual rates of 2.8 per cent). Motor vehicles grew at the manufacturing average of 2.3 per cent.

Value-added growth leading up to the global financial crisis was driven chiefly by the chemical and primary metal sectors, and associated strategies of dominant firms including increasing internationalization. The coke and refined petroleum, and basic chemicals sectors, accounting for 14 per cent of manufacturing value added, have been dominated by formerly state-owned Sasol. Sasol benefits from a legacy of state support, vertically integrated coal supply, and cheap natural gas from Mozambique, as well as monopolistic pricing and market conduct (Bell et al., 2018; and Chapter 4). Sasol has internationalized through a secondary listing on the NASDAQ and various expansion projects outside South Africa, the largest being its Lake Charles Chemicals gas-to-liquids project in Louisiana in the USA. However, the combination of vast cost and time overruns constructing the Lake Charles plant, combined with low oil prices, has created a debt crisis for Sasol (Theunissen, 2020), the resolution of which could have damaging consequences for South African manufacturing.

While basic iron and steel and non-ferrous metals grew significantly above average until the crisis, lacklustre growth after 2009 reflected a confluence of global steel and aluminium oversupply, weak domestic demand exacerbated by low public investment, and low investment in plant maintenance in primary steel. Rapid escalation of electricity prices and the unreliability of supply have precipitated the closure of many foundries (Rustomjee et al., 2018). Formerly state owned Iscor's 2001 unbundling saw its steel operations transferred to transnational ArcelorMittal with the contractual right to iron-ore supply on concessional terms from Anglo subsidiary Kumba that had acquired Iscor's iron-ore assets. Concurrently, ArcelorMittal South Africa (AMSA) exerted its monopoly power to charge domestic customers import parity prices (Roberts and Rustomjee, 2010), as touched on in Chapter 3. Rather than the anticipated efficiencies the state naively assumed would flow from foreign ownership, AMSA systematically underinvested amid multiple plant failures and escalating inefficiencies, extracting as much cash as possible to its global parent (Zalk, 2017). These inefficiencies were brutally exposed after world steel prices fell in the aftermath of the 2008 global financial crisis, throwing the South African steel industry into deep crisis. As part of Anglo's restructuring strategy to meet shareholder expectations that it become a 'focused mining group' it sold off the second-largest steel producer to Evraz in 2007, which, like AMSA, failed to invest and extracted cash to help service the debt of the global group (Zalk, 2017; Rustomjee et al., 2018).

Three main diversified manufacturing sectors recorded meaningful real value-added growth: motor vehicles and parts, food and beverages, and machinery, with the remainder collectively little larger in real terms than they were in 1994. Chapter 3 highlights how industrial capabilities in machinery were developed to service the mining sector. However, substantial industrial capabilities and opportunities have been lost through Anglo and Rembrandt/Remgro's disposal of their most significant engineering subsidiaries: Dorbyl, Boart Longyear, and Scaw Metals over the 2000s (Zalk, 2017). Chapter 4 provides a contrast between South Africa and Thailand's plastics industry, demonstrating how tight integration with the latter's automotive policy has driven a far more dynamic trajectory than in South Africa. Chapter 5 highlights how the automotive sector has attracted substantial foreign investment by assemblers and first-tier original equipment manufacturer (OEM) suppliers through South Africa's flagship sector policy programme, but that rising exports have not been accompanied by adequate increases in domestic value added on a per vehicle basis.

Food and beverages has been one of the few diversified manufacturing sectors where the main firms have domestic market power, dominated by a handful of large producers (Chisoro-Dube et al., 2018). It is notable that two major sub-sectors—sugar and poultry—were among the few that secured sustained import protection amid the general slashing of industrial tariffs during the 1990s. Remgro (previously Rembrandt), the second-largest business group at the end of the apartheid era and co-founder with Anglo of the South Africa Foundation that advocated the liberalization of various markets, retained substantial interests in both sectors, and food and beverages more generally (Mondliwa et al., 2017). Concentration in food and beverages has overlapped with, and mutually reinforced, market dominance in the supermarket sector, as large producers have offered terms to retailers which cannot be matched by smaller producers (Bosiu et al., 2017a).

Manufacturing job losses have been more pronounced in heavy-industry (−0.7 per cent (CAGR)) than diversified manufacturing (−0.4 per cent) (Table 2.2). The dominant explanation given for poor manufacturing employment performance is that inordinate labour-market protections were extended over the 1990s, raising unskilled workers' wages, while weak vocational education has led to a shortage of skilled workers and raised their wages (Levinsohn, 2008; Kaplan, 2015a and 2015b; Nattrass and Seekings, 2019). While South Africa is clearly not a very low-wage manufacturing economy, various indicators cast doubt that its uniquely high unemployment is explained predominantly by market inflexibility. First, nominal international wages in tradable sectors are highly sensitive to exchange rate movements. Periods of overvaluation push up relative wage costs in dollar terms, even as labour productivity has roughly matched Rand increases in the wage bill (Rodrik, 2008; Zalk, 2014).

Second, there is no obvious relationship between measures of labour-market rigidity and unemployment across a range of developing countries. A number of other middle-income countries have been ranked with similar levels of labour market rigidity as South Africa over the past two decades but have not experienced anywhere near the levels of unemployment that South Africa has.[1] Far more plausible is that low profitability and correspondingly tepid rates of investment in diversified manufacturing in general, even while there have been higher investment rates in capital-intensive heavy industries, are the primary factors in poor manufacturing employment growth. Third, while there are clearly deep problems with both South Africa's education and vocational training system, the greatest constraint cited by firms for unutilized capacity and in business confidence surveys is lack of demand. This is in no way to suggest that skills formation is irrelevant. Rather, a poorly performing secondary and vocational education system has provided, at best, no particular advantage to South African manufacturers. Indeed, inadequate skills would likely become a more significant constraint with any acceleration of manufacturing growth. Furthermore, Chapter 12 emphasizes that increasing technological sophistication and digitalization of production systems mean that the intensity and complexity of skills required are set to rise, both in manufacturing and in progressively more integrated ancillary service sectors, such as data mining.

South Africa remains heavily dependent on primary and semi-processed mineral exports, accounting for 57 per cent of merchandise exports in 2019, while aggregate export growth and diversification have been lacklustre (Chapter 1). Import growth and dividend outflows have outstripped export growth with the balance-of-payment constraint increasingly financed by short-term capital inflows (Strauss, 2017). Agricultural export growth has been driven predominantly by the horticulture sector, particularly of high-value fresh fruit (Chapter 6).

The following section turns to the phases and processes of industrial restructuring that have given rise to the limited post-apartheid structural transformation described above.

2.3 Phases and Processes of Industrial Restructuring and Policy

Three phases of post-apartheid industrial restructuring and policy can be identified, reflecting both significant continuity since the 1990s, particularly with respect to macroeconomic policy, as well as important policy shifts.

---

[1] See for example, World Bank measures of labour market rigidity reviewed in Zalk (2017).

2.3.1   Phase 1: Core Bargains, Liberalization, and Stabilization

South African deindustrialization began in the early 1980s due to an inability to develop internationally competitive manufacturing sectors outside of the heavy 'mineral-energy-complex' industries built up under apartheid (Fine and Rustomjee, 1996). Profitability of the handful of private conglomerates that dominated the economy faltered together with private and public investment, amid a deepening political and economic crisis (Morris, 1991).

The orthodox orientation of economic policy which has prevailed to a greater or lesser degree in the post-apartheid period—with its emphasis on macroeconomic 'stability', Anglo-American-style capital markets, and the removal of market distortions—was effected through processes of contestation and accommodation during South Africa's transition from apartheid to democracy. From the late 1980s, dominant conglomerates sought to secure policies that would restore profitability and, above all, maximize their freedom to restructure capital domestically and abroad (Zalk, 2017). Their central contention was that efficient capital allocation and higher fixed investment would best be secured, not by state-directed restructuring, but by further deepening Anglo-American-style capital markets in which shareholders and lenders overwhelmingly shape capital-allocation strategies (South African Foundation, 1996). A multi-pronged effort was pursued to legitimate this objective. This included relentless lobbying of senior African National Congress (ANC) leaders and economic policy office-bearers (Spicer, 2016), rhetorical and ideological appeals to the benefits of 'free markets' (South African Foundation, 1996), and the initiation of narrow-based black economic empowerment (BEE) asset transfers to politically influential individuals (Kantor, 1998) in a series of highly leveraged 'first generation' BEE deals.

Momentum for a putatively market-led restructuring was bolstered by selective appeals to scholarship contending that apartheid industrialization had failed due to a range of product and factor market distortions, which incentivized capital-intensive investment while disincentivizing the employment of unskilled labour (Lipton, 1986; Nattrass, 1989; Holden, 1992; Fallon and de Silva, 1994). Overlaid upon this market distortions thesis were various ideological claims, inadequately substantiated by empirical evidence. These included that public investment crowded out private investment, that macroeconomic stabilization of public debt and inflation would raise investment via an ill-defined 'business confidence', and that South Africa's industrial import tariff structure was high relative to developing-country peers (Macroeconomic Research Group, 1993; Michie and Padayachee, 1998; Weeks, 1999).

The adoption of the Growth, Employment, and Redistribution (GEAR) strategy reflected this confluence of interests, selective reliance on scholarship, and ideology. Neither the surge in private investment in export-oriented manufacturing nor the 600,000 jobs predicted by GEAR materialized. The concurrent adoption of legislation strengthening de jure worker protection is often conveyed as inconsistent with GEAR's liberalizing thrust (Nattrass, 1998). However, it is doubtful whether GEAR could have been politically feasible without it (Jonas, 2019), while extensive outsourcing and casualization have in practice weakened de jure worker protections (Tregenna, 2010).

Trade liberalization was intended to induce manufacturers to shift from 'excessively' profitable domestic markets to less profitable (but presumably not loss-making) export markets. Average manufacturing tariffs were cut from 28 per cent in 1990 to 23 per cent in 1994 and 8 per cent by 2004 (Edwards and van de Winkel, 2005). These went well beyond the reductions South Africa had committed to when it joined the World Trade Organization (WTO) in 1993 (Davies, 2019).

In the absence of any overarching manufacturing strategy, particularly for underdeveloped diversified sectors outside heavy-industry, industrial policy was relegated to a set of dispersed incentives supposed to assist firms adjust to trade liberalization. Only two sector-specific programmes were formalized: the Motor Industry Development Programme (MIDP) (Chapter 5) and a Duty Credit Certificate Scheme (DCCS) for clothing and textiles. In parallel, and stark contradiction with their disavowal of state intervention, private conglomerates secured extensive public support for heavy-industry expansions throughout the 1990s, supported by tax incentives, co-funding by the Industrial Development Corporation (IDC), and cheap electricity (Zalk, 2012 and 2014).

Similarly, the 'free market' commitment of large business groups was contradicted by their intense contestation of a revised Competition Act, which succeeded in circumscribing the competition authorities' ability to deal with anticompetitive conduct and not to tackle the pre-existing market concentration directly (Makhaya and Roberts, 2013).

Although the envisaged privatization was only partially implemented, a general de-emphasis of public fixed investment prevailed as SOCs were commercialized with a view to selling them to BEE investors. Low public investment meant the social infrastructure envisaged by the Reconstruction and Development Programme (RDP)[2] did not meaningfully materialize. This translated into weak demand for infrastructure-linked sectors, such as steel and engineering (Zalk, 2017). The commercialization of SOCs entrenched existing biases in the provision of electricity, rail, and ports in favour of the export of primary and semi-processed mineral commodities, rather than diversified manufacturing exports (Department of Trade and Industry, 2018a).

From the early 1990s, influential institutional investors secured the long-desired unbundling of apartheid-era conglomerate structures, shifting the

---

[2] The RDP was a socioeconomic programme of the incoming ANC government that envisaged large-scale investment to address social and infrastructural backlogs.

balance of power from founding families to shareholders, with the objective of 'unlocking shareholder value' and paving the way for greater internationalization (Malherbe and Segal, 2001; Chabane et al., 2006). Capital-account liberalization and offshore listings would, proponents argued, attract foreign direct investment and provide access to cheaper international capital to invest domestically (Walters and Prinsloo 2002). However, offshore listings by major corporations acted as a platform for international expansion rather than raising funds for investment in South Africa (Chabane et al., 2006). Most prominent was Anglo's listing on the London Stock Exchange (LSE) in 1999, with two of its biggest industrial subsidiaries, South African Breweries (SAB), and paper, pulp, and packaging producer, Mondi. Rising demands for Anglo to unlock value for shareholders by becoming a focused mining company saw it dispose of its remaining industrial subsidiaries, including chemicals producer AECI, bottler Bevcon (Mohamed 2020) and its steel and engineering investments (together with co-investor Remgro)—with profoundly damaging effects on industrial capabilities in the sector.

Rather than attracting long-term foreign direct investment, potentially invest-able long-term capital has been drained through offshore listings and rising ownership by foreign institutional investors. The associated stream of dividend outflows has become a substantial part of a persistent current-account deficit (Strauss, 2017). Long-term sources of capital have been replaced by more volatile short-term portfolio flows into South Africa's expanding stock, bond, and money markets (Hassan 2013). Illegal capital flight is said to have exacerbated the exit of long-term capital (Ashman et al., 2011; Ndikumana, 2016) although estimates of its extent and magnitude are contested (Östensson, 2018).

In the context of legislation that did not empower the competition authorities to deal with the pre-existing monopolistic market structures, the unbundling of highly concentrated apartheid-era conglomerates across the economy was followed by consolidation of control within industries, in which high levels of profitability could generally be secured. Heavy industries including petrochemicals, carbon and stainless steel, and aluminium retained their ability to impose monopolistic pricing on downstream customers (Roberts and Zalk, 2004; Zalk, 2017; Rustomjee et al., 2018). As discussed in Chapter 9, large business groups have often incorporated BEE partners to help entrench their market dominance, rather than open up space in the economy for smaller and black-owned entrants (Bell et al., 2018).

By the end of the 1990s, many 'first generation' BEE deals, which served to bolster the legitimacy for an overwhelmingly orthodox policy path, collapsed in the wake of the 1997/8 Asian financial crisis. A brief period that saw black ownership on the Johannesburg Stock Exchange (JSE) rise and peak at around 7 per cent was rapidly reversed (Mcgregor's, various years). This prompted the establishment of a BEE Commission that in 2001 called for BEE to be included in legislation rather than left to the discretion of large business groups. The limitations of this 'stabilization' phase in the 1990s became increasingly apparent as fixed investment fell, unemployment and inequality soared, and BEE ambitions remained unrealized.

2.3.2 Phase 2: The Illusion of Progress, the Ostensible Shift to a 'Developmental State', and the Introduction of Industrial Policy

The 2000s saw both continuity of orthodox policy and some significant shifts. Two main groupings in and around the ANC challenged the direction of policy, but for different fundamental reasons. The first sought a shift to East Asian-style intervention to reverse deindustrialization and associated job losses. The second grouping wanted the state to reorient its procurement, licensing, and regulatory powers in their favour. The government belatedly recognized that public investment was essential to crowd in private investment (Presidency, 2006) and public investment began to increase, particularly to address a mounting backlog in electricity supply Concurrently prepare for the country's hosting of the 2010 World Cup. Concurrently BEE became increasingly entrenched in legislation, policy, and procurement practices of the state and SOCs.

Meanwhile, corporate restructuring bore fruit as 'value' was increasingly disgorged to shareholders through dividends and share buybacks. Based on estimates by Wesson (2015), dividends to and repurchases from institutional investors on the JSE between 1999 and 2009 were equivalent to 17 per cent of total gross fixed formation (GFCF) or 61 per cent of manufacturing GFCF over the corresponding period. This is a lower-bound estimate as it excludes firms that form part of two of the largest sectoral indices of the JSE: basic materials and financials, as well as formerly South African companies listed offshore. Thus, it excludes Anglo's large-scale programme between 2005 and 2008 to repurchase shares from LSE investors (Coulson, 2009), which coincided with the destructive unbundling of its steel and engineering businesses discussed above. Sizeable transfers also accrued to beneficiaries of BEE deals. Based on estimates by Theobald et al. (2015) the net value transferred to beneficiaries of BEE deals from the one hundred largest JSE-listed firms between 2000 and 2014 was equivalent to 8 per cent of total GFCF and 29 per cent of manufacturing GFCF over the same period (Zalk, 2017). Thus, very sizeable (and conservatively estimated) flows of potentially investable funds have accrued as rents or rent-like transfers to both entrenched and new shareholders. But these have not translated into levels or patterns of fixed investment capable of shifting South Africa onto a structurally transformed growth path.

Despite low investment and exceptionally high unemployment and inequality, macroeconomic policy continued to be cast as 'state of the art' and declared a success in terms of intermediate measures such as lower inflation, fiscal deficits, and tariffs. Weak manufacturing performance was attributed to a lack of 'microeconomic reforms', particularly labour market deregulation, deeper trade liberalization, incomplete privatization, and limited competition (Edwards and van de Winkel, 2005; Du Plessis and Smit, 2007). A 'Microeconomic Reform Strategy' echoed the dogma of irreproachable macroeconomic policy, emphasizing further microeconomic reforms and an ill-defined shift towards greater manufacturing 'knowledge intensity'. The latter was not, however, accompanied by any meaningful sector strategies beyond automotives, and clothing and textiles. Over this period, the IDC shifted its emphasis from financing capital-intensive mega-projects to BEE ownership transfers that were delinked from new industrial investment capacity (Mondi and Roberts, 2005).

Although the 2000s saw a brief period of improvement in GDP, investment and employment, this was driven by an unsustainable confluence of the global commodity boom, a surge in short-term capital inflows, and a domestic consumption-led boom underpinned by unsustainable increases in household debt (Bell et al., 2018). The disjuncture between industrial and macroeconomic policy over this period was manifested most starkly by the failure to act meaningfully against prolonged currency overvaluation, which dramatically eroded the competitiveness of diversified manufacturing industries (Zalk, 2014). Furthermore, rail and port SOCs Transnet and Portnet have favoured bulk primary and semi-processed commodity exports over diversified value-added exports. Port unit costs are considerably higher than developing-country comparators and exceed those of either primary commodity exports or the imports of manufactured goods (Ports Regulator, cited in Department of Trade and Industry (2018a: 58)).

The belated adoption by the Mbeki administration (1999–2008) of the 'developmental state' nomenclature in the second half of the 2000s represented more an attempt to shore up legitimacy within the ANC than present a serious policy alternative (Fine, 2010). However, it was inadequate to stave off the accession of Jacob Zuma to the Presidency in 2008, supported by an uneasy coalition of ANC factions: one envisaging a shift from orthodox policies, the other eyeing unproductive accumulation opportunities through the state. On the cusp of this transition, Cabinet adopted the first formal, overarching, post-apartheid industrial policy, the 2007 National Industrial Policy Framework (NIPF) (Department of Trade and Industry, 2007). The NIPF's core objective was to guide and facilitate government-wide policy aimed at the reversal of deindustrialization and the diversification of manufacturing beyond heavy-industry.

2.3.3 Phase 3: Industrial Policy—Formally Embraced, Undermined in Practice

The introduction of the NIPF and a series of rolling Industrial Policy Action Plans (IPAPs) marked a consequential policy shift. It raised fundamental questions about the appropriateness of orthodox policies in light of weak domestic invest-ment and manufacturing performance since 1994 and the onset of the global financial crisis in 2008. In order to reverse a growth path 'driven by unsustainable increases in credit extension and consumption, not sufficiently underpinned by growth in the production sectors of the economy' (Department of Trade and Industry, 2010: 4), it highlighted the need for supportive macroeconomic policy, scaled-up industrial financing including via development banks like the IDC, the strategic use of trade policy instruments, and the leveraging of public procurement.

The automotive sector, supported by the Automotive Production Development Programme (APDP) and notwithstanding the weaknesses discussed in Chapter 5, has grown to become the leading export sector outside of heavy-industry. The Clothing and Textile Competitiveness Programme (CTCP) has helped to stabilize the sector after mass job losses during the 1990s, through rapid productivity growth and the better integration of manufacturers in retail supply chains. The agroprocessing, metals and machinery, film, and business-process industries have also been supported. These measures have helped to avert even deeper deindus-trialization. However, notwithstanding formal adoption of the policy by the Cabinet in 2007, industrial policy and structural transformation have been undermined in practice in three main ways.

First, monetary and fiscal policy have been misaligned with structural trans-formation and industrial policy. National Treasury took over five years to imple-ment Cabinet-mandated regulations enabling the designation of publicly procured products for domestic manufacture. No real increase in on-budget industrial financing materialized until the 2009/10 financial year (Zalk, 2014) and these have subsequently been reversed with the Department of Trade, Industry, and Competition's (DTIC) incentives budget declining by 19 per cent in real terms between 2012/13 and 2018/19 (Zalk 2014; Department of Trade and Industry, 2018b). Since the introduction of the NIPF, the IDC has raised its levels of disbursements. However, its ability to provide long-term concessional funding has been constrained by limited access to low-cost funding streams, in the face of rising costs of capital (Goga et al., 2019), that have been the lifeblood of successful development banks elsewhere in the world (Griffith-Jones and Ocampo, 2018).

Second, discordant objectives for an expanded role for the state and SOCs became increasingly manifest, particularly with respect to the exercise of the state's licensing and procurement powers. The DTIC and the Economic Development Department (EDD) envisaged an expanded role of the state and SOCs to reverse deindustrialization and place it on a more diversified path (Economic Development Department, 2011). However, much of government and the SOCs placed particular emphasis on BEE ownership transfers with limited regard to structural transformation and employment considerations. For instance, the 2002 Mining Charter (Republic of South Africa, 2002) required a minimum

25 per cent black ownership and to cascade these ownership requirements to mining suppliers, often sucking in imports from 'empowered' importers (Zalk 2014 and 2017; and Chapter 9). Efforts to forge a stronger link between BEE and the development of productive capabilities included introducing enterprise and skills development elements into a revised Broad-Based Black Economic Empowerment (BBBEE) Act (Republic of South Africa, 2014) and a black industrialist programme to support active black ownership in manufacturing (Department of Trade and Industry, n.d.; and Chapter 9). However, this effort has come up against lobbying for the inclusion of importers rather than manufacturers, limited budget, and lack of support from SOCs in procuring from bona fide black manufacturers (Vilakazi, 2020; and Chapter 9).

Rising corruption and maladministration under the Zuma administration (2009–18) further weakened manufacturing. Many SOCs and government departments have not complied with local content requirements (Department of Trade and Industry, 2018a). The most conspicuous lost opportunity was the subornment of SOCs Transnet and Prasa's rail recapitalization programme to renew their ageing freight and passenger rail fleets. Widespread irregularities and corruption in contracts to acquire rolling stock, have invariably involved the minimization of local content in favour of imports. (Bhorat et al., 2017; Crompton et al., 2017).

Corruption and maladministration have been accompanied by a generalized deterioration in the public provision of electricity, rail, and port services. Electricity prices increased more than 240 per cent above inflation between 2004 and 2017 (Statistics South Africa, cited in Department of Trade and Industry (2018a: 57)) as Eskom's debt surged due to massive capital cost overruns and maladministration. Periodic electricity supply outages have had an extremely adverse impact on manufacturing and mining. State guarantees on Eskom's debt have become so large that they have triggered a sovereign credit rating downgrade to sub-investment level, with an associated increase in the cost of debt (South African Reserve Bank, 2020).

2.4 Conclusions

This chapter traces how the post-apartheid political settlement and associated policies and institutions have been shaped by a confluence of interests, selective appeals to scholarship, and ideology. These policies and institutions have given rise to a range of rents and rent-like transfers including monopolistic profits as well as via BEE deals. However, these rents have not been adequately channelled into levels of fixed investment or increasing return sectors capable of shifting the economy onto a path of decisive structural transformation. Corporate and industrial restructuring has been associated with a 'high-profit-low-investment' economy and deepening deindustrialization. Low investment has prevailed, notwithstanding the rapid growth and high profitability of the finance sector, with institutional investors the major beneficiaries of these monopoly rents. Within a context of low overall fixed investment, capital has shifted away from the two major tradable sectors essential for structural transformation and job creation: agriculture and an increasingly low-profitability manufacturing sector. Together with mining, these tradable sectors have experienced large declines in employment. Rather, investment has moved predominantly to limited-tradability services sectors.

Industrial policy interventions have played an important role in supporting growth, competitiveness, and jobs in a number of diversified manufacturing sectors, particularly automotives, and clothing and textiles. However, increasingly internationalized heavy industries have continued to dominate through their weight in manufacturing investment and value added, their ability to impose monopolistic pricing for their output on downstream industries, and a continued reliance on mining and mineral processing for close to two-thirds of South Africa's merchandise exports. Rather than 'excessive' worker protections, poor manufacturing employment outcomes are mainly due to low rates of manufacturing investment, with low and declining profitability and weak demand.

Low investment, job losses, and limited black participation in the 'commanding heights' of the economy from the mid-1990s spurred the political impetus for a stronger role for the state during the 2000s and 2010s. In this context the formal introduction of industrial policy in 2007 reasserted the centrality of structural transformation, supported significant sectoral advances, and helped avert even deeper deindustrialization. However, industrial policy has been undermined by the disarticulation between the policy objective of structural transformation, subordinated to the domain of 'microeconomic reforms' on the one hand, and macroeconomic and other economy-wide policies and institutional arrangements on the other. Monetary, fiscal, and financial policy as well as policies to advance black ownership have generally been disconnected from the economy-wide imperative of structural transformation. Strategic SOCs, particularly those providing electricity, rail, and port infrastructure as well as technical and vocational educational and training (TVET) institutions, have at best provided no particular advantage to diversified manufacturing sectors. Rising corruption and maladministration have fundamentally weakened these SOCs, increasing costs and further lowering efficiencies for diversified manufacturing in particular. The emerging cornerstone of industrial policy and structural transformation, under the 'New Dawn' of the Ramaphosa administration that commenced in 2018, are sector master plans to be forged through social compacts between the state, business, and labour (Republic of South Africa, 2020). There is a danger that these continue to be relegated to the domain of 'microeconomic reforms' rather than elevated as an economy-wide imperative that enjoys appropriate and coherent support across the state and SOCs.

Despite its own specificities, the South African case has important similarities with and some implications for other MIDCs. These include the need to ensure that industrial policy and structural transformation are treated as economy-wide rather than 'microeconomic' imperatives. This implies that associated policies and institutions, including fiscal and monetary policy, are supportive of structural transformation. For resource-dependent countries, this includes managing resource rents over the commodity cycle: sterilizing and saving commodity wind-falls during the peak and deploying these savings in a counter-cyclical way when the cycle turns downwards. Policy space needs to be preserved to use trade and other policy instruments strategically in engagements with global, regional, and bilateral trade and investment negotiations. The sequencing and orientation of financial-sector policy and regulation should focus on mobilizing finance and channelling it to productive investment in increasing return sectors rather than uncritical 'financial deepening'. Taxation and other policies have a role to play in encouraging the reinvestment of retained earnings rather than maximizing their disgorgement to shareholders. Development banks have a critical role to play and require access to concessional sources of funding to help underwrite the lengthy and risky process involved in firms acquiring industrial capabilities. Finally, the South African experience reflects how the failure to foster meaningful structural transformation can help create fertile conditions for unproductive rent-seeking and corruption to flourish.

References

Aghion, P., M. Braun, and J. Fedderke (2008). 'Competition and productivity growth in South Africa.' *Economics of Transition* 16(4): 741–68.

Akyüz, Y. and C. Gore (1996). 'The investment-profits nexus in East Asian industrial-ization.' *World Development* 24(3): 461–70.

Amsden, A. H. (2003). *The Rise of 'The Rest': Challenges to the West from Late-Industrializing Economies.* Oxford: Oxford University Press.

Ashman, S., B. Fine, and S. Newman (2011). 'Amnesty International? The nature, scale and impact of capital flight from South Africa.' *Journal of Southern African Studies* 37(1): 7–25.

Bell, J., S. Goga, P. Mondliwa, and S. Roberts (2018). 'Structural transformation in south africa: moving towards a smart, open economy for all.' Centre for Competition, Regulation and Economic Development. Johannesburg: University of Johannesburg.

Bhorat, H., M. Buthelezi, I. Chipkin, S. Duma, L. Mondi, C. Peter, M. Qobo, et al. (2017). 'Betrayal of the promise: how South Africa is being stolen.' State Capacity Research Project. Johannesburg: University of Johannesburg.

Bosiu, T., R. Das Nair, and A. Paelo (2017a). 'The global food value chain and compe-tition law and policy in BRICS countries: insights from selected value chains in

South Africa.' Working Paper 21/2017. Centre for Competition, Regulation and Economic Development. Johannesburg: University of Johannesburg.

Bosiu, T., N. Nhundu, A. Paelo, M. O. Thosago, and T. Vilakazi (2017b). 'Growth and strategies of large and leading firms—top 50 firms on the Johannesburg Stock Exchange (JSE).' Working Paper 17/2017. Centre for Competition, Regulation and Economic Development. Johannesburg: University of Johannesburg.

Buthelezi, T., T. Mtani, and L. Mncube (2019). 'The extent of market concentration in South Africa's product markets.' *Journal of Antitrust Enforcement* 7(3): 352–64.

Chabane, N., A. Goldstein, and S. Roberts (2006). 'The changing face and strategies of big business in South Africa: more than a decade of political democracy.' *Industrial and Corporate Change* 15(3): 549–77.

Chisoro-Dube, S., R. das Nair, and M. Nkhonjera (2018). 'Structural transformation to grow high value exports and jobs: the case of fruit.' Industrial Development Think Tank: Policy Briefing paper 2/2018. Centre for Competition, Regulation and Economic Development. Johannesburg: University of Johannesburg.

Coulson, M. (2009). 'Anglo's disastrous share buyback.' *Miningmx*. 6 March 2009, https://www.miningmx.com/uncategorized/20523-anglo-s-disastrous-share-buyback.

Cramer, C. and J. Sender (2015). 'Agro-processing, wage employment and export revenue: opportunities for strategic intervention.' Trade and Industrial Policy Strategies. Pretoria: TIPS.

Crompton, R., J. Fessehaie, L. Kaziboni, and T. Zengeni (2017). 'Railway locomotives and Transnet: a case study.' Working Paper 9/2017. Centre for Competition, Regulation and Economic Development. Johannesburg: University of Johannesburg.

Davies, R. (2019). *The Politics of Trade in the Era of Hyperglobalisation: A Southern African Perspective*. Geneva: South Centre.

Department of Trade and Industry (2007). 'National industrial policy framework.' Department of Trade and Industry, Republic of South Africa. Pretoria: DTI.

Department of Trade and Industry (2010). 'Industrial policy action plan 2010/11–2012/13.' Department of Trade and Industry, Republic of South Africa. Pretoria: DTI.

Department of Trade and Industry (2018a). 'Industrial policy action plan 2018/19–2020/21.' Department of Trade and Industry, Republic of South Africa. Pretoria: DTI.

Department of Trade and Industry (2018b). 'Concept note: placing structural transformation at the centre of economic revival under the new dawn.' Department of Trade and Industry, Republic of South Africa. Pretoria: DTI.

Department of Trade and Industry (n.d.). 'Black industrialists policy.' Department of Trade and Industry, Republic of South Africa. Pretoria: DTI.

Di John, J. and J. Putzel (2009). 'Political settlements: issues paper.' Governance and Social Development Resource Centre. Emerging Issues Research Service. Birmingham: GSDRC.

Du Plessis, S. and B. Smit (2007). 'South Africa's growth revival after 1994.' *Journal of African Economies* 16(5): 668–704.

Economic Development Department (2011). 'New growth path.' Economic Development Department, Republic of South Africa. Pretoria: EDD.

Edwards, L. and T. van de Winkel (2005). 'The market disciplining effects of trade liberalisation and regional import penetration on manufacturing in South Africa.' Working Paper 1/2005. Trade and Industrial Policy Strategies. Pretoria: TIPS.

Fallon, P. and L. A. P. de Silva (1994). 'South Africa: economic performance and policies.' Discussion Paper No. 7. Informal Discussion Papers on Aspects of the South African Economy. Washington, DC: World Bank.

Faulkner, D., C. Loewald, and K. Makrelov (2013). 'Achieving higher growth and employment: Policy options for South Africa.' South African Reserve Bank Working Paper 13(03).

Fedderke, J., C. Kularatne, and M. Mariotti (2007). 'Mark-up pricing in South African industry.' *Journal of African Economies* 16(1): 28–69.

Fedderke, J., N. Obikili, and N. Viegi (2018). 'Markups and concentration in South African manufacturing sectors: an analysis with administrative data.' *South African Journal of Economics* 86: 120–40.

Fine, B. (2010). 'Can South Africa be a developmental state.' In O. Edigheji (ed.), *Constructing a Democratic Developmental State in South Africa: Potentials and Challenges*, 169–82. Cape Town: Human Sciences Research Council.

Fine, B. and Z. Rustomjee (1996). *The Political Economy of South Africa: From Minerals-energy Complex to Industrialisation*. New York: Routledge.

Gerschenkron, A. (1962). *Economic Backwardness in Historical Perspective: A Book of Essays*. Cambridge, MA: Harvard University Press.

Goga, S., T. Bosiu, and J. Bell (2019). 'Linking IDC finance to structural transformation and inclusivity in post-apartheid South Africa.' *Development Southern Africa* 36(6): 821–38.

Griffith-Jones, S. and J. A. Ocampo, eds (2018). *The Future of National Development Banks*. The initiative for policy dialogue series. Oxford: Oxford University Press.

Hassan, S. (2013). 'South African capital markets: an overview.' Working Paper No. WP/13/04. South African Reserve Bank Working Paper Series. Pretoria: South African Reserve Bank.

Hausmann, R., J. Hwang, and D. Rodrik (2005). 'What you export matters.' Working Paper No. 11905. National Bureau of Economic Research. Cambridge, MA: NBER.

Hirschman, A. O. (1971). 'Political economics and possibilism.' In J. Adelman (ed.), *Bias for Hope: Essays on Development and Latin America*. New Haven: Yale University Press.

Holden, M. (1992). 'Trade reform: finding the right road.' *South African Journal of Economics* 60(3): 149–56.

International Monetary Fund (2011). 'South Africa: 2011 Article IV consultation— staff report; staff supplement; public information notice on the executive board discussion; and statement by the Executive Director for South Africa.' No. 11/258. Country Report. Washington, DC: IMF.

International Monetary Fund, African Dept. (2014). 'South Africa: staff report for the 2014 Article IV consultation.' No. 14/338. Country Report. Washington, DC: IMF.

International Monetary Fund, African Dept. (2016). 'South Africa: 2016 Article IV consultation-press release; staff report; and statement by the Executive Director for South Africa.' No. 16/217. Country Report. International Monetary Fund. Washington, DC: IMF.

Jonas, M. (2019). *After Dawn: Hope after State Capture*. Johannesburg: Picador Africa.

Kaldor, N. (1967). *Strategic Factors in Economic Development*. Ithaca: Cornell University Press.

Kantor, B. (1998). 'Ownership and control in South Africa under black rule.' *Journal of Applied Corporate Finance* 10(4): 69–78.

Kaplan, D. (2015a). 'The structure and performance of manufacturing in South Africa.' In W. Naudé, A. Szirmai, and N. Haraguchi (eds), *Structural Change and Industrial Development in the BRICS*. Oxford: Oxford University Press.

Kaplan, D. (2015b). 'Manufacturing in post-apartheid South Africa: performance and policy.' In J. Weiss and M. Tribe (eds), *Routledge Handbook of Industry and Development*. New York: Routledge.

Kerr, A. and M. Wittenberg (2019). 'Earnings and employment microdata in South Africa.' Paper No. 2019/47. WIDER Working Paper. Helsinki: UNU-WIDER.

Khan, M. and S. Blankenburg (2009). 'The political economy of industrial policy in Asia and Latin America.' In M. Cimoli, G. Dosi, and J. E. Stiglitz (eds), *Industrial Policy and Development: The Political Economy of Capabilities Accumulation*. Oxford: Oxford University Press.

Khan, M. H. and K. S. Jomo, eds (2000). *Rents, Rent-Seeking and Economic Development: Theory and Evidence in Asia*. Illustrated edition. Cambridge: Cambridge University Press.

Levinsohn, J. A. (2008). 'Two policies to alleviate unemployment in South Africa.' Center for International Development at Harvard University. Cambridge, MA: CID.

Lipton, M. (1986). *Capitalism and Apartheid: South Africa, 1910–1986*. Aldershot: Wildwood House.

Macroeconomic Research Group (1993). 'Making democracy work: a framework for macroeconomic policy in South Africa.' A Report to Members of the Democratic Movement of South Africa. Bellville: Centre for Development Studies.

Makhaya, G. and S. Roberts (2013). 'Expectations and outcomes: considering competition and corporate power in South Africa under democracy.' *Review of African Political Economy* 40(138): 556–71.

Malherbe, S. and N. Segal (2001). 'Corporate governance in South Africa.' Presented at the TIPS Annual Forum, Muldersdrift.

Mcgregor's (various years). *Who Owns Whom*. Johannesburg: Mcgregor's.

Michie, J. and V. Padayachee (1998). 'Three years after apartheid: growth, employment and redistribution?' *Cambridge Journal of Economics* 22(5): 623–36.

Mondi, L. and S. Roberts (2005). 'The role of development finance for industry in a restructuring economy: a critical reflection on the Industrial Development Corporation of South Africa.' *Opportunities and Challenges*. Presented at the TIPS Annual Forum.

Mondliwa, P., N. Nhundu, A. Paelo, M. Thosago, and T. Vilakazi (2017). 'Growth and strategies of large and leading firms—Remgro Limited.' Working Paper 11/2017. Centre for Competition, Regulation and Economic Development. Johannesburg: University of Johannesburg.

Morris, M. (1991). 'State, capital and growth: the political economy of the national question.' In S. Gelb (ed.), *South Africa's Economic Crisis*. Cape Town: Zed Books.

Nattrass, N. (1989). 'Post-war profitability in South Africa: a critique of regulation analysis in South Africa.' *Transformation: Critical Perspectives on Southern Africa* 9: 66–80.

Nattrass, N. (1998). 'Growth, employment and economic policy in South Africa: a critical review.' Africa Portal. Johannesburg: Centre for Development and Enterprise (CDE).

Nattrass, N. and J. Seekings (2019). *Inclusive Dualism: Labour-Intensive Development, Decent Work, and Surplus Labour in Southern Africa*. Oxford: Oxford University Press.

Ndikumana, L. (2016). *Trade Misinvoicing in Primary Commodities in Developing Countries: The Cases of Chile, Côte d'Ivoire, Nigeria, South Africa and Zambia*. Geneva: UNCTAD.

Ocampo, J. A., C. Rada, and L. Taylor (2009). *Growth and Policy in Developing Countries: A Structuralist Approach*. Initiative for Policy Dialogue at Columbia University. New York: Columbia University Press.

Östensson, O. (2018). 'Misinvoicing in mineral trade: what do we really know?' *Mineral Economics* 31(1): 77–86.

Presidency (2006). *Accelerated and Shared Growth Initiative—South Africa (ASGISA): A Summary*. Presidency, Republic of South Africa.

Quantec (n.d.). 'South African standardised industry indicator database, sources and description.'

Republic of South Africa (2002). 'Mineral and Petroleum Resources Development Act 28 of 2002'. Government Gazette.

Republic of South Africa (2014). 'Broad-Based Black Economic Empowerment Amendment Act, 2013.'

Republic of South Africa (2020). 'President Cyril Ramaphosa: 2020 State of the Nation Address.'

Ritchken, E. (2018). 'The gold of the 21st century.' In S. Valiani (ed.), *The Future of Mining in South Africa: Sunset or Sunrise?* Sandton: Mapungubwe Institute for Strategic Reflection.

Roberts, S. and Z. Rustomjee (2010). 'Industrial policy under democracy: apartheid's grown-up infant industries? Iscor and Sasol.' *Transformation: Critical Perspectives on Southern Africa* 71(1): 50–75.

Roberts, S. and N. Zalk (2004). 'Addressing market power in a small, isolated, resource-based economy: the case of steel in South Africa.' CrC 3rd International Conference.

Rodrik, D. (2008). 'Understanding South Africa's economic puzzles.' *Economics of Transition* 16(4): 769–97.

Rodrik, D. (2012). 'Unconditional convergence in manufacturing.' *The Quarterly Journal of Economics* 128(1): 165–204.

Rustomjee, Z., L. Kaziboni, and I. Steuart (2018). 'Structural transformation along metals, machinery and equipment value chain—developing capabilities in the metals and machinery segments.' Working Paper 7/2018. Centre for Competition, Regulation and Economic Development. Johannesburg: University of Johannesburg.

South African Foundation (1996). *Growth for All: An Economic Strategy for South Africa*. Johannesburg: South African Foundation.

South African Reserve Bank (2020). 'Quarterly bulletin 295.' Pretoria: South African Reserve Bank.

Spicer, M. (2016). 'Government and business—where did it all go wrong?' *Business Day*, 15 November 2015, https://www.businesslive.co.za/rdm/politics/2016-11-15-government-and-business—where-did-it-all-go-wrong/.

Storm, S. (2018). 'Financialization and economic development: a debate on the social efficiency of modern finance.' *Development and Change* 49(2): 302–29.

Strauss, I. (2017). 'Understanding South Africa's current account deficit: the role of foreign direct investment income.' *Transnational Corporations* 23(2): 49–80.

Szirmai, A., W. A. Naudé, and L. Alcorta, eds (2013). *Pathways to Industrialization in the Twenty-First Century: New Challenges and Emerging Paradigms*. UNU-WIDER studies in development economics. Oxford: Oxford University Press.

Theobald, S., O. Tambo, P. Makuwerere, and C. Anthony (2015). 'The value of BEE deals: a study of the total value created for beneficiaries through BEE deals conducted by the 100 largest companies on the JSE.' Intellidex, https://www.intellidex.co.za/wp-content/uploads/2015/06/Intellidex-report-The-Value-of-BEE-Deals.pdf.

Theunissen, G. (2020). 'A billion here and a billion there: how Sasol came to sell 50% of its Lake Charles megaproject.' 2 October 2020. *BusinessInsider*, https://www.businessinsider.co.za/what-you-need-to-know-about-sasols-huge-lake-charles-project-2020-10.

Thirlwall, A. P. (1983). 'A plain man's guide to Kaldor's growth laws.' *Journal of Post Keynesian Economics* 5(3): 345–58.

Thirlwall, A. P. (2002). *The Nature of Economic Growth: An Alternative Framework for Understanding the Performance of Nations*. Cheltenham: Edward Elgar.

Tollison, R. D. (1982). 'Rent seeking: a survey.' *Kyklos* 35(4): 575–602.

Tregenna, F. (2010). 'How significant is intersectoral outsourcing of employment in South Africa?' *Industrial and Corporate Change* 19(5): 1427–57.

UNCTAD (2016). 'Beyond austerity: towards a global new deal.' Trade and Development Report. New York and Geneva: United Nations.

Vilakazi, T. (2020). 'Black industrialists—it's not just about funding.' Industrial Development Think Tank: Policy Briefing paper 17/2020. Centre for Competition, Regulation and Economic Development. Johannesburg: University of Johannesburg.

Walters, S. and J. Prinsloo (2002). 'The impact of offshore listings on the South African economy.' Johannesburg: South African Reserve Bank.

Watermeyer, R. and S. Phillips (2020). 'Public infrastructure delivery and construction sector dynamism in the South African economy.' Background Paper. NPC's Economy Series. Pretoria: NPC.

Weeks, J. (1999). 'Commentary. Stuck in low GEAR? Macroeconomic policy in South Africa, 1996–98.' Cambridge Journal of Economics 23(6): 795–811.

World Bank (2008). 'The growth report: strategies for sustained growth and inclusive development.' Washington, DC: World Bank.

World Bank (2011). 'South Africa economic update: focus on savings, investment and inclusive growth.' Paper No. 63539, pp. 1–60. Washington, DC: World Bank.

Zalk, N. (2012). 'South African post-apartheid policies towards industrialization: tentative implications for other African countries.' In A. Noman, J. Stiglitz, H. Stein, and K. Botchwey (eds), Good Growth and Governance in Africa: Rethinking Development Strategies, 345–71. Oxford: Oxford University Press.

Zalk, N. (2014). 'Industrial policy in a harsh climate: the case of South Africa.' In J. M. Salazar Xirinachs, I. Nübler, and R. Kozul-Wright (eds), Transforming Economies: Making Industrial Policy Work for Growth, Jobs and Development. Geneva: ILO.

Zalk, N. (2017). 'The things we lost in the fire: the political economy of post-apartheid restructuring of the South African steel and engineering sectors.' PhD Thesis. University of London, School of Oriental and African Studies.

Zalk, N. (2019). 'Hiding in plain sight: high-value agriculture's large-scale potential to grow jobs and exports.' Econ3x3.org, https://www.econ3x3.org/article/hiding-plain-sight-high-value-agriculture%E2%80%99s-large-scale-potential-grow-jobs-and-exports.

3

Metals, Machinery, and Mining Equipment Industries in South Africa

The Relationship between Power, Governance, and Technological Capabilities

Antonio Andreoni, Lauralyn Kaziboni, and Simon Roberts

3.1 Introduction

The metals, machinery, and mining equipment industries have been at the heart of South Africa's industrial ecosystem for many decades. This is due to the importance of mining in the country for more than a century and the close demand- and supply-side linkages with metals and machinery production. These industries include basic iron and steel, non-ferrous metals, fabricated metal products, and a diverse array of machinery and equipment manufacturing. The industries are characterized by well-established technological capabilities developed through linkages with mining and extensive state support under apartheid. During apartheid, there was particularly extensive support for basic metals production.

The industries continue to be crucial to the South African economy for several reasons. They make up a very substantial part of manufacturing, accounting in 2019 for 19 per cent of manufacturing value added and 23 per cent of employment, with employment mainly in downstream fabricated metals products, and machinery and equipment. They also provide intermediate products to other sectors across the economy. The industries are central to the processes of learning and technological change, and are critical for convergence between the ICT, and machinery and equipment industries in the context of the fourth industrial revolution (Min et al., 2018). As such, machinery and equipment are 'root industries' for any strategy that seeks to diversify the domestic economy towards higher value adding and more sophisticated activities, while creating jobs (see Chapter 12).

This chapter analyses the restructuring and development of these complex value chains in post-apartheid South Africa, from 1994 to 2019. In section 3.2, key turning points in this development are identified, in relation to the initial phase of the liberalization of the economy, the growth in demand associated with

Antonio Andreoni, Lauralyn Kaziboni, and Simon Roberts, *Metals, Machinery, and Mining Equipment Industries in South Africa: The Relationship between Power, Governance, and Technological Capabilities* In: *Structural Transformation in South Africa: The Challenges of Inclusive Industrial Development in a Middle-Income Country*. Edited by: Antonio Andreoni, Pamela Mondliwa, Simon Roberts, and Fiona Tregenna, Oxford University Press. © Oxford University Press 2021. DOI: 10.1093/oso/9780192894311.003.0003

the global commodities boom in the 2000s, and the period of adjustment from 2008, after the financial crisis, until 2019. Notwithstanding major changes, the overall record is of a basic steel industry that performed better in terms of value added relative to the more diversified downstream industries.

Section 3.3 involves a critical examination of the engagement of the post-apartheid state with the main companies producing basic metals—the key inputs for downstream manufacturers of metal products. The principal firm was the major basic-steel producer Iscor, which became ArcelorMittal South Africa (AMSA). This is followed by a discussion on the use of procurement as a demand-side industrial policy, given the importance of infrastructure and investments by state-owned enterprises and mining companies as buyers of metal products and machinery.

In section 3.4 the focus turns to the downstream mining machinery and equipment industry. While South Africa has strong production capabilities, these have been eroded. The section includes a reflection on the challenges in terms of technologies, changing ownership, and governance arrangements in production systems, and an examination of the related changes in the domestic environment. Conclusions and implications for industrial policy are set out in section 3.5.

3.2 Missed Opportunities for Structural Transformation

The metals, machinery, and mining equipment value chains serve a critical role in South Africa as a source of employment, output, and high-value products. In 2019, the industries accounted for the largest source of formal employment in manufacturing, contributing a total of 284,000 direct jobs, of which 228,000 were in the machinery and equipment, and fabricated metal products industries. The industry's strong linkages with support industries such as engineering services, transport, and logistics generate further employment. While the upstream capital-intensive basic metals industry saw output growth alongside shrinking employment, the growth of output in the diversified machinery and equipment industry was accompanied by employment growth, highlighting its labour-absorbing characteristics.

3.2.1 Mapping the Metals to Machinery and Equipment Value Chains

The metals, machinery, and equipment value chains are quite complex, with backward and forward linkages underpinned by integrated production systems. The upstream segment begins with the mining and production of mineral ores, including iron ore, chrome, manganese, and other related mining activities that feed into both basic ferrous and non-ferrous production. The basic metals go

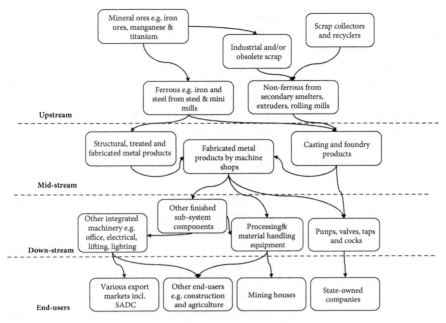

Figure 3.1 Metals to machinery and equipment value chain

Note: The arrows are only illustrative of the main linkages and supplies of, for example, pumps and valves are supplied to a range of customer groupings.

Source: Adapted from Rustomjee et al., 2018.

through various processes of value addition, until being manufactured into sophisticated products and components including pumps and valves, material handling equipment, mineral processing, and earthmoving equipment (see Figure 3.1). These are demanded by mining houses, utility providers (including state-owned companies in energy and transport), and other sectors such as agriculture and construction. The mining sector is the largest user of these inputs, directly accounting for 24 per cent of domestic demand in 2019 and further demand for metals and machinery components (Quantec, 2020), as they are embodied in intermediate goods.[1]

Steel is by far the most important basic metal, followed by aluminium and other non-ferrous metals. Primary steel production is a large-scale, capital- and energy-intensive industry, with strong backward linkages to iron ore, coal, and electricity, as well as scrap metal (used in mini-mills for producing long steel products). Basic steel is widely traded, notwithstanding substantial transport costs, as is aluminium. Cast-metal products are produced in foundries, melting steel and other metals to produce components that are used in a range of

---

[1] It is important to note that the Quantec data are not official statistics. They have been compiled including data from Statistics South Africa, with some computations by Quantec, and this should be borne in mind.

downstream finished manufactures. The cost and quality of steel, as a key input, is a major contributor to the competitiveness of downstream fabrication of a range of metal products.

Basic steel production in South Africa has been dominated throughout the period by the steel plants of by the formerly state-owned Iscor, which became ArcelorMittal South Africa (AMSA). Acerinox is the major stainless-steel producer, while there were a few very large aluminium smelters. Iscor's first plant came into production in Pretoria in 1934 (Zalk, 2017). Following its privatization in 1989, Iscor continued to receive substantial government support in the 1990s and was the subject of a major government-sponsored restructuring strategy resulting in its acquisition to become AMSA (Roberts and Rustomjee, 2009; Rustomjee et al., 2018). Other steel producers then included Highveld Steel and Vanadium, using iron ore as the main feedstock, and Scaw Metals, manufacturing from scrap metal. Both companies were part of the Anglo American conglomerate until the 2000s. Parts of Highveld Steel were taken over by Evraz in 2006, while parts of Scaw were acquired by the IDC following the downturn after 2008 (Rustomjee et al., 2018).

Downstream products have strong backward linkages with the upstream steel producers and foundries that provide fabricated metal products as key inputs into machinery and equipment production. In addition to basic metal products from which intermediate components are manufactured, there are a range of cast products made by foundries. These cast components can be manufactured from alloys and are important for the automotive industry. The key components sold to the industry include a combination of low-tech, medium-tech, and high-tech components, illustrating some level of structural transformation.

Despite the importance of the foundry industry at the midstream level as producer of cast components, its capabilities were severely eroded after the opening up of the economy in 1994. The industry continued to struggle competitively, resulting in a dramatic decline in the number of foundries and levels of output, particularly between 2008 and 2016, when the number of foundries fell by 38 per cent and output declined by 15 per cent (Rustomjee et al., 2018). The weakening capabilities are partly explained by the lack of any substantial investment in capital and technology upgrading in the two decades up to 2020, coupled with increasing import competition from Asia and Europe.

In South Africa, the local mining machinery and equipment industry, which is the most imprtant downstream segment, is characterized mainly by medium-sized local companies that are highly specialized in specific product segments, including underground and surface mining equipment, off-road specialized equipment, mineral processing, and material handling. These firms compete with global original equipment manufacturers (OEMs) which have increased their share of the South African and Southern African markets. The South African producers have innovative and advanced technological capabilities in deep-level mining, including rock mechanics, shaft sinking, refrigeration, ventilation, pumping, and hoisting systems, and drilling and blasting (Fessehaie, 2015; Andreoni and Torreggiani, 2020). Some of the domestic manufacturers supplying equipment to the mining houses have backward linkages to foundries providing metal casting and to suppliers of components such as pumps, valves, and conveyor systems, as well as with related services, especially in engineering, and product-system and software design (Phele et al., 2005; Phele and Roberts, 2005).

3.2.2 Competitiveness and Structural Transformation

Structural transformation in the industry requires better performance in diversified downstream activities, instead of in the upstream, capital- and energy-intensive basic metals industries. Despite the downstream sector accounting for a larger proportion of value added in total manufacturing, the relatively stronger growth in value added through the 1994–2008 period was observed in the upstream basic metals industries (Table 3.1).

Major investments were made in the basic iron and steel industries in the early 1990s and in the non-ferrous metals industry in large aluminium smelters in the early 2000s, as reflected in the average rates of investment (Table 3.1). The continuation of support to the main producers underpinned high average growth in value added in basic metals industries from 1994 to 2002, alongside major restructuring efforts to reduce employment. The upstream industry growth reflected the strength of path-dependency effects in response to liberalization, and how the balance of interests in favour of concentrated incumbents influenced policy (Goga et al., 2020). This path dependency is evident in the capital-intensive upstream industries continuing to attract higher levels of investment through the period as a whole, accounting for the great majority of real gross fixed capital investment (in constant 2010 prices) in the metals and machinery industries overall.

The commodities boom in the 2000s further drove growth in steel value added, with an 11.8 per cent compound annual average growth rate in the 2002–8 period. The growth in mining activity in other parts of Southern Africa increased demand for machinery and equipment in this period and saw average annual growth in value added in this industry of 5.7 per cent from 2002 to 2008, even while import penetration increased to 67.6 per cent of domestic consumption (Table 3.1). The import penetration, especially from China and including in cast metal components, eroded capabilities even while overall the industry grew in both output and employment. This impact is evident in the decade following the financial crisis, when production stagnated, notwithstanding a few areas of excellence in machinery and equipment, which regained competitiveness following investments in capabilities (Barnes et al., 2019).

Table 3.1 Performance across the metals, machinery, and mining equipment industry grouping

	Period	Basic iron and steel	Basic non-ferrous metals	Fabricated metal products	Machinery and equipment
Value added (Rbn)	1994	9.2	7.8	16.5	12.5
(% share of total		(3.8%)	(3.3%)	(6.8%)	(5.2%)
manufacturing)	2019	16.7	11.8	21.3	21.7
		(4.4%)	(3.1%)	(5.6%)	(5.7%)
Average value-added	1994–2002	3.9%	7.9%	2.7%	2.4%
growth	2002–8	11.8%	3.8%	0.7%	5.7%
	2008–19	−3.3%	−3.7%	0.1%	0.3%
Employment (in	1994	80	27	118	97
thousands)		(5.5%)	(1.8%)	(8.1%)	(6.6%)
(% share of total	2019	32	15	104	124
manufacturing)		(2.7%)	(1.2%)	(8.5%)	(10.1%)
Average employment	1994–2002	−5.4%	−3.7%	−1.5%	−0.2%
growth	2002–8	−0.7%	2.3%	1.8%	3.9%
	2008–19	−3.8%	−3.8%	−1.0%	0.3%
Average investment	1994–2001	41.0%	31.6%	9.4%	9.4%
(gross fixed capital	2002–8	37.2%	36.2%	11.2%	10.0%
formation	2009–19	34.1%	43.7%	9.9%	9.4%
as % of gross value					
addition)					
Imports as % of	1994	10.4%	11.7%	13.8%	54.0%
domestic	2002	7.7%	22.3%	19.1%	57.4%
consumption	2008	25.9%	66.9%	24.5%	67.6%
	2019	13.8%	39.9%	24.3%	69.1%
Exports as % of	1994	45.1%	29.1%	5.1%	14.2%
domestic	2002	35.6%	38.9%	10.0%	22.2%
output	2008	67.0%	57.2%	12.7%	27.4%
	2019	37.2%	42.6%	15.0%	40.4%

Note: The imports and export measures for fabricated metal products are for 'Other fabricated metal products'.
Source: Quantec data and authors' calculations.

The downstream industries have not had a major coordinated industrial policy programme of support and services, including targeted skills and technology support through institutions of industrial policy. Instead, there has been an evolving mix of ineffective incentives and initiatives. These include investment incentives in the 1990s, the bulk of which went to the basic metals producers rather than diversified downstream and labour-absorbing producers (Roberts and Rustomjee, 2009). There were also technology support measures under the Integrated Manufacturing Strategy and the Advanced Manufacturing Technology Strategy (Machaka and Roberts, 2003). Cluster developments were championed by the South African Capital Equipment Export Council (SACEEC), established in 2000 as a public-private partnership between the industry and the Department of Trade, Industry, and Competition (DTIC), but the emphasis was on driving market access through public procurement, export promotion, and marketing initiatives, such as international trade fairs.

In fact two separate developments worked against diversifying the industrial base. First, substantial engineering capabilities in subsidiaries of the major conglomerates, led by Anglo American and including its Dorbyl business, were eroded when the conglomerates unbundled and a short-term asset stripping took place (Zalk, 2017; Rustomjee et al., 2018). Second, the procurement policies, including under black economic empowerment (BEE) provisions in the 2000s to favour black suppliers, did not measure local value added and led to black entrepreneurs setting up as local suppliers for multinational producers importing into South Africa (Chapter 9).

3.2.3 Trade Performance and the Poor Performance of Machinery and Equipment

The opening-up and international reintegration of the South African economy from 1994 saw the basic metals industries (iron and steel, and non-ferrous metals) maintain trade surpluses while the trade deficit in machinery and equipment reduced somewhat, as the real exchange rate depreciated in line with the unwinding of protection measures (Figure 3.2). Fabricated metal products maintained

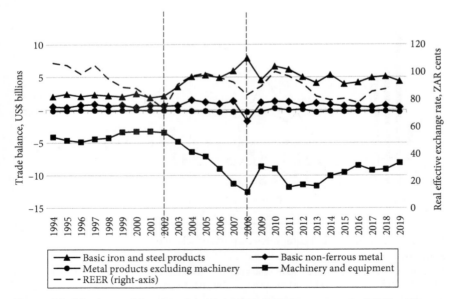

Figure 3.2 Metals, machinery, and equipment trade balances, nominal US$ millions
Source: Trade Map and South African Reserve Bank, accessed in March 2020.

roughly balanced trade throughout the entire 1994–2019 period, as exports were similar to imports.

From 2002, as the commodity boom took hold and international commodity prices increased substantially, the trade surplus in basic steel quadrupled. However, while robust domestic demand meant that the machinery and equipment industry continued to grow output and employment, under the stronger commodity-supported currency it could not compete with the massive import penetration. The currency appreciation made it more attractive for domestic demand to be met by relatively cheaper imports. The increase in the trade deficit from 2002 to 2008 was equivalent to the domestic value-added of the industry in 2008, which supported 100,000 direct jobs.

The global financial crisis saw a sharp decline in the output of both basic metals and fabricated metals as prices collapsed. While the trade balance in machinery and equipment improved somewhat, as imports declined, the hollowing out of capabilities in the previous period from 2002 to 2008 meant that performance continued to be weak overall, and value added in 2019 remained lower than ten years earlier.

The failure to maintain and grow from a strong industrial base in machinery and equipment is most evident in the declining competitiveness in the Southern African region, which accounts for the great majority of South Africa's exports of these products. For example, in Zambia, which has been one of the largest export markets for South Africa, market share fell from above 60 per cent in 2002 to around 30 per cent in 2019 (Figure 3.3). Shares are higher in Botswana, Namibia,

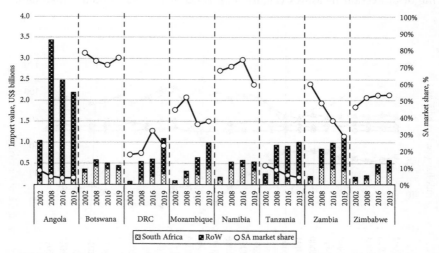

Figure 3.3 Machinery and equipment imports of selected SADC countries from South Africa versus the rest of the world, in US$ billions

Note: Due to lack of data, Angola import values for 2002, 2008, and 2019 are represented by 2004, 2009, and 2019; and Tanzania import values for 2019 are represented by 2018 import values.

Source: ITC Trade Map (https://www.trademap.org/); authors' calculations.

and Zimbabwe, but these are smaller markets. In the largest importer in the region, Angola, South Africa's share of machinery imports is very small, as it is too in Tanzania.

South Africa's poor performance in the Southern African Development Community (SADC) has been especially concerning as, in 2019, other SADC countries collectively accounted for a larger market in terms of mining activity than South Africa itself. This suggests the need to urgently build strong regional value chains for South Africa to regain the lost ground in machinery and equipment exports.

The lack of structural transformation at the downstream segments represents lost opportunities for these industries to move towards higher-value and relatively complex products. While there have been businesses with existing islands of competitiveness, overall, the downstream industries have failed to build on these capabilities.

3.3 Steel and Metal Products: Industrial Policies, Power, and Governance

To assess how interests have shaped policies to maintain economic power, this section involves an examination of the industrial policy, power, and governance dynamics along the value chain from steel producers to fabricators of metal products. In particular, the grand bargains struck by government with the steel industry and the implications for the supply of inputs to downstream industries are analysed. On the other side, the impact of procurement policies working through demand by state-owned companies for metals and machinery products are assessed.

The first democratic government in 1994 adopted a set of policies to support the manufacturing industry, including incentives and investment support programmes.[2] In reality, the greater share of these incentives went to the upstream basic industries (Mondi and Roberts, 2005; Roberts and Rustomjee, 2009; Black and Roberts, 2009). At the same time, the steel industry was facing very low international steel prices and the challenges of restructuring the local producers, while globally there were shifts from national to transnational ownership and consolidation.

The government's strategy for the steel industry in the late 1990s involved a grand bargain struck with the main steel producer, where low input costs in terms of energy and iron ore were ensured, along with support for investment and for

---

[2] Investment support programmes included the IDC's Global Player Fund, a tax holiday programme and accelerated depreciation allowance tax incentive scheme under section 37E of the Income Tax Act.

local consolidation. This competitive restructuring upstream was envisaged to be the foundation for growing downstream steel-using industries led by fabricated metal products and machinery. These industries were also supported in the later period by government preferential procurement policies, which are described and evaluated below. Against this background and in the context of the government's approach, a question that needs to be asked is why so little changed in the overall structure of the metals and machinery industries. Specifically, how does one explain the fact that, on average, upstream capital-intensive industries continued to grow more strongly than the downstream industries?

3.3.1 The Big Steel Bargain: Government Support and Conditionalities for Upstream Producers

As part of achieving a rapid restructuring of the basic steel industry in the late 1990s to improve production efficiencies, upgrade plant, rationalize employment numbers, and reduce the number of grades manufactured, the government supported acquisitions of strategic equity stakes by transnational corporations (TNCs). The government did this through its ownership in Iscor (held by the IDC) and different forms of industrial policy support. The rationale was to ensure the local acquisition of international technology, expertise, and capital essential for the rapid upgrade of local production.

Under this strategy, Lakshmi Mittal's LNM (later Mittal Steel) acquired a stake in Iscor, following the vertical separation of the steel-making from the mining parts of the business. The separation ensured the supply of iron ore for twenty-five years at cost plus a 3 per cent management fee which, along with cheap energy in the form of coal and electricity, meant Iscor's plants were among the lowest cost in the world (Roberts, 2008).

Government support for the Mittal acquisition represented the first 'grand bargain' (Rustomjee et al., 2018) and was linked to a business assistance agreement which provided various incentives, including additional shareholding related to investment and upgrading steps (Zalk, 2017). Through the agreement, Mittal gained sole control of an effective local monopolist in flat steel products in 2003, given the additional absorption of Saldanha Steel in 2002 in which Iscor had already held a 50 per cent stake. The acquisitions were approved based on the company moving to a 'developmental steel price' for local customers. However, the nature of the developmental steel price was not specified nor agreed with government.

Instead, it fell to competition law to discipline the exercise of market power over local downstream customers by Mittal Steel South Africa before it became AMSA.[3] The competition authorities duly uncovered various cartels in which

---

[3] There are other producers in long steel products.

AMSA had been engaging with its competitors, where it had them in long-steel products. For instance, the reinforcing bar price-fixing cartel, which lasted from 1999 to 2008, led to average prices being over 30 per cent above competitive levels (Mondliwa and Das Nair, 2019).

In most flat steel products AMSA faced no local competitor and explicitly priced at an import parity level until 2019, calculated as the landed price of imported steel, generally to inland customers, including all the imputed transport and related costs and a 5 per cent 'hassle factor' (Roberts, 2008). This was notwithstanding around 40 per cent of AMSA's production being exported, while the local import parity-based prices were around 40–60 per cent above the export prices being earned by AMSA for the same products. The high prices directly undermined the competitiveness of producers of downstream products using steel as an input. In March 2007, The Competition Tribunal found in favour of a complaint by two mining companies that this pricing was excessive and a contravention of the Competition Act. Two years later, The Competition Appeal Court overturned the decision on the grounds that the economic value against which prices needed to be evaluated had not properly been considered (Das Nair and Mondliwa, 2017).

Using competition law to address monopoly pricing by a business that had received extensive government support ignored direct policy levers which could have been used to discipline the conduct of AMSA. Mining licences were a potential tool as clause 8 of the standard mining licence in South Africa stated that minerals and derivative products were to be sold at competitive and non-discriminatory prices (Rustomjee et al., 2018). This, in effect, would have required factory gate prices for downstream steel customers of AMSA (given its production from local iron ore) to ensure it did not discriminate between local and export customers.

Conditionalities on investment incentives were a second industrial policy lever. In this regard, the upstream capital- and energy-intensive basic metals (and basic chemicals) industries had received the bulk of the benefits from generous tax incentive programmes and development finance, while the downstream industries received a fraction of this support (Mondi and Roberts 2005; Black and Roberts, 2009; Roberts and Rustomjee, 2009). The upstream firms, however, evaded conditionalities. For instance, the 37E tax incentive legally obliged the upstream firms to sell steel at non-discriminatory export-parity prices to the domestic market. This was side-stepped by Saldanha Steel, which elected to export its production in its entirety rather than sell locally (Roberts and Rustomjee, 2009).

The business assistance agreement reached with Mittal on the purchase of its initial stake and the commitment to a 'developmental steel price' proved not to be effective. In addition, after the initial restructuring, Mittal extracted profits from the South Africa business while funding acquisitions and investments in developed countries (Zalk, 2017). This meant that the expected benefits from Mittal's ownership in South Africa were not realized.

When global steel export prices dropped again to a ten-year low in 2016, the industry, led by AMSA, placed government under pressure to provide support once again. To support the upstream industry, government struck a second 'grand bargain' with AMSA. AMSA committed to adopt a production cost-based formula for local pricing in exchange for the settlement of unresolved competition-related matters, increased tariff protection, and a policy directive that only South African steel be utilized in publicly funded infrastructure projects. The rationale for government included the protection of the remaining jobs in the steel industry and the importance of a local steel producer for value chain linkages upstream and downstream.[4]

The agreement favoured AMSA. Steel prices turned upwards in 2016, while AMSA's local monopoly power was further entrenched (as other small domestic producers were in or close to bankruptcy) and the agreement was only binding until 2022. The settlement of the anticompetitive charges across multiple competition cases for R1.5 billion (US$115 million) in 2016 was generous relative to the likely penalties, especially for the collusion charges. The steelmaker also received an additional steel tariff of 10 per cent that effectively increased the steel industry's safeguard measure to 22 per cent. While the pricing commitment was meant to protect local buyers, there is considerable scope for interpretation as to its terms (Rustomjee et al., 2018). Meanwhile, the labour-absorbing downstream industry was not protected by tariffs in the same way as the upstream industry.[5]

The concentration of employment in a few upstream firms supported the lobbying efforts by large steel companies, despite the much higher number of jobs in the relatively disorganized downstream industries. Tackling these inherent power dynamics is central to structural transformation.

3.3.2 The Effects of Poorly Enforced Public Procurement Policy

Public procurement is a significant source of demand in most economies and can be a key lever for industrial development. In South Africa procurement by state-owned companies is very important for the metals and machinery industry. Procurement policies can thus be effective industrial policy instruments for supporting local industry development, innovation, and technological upgrading (Edler and Georghiou, 2007; Georghiou et al., 2014; Lember et al., 2014; Tiryakioğlu and Yülek, 2015).

---

[4] See the DTIC presentation to the joint portfolio committees on trade and industry and economic development on 23 August 2016: https://www.thedti.gov.za/parliament/2016/Steel_Industry_Interventions.pdf.

[5] There is a lack of tariff support for the downstream industries, with 90 per cent of capital equipment duty-free (Rustomjee et al., 2018).

South Africa has leveraged public procurement, including by state-owned enterprises, through the designation of sectors and products for local content under the Preferential Procurement Policy Framework Act (PPPFA) of 2000 and the Competitive Supplier Development Programme. This followed the earlier National Industrial Participation Programme in 1995. Under the PPPFA the Department of Trade, Industry, and Competition is enabled to designate certain sectors whereby tenders will only be awarded to locally manufactured products with a prescribed minimum threshold of local content. The PPPFA also has BEE objectives to support businesses owned and controlled by black South Africans (Chapter 9). In 2007, the Department of Public Enterprises introduced the Competitive Supplier Development Programme (CSDP) to specifically support the development of local industrial capabilities.[6] While these different policy instruments were meant to complement each other, evidence suggests that their enforcement was weak (Mohamed and Roberts, 2008; Crompton et al., 2016). Instead of realizing the intended outcomes, weak enforcement also enabled significant rent extraction. A striking example was state-owned enterprise Transnet's procurement of 1,064 locomotives and its infamous outcomes.

3.3.2.1 The Case of Transnet: A Cautionary Tale

Transnet was supposed to be implementing the CSDP approach when it started to plan a major procurement of locomotives for its freight business in 2012. In July 2012, it issued a tender for 1,064 locomotives for its general freight business division, both electric and diesel. The procurement was required to comply with the earlier stated PPPFA's local content requirements, with thresholds of 55 per cent local content for diesel and 60 per cent for electric locomotives.

In 2014 Transnet placed the very large order for the 1,064 locomotives with four companies: Bombardier Transportation South Africa, China South Rail Zhuzhou Electric Locomotive Company (CSR), General Electric South Africa Technologies, and China North Rail Rolling Stock South Africa (Pty) Ltd (CNR).[7] All four had BEE partners. The two Chinese firms, which subsequently merged, secured permission to build a relatively large number of locomotives outside of South Africa for an initial period. However, while Transnet had developed an ambitious three-phased approach for localization, by the end of 2019 there was limited evidence of investments being made in South African manufacturing, while costs had escalated substantially.

Widespread issues of corruption and non-compliance were subsequently uncovered and subject to scrutiny at the Zondo Commission of Inquiry into State

---

[6] The Competitive Supplier Development Programme (CSDP) provided for SOEs to design supply and demand side measures with government for OEM suppliers to develop localized first- and second-tier suppliers, so building the domestic supply chain. The CSDP was coordinated by the Department of Public Enterprises (Crompton et al., 2016).
[7] The order was for R50 billion (around US$5 billion at the time).

Capture, which started in the middle of 2018 and was due to wrap up in early 2021. In January 2018, Transnet made attempts to remedy instances of non-compliance in agreements with the Bombardier and General Electric suppliers, while in December 2019 Transnet launched a court case to declare the contracts with the Chinese suppliers as being unlawful and set aside.[8]

Through this procurement, the foreign OEMs held the potential to develop industrial capabilities and improve manufacturing suppliers in South Africa, as the procurement terms required supplier development initiatives that would encourage technology transfer, skill transfer, and improved quality standards (Crompton et al., 2016). However, in addition to the concerns about corruption, the incentives for OEMs to invest to establish South Africa as a platform and innovation hub were also undermined by Transnet Engineering's own ambition to become an OEM. This placed Transnet in a conflicted position as it was both customer and competitor. (Mondliwa and Das Nair, 2019)

The procurement process was fraught with problems that reflect the under-lying challenges in developing effective industrial policy (Crompton and Kaziboni, 2020). Public procurement involving such large sums requires a num-ber of institutional conditions to be in place, which were largely lacking in South Africa. These include a lack of clear guidelines, weak verification and enforce-ment processes, insufficient coordination between the relevant government departments, and capacity constraints at the governing department (Rustomjee et al., 2018). The ongoing changes to procurement rules, to the BEE codes,[9] and to incentive procedures greatly increased the risks and uncertainty for investment, while making it easier to capture rents through the procedures being bypassed. And the verification of local content requires a competent and well-resourced verification agent to conduct verification checks at various points in the process. If non-compliance at any stage is detected there needs to be a functional enforce-ment agency with the necessary policies and procedures to address it.

3.4 Mining Machinery and Equipment: Technological Capabilities, Power Asymmetries, and the Missing Ecosystem Ingredients

The mining machinery and equipment segment is the most significant part of the machinery and equipment industry in South Africa, and includes niches of technological excellence. The downstream industry has established capabilities thanks to the backward linkages from mining to local producer, and lateral

---

[8] https://www.news24.com/fin24/companies/industrial/transnet-wants-court-to-clear-r54bn-unlawful-contract-for-1064-locomotives-20,191,217. As of September 2020, the extensive allegations relating to corruption and state capture including relating to this contract were still under inquiry.

[9] These were last revised in 2017; see Chapter 9 for more on this.

migration of capabilities of generic technologies used in other sectors such as construction, agriculture, and general manufacturing (Walker and Minnitt, 2006; Dolo et al., 2018).

By drawing on extensive firm-level research, this section examines the impact of technology changes, notably digitalization, and the relationships with the governance of production systems. In particular, engineering, procurement, and construction management (EPCM) companies which provide full package solutions to mining companies have grown in importance while the larger South African engineering businesses have been divested from the industrial conglomerates (Jourdan, 2014). These changes have coincided with increased international consolidation in the industry and the growing importance of large multinational enterprises in the Southern African markets. As the developments in the global industry affect companies in all countries, some governments have supported their domestic companies to capture domestic value addition, technology spillovers, and the employment dividend. Considered against selected international examples, it is clear that in South Africa there are a number of missing ingredients, coupled with poor policy design.

3.4.1 Technological Capabilities and the Digitalization of Mines

The technological changes with the digitalization of production, design, and coordination along supply chains (see Chapter 12) have had major impacts on machinery and equipment for the mining industry. The developments encompass advanced capabilities in design, additive manufacturing, and rapid prototyping and sensor technologies for predictive maintenance and conditional monitoring. These technological advancements potentially open the way for more effective supply-chain integration, process efficiencies, and collective upgrading for both larger and smaller firms. The lead mining machinery and equipment firms in South Africa have developed advanced capabilities, improving supply-chain integration and upgrading, to offer customized solutions to enhance the performance for the end users, that is, the mines.

In mineral processing equipment the customization often depends on the environments and mineral being mined. This means that, when coupled with the analysis of data on performance in different settings (including through machine learning), additive manufacturing can drastically reduce the time to upgrade machinery for specific requirements. For example, one company managed to reduce the time for customization from six to eight weeks to not more than three days (Kaziboni et al., 2019).

Digitalization extends beyond product design, testing, and customization to integrating sensors across businesses, allowing remote monitoring and real-time data collection. Together with cloud computing, big-data analytics and machine learning have made predictive maintenance of these machines and consumables possible, allowing for the rate of wear and tear to be tracked (Barnes et al., 2019). Thanks to these innovations, mining companies can prevent unplanned downtime and reduce operating costs, while lead firms can pre-determine consumable requirements by customers, thereby reducing stock-holding and manufacturing waste. This is especially valuable as after-market services and components represent the most profitable segment of the value chain (Fessehaie, 2015). Realizing the benefits requires connectivity and bandwidth at reasonable cost; personnel with specific skills such as data analysts, scientists, and artisans with IT capabilities; and an appropriate policy environment governing data. South Africa faces challenges in each of these (Chapter 12).

While lead firms have developed integrated supply-chain systems and structures, smaller firms are lagging. Smaller manufacturers of mineral process equipment are still in the early stages of integrating their supply chain and their challenges are seldom about the implementation of advanced applications, but more around basic elements of internal systems and processes related to ordering, standardized quoting, and stock-taking applications. Optimizing linkages between firms requires an integration of systems that allows access to information and data across firms within a single ecosystem to support capability upgrading. This shows that capabilities are not limited to technologies and skills, but also include internal systems, structures, routines, and working practices.

An example of the potential benefits from digitalization across a lead firm and its suppliers and customers is the case of Multotec, an international OEM of South African origin that engineers minerals processing machinery. Multotec has built its capabilities based on customized solutions for mines in South Africa (Gostner et al., 2005). Working with customers and suppliers it has demonstrated how an internationally integrated firm can be an important source of demand-driven innovation back to components manufacturers. Its suppliers have become globally competitive (and certified) to service both the lead firm and other clients (Kaziboni et al., 2019). Such experience is, however, not common and it has required the company to build internal technical training and testing facilities which would not be viable for smaller businesses to develop.

Power asymmetries and fragmentation in the South African mining equipment value chain have further limited the opportunities for collaboration and technological upgrading (Rustomjee et al., 2018). The discussion turns to these implications.

3.4.2 Power Asymmetries: Global Consolidation and Domestic Fragmentation

Similar to other advanced manufacturing industries, the 2000s and 2010s saw significant consolidation in the machinery and equipment industry. Already in

2009, the six global leading companies accounted for one-quarter of total world production of these mining technologies. In the decade 2010–20, intense M&A activity drove consolidation along global value chains, and across the main industry segments, with signs of new competitive pressure coming from China globally in segments such as yellow metal vehicles (Andreoni and Torreggiani, 2020). Chinese producers also increased their penetration into Southern African markets, including in areas such as castings (components of machines).

Against this backdrop, mining machinery and equipment firms in South Africa have remained largely fragmented, while major multinational OEMs such as Sandvik, Epiroc, Caterpillar, and Komatsu continued to consolidate their market shares and leverage their global supply chain to provide mining houses with highly competitive solutions. In 2018, for example, in the underground equipment segment, Sandvik and Epiroc together held around 70 per cent of the local market (Smeiman, 2018), especially for certain mineral commodities; their regional presence in Southern Africa has been equally significant. The multinational OEMs have some fabrication and assembly in South Africa, but mining machines are mainly produced abroad: in Europe and the USA for high-end products, and in India and China for lower-end equipment, including over ground vehicles and basic mineral processing technologies, and components such as valves. Some local engineering companies manufacture components under licence for OEMs.

The power of the OEMs allows them to directly deal with mining houses, providing machines, customized financial packages, and after-sale services. In contrast, the relationship between small and medium-size South African OEM companies and mining houses is often intermediated by specialized engineering contractors under EPCM (engineering, procurement, and construction management) or so-called EPC (engineering, procurement, and construction) arrangements—with the main difference related to the allocation of cost risks. These specialized engineering companies are very powerful as they are responsible for making procurement decisions for the mining houses, as part of their design of the overall mining solution. Being excluded from their sourcing strategies means being excluded from the main source of demand in this market (Andreoni and Torreggiani, 2020).

There are a number of more established South African OEMs and local suppliers with high local content and export capabilities, which have both direct and mediated relationships with mining houses and junior mines (notable examples are AARD for underground equipment, Bell Equipment for surface equipment, and Kwatani and Multotec for mineral processing) (Andreoni and Torreggiani, 2020). They have a regional and international footprint in terms of markets, as well as strong supply-chain linkages with several tiers of components producers along the domestic metal value chain. They have also made domestic investments in new digital technologies and, in some cases, have managed to upgrade their domestic suppliers. Unfortunately, these are also the companies whose supply of metals is negatively impacted by the market power in supplier industries, discussed in section 3.3.

Within this ecosystem, with the exception of the very few leading South African OEMs, in the 2000s smaller and less well-established mining equipment companies operating as OEMs, or component suppliers and assembly, were located in fragmented production systems and became increasingly uncompetitive. Several key factors explain this (Andreoni and Torreggiani, 2020): limited cooperation between project houses and suppliers, particularly towards smaller equipment suppliers that could not supply at scale; the balance of power along the supply chains from metals inputs to machinery producers, often resulting in frequent and sudden price increases imposed on equipment manufacturers; insufficient financial resources on the part of local manufacturers to invest in formal R&D activities compared to large international OEMs; the unavailability or cost of local components which presented challenges in meeting local content requirements; and severe skills shortages in the sector and inadequate training provision.

The objectives of BEE and localization for the sector have presented several challenges. The Broad-Based Black Socio-Economic Empowerment Charter for the South African Mining and Minerals Industry, known as the Mining Charter, was introduced in 2004, with subsequent amendments and revisions to the targets. Its core objectives included building links between mining companies and suppliers, and supporting local capabilities and skills. The Mining Charter introduced a scorecard system for mining right holders which, as of 2018, had the following six criteria: (1) ownership participation by historically disadvantaged persons; (2) employment equity, promoting fair treatment and equal opportunities in the workplace; (3) human resources development and capacity building for employees and local communities; (4) procurement and enterprise development aimed at locally empowered businesses; (5) mine community development; and (6) housing and living conditions for mine employees. While targets can be met within a transition period, the non-compliance with any one of the above obligations can lead to the withdrawal (or the suspension) of the mining permit. The 'procurement, suppliers and enterprise development' requirement alone accounted for 40 per cent of the 2018 scorecard. The 2018 revision tightened the requirements for local content and established conditions on domestic sourcing of capital equipment, consumables, and services (80 per cent with preferential conditions), as well as a minimum of 70 per cent of total R&D budget to be spent on South Africa-based R&D entities.

The promotion of local sourcing in the Charter, along with a number of other government and industry-led initiatives to support increased domestic value addition and boost R&D activities, have been undermined by the exploitation of loopholes. The provisions have to a large extent been met by intermediaries who may be sourcing imported products (possibly assembled in South Africa)

(Rustomjee et al., 2018). In addition, the tariff schedule that the South African government negotiated for equipment and components used in mining operations tended to protect a number of key industrial components for domestic OEMs raising their local costs (such as tyres and some steel components). In doing so, trade policy undermined the cost-competitiveness of the local machinery and equipment manufacturers. By comparison, final products, such as assembled machinery and equipment, were generally given access to the domestic market at zero or very low tariffs.

There is also a lack of appropriate skills in the sector. Skills development has been largely managed through the relevant Sector Education and Training Authority (SETA), that is, the Manufacturing, Engineering, and Related Services Authority (MERSETA), and, more specifically, the Metal Chamber of MERSETA. It is responsible for quantifying occupational shortages, identifying skill gaps, determining skills priorities, and developing an appropriate educational offer for specific clusters of industries. However, as discussed in Chapter 12, institutional challenges in delivering appropriate skills, especially in the digital space, remain.

3.4.3 Missing Ingredients: Comparative International Insights for Better Ecosystem Development

Important insights into the key missing ingredients are provided by comparisons with other countries which have successfully supported machinery equipment clusters. These include Chile and Australia, where South African companies are also active, as well as Finland. The comparative assessments help to evaluate alternative policies and institutional forms used to support local content, effective trade policy, and R&D efforts (Steuart, 2019; Andreoni and Torreggiani, 2020).

In terms of procurement and local content, by ensuring commitments on the part of buyers, supply industries have been incentivized to make the investments required to upgrade capabilities. Australia's local-content policies have been defined at the national as well as the state level. This has enabled strong growth in the country's Mining Equipment, Technology, and Services (METS) industry. The overarching principle guiding the framework has been to offer 'full, fair and reasonable' access to employment and tendering opportunities to Australian firms and individuals (World Bank, 2015). The emphasis has been on equitable opportunity, and on monitoring and reporting, which means that procurers are effectively held accountable. This has been supported by funds for suppliers to work with project developers to identify supply opportunities for 'capable and competitive' Australian firms, especially SMEs. Finland has an even more hands-on approach to local content under its green-mining objectives. It requires foreign companies to establish affiliates in Finland and access to funding from public sector bodies is conditional on firms being registered in Finland. There are detailed requirements on firms including domestic value addition, technology transfer, and local R&D spending. This is also a preferential price premium for local suppliers (OECD, 2017).

Local procurement priorities have mostly required an aligned and strategic trade policy. In Australia, for example, there were arrangements under the Enhanced Project By-Law Scheme (EPBS) from 2002 to 2016 for duty-free importation of eligible goods identified as strategic and not produced in Australia. In a quid pro quo, these concessions were, however, contingent on the project houses developing and implementing approved Australia Industry Participation plans. This contrasts with South Africa, where, despite advanced technological capabilities, trade policy has not protected final products, such as assembled machinery and equipment.

R&D tax incentives have been widespread across all countries, with some having targeted incentives linked to the upgrading of suppliers. In Chile, for instance, the economic development agency (CORFO) has granted incentives to large companies participating in supplier development. In the Antofagasta region this has supported a collaborative effort across the stakeholders in the ecosystem, including ten large mines and two regional universities, the establishment of an industry association, a vendor qualification system, and a supplier database. By 2015 this vendor model was being used by twenty purchasing companies in mining, oil, and gas industries, and accounted for over 2,500 suppliers (World Bank, 2015). The model has evolved to a hybrid incentive and procurement scheme with mining companies and potential suppliers who could form a collaborative cluster to work on solutions together with local universities and public institutions.

In building R&D-rich ecosystems, intermediate technology and business services are the capabilities 'glue'. Local 'intermediate technology institutions' are essential for this glue to stick. These include institutional arrangements interfacing with universities, engineering and design services businesses, and hybrids supporting advanced manufacturing. In Australia a whole range of encouragement activities were offered for the evolution of collaborative institutional arrangements, such as through accelerators, hackathons, challenge platforms, and cluster programmes. These supported the establishment and growth of a network of public-private technology intermediate institutions in the ecosystem.

3.4.3.1 South Africa's Attempts to Address the Constraints
In the context of R&D and skills, as part of the Mining Phakisa initiative launched in 2015, the Mandela Mining Precinct was established in Johannesburg as a central hub for industry-specific R&D initiatives, alongside the promotion of the Mining Equipment Manufacturers of South Africa (MEMSA) association in 2016. MEMSA is an industry cluster body supporting the absorption and diffusion of technologies and collaborations across local OEMs and their suppliers and promises to impact on the fragmentation of the local industry.

With the establishment of the Mandela Mining Precinct, South Africa started equipping the industry with an important institutional solution to some of the binding constraints noted above in terms of technological innovation and upgrading. An intermediate technology institute like the Precinct can support companies in achieving appropriate functional, technical, and performance specifications, by innovating on several technologies and solutions offered by local OEMs. It may also provide support in the standardization process, making sure local OEMs develop solutions to capture the value of post-sale services. The extent to which these initial steps in the right direction are going to be effective in South Africa will depend on their sustained support, and the adoption of a full package of aligned measures cutting across the Mining Charter and relevant institutions.

3.5 Conclusions and Opportunities for Industrial Policy in the Metals and Mining Machinery and Equipment Industries

The metals, machinery, and equipment industries are at the heart of South Africa's industrial economy. The performance in these industries over the 1994 to 2019 period has demonstrated the challenges facing the country in redirecting the path of structural transformation and points to the key reasons why it has largely failed to overcome these challenges. As the 'big steel' case highlights, the entrenched power of the upstream firms continued to drive the agenda and shape the overall development of the industries. Downstream in the value chain, as is evident in the mining machinery and equipment industry, there was extensive international integration, in terms of ownership, technology, and trade. However, this was accompanied by increasing import penetration, persistent industry fragmentation, and ineffective and poorly coordinated policy and institutional support.

The industry record underlines the importance of understanding how and through what mechanisms power is exercised. A significant proportion of the support directed at strengthening the metals, machinery, and equipment value chain has benefited the capital-intensive upstream businesses, despite the potential to build on downstream capabilities and the opportunities which digitalization has presented. Additionally, the absence of a cohesive downstream industry able to lobby for government support has undermined the industry-level cluster efforts aimed at bolstering the industry. Lead firms can play a critical role in learning and building capabilities across their supplier networks. The lead upstream firms (in basic metals) have been instead largely oriented to protecting rents, particularly in the context of the challenges posed by international volatility (Rustomjee et al., 2018). Conditionalities needed to be strongly enforced along with moves to ensure cost-based mining inputs to steel-making and the removal of tariff protection.

At the same time, some lead firms in machinery and equipment have managed to sustain capabilities thanks to efforts to continuously invest in infrastructure, skills, and technology, including adopting digitalization. However, these have represented islands of capabilities rather than anchoring wider clusters of competitive capabilities. After 2008, the South African domestic market for machinery and equipment also started to shrink with the end of the commodities boom, while import penetration continued to be high despite various local content and procurement policies.

There was clearly a lack of an overarching strategy in this period that would locate procurement policies within the wider ecosystem as well as appropriate policies to increase domestic value addition, technology development, and upgrading (Andreoni and Torreggiani, 2020). This would require overcoming the fragmentation of policies being pursued by different departments and targeting the policies based on a thorough assessment of the products and services in order to impact on quantity, quality, and price competitiveness parameters. Monitoring compliance is also clearly important. Exports became increasingly significant for the companies that managed to sustain themselves through the prolonged slump. Export performance should have been incorporated into the targets in order to impact on the production decisions of the international and domestic OEMs affected by local content requirements. The international OEMs should also have been able to 'link back' local suppliers into their exclusive supply chains, thus 'powering' the local company.

Tariffs need to be consistent with the assessment of the local supply-chain capabilities and specific product segments for which domestic producers have a chance to be competitive internationally. This assessment should start from the analysis of the additionality of the current tariff, that is, the identification of the real beneficiaries of tariffs along the extended metal, mining equipment value chain. Trade policy should prioritize those intermediate and final product segments in which existing companies have already developed distinctive capabilities and are close to the international price competitiveness benchmark.

Rebuilding overarching institutions of industrial development is a central means to integrating fragmented initiatives and building a strong coalition for the downstream industries. The Mandela Mining Precinct has the potential to be elevated to a specialized intermediate technology institute focusing on the opportunities offered by the mega trends in global mining, addressing the challenge of scaling up national OEMs and their suppliers, and promoting collaboration across domestic players, including collaborative challenge-driven efforts for diversification. As discussed in section 3.4, effective engagement with digitalization is essential, including building the specialized digital skills base. The institute can provide this combined technology and skills development functions, focusing on the targeted training of task forces of specialized technicians and engineers in collaboration with universities and technical and vocational education and training (TVET) colleges.

Capturing the opportunities offered by the global technology and industry megatrends is conditional on increasing the scaling-up capability of the domestic OEMs and suppliers. This includes the lateral migration of capabilities in processes common to machinery and equipment across different applications such as food processing. These scaling-up challenges can be addressed by providing dedicated technology services as well as providing companies with access to quasi-public good technologies such as data systems, testing facilities, and pilot lines for virtual design and prototyping of mining solutions, complemented by the financing and skills for investing in capabilities.

While policy instrument design and governance frameworks are critical, the effective implementation and enforcement of any industrial policy will depend on the extent to which the policy is able to promote the emergence of a new coalition of productive interests, or offer the existing powerful groups alternative and more productive ways to operate in the economy. This is the ultimate 'feasibility' test for the policy.

References

Andreoni, A. and S. Torreggiani (2020). 'Mining equipment industry in South Africa: global context, industrial ecosystem and pathways for feasible sectoral reforms.' CCRED Working Paper 3/2020. Johannesburg: CCRED.

Barnes, J., A. Black, and S. Roberts (2019). 'Towards a digital industrial policy for South Africa: a review of the issues.' Industrial Development Think Tank.

Black, A. and S. Roberts (2009). 'The evolution and impact of industrial and competition policies.' In J. Aron, B. Kahn, and G. Kingdon (eds), *South African Economic Policy under Democracy*. Oxford: Oxford University Press.

Crompton, R., J. Fessehaie, L. Kaziboni, and T. Zengeni (2016). 'Railway locomotives and Transnet: a case study.' Johannesburg: The Centre for Competition, Regulation and Economic Development.

Crompton, R. and L. Kaziboni (2020). 'Lost opportunities? Barriers to entry and Transnet's procurement of 1064 locomotives.' In T. Vilakazi, S. Goga, and S. Roberts (eds), *Opening the Economy: Barriers to Entry and Competition*. Cape Town: HSRC Press.

Das Nair, R. and P. Mondliwa (2017). 'Excessive pricing under the spotlight: what is a competitive price?' In J. Klaaren, S. Roberts, and I. Valodia (eds), *Competition Law and Economic Regulation: Addressing Market Power in Southern Africa*. Johannesburg: Wits University Press.

Dolo, S., M. Odendaal, and G. Togo (2018). 'South Africa: Horizontal linkages-building expertise by overcoming country-specific constraints (Case Study).' IGC

Guidance for Governments: Leveraging Local Content Decisions for Sustainable Development. Winnipeg: IISD.

Edler, J. and L. Georghiou (2007). 'Public procurement and innovation—resurrecting the demand side.' *Research Policy* 36(7): 949–63.

Fessehaie, J. (2015). 'South Africa's upstream industries to mining: import substitution opportunities and impact of regulatory frameworks.' Background Paper for the Mining Phakisa.

Georghiou, L., J. Edler, E. Uyarra, and J. Yeow (2014). 'Policy instruments for public procurement of innovation: choice, design and assessment.' *Technological Forecasting and Social Change* 86: 1–12.

Goga, S., P. Mondliwa, and S. Roberts (2020). 'Economic power and regulation: the political economy of metals, machinery and equipment industries in South Africa.' In E. Webster, D. Francis, and I. Valodia (eds), *Inequality Studies from the Global South*, 75–98. London: Routledge.

Gostner, K., S. Roberts, A. Clark, and I. Iliev (2005). 'Resource-based technology innovation in South Africa.' Employment Growth and Development Initiative Working Paper, October 2005. Pretoria: Human Sciences Research Council.

Jourdan, P. (2014). 'The optimisation of the developmental impact of South Africa's mineral assets for building a democratic developmental state.' *Mineral Economics* 26(3): 107–26. Https://link.springer.com/content/pdf/10.1007/s13563-013-0037-1.pdf.

Kaplan, D. (2011). 'South African mining equipment and related services: growth, constraints and policy.' Making the Most of Commodities Programme (MMCP), Volume MMCP Discussion Paper 5.

Kaziboni, L., M. Nkhonjera, and S. Roberts (2019). 'Machinery, equipment and electronic control systems: leading reindustrialisation in Southern Africa.' Digital Industrial Policy Framework Issues Paper 1, CCRED. Johannesburg: University of Johannesburg.

Lember, V., R. Kattel, and T. Kalvet (2014). 'Public procurement and innovation: theory and practice.' In V. Lember, R. Kattel, and T. Kalvet (eds), *Public Procurement, Innovation and Policy*, 13–34. Berlin and Heidelberg: Springer.

Machaka, J. and S. Roberts (2003). 'The DTI's new "integrated manufacturing strategy": comparative industrial performance, linkages and technology.' *South African Journal of Economics* 71(4): 679–704.

Min, Y. K., S. G. Lee, and Y. Aoshima (2018). 'A comparative study on industrial spillover effects among Korea, China, the USA, Germany and Japan.' *Industrial Management & Data Systems* 119(3): 454–72.

Mohamed, G. and S. Roberts (2008). 'Weak links in the BEE chain? Procurement, skills and employment equity in the metals and engineering industries.' *Journal of Contemporary African Studies* 26(1): 27–50.

Mondi, L. and S. Roberts (2005). 'The role of development finance for industry in a restructuring economy: a critical reflection on the Industrial Development

Corporation of South Africa.' Presented at Trade and Industrial Policy Strategies Annual Forum, Johannesburg, 30 November – 1 December 2005.

Mondliwa, P. and R. das Nair (2019). 'Overcharge estimates in the South African reinforcing bar cartel.' In J. Klaaren, S. Roberts, and I. Valodia (eds), *Competition and Regulation for Inclusive Growth in Southern Africa*. Johannesburg: Wits Press.

OECD (2017). *The Next Production Revolution*. Paris: OECD.

Phele, T. and S. Roberts (2005). 'The impact of the minerals sector on industrial competitiveness: linkages and the development of capabilities in the capital equipment industry in South Africa.' Mimeo, presented at Globelics Conference, Pretoria, 2005.

Phele, T., S. Roberts, and I. Steuart (2005). 'Industrial strategy and local economic development: the case of the foundry industry in Ekurhuleni Metro.' *South African Journal of Economic and Management Sciences* 8(4): 448–64.

Roberts, S. (2008). 'Assessing excessive pricing: the case of flat steel in South Africa.' *Journal of Competition Law and Economics* 4(3): 871–91.

Roberts, S. (2020). 'Assessing the record of competition law enforcement in opening up the economy.' In T. Vilakazi, S. Goga, and S. Roberts (eds), *Opening the Economy: Barriers to Entry and Competition*. Cape Town: HSRC Press.

Roberts, S. and Z. Rustomjee (2009). 'Industrial policy under democracy: apartheid's grown-up infant industries?' *Iscor and Sasol. Transformation* 71: 50–75.

Rustomjee, Z., L. Kaziboni, and I. Steuart (2018). 'Structural transformation along metals, machinery and equipment value chain—developing capabilities in the metals and machinery segments.' CCRED Working Paper 7/2018. Johannesburg: CCRED.

Smeiman, M. (2018). 'Opportunities in mining industrialisation. phase one: a high-level business case to focus industrial development.' Mining Industrialisation Business Case presented at the Department of Trade and Industry in May 2018.

Steuart, I. (2019). 'A critical review of international cluster and other sector-support initiatives in the mining equipment & machinery sector.' The Industrial Development Think Tank (IDTT).

Tiryakioğlu, M. and M. A. Yülek (2015). 'Development-based public procurement policies: a selective survey of literature, cross-country policy experience and the Turkish experience.' *The European Journal of Social Science Research* 28(3): 344–59.

Walker, M. I. and R. C. A. Minnitt (2006). 'Understanding the dynamics and competitiveness of the South African minerals inputs cluster.' *Resources Policy* 31(1): 12–26.

World Bank (2015). 'A practical guide to increasing mining local procurement in West Africa.' World Bank, KAISER EDPI, and Australian Government.

Zalk, N. (2017). 'The things we lost in the fire: the political economy of post-apartheid restructuring of the South African steel and engineering sectors.' Unpublished PhD Thesis, Department of Economics, School of Oriental and African Studies, University of London.

4

Leveraging Plastics Linkages for Diversification

An Assessment of Backward Linkages from Polymers and Forward Linkages to the Automotive Industry

Jason Bell, Lorenza Monaco, and Pamela Mondliwa

4.1 Introduction

At the core of structural transformation is the diversification of an economy, generally based on linkages to support cumulative productivity increases. In the early 1990s, South Africa's industrial core was made up of a set of sectors spanning mining, energy, and various heavy industries. The strong input-output linkages between them, but weaker linkages with other manufacturing sectors, resulted in an economic structure that has been identified as the minerals and energy complex (MEC) (Fine and Rustomjee, 1996). An assessment of South Africa's structural transformation over the post-apartheid period from 1994 to 2019 necessarily entails an evaluation of the extent to which the economy has diversified away from the MEC core and towards more diversified downstream industries within the MEC.

This chapter analyses the development of the downstream plastic products industry, which has strong backward linkages to the upstream, petroleum industry for its main material inputs. At the same time, plastic products are a diverse set of manufactured goods for final and intermediate use and, as such, the sub-sector has strong forward linkages to the rest of manufacturing, with 54 per cent of output consumed by the range of manufacturing sub-sectors in 2019. While the upstream petrochemicals activities and some downstream manufacturing activities that consume plastic products, such as the automotive industry, have grown throughout the 1994–2019 period, plastic products have recorded poorer performance (Chapter 1). The plastic products sub-sector grew between 1994 and 2002, but declined thereafter, with weak performance in terms of output, value added, and investment, as with other diversified manufacturing activities (Mondliwa and Roberts, 2019).

Jason Bell, Lorenza Monaco, and Pamela Mondliwa, *Leveraging Plastics Linkages for Diversification: An Assessment of Backward Linkages from Polymers and Forward Linkages to the Automotive Industry* In: *Structural Transformation in South Africa: The Challenges of Inclusive Industrial Development in a Middle-Income Country*. Edited by: Antonio Andreoni, Pamela Mondliwa, Simon Roberts, and Fiona Tregenna, Oxford University Press. © Oxford University Press 2021. DOI: 10.1093/oso/9780192894311.003.0004

This raises two important questions. The first is why the growth of those industries requiring plastic components, such as automotive, has not acted as a demand pull. This question is analysed through a comparative assessment of the South African and Thai plastic automotive component industries. The focus is on how the two countries have attempted to foster technological upgrading and production capability accumulation by leveraging linkages to the automotive industry. While both South Africa and Thailand have embarked on targeted industrial policy to grow their automotive industries, very different results in terms of upgrading in the linked components industries have been observed, and Thailand is currently significantly more competitive (on South Africa, see Chapter 5).

The second is why the growth of the upstream polymer industry—in part due to South Africa's cost advantages in the production of basic petrochemical inputs—has not supported growth of plastic products. This is assessed through an analysis of the vertical relationships between the upstream polymer industry dominated by Sasol, and downstream plastic producers. The analysis focuses on the extent to which pricing decisions by the lead firm and policy (including regulatory decisions) in the upstream polymer industry have had an impact on the growth path of the downstream industry.

Overall, the chapter considers the role of policies, lead firm strategies, and governance in facilitating technological upgrading and the accumulation of productive capabilities necessary for the formation of linkages.

The rest of the chapter is organized as follows. Section 4.2 discusses the dynamics of structural transformation through linkages by reflecting on existing literature. Section 4.3 provides an overview of the structural change patterns in the linked petroleum, basic chemicals, and plastic industries. Through a comparison of South Africa and Thailand, section 4.4 assesses technological and production capability accumulation in plastic automotive components with a focus on the importance of the linkage to the automotive industry. Section 4.5 presents an analysis of the backward input linkages to the polymer industry with a focus on the lead firm, Sasol. Concluding remarks are made in section 4.6.

4.2 Structural Transformation through Exploiting Forward and Backward Linkages

The premise of growth through linkages stems from the early contributions by Hirschman (1958), which demonstrated the significance of backward linkages to input producers and forward linkages to markets for intermediate products in supporting structural change and productivity growth necessary for economic development. Linkages create multiplier effects, such that support for final goods producers can increase the range of components or inputs produced, broadening the industrial base and attracting the entry of further final goods producers in an economy (Baldwin and Venables, 2015). Country comparisons have shown that those countries that have strong production linkages with both domestic and foreign suppliers have been more successful in changing the structure of their economies and achieving economic development (Haraguchi and Rezonja, 2015).

In resource-rich countries like South Africa, backward and forward production linkages from the resource industries provide an important and often unrealized potential for industrial development (Morris et al., 2012) and thus for structural change. This is because successful economic development is essentially an incremental unfolding of linkages between related economic activities. This process is supported by an accumulation of capabilities including technological upgrading (Tregenna, 2012).

Many plastic products are intermediate components, which rely on linkages with input suppliers and with downstream industries. Literature on value chain governance shows how corporate power exercised by large and lead firms shapes the distribution of profits and risks in an industry, and how this alters the upgrading prospects of firms in developed and developing economies that are included in (or excluded from) the supply chain (Gereffi and Lee, 2016). Lead firms play a crucial role by defining the terms of participation in value chains, by incorporating or excluding actors, and by determining how, when, where, and by whom value is added (Gereffi and Lee, 2016).

While much attention has been paid to governance within global value chains (GVCs), a number of similar dynamics are also present in domestic value chains. First, firms with market power can exploit the downstream businesses reliant on the products as inputs through charging high prices, and can also leverage this power to undermine downstream rivals (Goga et al., 2020; Mondliwa et al., 2021). Distortions in input markets have been found to explain productivity differences within value chains and in the competitiveness of sectors (Acemoglu et al., 2007; Jones, 2013). Second, market power often translates into political power, whereby dominant firms can influence policy and regulation in their favour (Zingales, 2017; Goga et al., 2020). Third, firms also share knowledge and practices vertically through the supply chain, and large and lead firms often drive this process (as discussed in the Thai case in section 4.4). In this regard, the strategies of large and lead firms, as well as their capabilities, can have an impact on the propensity for positive linkage development along value chains.

While the GVC approach brings out elements of learning from geographically dispersed and vertically fragmented production networks (Gereffi et al., 2005), clustering analytical frameworks emphasize the importance of co-location and the creation of dynamic linkages for achieving increased competitiveness, as well as the upgrading of firms (Porter, 2000). These clusters can include firms in vertical or horizontal relationships. The emphasis is on collaboration among different stakeholders to take advantage of interdependencies in the production process (Götz and Jankowska, 2017). In particular, small firms in horizontal clusters are supposedly able to overcome some of the major constraints they usually face: lack of specialized skills, difficult access to technology, inputs, markets, telecommunication, credit, and external services (Giuliani et al., 2005). Participation in a cluster allows for collective benefits (positive externalities) for firms engaging in similar activities. These include, for example, the pooling of skilled labour and facilities, including testing and research facilities for design and product development. In the analysis here, value chains are used to capture the vertical relationships, and clusters are used to capture the horizontal relationships between firms.

Technological 'learning' and developing production capabilities are areas in which collective action by government and firms play an important role. International experience in the development of local industrial clusters or upgrading within value chains demonstrates the importance of the public sector in creating appropriate institutions and an enabling policy environment (see, for example, Best, 2001; Lema et al., 2018). In this regard, industrial policy is critical. Industrial policies can play an important role in developing linkages either through solving market failures, developing supportive institutions, or engaging in the process of discovery. When effectively coordinated, industrial policy incentives can promote both the breadth of linkages (the proportion of inputs sourced locally or outputs processed locally) and the depth of linkages (the extent of their domestic value added) (Morris et al., 2012).

4.3 Structural Change Dynamics within the Chemicals and Plastic Products Industry Grouping

The chemicals and plastic products industry grouping has been an important part of South Africa's industrial core throughout the twenty-five-year period under review (1994–2019). In 2019, the industry grouping accounted for 24 per cent of manufacturing value added (up from 16 per cent in 1994), 18 per cent of manufacturing exports (up from 16 per cent in 1994), and 13 per cent of manufacturing employment (up from 7 per cent in 1994). The broader chemicals and plastic products grouping is made up of a range of value chains. These include a wide range of activities, from resource extraction (crude oil, coal, and natural gas) and refining, to various levels of basic chemicals processing to produce industrial and consumer products, including plastic products. This chapter focuses on only one of these value chains—the petrochemical co-products to polymers (one of the many basic chemicals), to plastic products and the linked automotive assembly industry.

Plastic products are an important area of focus: they have been identified as having high potential for pulling along growth and are thus important for cumulative productivity increases (Tregenna, 2012); they are relatively more labour-absorbing (Table 4.1), which is a priority for South Africa's industrial policy; and, constituting mostly intermediate products, they are central in diversified manufacturing through their extensive forward linkages (Figure 4.1).

The petrochemical value chain in South Africa is characterized by highly concentrated upstream manufacture of polymer chemicals, closely linked with the processing of petroleum products, and lower levels of concentration in the downstream manufacture of plastic products. There are only two polymer producers in

Table 4.1 Performance of the chemicals and plastic products sub-sectors

		Coke and refined petroleum	Basic chemicals	Other chemicals	Plastic products
Value added R'bn) (% share of total manufacture)	1994	10 (4.4%)	8 (3.5%)	12 (4.9%)	8 (3.2%)
	2019	35 (9.3%)	17 (4.6%)	26 (7.0%)	11 (3.0%)
Employment (in thousands) (% share of total manufacture)	1994	18 (1.1%)	26 (1.5%)	37 (2.1%)	44 (2.6%)
	2019	27 (1.8%)	28 (1.8%)	83 (5.5%)	59 (3.9%)
Avg. valued-added growth	1994–2002	6.9%	6.5%	6.5%	5.6%
	2002–8	4.6%	2.6%	6.3%	−1.1%
	2008–19	3.8%	0.8%	−0.6%	0.1%
Avg. employment growth	1994–2002	−4.4%	−1.1%	0.7%	3.4%
	2002–8	17.4%	2.1%	8.8%	0.0%
	2008–19	−1.9%	0.5%	2.3%	0.5%
Avg. investment (gross fixed capital formation, % of gross value added)	1994–2002	35.5%	57.3%	15.9%	17.3%
	2002–8	36.5%	64.7%	15.0%	20.4%
	2008–19	30.0%	52.7%	13.1%	17.9%
Imports as % of domestic demand	1994	5.6%	57.6%	32.5%	11.4%
	2002	7.1%	24.3%	21.3%	11.2%
	2008	20.4%	36.2%	27.1%	19.8%
	2019	29.4%	37.4%	25.2%	33.7%
Exports as % of domestic output	1994	33.4%	20.5%	5.8%	2.6%
	2002	21.5%	17.8%	8.1%	4.4%
	2008	13.6%	36.0%	11.7%	9.4%
	2019	27.1%	46.1%	20.5%	16.6%

Notes:

1. It is important to note that the Quantec data are not official statistics. They have been compiled including data from Statistics South Africa, with some computations by Quantec, and this should be borne in mind.
2. Value figures are in ZAR millions (constant 2010 prices).
3. Growth is calculated as compound average growth rates.
4. Employment numbers include informal jobs.

Source: Quantec, authors' calculations.

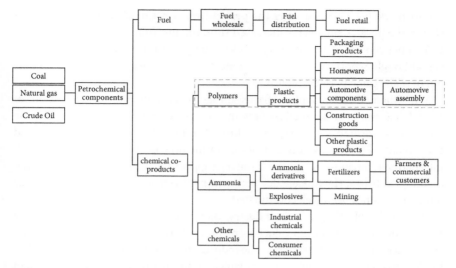

Figure 4.1 The petrochemical value chain
Source: Adapted from Mondliwa et al. (2020).

South Africa—the formerly state-owned Sasol, with a 60 per cent share of the commonly used polypropylene input, and Safripol, with the remaining 40 per cent. Sasol's power comes from it holding a monopoly position in important monomers such as propylene which are chemical co-products from refining and are used in the production of polymers.

In contrast, the manufacture of plastic products is characterized by relatively low-scale economies with many of the producers being small and medium-sized firms. Plastic production itself is diversified, with products differentiated by the sectors into which they form inputs, such as motor vehicles, building materials, electrical products, and packaging (Figure 4.1).

Over the twenty-five-year period under review (1994 to 2019), the upstream coke and refined petroleum products and basic chemicals sub-sectors recorded strong overall performance in terms of value-added growth, supported by relatively high levels of investment (Table 4.1). By comparison, the plastic products sub-sector performed well in the earlier part of this period with average annual growth in value-added of 5.6 per cent between 1994 and 2002, and employment growth of 3.4 per cent. However, the plastic products sub-sector lagged other industries in the value chain thereafter. There have been relatively low levels of investment in plastic production, as gross fixed capital formation averaged around 17 per cent to 20 per cent of value added.

South Africa's trade liberalization appears to have benefited the upstream basic chemicals sub-sector, with improved competitiveness in both domestic and export markets.[1] However, after the period from 1994 to 2002, import penetration in the plastics sub-sector increased substantially, from 11.2 per cent in 2002 to 33.4 per cent in 2019, reflecting a loss in competitiveness in the domestic market, although exports also increased somewhat to 16.6 per cent of domestic output over the same period (Table 4.1).

Why then, despite South Africa's initial success in plastic production in 1994–2002 and cost competitiveness in the upstream polymer inputs, has the industry performed so poorly over time? The liberalization of protection had been assumed to improve the capabilities of the downstream industries, through international integration and the industry support measures provided. However, as analysed below, the linkage development has been weak and industrial policy interventions not been well coordinated.

Within the plastic products industry, there has also been a failure to move towards the more complex product segments such as components for automotive, electronics, and medical products. The industry has continued to be dominated by the less tradable packaging segment, which continued to account for more than half of the sub-sector's output, signifying poor diversification (Beare et al., 2014; Bell et al., 2018). Though packaging is the largest segment in most countries (for example, around 40 per cent in the EU), the share in South Africa is particularly high. This matters for understanding capabilities and competitiveness of plastic production as packaging is relatively less traded and, as such, benefits from some protection from import competition.

While the industry's import penetration increased over the period, the overall picture masks important trends within the sub-sector. Import penetration appears to have increased most in the more sophisticated automotive components, medical, and sports and leisure segments, at over 70 per cent in 2013 (Mondliwa, 2018). And, instead of plastic product exports becoming more diverse over time, they have become more concentrated in lower-value segments (Beare et al., 2014).

The rest of the chapter assesses the developments in more detail: first, by conducting a comparative analysis of technological upgrading in the plastic automotive components segment in Thailand and South Africa in section 4.4; and, second, by assessing how market power, governance dynamics along the value chain, and industrial policy have supported or undermined development along linkages between upstream polymers and downstream plastic products, in section 4.5.

Plastic automotive components represent an important segment due to their relative complexity and potential for upgrading through forward linkages. In addition, the policy framework that supports the automotive sector was meant to

---

[1] The increased import penetration in coke and refined petroleum is a result higher imports of fuel blending components to meet clean fuels specifications.

support upgrading in linked industries and the framework did support increased output and South African exports of assembled vehicles implying growing demand for components.

4.4 Leveraging Forward Linkages to the Automotive Sector: A Comparative Analysis of Plastic Automotive Components in South Africa and Thailand

Thailand presents a successful case study of fostering linkages between the automotive industry and the development of plastic and other automotive components (Black et al., 2018; Monaco et al., 2019). Leveraging this linkage, the Thai plastic automotive components segment has experienced high growth rates relative to South Africa. For example, between 2001 and 2018, Thailand grew exports of motor vehicle bumpers and their parts, such as fittings, at a compound average growth rate of 16 per cent, while South Africa's exports grew by a more modest 2 per cent.[2]

This linkage has supported the diversification of plastic production in Thailand with the plastic automotive component segment increasing its contribution to total plastic production volumes to 8 per cent in 2018. South Africa compares poorly in this area, with the plastic automotive component segment accounting for only 4 per cent of total production, with the majority of production focused on packaging and less sophisticated plastic product segments. In terms of the number of firms, 16 per cent of the 5,000 Thai plastic products firms manufacture automotive components (Monaco et al., 2019), compared to a much smaller share of the 1,800 South African firms.

While Thailand's proximity to the developed ASEAN regional market demand has allowed it to achieve scale economies and is an important contributor to its success (Monaco et al., 2019), this has not been the only success factor. The automotive component industry has built robust technological capabilities through strong collaborations—both vertically through the value chain and horizontally through clusters (Monaco et al., 2019). In addition, the state and industry associations have played an important role in both facilitating inter-firm collaborations and coordinating policy incentives for development of the component industry (Monaco et al., 2019). These factors have allowed Thailand to leverage participation in the automotive GVC to grow plastic and other automotive component production. The focus is on understanding the drivers of success and failure in leveraging these linkages.

---

[2] South Africa also focuses more on the actual bumpers rather than the more sophisticated fittings, suggesting relatively weaker capabilities.

The comparison comprises two main parts. First, the accumulation of technological capabilities in both Thailand and South Africa's plastic automotive component manufacturers are compared. This includes a discussion of the role played by firm collaborations in horizontal clusters, and the role played by vertical integration through the value chain in supporting capability upgrading.

Second, the factors that have supported the formation of the horizontal and vertical collaborations and technological upgrading more generally are discussed. This includes a discussion of how targeted automotive industrial policies have been leveraged to develop automotive components, the role of the state in the coordination of policies for capability upgrading, and the interactions between the state and the multinational original equipment manufacturers (OEMs) that govern automotive value chains.

4.4.1 Technological Capabilities and Competitiveness

As many plastic products are of intermediate goods, demand linkages to industries that require these as inputs are important.[3] Among the potential benefits of participation in the automotive GVC are the opportunities to meet increased domestic demand and the upgrading of technological and other capabilities of the supply chain (Gereffi, 2019). Technological capabilities are also important factors for countries to upgrade within GVCs and for linking back into the domestic economy.

4.4.1.1 The State of Technology Infrastructure

The technology divide is the overwhelming difference in competitiveness between South African and Thai firms. Since the 1980s, Thai firms have made significant improvements in both production and operational management techniques (Monaco et al., 2019). Overall, the Thai firms were operating with up-to-date technology infrastructure (e.g. machines, moulds). Thai plastic auto component suppliers have gradually introduced robotics and other technologies linked to the fourth industrial revolution, such as the internet of things (Monaco et al., 2019). The Thai firms also demonstrated the capacity to innovate, due in part to investment in research and development, and testing and prototyping facilities, all supported by synergies between the plastic industry and government centres such as the Plastics Institute of Thailand (PITH).

Evidence from the South African plastic automotive component suppliers tells a starkly different story. In terms of technology infrastructure, there are differences among the local subsidiaries of multinational corporations (MNCs),

---

[3] This section builds on fieldwork conducted in Thailand for the IDTT during October 2018 (see Monaco et al., 2019).

local small and medium-sized firms, and large domestic firms. Local subsidiaries of MNCs tended to have newer machines, their own tool rooms, and were already using technologies linked to the fourth industrial revolution, with some degree of technology adaptation taking place in the domestic production facilities (Bell et al., 2019). However, strategies for technological upgrading are developed in the home countries and most research and development occurs in the MNCs' headquarters abroad. The large domestic firms were also relatively up to date in terms of technology used, had their own tool rooms, and some degree of R&D that was mainly focused on adaptation. In contrast, the small and medium-sized firms (SMEs) had little engagement with technology changes, the firms tended not to have tool rooms, and had no formal R&D activity (Bell et al., 2019). Regarding age of machinery, South African firms had machines with an average age of around eighteen years which is old compared to the norm of replacing machinery after seven to ten years of use (Bell et al., 2019).

The analysis of technology infrastructure also considered the origins of the machinery used by firms, where European moulding machines are reported to have better precision, an important quality for more complex plastic products. South African firms appear to be shifting towards the use of Chinese machines, as they are relatively cheaper. In 1994, 60 per cent of imports of moulding machinery were from Europe, while in 2018 the bulk of moulding machines (55 per cent) were coming from China (Bell et al., 2019), with the change largely driven by cost differences. South African firms also have a far lower propensity to invest in R&D, opting for short-term solutions to problems rather than investing time and resources into building strong R&D capabilities as the Thai firms do (Garisch, 2016). Financial constraints are cited as the main reason for the reluctance to upgrade their technological infrastructure. This is largely because the local South African firms, particularly the SMEs, are trapped in a vicious circle of low margins (partly from the polymer input prices), low levels of investment in up-to-date technology, and poor competitiveness (Mondliwa, 2018).

4.4.1.2 Technological Capabilities Can Be Achieved through Vertical and Horizontal Collaborations

One way in which downstream plastic product manufacturers can realize improvements in technological capabilities and R&D capacity is through an acquisition or joint venture with an innovative firm. In Thailand, the increasing adoption of technology has been facilitated through vertical collaborations between Thai component manufacturers and MNCs, in particular Japanese OEMs (Monaco et al., 2019). Partnerships between the OEMs and local firms have improved management and production techniques through continuous human resource development, employee training and education in new technologies, connection with external markets, and through the attention paid to improving efficiency in the manufacturing process. Similarly, collaboration in

R&D, testing, and prototyping facilities has been crucial for improving and maintaining quality and standards, as well as allowing Thai firms to become leaders in innovation. This means that Thai firms are significantly more competitive in the auto components export market (Monaco et al., 2019).

The successful vertical collaborations between local and foreign-owned firms in Thailand have been complemented by horizontal collaborations in the form of clusters. The potential for a cluster to jointly develop technological capabilities is strongly connected to the quality and strength of linkages developed. As such, the development of industrial clusters has been considered crucial for the development of industries, such as the automotive industry, where the components are heavy and bulky, and just-in-time manufacturing is necessary to improve competitiveness (Kuroiwa et al., 2017). The locating of firms in clusters together with organizations that support innovation can promote the 'interactive learning' process, which in turn provides an opportunity for local firms to upgrade their capabilities (Malmberg and Maskell, 2006). The Thai state's cluster programmes have been designed to attract increasingly larger amounts of FDI and facilitate technological upgrading within the automotive industry by positioning large OEMs within a close geographical proximity to small and medium-sized component manufacturers. Automobile and auto parts producers have been encouraged to locate their operations in Bangkok and the surrounding central area (Techakanont and Charoenporn, 2011). Combined with the involvement of Japanese capital, this has fostered the strong growth in technological capabilities in these sectors.

In contrast, there has been limited collaboration for 'learning' and building capabilities in the plastic products and automotive industries in South Africa. Some success was observed in the Durban Automotive Cluster where there is a vertical cluster championed by Toyota and which includes various players in the value chain (Black et al., 2018). The success is limited, however, as spinoffs in other provinces such as Gauteng and the Eastern Cape have not been as effective.

Linkages between private and public investments in R&D and innovation have also been more successful in Thailand, where they have been coordinated by the PITH. In South Africa, the plastic products sector has a limited number of laboratories conducting R&D and testing of locally produced products for exports (IPAP, 2018). A partnership between Plastics SA and the Council for Scientific and Industrial Research (CSIR) was formed to encourage innovation and the use of new technologies in the plastic industry in 2018. However, the project is focused more on the recycling of polymers and bio plastic inputs.[4] While these are important for sustainability, there is still insufficient focus on innovation related to the final plastic products.

---

[4] https://www.crown.co.za/environment/7533-plastics-sa-overcoming-challenges-with-collaboration-and-innovation.

4.4.2 The Role of Industrial Policy and Governance by OEMs

The analysis above points to the important role played by vertical and horizontal collaboration in building technological capabilities in Thailand. This section discusses the role of policy interventions in the automotive industry, the importance of policy coordination, and the governance role of multinational OEMs in facilitating these collaborations in Thailand and South Africa.

4.4.2.1 Thailand

In terms of policies, both South Africa and Thailand have been through iterations of industrial policy targeted at developing automotive industries, including the linked automotive components. The Thai Automotive Masterplan has offered several incentives that have facilitated an influx of foreign investment from global multinational assemblers who set up large-scale production facilities in the country. The establishment of a world-class domestic automotive components industry was in part due to the local content policy that was part of the Masterplan. Though the local content policy was initially opposed by the larger Japanese assemblers, negotiations involving the state, the assemblers, and component manufacturers led to its adoption. Lobbying by the industry associations representing domestic automotive components manufacturers played an important role in influencing the policy decisions (Poapongsakorn and Tangkitvanich, 2001).

A number of complementary incentives and policies have aided in the execution of the Thai Masterplan. These include the development of infrastructure in the form of special economic zones and industrial parks, education and training in firms, and the provision of finance for the purchase of up-to-date technologies. The Thai state has coordinated many of these incentives through various cluster initiatives that have linked locally owned Thai auto component manufacturers with large, multinational auto assemblers.

This suggests that the political economy dynamics in the Thai economy have significantly enabled the success of the Thai auto component sector. Specifically, the Thai state and the various associations and institutions in the automotive industry have complemented the presence of a strong regional market to realize the success of the Thai Masterplan (Monaco et al., 2019).

The governance role of MNCs and the ability of the state to shape their orientation have also been critical for developing plastic and other automotive components. At the global level, the significant size and power of large multinational automotive assemblers affects multiple levels within the supply chain and the broader institutional setting in which the industry operates. Owing to their dominant positions, these large multinational assemblers can affect investment (Monaco et al., 2019). This determines both the rate and success of the development of the national supply chain, particularly in the context of technological upgrading.

Similarly, these large and dominant assemblers can influence the policy space in which the state operates. The bargaining dynamics between the state and large multinationals are crucial for understanding supply-chain development (Monaco et al., 2019). Owing to a number of institutional arrangements and the formation of a strong coalition between the state and the multinational companies, Thailand has been able to grow its auto component sector around its automotive sector. The attraction of FDI has therefore been a key part of Thailand's success, acting as a catalyst for knowledge diffusion and the local capability building (Techakanont and Terdudomtham, 2004). Many of Thailand's SMEs that make up the bulk of its component manufactures have been developed as part of joint ventures with Japanese OEMs (Monaco et al., 2019).

4.4.2.2 South Africa

In South Africa, the political economy dynamics and their effect on the auto components sector have been very different.

South Africa's policy frameworks for developing a globally competitive auto industry took the form of the Motor Industry Development Programme (MIDP), which ran from 1995 to 2012, and the subsequent Automotive Production Development Programme (APDP), from 2012 to 2020. Neither the MIDP nor the APDP achieved the expected development of the local industry with South Africa's production of assembled automobiles only accounting for 0.65 per cent of the global market. The levels of local content in the domestic automotive industry have remained low (Chapter 5). The rebate mechanism, which allowed the OEMs to increase imports of components as long as exports were also increasing, has been the chief policy weakness, as it has undermined the increasing of local content (Black et al., 2018). For example, in 2016, as much as 60 per cent of the components used in production in South African plants were imported. Other factors contributing to this are low domestic and regional demand of assembled automobiles in the domestic industry.

The political economy dynamics in South Africa have not been supportive of the development of the automotive industry, especially automotive components. The South African state has failed both to realize its developmental agenda and to reconcile it with the interests of the global assemblers. While the state has assumed an interventionist role in the auto industry, this has meant that the MNCs have been in a strong bargaining position with the state for incentives, given their hegemonic positions in the local supply chain (Black et al., 2018). The South African automotive components industries have been reliant on the strategies of the multinational assemblers.

The experience in South Africa has led to the Auto Masterplan 2035, launched in 2020, which was largely inspired by the Thai version. Under this framework, the state is seeking to achieve local-content levels of 60 per cent across all assembled vehicles as well as doubling employment levels in the sector and increasing its competitiveness. It is too soon to comment on the success of the strategy.

With regards to the development of automotive components, poor coordination among different government departments responsible for executing policy incentives in the 1994–2019 period has further undermined this development. The National Industrial Policy Framework (2007) and the iterative Industrial Policy Action Plans (IPAPs, 2010–19) have sought to leverage linkages to the growing automotive industry to develop plastic automotive components. However, the political economy dynamics have not been supportive of this. For example, the local compounding industry, which produces automotive polymer grades was undermined by polymer pricing (discussed further below). An analysis of the cost competitiveness of the local industry showed that while the conversion cost and additive costs were comparable with global compounders, the local firms were paying 30 per cent more for polypropylene, which accounted for 80 per cent of the raw material cost (Mondliwa, 2018). The result is that, over time, the compounding level of the value chain lost competitiveness and firms largely exited the market. This meant the automotive plastic converters have had to switch to imported automotive grade polymers, which has obviously reduced the local content of the plastic components and, in turn, the incentive for assemblers to source locally.

The funding and incentive programmes have also reinforced South Africa's sub-sectoral composition rather than targeting the sub-sectors that the country was seeking to develop, such as automotive components (Beare et al., 2014).

4.5 Leveraging Backward Linkages to Polymers

To assess how interests have supported or undermined development along linkages between upstream polymers and downstream plastic products, this section examines industrial policy, market power, and governance dynamics along the value chain in South Africa.

4.5.1 The Role of Industrial Policy in Supporting Linkages and Structural Transformation

Structural change requires industrial policy to support the development of capabilities in new activities rather than allocating resources in line with the existing economic structure. For successful structural change within the plastic products value chain, industrial policy has an important role to play to support the more diversified plastic products industry including higher value added and more sophisticated goods, such as automotive components. Despite the prioritization of the plastic products industry, from 2007, by the Department of Trade, Industry, and Competition (DTIC), incentives have continued to disproportionately flow towards the upstream basic chemicals production—suggesting that the distribution of power within the economy does not support diversification. The section considers the distribution of industrial incentives between 1994 and 2007 (the year that the National Industrial Policy Framework was launched), and then in the period between 2007 and 2019.

In the 1994–2007 period, while there was no overarching industrial policy, a range of industrial policy support measures such as development finance and export incentives were made available to firms. These included loans extended by the Industrial Development Corporation, the General Export Incentive Scheme running from 1994 to 1997, and various tax incentives for investment. These measures were disproportionately awarded to the upstream firms, including Sasol. For example, Sasol received the lion's share of financing provided to the chemicals and plastic products industry grouping (Mondi and Roberts, 2005; and Gumede et al., 2011). Sasol was already internationally competitive by 1994 and able to finance further investments from its profits (Bell et al., 2019). This bias towards upstream producers continued in the 2000s, as Sasol alone received 22 per cent of the entire Strategic Investment Programme (SIP) incentive programme (Mondliwa and Roberts, 2019). Other beneficiaries were upstream basic steel industries. Very few plastic products firms benefited from these incentives. This distribution of incentives reinforced the economic structure rather supporting diversification.

Though the plastic products industry was prioritized in the post-2007 period, this did not result in substantial support for the industry. Instead, in terms of incentives and initiatives, most support continued to be biased towards upstream firms. Where the industry has benefited from government incentives, these have tended to go towards larger firms, primarily in the packaging industry (Beare et al., 2014; IPAP, 2016). This means that industrial policy has not supported diversification within the plastic products industry, but has instead reinforced the existing structure.

It was only in 2019, that the Industrial Development Corporation (IDC) developed a targeted scheme for the downstream plastic production industry. Though this is an important development, finance alone is not the silver bullet for changing industry performance. Other factors and conditions need to be in place, including competitively priced inputs and the ability to source appropriate technology, such as machinery and moulds. Clusters initiatives are an important part of collective action to address common challenges relating to skills and capabilities. In 2016, a cluster programme was developed by the DTIC for this purpose and firms in the plastic products industry applied for cluster development support. However, the programme was shelved due to lack of funding.

While the DTIC has developed 'sector strategies', the success of these strategies depends on the coordination of interventions among the different departments overseeing the different areas, such as technology and skills development (Mondliwa, 2018). As a result of poor cross-department coordination, many of the interventions identified in the sector strategies have not been implemented.

4.5.2 Industrial Policy, Economic Regulation, and Implications for Market Power

Diversification in the plastic products value chain has not only been undermined by poor support for the development of capabilities in downstream plastic production. The significant support provided to Sasol, accompanied with weak or no conditionalities, has further entrenched the firm's market power and undermined the bargaining power of downstream firms.

A product of the planning legacy of apartheid, Sasol is the dominant petro-chemicals producer in South Africa, including of monomers and polymers. Acknowledging the implications of Sasol's dominant position for price negoti-ations with downstream industries, the apartheid government placed a number of conditions on the provision of state support and a favourable regulatory regime for liquid fuels. One condition required Sasol to sell intermediate chemical inputs, including polymers, at export parity levels (as determined to be the competitive level), and to support the growth of the downstream industries in other ways, such as through advice and technical support (Roberts and Rustomjee, 2009). But, instead of continuing the stance of applying strong conditionalities, in the post-apartheid period decisions taken by regulators and policymakers have been char-acterized by weak reciprocal mechanisms, or none at all. Sasol changed its pricing around 2002 once it became evident that it was not going to be held to commit-ments. As discussed below, this coincides with a decline in the performance of the downstream plastic products sector (Figure 4.2).

Two features of the post-apartheid policy regime stand out. First, the approach to fuel regulation from 2003 onwards has assumed away Sasol's vertical integration and the potential leveraging of market power from one product market to another. Price regulation applies only to fuel, and the chemical co-products that arise in fuel production are not regulated. This creates opportunities to extract monopoly prices in the unregulated product markets. At the same time, the upstream petrochemical activities have continued to benefit from a range of inherited advantages and regulations. These advantages filter through to the chemical co-products, such as monomers, which are priced at fuel alternative-value.[5] The generous fuel regulation means that downstream industries pay higher prices for co-products and by-products (Mondliwa et al., 2020).

---

[5] The imputed return to the product, if it were converted into fuel components, even while there are limits to the extent to which this could be done in practice.

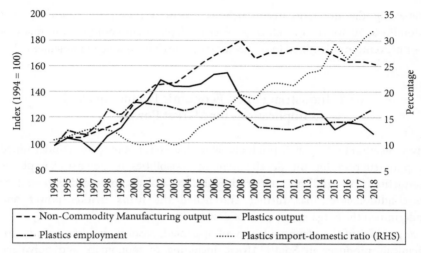

Figure 4.2 Turning point in the performance of the plastic products industry
Source: Authors' calculations using Quantec data.

Second is that there has been limited enforcement of conditionalities. For example, Sasol holds mineral rights to coal, which is used as an input for synthetic fuel production. The standard coal licence contains a condition that precludes price discrimination between domestic and export markets for coal and products beneficiated from coal. However, this condition has never been enforced for chemical products that are beneficiated from coal by Sasol. Another example is the condition placed on Sasol's release from repaying windfall gains from past regulation. Here, Sasol has committed to support and develop the downstream activities of the petrochemical value chain (Mondliwa and Roberts, 2019). However, rather than building strategic vertical partnerships with its customers for the development of new products, Sasol has instead taken a corporate social responsibility approach to the 'support for growth and competitiveness of the downstream sector' by establishing an incubator, which the government co-funded (Mondliwa and Roberts, 2019).

The state has therefore not succeeded in re-orienting Sasol's strategies to support downstream industry development. Sasol on the other hand has leveraged its market position to maximize its profits. The internationalization of the firm through its listing on the New York Stock Exchange in 2003, has also meant that these profits are increasingly distributed outside of the country as dividends (Chapter 10).

4.5.3 Input Linkages and Value Chain Governance: Pricing Power

Sasol has leveraged its market position to influence distribution of value in the value chain. The firm's vertical integration from the monomers to the polymers level of the value chain has allowed it to influence pricing outcomes in polymer production. Sasol is both the monopoly supplier of monomers (the input in the production of polymers) and the competitor to Safripol (the only other producer of polymers) in the supply of polymers. Sasol has been able to influence Safripol's pricing strategies in two ways. First, by limiting access to monomers, it has restrained Safripol's ability to expand and compete more aggressively with Sasol (Mondliwa et al., 2021). This has been done by adopting a pricing structure that resulted in higher prices as volumes increase. Collusion has also played a part, as Sasol and Safripol entered into a coordinated arrangement, which had the impact of indirectly fixing the polymer prices in the country based on Sasol's position as the monopoly monomer supplier.

Second, Sasol placed a condition on the 'gas to liquids' technology licence to PetroSA, precluding the state-owned firm from selling chemical co-products in the domestic market for the first twenty years of the licence agreement. This has effectively removed a potential competitor from the market, further entrenching Sasol's market power.

The impact of polymer pricing strategies on the performance of the plastic products industry can be observed in relation to the response to Sasol's change in pricing strategy in 2002/3. Between 1994 and 2002, when polymer prices continued to be priced at the required export parity levels as part of the historical conditions for state support, the plastic products industry performed reasonably well, with output growth in line with other diversified manufacturing production up until 2002 (Figure 4.2). However, 2002—when Sasol changed its pricing strategy from export parity to import parity—marked a turning point. It was then that the performance of the downstream plastic products industry started to lag that of other diversified manufacturing industries, with a marked decline in competitiveness and import penetration increasing, to reach 34 per cent by 2019 (Figure 4.1).

Input pricing is important for the wider development of capabilities, as the investments to build production and technological capabilities—necessary for becoming internationally competitive—are undermined by the input price effect on margins and profitability of downstream businesses. In plastic production in particular, the pricing of polymers is crucial for cost competitiveness, as polymers account for 50 to 70 per cent of variable production costs (Machaka and Roberts, 2003; Dobreva, 2006; Beare et al., 2014; Mondliwa, 2018). Though the pricing of the input may not be the only factor that led to the decline in competitiveness of industry, it is certainly an important one given that polymer inputs make up the largest component of variable cost.

Input linkages are not only important for input cost competitiveness: certain aspects of the innovation of plastic production require collaboration with polymer producers who are able to adapt the performance of polymers to specific design requirements. Since the days when Sasol was required to provide technical support to the downstream plastic industry there has been far less collaboration.

In order for industrial policy to succeed in driving development through linkages, it is important that it grapples with the vertical relationships in value chains, including the power distribution. This allows the policymaker to design policies that can tip the scales for large and lead firms like Sasol to work with downstream industries to develop capabilities and competitiveness.

4.6 Conclusions

At the core of structural transformation is diversification of an economy, generally based on linkages to support cumulative productivity increases. In the case of South African plastic products, this crucial development has been undermined by market power in the upstream petrochemicals industry, meaning high input prices, which are critical for the competitiveness of the industry as well as for building capabilities. The price pressures on an intermediary input product (polymers), have resulted in smaller margins, meaning that firms are unable to reinvest in up-to-date equipment and research and design, all of which are critical for building productive capabilities. These firms may find themselves in a vicious circle of competitiveness with low margins, low investment, and little development of capabilities.

With regards to the comparative analysis of Thailand and South Africa's automotive plastic components, the chapter highlights how, despite South Africa and Thailand both having policy frameworks to support automotive value chains, these have led to very different outcomes. This speaks to the importance of the design of industrial policy as well as the political economy dynamics that can support or undermine such policies. However, state policies alone do not provide a full explanation for either Thailand's relative success, nor South Africa's relative failure. The factors that explain the different trajectories include: the combination of vertical with horizontal integration in the form of participation in GVCs and the clustering effects which differed in the two countries; the presence of a larger and growing regional market for Thailand; and, a different role played by MNCs— Japanese firms in the case of Thailand. From a policy perspective, better coordination and more focused policy objectives also appear to have played an important role in Thailand's accumulation of technological capabilities and the development of deeper intersectoral linkages.

The complex and sometimes contradictory political economy dynamics in South Africa have been an important contributing factor in undermining the development of linkages. As the discussion has shown, in the period up to 2006, policy continued to support the upstream firms such as basic chemicals, with the lion's share of government incentives being channelled to these industries. Since 2007 onwards, industrial policy instruments have been deployed to target the plastic products industry and attempted to link the plastic automotive components to the automotive industry. However, poor coordination among multiple government departments and agencies has further weakened these initiatives.

The opportunity for 'linking back' into the domestic economy from automotive GVC participation has been further undermined by poor collaboration between firms, weak relationships with institutions that could support capabilities development, and conflicts within the value chain.

The chapter emphasizes the importance of understanding the performance of the plastic industry within the broader sectoral value chain. In the analysis of push dynamics from backward industries, it is shown that competitive outcomes at one level of the value chain can impact on the development of sectoral value chains. This happens through vertical linkages, which have the potential to promote or undermine structural transformation (see also Lee et al., 2018; Mondliwa et al., 2021). And crucially, as Zingales (2017) notes, the market power of firms translates easily into political power, which allows dominant firms to influence regulations and policy in their favour.

References

Acemoglu, D., P. Antràs, and E. Helpman (2007). 'Contracts and technology adoption.' *American Economic Review* 97(3): 916–43.

Baldwin, R. and A. J. Venables (2015). 'Trade policy and industrialisation when backward and forward linkages matter.' *Research in Economics* 69(2): 123–31.

Beare, M., P. Mondliwa, G. Robb, and S. Roberts (2014). 'Report for the plastics conversion industry strategy.' Research Report prepared for the Department of Trade and Industry.

Bell, J., L. Kaziboni, M. Nkhonjera, J. Nyamwena, and P. Mondliwa (2018). 'Firm decisions and structural transformation in the context of industry 4.0.' CCRED Working Paper 2018/12. Johannesburg: CCRED.

Bell, J., P. Mondliwa, and J. Nyamwena (2019). 'Technological change and productive capabilities in the plastics industry.' CCRED Working Paper 2/2019. Johannesburg: CCRED.

Best, M. (2001). *The New Competitive Advantage*. Oxford: Oxford University Press.

Black, A., J. Barnes, and L. Monaco (2018). 'Structural transformation in the auto sector: industrial policy, state-business bargaining and supply chain development.' A report for the Industrial Development Think Tank. Johannesburg: CCRED.

Dobreva, R. (2006). 'Value chains, market power and competitiveness: understanding the performance of the plastics sector.' In S. Roberts (ed.), *Sustainable Manufacturing? The Case of South Africa and Ekurhuleni*, 182–206. Cape Town: Juta.

Fine, B. and Z. Rustomjee (1996). *The Political Economy of South Africa: From Minerals-Energy Complex to Deindustrialization*. Johannesburg: Witwatersrand University Press.

Garisch, C. (2016). 'A study of innovation culture and capability in the South African plastics industry.' MerSETA Plastics Chamber Research.

Gereffi, G. (2019). 'Economic upgrading in global value chains.' In S. Ponte, G. Gereffi, and G. Raj-Reichert (eds), *Handbook on Global Value Chains*, 240–54. Edward Elgar Publishing.

Gereffi, G., J. Humphrey, and T. Sturgeon (2005). 'The governance of global value chains.' *Review of International Political Economy* 12(1): 78–104.

Gereffi, G. and J. Lee (2016). 'Economic and social upgrading in global value chains and industrial clusters: why governance matters.' *Journal of Business Ethics* 133: 25–38.

Giuliani, E., C. Pietrobelli, and R. Rabellotti (2005). 'Upgrading in global value chains: lessons from Latin American clusters.' *World Development* 33(4): 549–73.

Goga, S., P. Mondliwa, and S. Roberts (2020). 'Competition, productive capabilities and structural transformation in South Africa.' *European Journal of Development Research* special issue: 'Bringing production back into the development agenda.'

Götz, M. and B. Jankowska (2017). 'Clusters and industry 4.0—do they fit together?' *European Planning Studies* 25(9): 1633–53.

Gumede, W., M. Govender, and K. Motshidi (2011). *The Role of South Africa's State-Owned Development Finance Institutions (DFIs) in Building a Democratic Developmental State*. Pretoria: The Presidency.

Haraguchi, N. and G, Rezonja (2015). 'Structural change in the BRICS' manufacturing industries.' In W. Naudé, A. Szirmai, and N. Haraguchi (eds), *Structural Change and Industrial Development in the BRICS*, 29–65. Oxford: Oxford University Press.

IPAP (2016). 'Industrial policy action plan 2016/17–2018/19.' Pretoria: DTIC.

IPAP (2018). 'Industrial policy action plan 2018/19–2020/21.' Pretoria: DTIC.

Jones, C. I. (2013). 'Input–output economics.' In D. Acemoglu, M. Arellano, and E. Dekel (eds), *Advances in Economics and Econometrics: Tenth World Congress*, 2:419. Cambridge: Cambridge University Press.

Kuroiwa, I., K. Techakanout, and S. Keola (2017). 'Spatial distribution of automobile firms in Thailand.' BRC Research Report No. 17.

Lema, R., R. Rabellotti, and P. Sampath (2018). 'Innovation trajectories in developing countries: co-evolution of global value chains and innovation systems.' *The European Journal of Development Research* 30(3): 345–63.

Machaka, J. and S. Roberts (2003). 'The DTI's new "Integrated Manufacturing Strategy"? Comparative industrial performance, linkages and technology.' *South African Journal of Economics* 71(4): 679–704.

Malmberg, A. and P. Maskell (2006). 'Localized learning revisited.' *Growth and Change* 37(1): 1–18.

Monaco, L., J. Bell, and J. Nyamwena (2019). 'Understanding technological competitiveness and supply chain deepening in plastic auto components in Thailand: possible lessons for South Africa.' CCRED Working Paper 2019/01. Johannesburg: CCRED.

Mondi, L. and S. Roberts (2005). 'The role of development finance for industry in a restructuring economy: a critical reflection on the Industrial Development Corporation of South Africa.' Paper presented at the TIPS/DPRU Annual Forum on Trade and Uneven Development: Opportunities and Challenge.

Mondliwa, P. (2018). 'Capabilities, diversification and market power in industrial development: a case study of South African manufacturing and the plastics industry.' MCom dissertation, University of Johannesburg.

Mondliwa, P., S. Goga, and S. Roberts (2021). 'Competition, productive capabilities and structural transformation in South Africa.' *The European Journal of Development Research* 33(2): 253–74.

Mondliwa, P. and S. Roberts (2019). 'From a developmental to a regulatory state? Sasol and the conundrum of continued state support.' *International Review of Applied Economics* 33(1): 11–29.

Mondliwa, P., S. Roberts, and S. Ponte (2020). 'Competition and power in global value chains.' *Competition & Change*. IDO 1024529420975154.

Morris, M., R. Kaplinsky, and D. Kaplan (2012). '"One thing leads to another"—commodities, linkages and industrial development.' *Resources Policy* 37(4): 408–16.

Poapongsakorn, N. and S. Tangkitvanich (2001). 'Industrial restructuring in Thailand: a critical assessment.' In S. Masuyama, D. Vandenbrink, and S. Yue Chia (eds), *Industrial Restructuring in East Asia*, 109–38. Singapore: Institute of Southeast Asian Studies.

Porter, M. E. (2000). 'Location, competition, and economic development: local clusters in a global economy.' *Economic Development Quarterly* 14(1): 15–34.

Roberts, S. and Z. Rustomjee (2009). 'Industrial policy under democracy: apartheid's grown-up infant industries? Iscor and Sasol.' *Transformation* 71: 50–75.

Techakanont, K. and P. Charoenporn (2011). 'Evolution of automotive clusters and interactive learning in Thailand.' *Science, Technology & Society* 16(2): 147–76.

Techakanont, K., and T. Terdudomtham (2004). 'Evolution of inter-firm technology transfer and technological capability formation of local parts firms in the Thai Automobile Industry.' *Asian Journal of Technology Innovation* 12(2): 151–83.

Tregenna, F. (2012). 'Sources of sub-sectoral growth in South Africa.' *Oxford Development Studies* 40(2): 162–89.

Zingales, L. (2017). 'Towards a political theory of the firm.' *Journal of Economic Perspectives* 31(3): 113–30.

5

Government Policy in Multinational-Dominated Global Value Chains

Structural Transformation within the South African Automotive Industry

Justin Barnes, Anthony Black, and Lorenza Monaco

5.1 Introduction

The automotive industry has been regarded as one of South Africa's key industrial sub-sectors and attracted considerable state support.[1] Through a series of development plans, evolving from import protection during the apartheid era to progressive liberalization with the Motor Industry Development Programme (MIDP, 1995) and the Automotive Production and Development Programme (APDP, 2013), the industry was extensively restructured and became increasingly globally integrated. In the process, there was organizational and technological upgrading. However, the growth in finished vehicle exports was not accompanied by increasing local content, investment levels were modest by global automotive industry standards, and most capabilities resided within large multinational firms. These multinational corporations (MNCs), by and large, conducted research, design, and vehicle development in their home countries, and not in South Africa. Imports of vehicles and parts increased and the industry generally ran significant annual trade deficits. As a result, despite its important role in the South African manufacturing sector, spillovers have been modest and the industry has not developed into a competitive global hub.

This chapter reflects on constraints to localization. It does so by looking not only at structural impediments that hamper the process, but also at ownership and power relations between state and business, and at the distribution of power along the value chain. In particular, the question of bargaining between state

---

[1] The chapter draws on a rich set of data available thanks to the direct involvement of two of the authors in the formulation of previous and current auto plans, including the 2035 South African Automotive Masterplan. The authors would also like to acknowledge helpful comments by Tim Sturgeon and an anonymous referee.

Justin Barnes, Anthony Black, and Lorenza Monaco, *Government Policy in Multinational-Dominated Global Value Chains: Structural Transformation within the South African Automotive Industry* In: *Structural Transformation in South Africa: The Challenges of Inclusive Industrial Development in a Middle-Income Country*. Edited by: Antonio Andreoni, Pamela Mondliwa, Simon Roberts, and Fiona Tregenna, Oxford University Press. © Oxford University Press 2021. DOI: 10.1093/oso/9780192894311.003.0005

institutions and multinational carmakers is a key dynamic. It also analyses the potential for further deepening the automotive value chain in South Africa, considering the availability of resources, manufacturing infrastructure, and productive capabilities.

Section 5.2 of the chapter locates the South African industry in its international context. It then goes on in section 5.3 to trace the development of the domestic industry since 1960. The related questions of scale of production and structural change are examined in section 5.4. The development of the automotive industry has been driven by policy that has been the subject of intense state–business bargaining. This is the subject of section 5.5. The rest of the chapter is then focused on the supply chain. Section 5.6 considers the impact of growing foreign ownership and other factors on supply-chain development. In section 5.7 prospects for increased localization are assessed. Section 5.8 concludes.

5.2 The South African Automotive Industry in an International Context

The automotive industry is one of the world's largest manufacturing industries and has frequently been identified as emblematic of national industrialization. As such it has been the recipient of extensive state attention and support. Given the size and visibility of the sector, this is not altogether surprising and governments all over the world have tried to promote their domestic automotive industries in various ways.

In developing countries, these support measures initially included high tariffs on imported vehicles tied to local-content requirements. Indeed, the automotive industry was an important pillar in import substitution programmes, especially in larger countries (Humphrey et al., 1998). From the 1980s, again echoing global trends, support moved to the promotion of exports and was accompanied by trade liberalization. Direct investment support and a wide range of other incentives for local production were also put in place and countries (and regions within countries) competed fiercely to attract major plants, mainly to the advantage of investing multinational firms (Pavlinek, 2016). These pressures were enough to foment several waves of foreign direct investment, beginning early in the twentieth century when Ford and General Motors made dozens of investments across the globe, carrying through to a new surge in the 1990s as most large auto producers sought to build vehicles in large emerging markets (Sturgeon and Florida, 2004). Indeed, the rapid development of the industry in many global locations such as Brazil, Mexico, Turkey, and Thailand was driven by foreign investment, while the role of domestic first-tier suppliers declined (Barnes and Kaplinsky, 2000).

Many countries embarked on even more specific industrial policies. These included efforts to rationalize production by reducing the proliferation of makes and models being domestically assembled. The objective was generally to achieve economies of scale in order to encourage a deepening of the domestic supply chain. There were also policies to promote indigenous firms, often at great cost, as in the case of the Proton and Perodua projects in Malaysia. In other countries, such as in central Europe, Turkey, and Brazil, efforts were made to incentivize investments in R&D, with generally weak results. Automotive policies have fundamentally shaped the development of national industries, and policy instruments have often been highly contested.

In considering the effectiveness of state intervention, three patterns can be identified. The first are cases where an effective developmental state was able to harness domestic firms to gradually develop a globally competitive industry (e.g. South Korea). The second are cases where domestic rent-seeking dynamics dominated (e.g. Egypt).[2] The third are cases such as South Africa, where policy was driven by the interests of multinational corporations, potentially resulting in an adverse mode of incorporation into global markets (Black et al., 2020). In these latter cases governments had certain objectives—mainly GDP contribution, employment growth, technology transfer, and the generation of foreign exchange. But industry stakeholders—primarily the major multinational corporations (MNCs)—play a vocal and frequently influential role in the development of policy, tightly framed by their direct commercial interests, and to both good and bad effect. Major MNCs were therefore of specific and growing importance. A key issue was the interaction between the developmental ambitions of government and the strategies of major firms, whose decisions were based on optimizing their global position in an increasingly competitive world market.[3]

The bargaining power of governments is dependent on the size and dynamism of the domestic (or regional) market and on the capacity of the government bureaucracy to engage with MNCs. China, due to its huge market, obviously had exceptional leverage in this respect and was able to insist that MNCs raise local content, form joint ventures with domestic firms, and transfer technology to these firms. India and Brazil similarly were able to negotiate investments that aligned with state development priorities. Most other developing countries, including South Africa with its small local market, were in a far weaker bargaining position.

Industry outcomes in individual country contexts consequently depend in large part on what multinationals do. On the upside this could include developing the national industry as a major production hub within their global (or regional)

---

[2] See for example Black et al. (2020).
[3] For examples in different country contexts, see Doner (1991 and 2009); Miozzo (2000); and Pavlinek (2016).

networks, investing heavily in the supply chain, and even undertaking R&D. The downside would be more limited investment in basic assembly processes that meet minimum domestic policy requirements with limited investment in the supply chain. In some circumstances, local brands that are (at least initially) heavily dependent on foreign technologies might also emerge, probably with government support. But this was not the case in South Africa and MNCs became increasingly dominant in the component supply chain as well, reflecting a global trend (Sturgeon and Lester, 2004).

5.3 The Development of the South African Auto Industry since 1960

The early development of the South African auto industry was fundamentally shaped by protection. High tariffs were placed on finished vehicles, which, when combined with a rapidly growing market, attracted significant MNC investment, frequently in the form of joint ventures with local firms. These operations were very small in international terms and had correspondingly high unit costs. Production was aimed solely at the domestic market (Black, 2009).

The first in a series of local-content programmes was introduced in 1961. In later phases, the local-content requirement (on a mass basis) was raised to 66 per cent. By late 1986, there were seven assemblers producing over twenty basic model variants for a market of only 172,000 passenger cars. Low volumes meant that the industry was uncompetitive. Exports were minimal but there had been substantial development of a domestic supply base (Black, 1994; Duncan, 1997).

The Phase VI local-content programme, introduced in 1989, marked a significant change in direction by allowing exports to count as local content. Many component suppliers and all the vehicle assemblers instituted significant export drives. The level of protection on built-up vehicles, however, remained prohibitive with nominal protection of 115 per cent (100 per cent ad valorem plus 15 per cent surcharge). However, the Phase VI programme came in for increasingly heavy criticism from the component-producer federation, the National Association of Automotive Component and Allied Manufacturers (NAACAM), which was concerned about rising import competition (Black, 1994).

The advent of democracy in 1994 fundamentally shifted the automotive policy terrain in South Africa, culminating in the introduction of the MIDP in 1995. The MIDP abolished local-content requirements and introduced a tariff phase down at a steeper rate than required by the terms of South Africa's offer to the GATT. It also entrenched the principle of import–export complementation that had been initiated in Phase VI. Import–export complementation enabled assemblers to use import credits to source components at close to international prices—provided they exported either vehicles or automotive components. Declining nominal protection on finished vehicles was therefore largely compensated for by reduced protection for components, again as a result of strong pressure by vehicle producers, all of which were either foreign-owned or with licence agreements with MNCs.

The MIDP was devised as a form of a WTO Trade Related Investment Measure (TRIM), with very particular industrial policy objectives. With the proliferation of makes and models being produced in low volumes in South Africa, component firms had in turn been required to produce at volumes below minimum efficient scale. This rendered them largely uncompetitive, especially in supply-chain segments requiring high-cost and model-specific tooling and machinery, a feature that is pronounced in the automotive industry (Sturgeon et al., 2008). A key objective of the MIDP was, therefore, to increase the volume and scale of production through a greater level of specialization in terms of both vehicle models and components. This could be achieved by exports of locally produced, high-volume vehicles and automotive components that could earn import credits to be used to import either additional models for sale in the domestic market, or components required in vehicle assembly.

Until the early 1990s, high protection resulted in very low numbers of vehicle imports. With the liberalization that followed the introduction of the MIDP, total imports of vehicles and components grew rapidly. Nominal tariffs on light vehicles and automotive components were phased down gradually to 25 per cent in the case of vehicles and 20 per cent for components. These tariff reductions could not, on their own, explain the rapid increase in automotive imports. A key factor was that the MIDP enabled firms to rebate import duties by exporting.

Vehicle producers were happy to accept reductions in vehicle tariffs from very high levels but initially registered growing concerns about proposed reductions below 40 per cent. However, as they derived a growing proportion of their revenue from the importation of vehicles, much of their strategic behaviour shifted to optimizing their duty position. This was reflected in their firm-level strategies as well as interventions to influence government to ensure that the import credits they earned from exporting were only phased down very slowly. From 1996 to 2011, the average level of duty paid by vehicle manufacturers was only 0.6 per cent of the total value of their imports of vehicles and components over this period.

The growth of automotive exports was one of the most striking features of the development of the automotive industry under the MIDP. Its incentive structure strongly favoured exports. But the very strong supply response to changes in the policy regime is also partly attributable to the changing nature of the automotive industry value chain. From 1994 there was a process of investment or reinvestment by MNCs with all seven light-vehicle producers rapidly becoming 100 per cent foreign-owned. In addition to the benefits of exporting, one of the factors driving the takeover of domestically owned plants by licensors was the need to upgrade the South African plants in the face of growing competition. To achieve scale, exports were essential and this required the control that comes with wholly owned plants.

The MNCs were able to rapidly facilitate exports either from their own South African operations or from South African-based suppliers to their international operations. This enabled them to expand their exports and offset import duties on vehicles and auto parts. While trade and industrial policy provided significant support, especially for exports, substantial improvements in productivity were also evident. However, South Africa still lagged countries such as Thailand in terms of manufacturing costs (Barnes et al., 2017). Part of the competitiveness deficit can be accounted for by the relatively low availability of skills in South Africa, which is reflected in high skills premiums for technicians, artisans, professionals, and managers (Barnes et al., 2017).

A highly contested issue in the development of the automotive sector both in South Africa and other developing countries was the level of local content in domestically assembled vehicles. The South African government was keen to promote greater depth of supply-chain development by securing investment in first- and second-tier suppliers; this was one of the stated objectives of the APDP, which replaced the MIDP in 2013. As has been illustrated, the bargaining power of the MNCs ensured that it remained relatively easy to import vehicles and auto parts into the South African market while offsetting almost all duties (Barnes et al., 2017). Indeed, this did not help the established domestic component manufacturers and allow for deepening of the local supply chain. The aim of the 2035 South African Automotive Masterplan (SAAM), launched in 2019, was to build on the foundations established by the APDP, while simultaneously correcting its distortions and perceived development limitations. It set an ambitious objective of 60 per cent local content by 2035, which was a substantial increase on the level of only 38.7 per cent achieved in 2015 (Barnes et al., 2016).

Apart from a market and production growth boom in 2005–6, there was only a modest increase in investment in vehicle manufacturing. The expansion in investment in the component sector was also modest due to weak domestic demand and the lack of supply-chain competitiveness relative to other investment locations (Barnes et al., 2017). This was despite South Africa's automotive policy offering significant investment incentives in the form of the Automotive Investment Scheme (AIS).

The conversion of the MIDP to the APDP in 2013 heralded a significant change in government policy, with its explicit export support reoriented to production support, irrespective of market focus. This was embodied in the move to a Volume Assembly Allowance (VAA) for vehicle producers and a Production Incentive (PI) for vehicle producers and component manufacturers. The import credits that had been earned by exporting (under the MIDP) were, in terms of the APDP,

Table 5.1 South African production profile for major vehicle categories (2011–17)

Product	Market	2011	2013	2015	2017
Passenger vehicles	Domestic	124,736	113,364	112,566	100,354
	Export	187,529	151,893	228,459	230,957
	Total	312,265	265,257	341,025	331,311
	Export%	60.1%	57.3%	67.0%	69.7%
Light commercial vehicles	Domestic	108,704	127,188	140,310	136,438
	Export	84,125	121,345	102,664	105,862
	Total	192,829	248,533	242,974	242,300
	Export%	43.6%	48.8%	42.3%	43.7%
Medium and heavy commercial vehicles	Domestic	26,656	30,924	30,535	26,293
	Export	803	1,206	1,124	991
	Total	27,459	32,130	31,659	27,284
	Export%	2.9%	3.8%	3.6%	3.6%

Source: Adapted from Barnes et al. (2016): 32; AIEC (2018).

based on value added. The policy 'paradox' of rewarding local production with import rebates was therefore extended to 2020.

As indicated in Table 5.1, the share of exports in light vehicle production was high and tended to increase since the inception of the APDP. In respect of strategic choices, it would appear as if several carmakers identified the opportunity to increase their finished vehicle export programmes under the APDP as an alternative to deepening their local content. This appears to have been driven by international export opportunities, the ease of exporting relative to the arduous task of growing local supplier capabilities and competitiveness levels, and the ability of vehicle producers to inflate the level of rebates earned through the Volume Assembly Allowance (VAA). As the VAA is based on the sales value of finished vehicle production, as opposed to local value addition, carmakers can earn substantial rebates by exporting higher-value vehicles comprising predominantly imported components.

5.4 The Scale of Production and Structural Change

Overall, the targeted industrial policies in the auto industry yielded mixed results. The sector undoubtedly achieved improved industrial performance. From 1994 to 2014 it was the second-fastest growing manufacturing sub-sector in South Africa, although it slumped subsequently in response to a weakening economy (Bell et al., 2018: 7). Technological upgrading at vehicle assemblers and some first-tier automotive component manufacturers, higher volumes and a rationalization of products and platforms enabled significant improvements in productivity and rapidly rising exports. However, important structural weaknesses remained.

Undoubtedly, the growth in exports was strongly incentivized by the import–export rebate mechanisms designed as part of the MIDP; and continued with vehicle exports under the APDP. At the same time, the generous concessions on import duties granted to exporting firms reinforced a balance of power in favour of vehicle producers in relation to suppliers. Overall, the growing power of MNC lead firms, together with the increasing foreign ownership of first-tier suppliers operating within global contractual arrangements, blocked the deepening of the domestic value chain in South Africa. Local content either remained stable or tended to decline, with a concomitant contraction among second- and third-tier suppliers. The successful transition to export orientation produced a much more technologically sophisticated industry, while quality and productivity also improved significantly. Although the sub-sector continued to be highly subsidized, its structure did become more robust, more competitive, and more oriented to global markets.

The issue of the scale of production is, however, fundamental. The automotive industry remains highly scale intensive. In such industries, tariff protection in small domestic markets is likely to lead to the establishment of plants operating at below minimum efficient scale. Small-scale assembly raises costs and adds little value. Low-volume vehicle plants mean that in the absence of heavy protection, investment in component production is uneconomic beyond a very low level of local content. In a market with high effective rates of protection for vehicle assembly, it is economic for producers to build a wide range of models even in low volumes, to be able to supply a full model range to the domestic market. However, the implications for the component sector are highly adverse. The cost premium incurred by component makers for producing a wide range of products at low volume is considerable. Suppliers are, therefore, severely disadvantaged by the decision of assemblers to increase product variety. Given that automotive components comprise the heart of value addition within the industry, this imposes a binding constraint on industry development.

Essentially, what was sought in South Africa with the introduction of the MIDP was a shift from completely knocked down (CKD) assembly,[4] as was typically characteristic of vehicle production in protected developing country markets, through a 'transition stage' to 'full manufacturing' (Black, 2009). This transition is depicted in Table 5.2. CKD assembly involves relatively light investments but production costs are usually quite high, especially if a high level of localization is stipulated by government policy. Product variety makes traditional automation impractical. High local-content requirements would necessarily require much higher investment levels and would tend to encourage rationalization. In a protected market, the cost of tooling up for new models and domestic content also

---

[4] CKD assembly typically involves the assembly of imported 'kits' of components.

Table 5.2 Stages in the development of vehicle production in South Africa

Criteria	CKD assembly	Transition	Full manufacturing
Target market	Domestic	Domestic and export	Domestic and export
Level of integration with parent company	Low; import of CKD packs	Medium	High
Model line up	Many models	One or two	One or two
Derivatives	Limited to reduce costs	Full range to supply export market	Full range to supply export market
Local content	Generally low but may be quite high due to local content requirements	Moderate based primarily on cost factors	Medium to high
Quality	Below source plant	Equal to source plant	Equal to source plant
Production cost	High	Medium; penalties incurred by high logistics costs	Low
Domestic design	Local adaptations	None	None—may do global R&D in niche areas

Source: Black (2009: 491).

encourages assemblers to skip the introduction of new models. As a result, in many protected, emerging economy markets, models have continued in production long after they have been phased out in advanced country markets. In the CKD assembly stage, quality is also likely to be below international standards.

In the transition and full manufacturing stages (Table 5.2), where exports may become substantial, both quality standards and the number of derivatives offered need to be in line with international practice.[5] Production volumes per model also increase in the transition stage and under full manufacturing would approach world scale. Because firms are exporting, they would need access to components at world prices, so despite higher volumes in the transition stage, local-content levels may not increase. In the full manufacturing stage, much higher volumes would normally be attained, encouraging vehicle makers to localize components on an economic basis.

The South African automotive industry made considerable progress in achieving a reasonable level of scale with current average model volumes in the region of 65,000 units per annum, representing a huge improvement on levels well below 10,000 units at the advent of the MIDP, but below the 150,000 units that represent

---

[5] The term 'derivative' refers to the different permutations within a 'basic model'. Examples include engine size and body (e.g. saloon or hatchback) configurations.

fully integrated plants in large markets. Most vehicle producers could now be classified as having reached the 'full manufacturing stage' indicated in Table 5.2.[6] However, higher model volumes in the assembly sector were not accompanied by higher local content, despite evidence that the component industry did significantly improve its operational performance (Barnes and Black, 2014).

Considered as a whole, the supply chain remained underdeveloped and heavily reliant on imports. Overall, the desired process of productive transformation was not completed. Without major structural weaknesses being overcome and the balance of power moderated, the ambitious targets of the SAAM would always be difficult to meet.

5.5 Policy, Incentives, and State–Business Bargaining

The transformation of the South African auto industry from protection during apartheid to the post-apartheid globalization era can only be understood if embedded within the political economic context in which it occurred. Indeed, its most recent configuration can be interpreted as the outcome of specific policy choices, the product of international competitive pressure, and a balance of power between state institutions, MNCs, domestic firms, and organized labour. Such balance of power, and the institutional setting that accompanied it, are a direct product of the country's historical trajectory.

Overall, South Africa's industrial development path was highly conditioned by its apartheid legacy, and the way the globalization of its economy was negotiated also depended on this inheritance. The auto industry, in this sense, followed a rather peculiar path. First, it benefited from significant financial support received in the form of incentives—which other industrial sectors were not granted. Second, its development was also influenced by global integration being delayed by the pre-1994 sanctions period, although the eventual integration into international markets was quite rapid. Finally, the sector, being one of the most globalized, was also one of the most exposed to the demands of multinational firms, and to power bargaining dynamics between local institutions and foreign firms. Overall, both state–business bargaining and changing ownership strongly affected the policy space in the industry.

Since the end of apartheid, and of the white nationalist project that found its expression in the protection of infant industries, including the automotive industry (Duncan, 1997), the South African state was caught between forces pushing in different directions. On one side, the need to transform the socio-political-economic structure in a democratic sense called for a developmental project

---

[6] The exceptions are Nissan and Isuzu, which have so far failed to secure major export programmes that would enable them to achieve large volumes per model.

addressing the basic needs of a long-neglected majority population. On the other, the wish to catch up with the rest of the world, to compensate for 'wasted' time, resulted in an attempt to accelerate global integration. This directly affected the direction taken by the industrialization process, and the bargaining relationship between the state and multinational firms.

Tangri and Southall (2008) highlight how the coexistence of contrasting goals generated a tension that was often difficult to manage. In this sense, post-1994 ANC governments all clumsily steered between the declared aims of pursuing economic equity and redistributing wealth, while also advocating actions target-ing rapid economic growth by attracting corporate investment. Hamann, Khagram, and Rohan (2008) show how the apparent attempt to establish a form of 'collaborative governance' between state and business paradoxically entailed an active intervention of the state to limit its own powers. In their view, any move to regulate firm behaviour was constrained by the simultaneous need to operate within a framework that also worked in the firms' interests. In practice, what lay behind the negotiation of a governance space was always the condition for busi-ness to keep a hegemonic position. This was particularly evident in the auto industry, where global companies not only asserted their voice in relation to investment and productive strategies, but also defended their dominant role within the supply chain (Barnes et al., 2017).

The tensions had parallels to the Slovakian case described by Pavlinek (2016). In the development of the South African auto sector, the state played a crucial role in accommodating the strategic needs of foreign capital, to a point where the industry became overwhelmingly dependent on the directions taken by global investors (Hamann, Khagram, and Rohan, 2008). Analysing an FDI-driven, export-oriented strategy comparable to the one pursued by the South African auto industry in the post-apartheid era, Pavlinek (2016) warns against the dynam-ics typical of a 'dependent market economy', where the state actively sets the rules of the game to attract investors, but eventually sees its bargaining power signifi-cantly reduced. In this regard, while broadly compensating for the lack of domes-tic capital, strategies relying on foreign capital as a primary vehicle to promote national competitiveness and industrial restructuring end up limiting the domes-tic policy space. At a sectoral level, such strategies will be successful only if the shape taken by the targeted industry is in line with the investment strategies of the hosted MNCs. Overall, while possibly conducive to faster integration and more efficient restructuring, such policies can also be less sustainable as they are usually reliant on state incentives and can lead to patterns of uneven develop-ment. For example, as in the South African case, they can lead to the progressive erosion of local capabilities, whereby 'export-oriented foreign-owned factories often assemble high-tech, high quality goods with a relatively high value-added from components that are either imported or produced locally by other foreign firms' (Pavlinek, 2016: 575). The outcome of such strategies can be rapid industrial growth, but with the possible downside of truncated supply chains, control by foreign firms and reduced state bargaining power.

In the South African auto industry, the will of the government to compensate for delayed industrial development, and the consequent attempt to accommodate foreign companies to attract investment and technology, was reflected in the incentive mechanisms and in the generous concessions made to increasingly dominant MNC lead firms. As a result, the industry today is strongly influenced by the strategic direction set by the multinational assemblers, whose lobbying power weighs heavily on policy decisions (Masondo, 2018). In this sense, it is only by re-balancing the governance mechanisms of the supply chain that the conditions for a more sustainable structural transformation will be put in place.

Weak economic growth in South Africa and the resultant negligible growth in the domestic market further weakened the bargaining power of government in dealing with multinational firms. These firms were quick to point to a multitude of real constraints and difficulties which made it easier for them to extract further concessions from government.

5.6 Changing Ownership and Supply-Chain Development

In South Africa, these state–business bargaining dynamics limited the development of the supply chain. While foreign investment promoted industrial upgrading and international integration, local ownership and capabilities simultaneously declined (Barnes et al., 2017).

It became increasingly important for local firms to have links to global networks as a way of facilitating access to international markets. In South Africa, and indeed in other emerging markets, foreign-owned assemblers increasingly preferred to source components from joint ventures and wholly owned subsidiaries of their global suppliers rather than from domestically owned firms. The result for many South African firms was that they either needed to seek out an international partner or face the prospect of being confined to the aftermarket (Barnes and Kaplinsky, 2000).

With growing foreign ownership, the main conduits for technological upgrading were through transfers from foreign sources rather than an increase in domestic R&D. Domestic firms, under pressure to upgrade their technological and production capacities, turned to foreign sources through the establishment of joint ventures, for example. There was plenty of evidence that when local firms have come under the control of transnationals, existing R&D establishments are downsized or shut down (Lorentzen and Barnes, 2004; Black, 2011). It does not necessarily follow, however, that these firms downgrade technologically. This is because the shutting down of formal R&D facilities can be accompanied by the introduction of new specialized product and process technologies from their global networks that bring the firms closer to the world frontier.

Multinational vehicle producers have actively sought out component suppliers that are able to export and to supply components which meet the exacting standards of their own increasingly export oriented assembly operations. These MNC lead firms have therefore played a major role as conduits between domestic component firms and the international market by arranging export contracts for component suppliers by facilitating access to their global networks, brokering new investment, bringing in new technology, and accelerating the transfer of industry best practices in production organization to their suppliers.

There is no doubt that foreign ownership, as opposed to licensing arrangements, has in many cases been critical for vehicle producers to obtain major export contracts but the question is more complicated for component producers. A number of foreign-owned suppliers have established facilities in South Africa with the sole purpose of supplying component subsystems to domestic assemblers. A striking difference between foreign-owned and domestically owned firms has been that the former import a significantly larger share of their inputs. The main explanation is that many foreign component firms are 'systems integrators', supplying entire sub-assemblies to the vehicle manufacturer. This is more of an assembly than a manufacturing activity. Foreign firms are also clearly less embedded in the domestic economy although this may change over time as firms develop domestic linkages (Black, 2011).

As a consequence of such processes, the South African automotive value chain was now underdeveloped relative to leading international competitors. This is indicated schematically in Figure 5.1, which illustrates the large share of value addition by assemblers and first-tier suppliers in South Africa, with this essentially a function of the hollowing out of the second and third tiers of the supply chain. Overall levels of local content are low and have been declining with a strong rise in component imports. Table 5.3 indicates the extent of this trend over the period of the APDP. While South Africa increased the value of its vehicle assembly activities significantly over the period, the increase in vehicle assembly was accompanied by a R54.8 billion (US$ 2.2 billion) surge in automotive component imports, largely nullifying the assembly gains made.

As indicated in Table 5.4, component exports have expanded rapidly. From a low base of R3.3 billion (US$909 million) in 1995, component exports increased to R23 billion (US$3.6 billion) in 2005 and R53.7 (US$3.7 billion) by 2019. A key objective of the import-export complementation scheme under the MIDP was to assist component suppliers to generate higher volumes, which would make them more efficient, and able to compete in the domestic market against imports. A linked objective was that reduced production costs would have the added benefit of providing lower-cost inputs into the assembly industry. The objective of higher

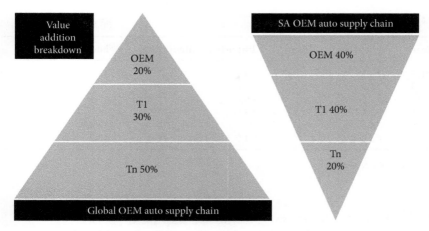

Figure 5.1 Value addition breakdown of global and South African automotive supply chains
Source: Barnes (2014).

component volumes has certainly been achieved at least in the sense that export development has usually been accompanied by higher volumes and specialization. Many component producers have also rationalized their product lines.

However, the nature of the component industry's export expansion also raises concerns. Firstly, the bulk of exports has consisted of catalytic converters. This export growth was certainly affected by the high subsidies the sector received as a result of the platinum group metals used in their production. In this sense, large export contracts were arranged by vehicle producers seeking to offset import duties on parts (and vehicle) imports through the rebate mechanism. So instead of promoting exports of parts in order to achieve economies of scale in the components which they were purchasing for their own assembly operations, the car-makers in many cases preferred to establish large-scale component export programmes of products, such as catalytic converters. These were for the most part disconnected from their own assembly operations. Another sub-sector that emerged in the early days of the MIDP was automotive leather, which in 1995 accounted for 30.7 per cent of component exports. This labour-intensive sector eventually went into decline with supply contracts being moved to central Europe, and two factories relocating to Lesotho. Such shifts were influenced by decreasing policy support to materials-based export-oriented sectors under the APDP and lower labour costs in neighbouring countries (i.e. Lesotho). Overall, the expansion of component exports was accompanied by a very low level of integration into the domestic industry, both in terms of supply to domestically assembled vehicles, and in terms of the local sourcing of sub-components and materials.

Table 5.3 Assembled vehicles

Year	Local content (Rbn)	Imported content (Rbn)	Local content (%)
2012	35.2	40.1	46.6
2013	37.9	54.6	40.9
2014	47.1	66.4	41.5
2015	52.9	83.8	38.7
2016	58.1	97.1	37.4
2017	61.2	94.9	39.2

Sources: SARS; NAAMSA.

Table 5.4 Major component export categories, 1995–2019 (R million)

	1995	2005	2015	2019	% 2019 total
Total	3,316	23,000	49,641	53,667	
Catalytic converters	389	9,935	20,326	20,359	37.9
Engine parts	102	1,000	3,941	4,345	8.1
Tyres	213	1,183	2,193	2,619	4.9
Engines	9	781	1,448	1,904	3.5
Radiators and parts	66	220	1,190	1,536	2.9
Transmission shafts/cranks	55	553	1,060	1,152	2.1
Automotive tooling	153	332	1,459	943	1.8
Other	2,329	8,996	18,024	20,806	38.8

Source: AIEC (various years).

5.7 The Prospects for Localization and Transformation in the Supply Chain

Given the structure of the South African automotive industry, attempts to secure sustainable industry growth need to be linked to two main challenges: increasing the level of localization, and developing the lower tiers of the auto supply chain. Indeed, this will also require strong intervention to re-balance governance assets and the balance of power between big and small players, multinational lead firms and component suppliers, and foreign and local firms. At the same time, any strategy to raise local content and develop local suppliers will also have to be connected to initiatives aimed at developing local ownership and increasing black participation in the industry.

The localization challenge is particularly pressing. At only 39.2 per cent local content in South African assembled vehicles in 2017, the ability of the South African automotive industry to realize its growth potential is being severely compromised. As a second-tier automotive producer, the domestic automotive industry has the potential to grow its local content to at least 60 per cent. This is based on the recognition that core drivetrain, powertrain, safety, and telematics technology is unlikely to be domestically sourced soon, but that there is substantial opportunity to increase local content in South African vehicles—as evidenced through the experiences of other second-tier automotive economies, such as Turkey, Thailand, and Brazil.

However, localization is a multidimensional challenge requiring a multifaceted response. At the most basic level it is associated with improving South Africa's factor cost profile (overheads, labour, and materials costs), along with the economy's ability to ensure technology and skills availability ahead of industry demand. Research completed for the South African Automotive Masterplan in 2016 emphasized the debilitating impact of exorbitant government-administered service price increases (such as electricity, rail, and port handling) on the operating costs of firms (Barnes et al., 2016).

As firms have shifted their business models to accommodate these increasing costs, domestic content has been lost, along with associated technologies and skills. Reversing this trend requires the stabilization of government-administered service costs, and the development of technology and associated skills.

Additional key elements relate to the creation of targeted specialization within the automotive value chain, and the potential to strategically link South Africa's materials base with automotive opportunities. Dealing with specialization first: unless firms can secure economies of scale within the domestic automotive industry, they are unlikely to be sufficiently competitive to deepen their value addition. Key then is identifying opportunities to secure improved economies of scale in the context of South Africa's comparatively small production volumes. This is partly a policy issue, but it also requires industry coordination and programmatic interventions. The South African automotive industry, working in partnership with national government, has established the Automotive Supply Chain Competitiveness Initiative (ASCCI) as the vehicle for identifying and responding to localization opportunities, and it is important that the industry and government collaborate on specific agreed-upon opportunities.

The objective of increasing local content is deeply intertwined with the challenge of promoting the transformation of the industry. This is part of a broader government ambition to strengthen local ownership of the country's productive assets, and to promote the participation of black industrialists in the development of national industry. The transformation of the sector is consequently included as a priority for firms looking to continue securing government support, and to access available incentives.

The idea of economic transformation, aimed at expanding the role of black ownership and control of the economy, has been part of the post-apartheid political project from the outset. The aim of achieving black economic empowerment (BEE) has informed numerous government programmes since 1994. However, the BEE policies of the first ten years of the post-apartheid era were, at best, considered ineffective, leading to only cosmetic adjustments of pre-1994 inequalities and economic imbalances. Early BEE policies were also strongly criticized, for resulting in the formation of a black industrial elite, without concretely addressing South Africa's much deeper structural disparities. Makgetla (2004), for example, highlights how economic restructuring post-1994 created very limited opportunities for black entrepreneurs, while the extreme concentration of ownership remaining largely unchanged (see also Freund, 2007).

The perception of limited policy reach (Ponte et al., 2007) led the South African state to reconsider the first package of BEE policies, in favour of an enlarged set of conditions for transformation. The 2000s thus saw the introduction of a 'broad-based black economic empowerment' (BBBEE) formula, which went beyond simple corporate ownership. The widened package entailed a long list of criteria, seen as crucial indicators of deeper transformation. These included ownership, management representation, employment equity, skills development, preferential procurement, enterprise development, and corporate social investment (Ponte et al., 2007; and Chapter 9). The objective was to promote more inclusive transformation, and to target a larger pool of potential beneficiaries. However, despite the revision of the original agenda, and the ambition to extend its reach, the implementation of BBBEE policies remains limited, and the transformation of South African industry remains slow.

In this regard, several weaknesses have been identified. Ponte and colleagues (2007) warned against the managerialization of the BEE agenda, which progressively shifted towards technical compliance, moving away from its initial focus on redistribution. Ultimately, such processes also transferred responsibilities from the state to the firms; with firms competing to tick boxes on their scorecards to win incentives. Despite critiques of its implementation and limited achievements, the idea of BEE remains crucial for the transformation of South Africa's post-apartheid industrial landscape. However, progress will not be achieved only by setting the right policy targets, but necessarily through the joint efforts of all the stakeholders involved in developing the industry.

Many initiatives have emerged, but the coordination between them needs to be significantly improved. Presently, all major stakeholders operating in the industry are exploring localization opportunities and have transformation programmes in place. The National Association of Automobile Manufacturers of South Africa (NAAMSA) has established a R6 billion (US$414 million) transformation fund (Engineering News, 6 November 2019). NAACAM is actively engaged in 'best practice education' via a black supplier development programme that is run jointly with the Automotive Supply Chain Competitiveness Initiative (ASCCI). NAACAM is also providing legal assistance to its members to assist in achieving compliance with the BBBEE scorecard. ASCCI endeavoured to target interventions aimed at building supplier capabilities, driving localization, and developing strategic insights into future opportunities for the value chain. All of these elements have transformation objectives. In Gauteng, the Automotive Industry Development Centre (AIDC) is promoting Automotive Incubation Centres linked to individual vehicle producers (the most advanced project being at Ford) and is also running a supplier development programme. In KwaZulu–Natal, the Durban Automotive Cluster (DAC) has tested a supplier development model based on the formation of joint-ventures between established component manufacturers and emerging black suppliers.

While a number of initiatives are in place, they face several difficulties. These are mainly related to the financial feasibility of identified localization opportunities and to technical barriers to localization (such as volumes, technology, global supply agreements, and the cost of testing). In addition, the uneven leverage of different stakeholders, pursuing diverse business strategies, does not facilitate the process, and further complicates the development of a common development strategy.

5.8 Conclusion

The South African automotive industry has undeniably achieved significant structural transformation since the end of apartheid. It has consolidated its manufacturing capacity, improved its productivity, increased exports, and upgraded its position in global value chains. However, this internationalization has not been accompanied by strong supplier development. Increasing foreign ownership, deteriorating local operating conditions (especially in respect of government administered services), and an unfavourable state–business bargaining relationship, have affected the development of the industry, leading to a supply chain heavily concentrated around MNC lead firms and first-tier suppliers, themselves mainly multinational firms. In the process, the second and third tiers of the automotive supply chain have declined.

Localization, transformation, and supply-chain development still emerge as key priorities for the future of the South African auto industry. In this regard, the 2035 Masterplan sets ambitious targets that could potentially be achieved, but that will also certainly require a significant effort on behalf of all stakeholders.

Supply-chain development will require major support for skills development and the technological advancement of local firms. In relation to black supplier development, ownership transactions, encouraging outsourcing to smaller suppliers and the establishment of joint-venture projects are all options worthy of further exploration. Another key requirement for the realization of the SAAM's objectives will be the recovery of the South African economy and the creation of a more favourable environment for both foreign and domestic investment.

References

Automotive Industry Expert Council (2018). *Automotive Export Manual* Pretoria: AIEC

Barnes, J. (2014). 'Localisation opportunities within OEM supply chains: what have we learnt from the AAS?' Presentation at the National Localisation Indaba. International Convention Centre, Durban, 5 June 2014.

Barnes, J. and A. Black (2014). 'The Motor Industry Development Programme 1995–2012: what have we learned?' International Conference on Manufacturing-Led Growth for Employment and Equality in South Africa, Johannesburg, South Africa, 20–21 May 2014.

Barnes, J., A. Black, D. Comrie, and T. Hartogh (2016). 'Challenges and opportunities: an analysis of the present position of the South African automotive industry.' Report 3 of 4 of the South African Automotive Masterplan Project. Compiled for the South African national government's Department of Trade and Industry, 28 September 2016.

Barnes, J., A. Black, and K. Techakanont (2017). 'Industrial policy, multinational strategy, and domestic capability: a comparative analysis of the development of South Africa's and Thailand's automotive industry.' *European Journal of Development Research* 29: 37–53.

Barnes, J. and R. Kaplinsky (2000). 'Globalisation and the death of the local firm? The automobile components sector in South Africa.' *Regional Studies* 34(9): 797–812.

Bell, J., S. Goga, P. Mondliwa, and S. Roberts (2018). 'Structural transformation in South Africa: moving towards a smart, open economy for all.' Overview Paper for Industrial Development Think Tank. University of Johannesburg: IDTT.

Black, A. (1994). *An Industrial Strategy for the Motor Vehicle and Component Sector.* Cape Town: University of Cape Town Press.

Black, A. (2009). 'Location, automotive policy and multinational strategy: the position of South Africa in the global automotive industry since 1995.' *Growth and Change* 40(3): 483–512.

Black, A. (2011). 'Trade liberalization, technical change and firm level restructuring in the South Africa automotive component sector.' *International Journal of Institutions and Economies* 3(2): 173–202.

Black, A., P. Roy, A. El-Haddad, and K. Yilmaz (2020). 'The political economy of automotive industry development policy in middle income countries: a comparative analysis of Egypt, India, South Africa and Turkey.' ESID Working Paper No. 143. Manchester: The University of Manchester, http://www.effective-states.org.

Doner, R. (1991). *Driving a Bargain: Automobile Industrialization and Japanese Firms in Southeast Asia.* Berkeley and Los Angeles: University of California Press.

Doner, R. (2009). *The Politics of Uneven Development: Thailand's Economic Growth in Comparative Perspective.* Cambridge: Cambridge University Press.

Duncan, D. (1997). *We Are Motor Men: The Making of the South African Motor Industry.* Scotland: Whittles Publishing.

Freund, B. (2007). 'South Africa: the end of apartheid & the emergence of the "BEE Elite."' *Review of African Political Economy* 34(114): 661–78.

Hamann, R., S. Khagram, and S. Rohan (2008). 'South Africa's charter approach to post-apartheid economic transformation: collaborative governance or hardball bargaining?' *Journal of Southern African Studies* 34(1): 21–37.

Humphrey, J., A. Mukherjee, M. Zilbovicius, and G. Arbix (1998). 'Globalisation, foreign direct investment and the restructuring of supplier networks: the motor industry in Brazil and India.' In M. Kagami, J. Humphrey, and M, Piore (eds), *Learning, Liberalisation and Economic Adjustment*, 117–89. Tokyo: Institute of Developing Economies.

Lorentzen, J. and J. Barnes (2004). 'Learning, upgrading, and innovation in the South African automotive industry.' *European Journal of Development Research* 16(3): 465–98.

Makgetla, N. (2004). 'The post-apartheid economy.' *Review of African Political Economy* 100: 263–81.

Masondo, D. (2018). 'South African business nanny state: the case of the automotive industrial policy post-apartheid, 1995–2010.' *Review of African Political Economy* 45: 1–20.

Miozzo, M. (2000). 'Transnational corporations, industrial policy and the "war of incentives": the case of the Argentine automobile industry.' *Development and Change* 31: 651–80.

Pavlinek, P. (2016). 'Whose success? The state–foreign capital nexus and the development of the automotive industry in Slovakia.' *European Urban and Regional Studies* 23(4): 571–93.

Ponte, S., S. Roberts, and L. van Sittert (2007). ' "Black economic empowerment", business and the state in South Africa.' *Development and Change* 38(5): 933–55.

Sturgeon, T. and R. Florida (2004). 'Globalization, deverticalization, and employment in the motor vehicle industry.' In M. Kenny and R. Florida (eds), *Locating Global Advantage: Industry Dynamics in a Globalizing Economy*, 52–81. Palo Alto: Stanford University Press.

Sturgeon, T. and R. Lester (2004). 'The new global supply-base: new challenges for local suppliers in East Asia.' In S. Yusuf, A. Altaf, and K. Nabeshima (eds), *Global Production Networking and Technological Change in East Asia*, 35–87. Oxford: Oxford University Press.

Sturgeon, T., J. Van Biesebroeck, and G. Gereffi (2008). 'Value chains, networks, and clusters: reframing the global automotive industry.' *Journal of Economic Geography* 8(3): 297–321.

Tangri, R. and R. Southall (2008). 'The politics of black economic empowerment in South Africa.' *Journal of Southern African Studies* 34(3): 699–716.

6

The Industrialization of Freshness and Structural Transformation in South African Fruit Exports

Christopher Cramer and Shingie Chisoro-Dube

6.1 Introduction

Clear evidence of the potential for stronger growth of the South African fruit industry, coupled with robust growth in global demand, makes it a central focus for any high-value agriculture-led growth strategy. In 2018, global fruit exports amounted to US$92 billion, up from US$73 billion in 2013 (a 26 per cent growth in value terms) (ITC Trade Map, 2019). Over the same period, South Africa's share in global fresh-fruit exports averaged 3 per cent, although the country commands higher shares in narrow product lines. For example, South Africa is the second-largest exporter of citrus after Spain, accounting for 10 per cent of global exports in 2018 (ITC Trade Map, 2019).

Although the spread of Covid-19 has disrupted many industries worldwide, exports of fruit have continued to grow amidst the crisis, accelerating the long-term growth trend.[1] In particular, the demand for citrus has boomed during the pandemic because of the fruit's high Vitamin C content. While global volumes of citrus imports between March and May 2020 (at the peak of the covid-19 pandemic) were not consistently higher than the previous season, their value averaged 13 per cent higher in the same period, compared to March to May 2019 (ITC Trade Map, 2020). South Africa has taken advantage of the Covid-19-related expansion in demand, increasing the volume and value of fruit exports. In value terms, South Africa's exports earned 114 per cent and 118 per cent more in March and April 2020 respectively, compared to the same months in 2019.[2]

---

[1] https://www.freshplaza.com/article/9216935/overview-global-lemon-market/; https://www.freshplaza.com/article/9220910/overview-global-stone-fruit-market/; https://www.freshplaza.com/article/9233712/overview-global-cherry-market/;https://www.freshplaza.com/article/9235863/overview-global-orange-market/.

[2] See ITC Trade Map, 2020; these are nominal values and the increase is partly due to the partly due to the depreciation of the Rand during this period. Also https://www.freshplaza.com/article/9209810/

Christopher Cramer and Shingie Chisoro-Dube, *The Industrialization of Freshness and Structural Transformation in South African Fruit Exports* In: *Structural Transformation in South Africa: The Challenges of Inclusive Industrial Development in a Middle-Income Country*. Edited by: Antonio Andreoni, Pamela Mondliwa, Simon Roberts, and Fiona Tregenna, Oxford University Press. © Oxford University Press 2021. DOI: 10.1093/oso/9780192894311.003.0006

The South African fruit industry has a high potential not only to ease the balance-of-payments constraint on growth, but also through high levels of labour demand to help address the high level of unemployment, particularly in rural areas (Cramer and Sender, 2015). However, to underpin sustainable growth of the fruit sub-sector, the industry (with policy support) needs to adapt to major advances in technology in what can be termed the 'industrialization of freshness' (Cramer and Sender, 2019). The industrialization of freshness hinges on fruit producers' ability to improve the quality of fruit and product shelf life through research and technology development. The goal to produce high-quality fruit for export markets is driving key technological changes—from inputs, production, packing, and storage, to marketing and distribution. Constant technology upgrading across these processes is critical for market access and developing timely, flexible, and speedy supply chains (Chisoro-Dube et al., 2019). Advances in technology have been a key mechanism through which structural transformation (a shift to higher productivity economic activity) towards higher-value crops has occurred in agriculture.

Despite evidence of dynamism in fruit production, effective structural transformation in the South African fruit industry has been constrained by widespread underinvestment in technical capacity and key infrastructure including water, telecommunications, and ports. The high levels of congestion and delays at South Africa's main ports, thanks to machinery breakdowns caused by ageing and worn out infrastructure, have hampered port operations and increased costs for fruit exporters. Similarly, the historical underinvestment in water resources and inadequate maintenance of water infrastructure, especially in rural areas, have caused water shortages in agriculture, forcing the industry to be conservative with new plantings. While growers have adopted on-farm production technologies to respond to the impacts of droughts and growing susceptibility of crops to pest and diseases imposed by climate change, poor internet and cell-phone connectivity in rural areas (exacerbated by low levels of investment in broadband penetration) has limited the use of such technologies. In addition to the infrastructure challenges, limited technical capacity and know-how at the quarantine laboratories of the Department of Agriculture, Land Reform, and Rural Development for clearing exotic pests and diseases makes the process of importing new varieties cumbersome, and delays commercial production.

The results from sector-wide interviews for this research suggest an underlying tension that has been constraining the deepening of structural transformation in fruit production in South Africa. The government's priority with regards to fruit (and agriculture more broadly) has been more focused on transformation in the

increased-global-demand-for-citrus-bodes-well-for-the-2020-export-season/; https://www.freshplaza.com/article/9225032/overview-global-blueberry-market/; https://www.freshplaza.com/article/9216133/south-african-2020-export-season-shows-strong-increase-in-global-citrus-demand/.

racial demographics of ownership in the industry. Through its black economic empowerment (BEE) policy, it has prioritized the participation of small and medium-sized black-farmer businesses (see Chapter 9). The industry's priority on the other hand, has been around quality, growth, and increased market access. This entrenched standoff has created an investment vacuum in key infrastructure and technical capacity within the industry, limiting overall growth.

In this chapter, evidence from South Africa's fruit industry is used to illustrate how advances in technology and industrial processes have driven a shift towards high-value crops and the accessing of high-value export markets in developed countries. The chapter also highlights the constraints on greater structural transformation in the sector. For although South Africa is an established exporter of fresh fruit, the country's performance lags behind key competitors. Indeed, South Africa has not been able to match the growth rates in fruit exports achieved by countries such as Mexico, Chile, and Peru.

The chapter draws largely on insights from interviews with some fifty industry stakeholders and government officials in different fruit-growing regions for a number of research projects conducted between 2017 and 2020.[3] The first project in 2017 formed part of a broader research programme on regional industrialization commissioned by the Department of Trade, Industry, and Competition (the DTIC) and coordinated by Trade and Industrial Policy Strategies (TIPS).[4] Eleven firms in the fruit industry were interviewed. The second project (2018–19) formed part of a series of studies on the challenges of industrialization in South Africa undertaken by the Industrial Development Think Tank (IDTT) housed in the Centre for Competition, Regulation, and Economic Development (CCRED) in partnership with the South African Research Chairs Initiative (SARChI) in Industrial Development at the University of Johannesburg. The IDTT project interviewed twelve firms in the fruit industry. CCRED also hosted a Dialogue on Industry 4.0 and the fruit sector, held on 22 October 2018. The third project (2019–20) was on innovation and inclusive industrialization in agriculture and agroprocessing and was funded by the UK Economic and Social Research Council's (ESRC) Global Challenges Research Fund. This two-year collaboration between researchers from the University of Edinburgh, the University of Johannesburg, and the Economic and Social Research Foundation, Tanzania, had by late 2020 amassed interviews with over thirty firms in the fruit industry in South Africa.

---

[3] Chisoro-Dube et al. (2018a); Chisoro-Dube et al. (2018b); Chisoro-Dube et al. (2019); and Innovation & Inclusive Industrialisation in Agro-Processing Project available on https://iiap.info/.

[4] Trade & Industrial Policy Strategies (TIPS) is an independent, non-profit, economic research institution established in 1996 to support economic policy development. TIPS undertakes quantitative and qualitative research, project management, dialogue facilitation, capacity building, and knowledge sharing. Its areas of focus are: trade and industrial policy, sustainable growth, and inequality and economic inclusion.

Section 6.2 sets out a conceptual framework for understanding structural transformation in agriculture. Section 6.3 describes the performance of South Africa's fruit industry in global markets and how South Africa has fallen behind competitor producers. Section 6.4 shows how South Africa's fruit industry is leveraging research and technology to produce high-quality fruit for export markets, showing in detail how fresh-fruit exporting has become increasingly industrial, while also embodying the process of 'servicification'. Section 6.5 discusses the infrastructural and technical capacity constraints limiting effective structural transformation of the South African fruit industry. Section 6.6 concludes and pulls together some of the key policy weaknesses and implications touched on in sections 6.3 and 6.5.

6.2 Structural Transformation in Agriculture; and Power and Upgrading in Global Value Chains

The process of structural change entails a shift of resources (capital and labour) from less productive to more productive sectors, either through upgrading within a sector or across sectors (Storm, 2015); and it involves integrating into the international economy through trade and technology relationships (Lall, 2004; Khan and Blankenburg, 2009; Hausman et al., 2014).

Economists have historically tended to associate industrial processes with manufacturing and not with agriculture (Kuznets, 1973; Syrquin, 1988; Samaniego and Sun, 2016; Mijiyawa, 2017). Hence, the process of economic development is often simplified to refer to a shift of resources out of low-productivity agricultural activities into higher-productivity manufacturing activities and urban services, with manufacturing viewed as distinct from agriculture. But the boundaries between agriculture and manufacturing, and processed and unprocessed agricultural products, are becoming less distinct. This is partly as a result of agriculture employing more sophisticated technology and transforming the structure of production (Page, 2014; Cramer and Sender, 2015).

A shift to higher-productivity economic activity entails building industrial capabilities. The term 'industrial' in Young's (1928) definition captures the extent to which certain kinds of productive activity are characterized by an increasingly intricate nexus of specialized undertakings that has inserted itself between the producer of raw materials and the consumer of the final product. This definition places more emphasis on the forms of industrial organization at play and what Young termed the 'roundabout' nature of production, than on whether or not production takes place in factories (Cramer et al., 2018). Industrial capabilities, on the other hand, entail the accumulation of knowledge and skills both at an individual and organizational level. While developing such capabilities requires education and formally acquired skills, of equal importance are capabilities associated with the problem-solving knowledge embodied within organizations. These capabilities include production technologies, marketing, labour relations, and 'dynamic capabilities' of search and learning (Cimoli et al., 2009). Similarly, at the level of national late development, Amsden (2001) emphasizes the role of learning in building technological capabilities, which she classifies into production capabilities, project execution capabilities (investment capabilities), and innovation capabilities.

Structural change in agriculture entails building exactly these kinds of capability, and developing the intricacy and 'roundaboutness' of the nexus of production in moving to higher-value agricultural production—improving yields, ensuring a reliably consistent supply of higher-quality products, perfecting ripeness at the point of consumption, improving the shelf life of the product and logistics coordination, and related undertakings that together may be called the 'industrialization of freshness' (Cramer and Sender, 2019). This requires that agriculture systems become more capital intensive, more productive, and better integrated with other sectors of the economy through markets (FAO, 2017).

It is important therefore to appreciate the close linkages between manufacturing and 'unprocessed' agriculture, even as the distinctions between them fade. The manufacturing sector remains a key source of technology-driven productivity growth, innovation, and learning for the agricultural sector, as manufacturing activities easily lend themselves to mechanization and processing (relative to other economic activities) (Andreoni and Chang, 2016). Developments in manufacturing industries and their dynamic linkages are key in producing agricultural machinery and equipment, agrochemicals, and mechanized warehousing—all necessary for developing the agricultural sector.

Structural change in agriculture has important implications for industrialization. Internationally, there have been several successful experiences of sustained economic growth and structural change that have been centred on agriculture (Cramer and Sender, 2015). This is evident in countries such as Mexico, Chile, Peru, and Brazil. Yet South Africa has not been able to match the growth rates achieved in agricultural exports in these countries. Part of the difficulty in achieving greater structural transformation in agriculture relates to the widespread underinvestment in infrastructure—ports, water, and telecommunications, and technical capacity.

Alongside the domestic challenges of underinvestment in key infrastructure and technical capacity, the nature of fresh-fruit production as an export-oriented industry means that access to developed-country markets becomes increasingly dependent on the ability to integrate into the global commodity chains of core or lead firms based in high-income countries (Gereffi, 1994; Gereffi and Fernandez-Stark, 2011; Gereffi and Lee, 2016; Dallas et al., 2018). In these global value chains (GVCs), participation of firms from low-income countries is not governed just by national trade and other policies but also by the strategic decisions of the core firms in the value chains (Nolan et al., 2008). The role played by powerful 'lead' firms in coordinating production activities and shaping the distribution of profits and risk within an industry is central to understanding governance structures in global industries (Gereffi and Lee, 2012). Lead firms in GVCs control production through setting and enforcing product and process parameters including standards and protocols that must be met by other players operating in the value chain. This includes controlling decisions about what to produce, how to produce, and how much to produce (Humphrey and Schmitz, 2002; Gereffi and Fernandez-Stark, 2011).

Thus, these 'systems integrators' (Nolan et al., 2008) are at the apex of extended value chains and they actively select the suppliers most able to meet strict requirements that are the condition of their participation in the 'systems integrators' supply chains. These firms interact in the deepest, most intimate fashion with the major segments of the value chain, both upstream and downstream, exerting intense pressure across the whole supply chain to minimize costs and stimulate technical progress (Nolan et al., 2008).

6.3 Performance of South Africa's Fruit Industry in Global Markets

South Africa's exports of fresh fruit grew at an annual compound rate of 6 per cent between 2013 and 2018, in value terms (Figure 6.1).[5] The growth in exports has been coupled with a corresponding increase in direct jobs in fruit farming, with an estimated 241,676 jobs in 2018,[6] up from 179,948 jobs in 2015,[7] with many more in related activities.

Nonetheless, South Africa lags behind key competitors such as Chile, Mexico, and Peru. This is especially the case for high-value and fast-growing fruits, such as avocados and berries (Figures 6.2 and 6.3). In volume terms, between 2013 and 2018, South Africa's exports of avocados grew at a compound annual growth rate (CAGR) of 8 per cent, compared to 26 per cent in Peru and 14 per cent in Mexico. Similarly, in the same period, South Africa's exports of berries in volume terms grew at 6 per cent compared to 68 per cent in Peru (although from a low base) and 8 per cent in Mexico.

South Africa's export fruit bowl is relatively concentrated relative to competitor countries. Citrus, grapes, and apples and pears together account for 91 per cent of total South African fruit exports, in both value and volume terms, and these are

---

[5] ITC Trade Map, 2019 HS Codes for fruits used are 0810, 0803, 0805, 0804, 0806, 0808, 0809, 0807, 0813.
[6] https://fruitsa.co.za/wp-content/uploads/2019/09/A5-Fruit-SA-Stats-Booklet_2018.pdf.
[7] CCRED (2018) Policy Brief: 'Structural transformation to grow high-value exports and jobs: the case of fruit.'

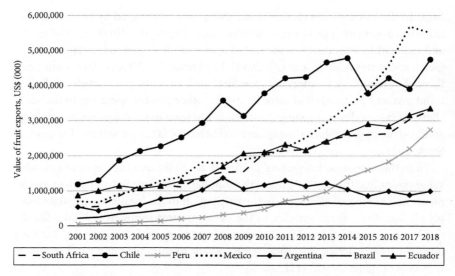

Figure 6.1 Value of fruit exports from South Africa and competitors, 2001–18
Source: ITC Trade Map, 2019.

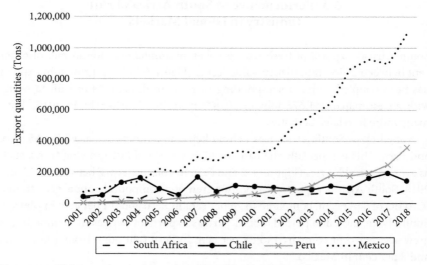

Figure 6.2 Volume of avocado exports from South Africa and competitors
Source: ITC Trade Map, 2019.

relatively large-volume, lower-value fruits. Competitors such as Chile and Peru have far more diversified export baskets with a wider range and proportion of higher-value fruits such as avocados, berries, cherries, guavas, and mangoes. Although South Africa exports larger volumes than competitors such as Chile,

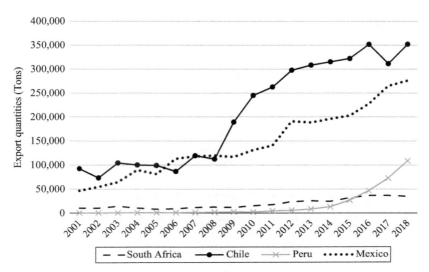

Figure 6.3 Volume of berries exports from South Africa and competitors
Source: ITC Trade Map, 2019.

the value of Chile's fruit exports is much higher than that of South Africa's fruit exports. Similarly, although Peru has much lower volumes of fruit exports than South Africa, it is fast approaching the equivalent of South Africa's export values (Figure 6.1).

However, some diversification has been under way: South Africa is shifting production to high-value and globally in-demand fruits within fruit varieties. For example, within the citrus category, South Africa is shifting from oranges to higher-value fruit varieties such as clementines and mandarins, and lemons and limes, which are among South Africa's fastest-growing exports. Between 2013 and 2018, South Africa's exports of lemons and limes grew at a CAGR of 12 per cent in volume terms. However, this is still slower growth than in key competitors: in volume terms, Chile expanded exports of lemons and limes at a CAGR of 22 per cent, and Peru at a CAGR of 26 per cent (although they are both from lower bases than South Africa) (Figure 6.5). And in the same period, while South Africa's exports of clementines and mandarins grew at a CAGR of 14 per cent in volume terms, Chile recorded a higher export growth rate of 23 per cent (Figure 6.4).

In addition to diversifying the fruit export basket, South Africa needs to diversify its export markets. The Netherlands and the United Kingdom account for 34.6 per cent of South Africa's total fruit exports in value terms (Figure 6.6). However, between 2013 and 2018, the growth of South Africa's volume of exports to the European Union grew at an annual compound rate of less than 2 per cent. With the European market clearly stagnating, Asian countries represent markets

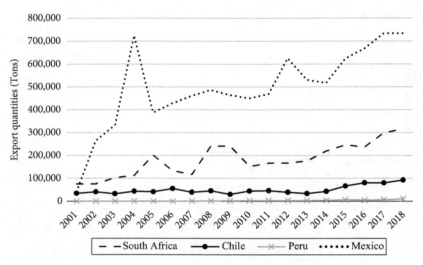

Figure 6.4 Volume of exports from South Africa and competitors: clementines and mandarins

Source: ITC Trade Map, 2019.

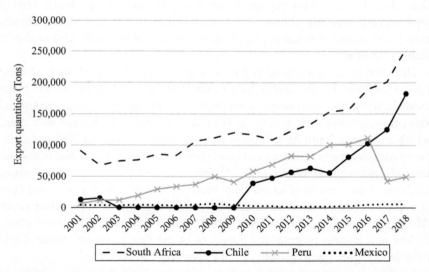

Figure 6.5 Volume of exports from South Africa and competitors: lemons and limes

Source: ITC Trade Map, 2019.

where most of the future growth is likely to come from. Yet South Africa has not done well in opening up access to these markets.

Currently, only a few fruits from South Africa are being exported into China. Gaining access into markets such as China takes a long time, and negotiations

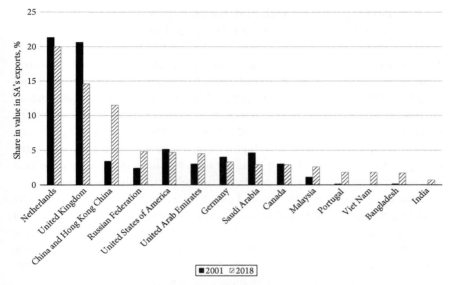

Figure 6.6 South Africa's fruit export markets: 2001 and 2018
Source: ITC Trade Map, 2019.

can be protracted. For example, it took eighteen years for South Africa's apples to gain access into China. Sanitary and phytosanitary issues have been a key reason for the slow and limited access. This was mainly due to the government's apparent limited technical and diplomatic expertise and agility. It did not capitalize on industry research and information to negotiate market access and to demonstrate to potential trading partners that South African fruits do not pose a risk of diseases and pestilence to importing countries (Cramer and Sender, 2015; Chisoro-Dube et al., 2019). Discussions have been under way for pears and avocados, supposedly the next in line. The trend seems to have been negotiating one fruit at a time, with protocols approved for citrus in 2004, table grapes in 2007, and apples in 2014. Even negotiations to amend existing protocols to change shipment methods are slow. For example, in 2015 the South African citrus industry asked China for specialized reefer (break bulk) vessel shipments to be allowed in terms of the 2004 protocol. After years of negotiating the technical details, the first break-bulk vessel with citrus left South African shores only in May 2019 (Chisoro-Dube et al., 2019).

The share in value of South Africa's fruit exports to China and Hong Kong has shown substantial growth, from 3.4 per cent in 2001 to almost 12 per cent in 2018. However, of the total value of fruit exports from South Africa to China and Hong Kong, citrus fruit has accounted for 85 per cent. With South Africa's exports to China concentrated on citrus, maximizing market access into such fast-growing markets would require a diversification of fruit exports.

6.4 Leveraging Research and Technology for the Production of High-Value Fruit and Access to Export Markets

The expansion of South Africa's fruit industry has been underpinned by research, innovation, and technological developments.[8] Growing customer demands and complex sanitary and phytosanitary standards in different markets require quality improvements and regulatory compliance at each level of the value chain. And the effects of climate change on fruit production complicate the ability of producers to meet these requirements. In a highly competitive global market, structured through relationships in GVCs, it is exactly these pressures that drive responses at firm and government levels that accelerate the industrialization of freshness.

Firms are innovating, learning, and adopting technological solutions to meet escalating requirements. Learning is a dynamic process; a solution at one level of the chain necessitates changes at other levels. For example, while biotechnology is key to responding to climate change threats, it is also at the heart of addressing issues of fruit quality through the development of genetically improved varieties necessary for complying with phytosanitary standards.

Major developments in research and technology in South Africa's fruit industry have been in the areas of biotechnology and on-farm production technologies. These include irrigation and precision farming methods, disease and pest management, and post-harvest production technologies such as digital platforms and the internet of things for sorting, grading, and cold storage. These new technologies are transforming the structure of fruit production, offering scope for greater productivity through improved yields, speed, shelf life and quality, and transparency and traceability along the value chain.

The growing complexity of fruit production and exporting also means that financing requirements are increasingly complex and often involve the need for long-term or 'patient' finance before returns are reaped (for example, on investments in R&D). And the increasingly intricate, roundabout character of fruit exporting also means that there are evolving requirements for public investment in key infrastructure and technical capacity that the evidence suggests have not adequately been met (see below, section 6.5). The rest of this section illustrates some of these knowledge-intensive industrial processes at play in the production of export-quality fruit.

6.4.1 Biotechnology

Upstream in the value chain, the impacts of climate change, weather variability, and diseases and pathogens have driven investments in advanced breeding

---

[8] Section 6.4 draws from interviews discussed in the introductory section.

technologies for growing varieties that are adaptable to local climate conditions, with improved resistance to diseases and pests such as insects, weeds, and pathogens. Advances in biotechnology also ensure that new varieties can be bred according to specific characteristics such as taste, visual appearance, shelf life, seasonality, yield, climatic resilience, and soil-type suitability. These advances may also affect labour requirements. New varieties enable growers to meet changing international preferences, and extend the growing seasons which supports year-round supply to different markets.

Integrating advanced genetic seed material into South African fruit production draws firms in South Africa into the domain of leading global firms. The berry industry provides a good example. The industry currently imports its main varieties from the USA (developed at the universities of Florida and Georgia) and Australia (from Costco Wholesale). These are the Costa and Driscoll, OZblu and Mountain Blue Orchards (MBO) cultivar range. These imported varieties are owned by three leading producers: Haygrove, United Exports, and BerryWorld. These producers have the breeding licences to produce new plants and seedlings from the parent plant, and they have contracts with the universities and Costco to disseminate the tree seedlings. Improved berry varieties have higher yields and are sweeter than old varieties. They fetch higher prices and perform better on export markets. Given their shorter shelf life, the older varieties are transported via air, while the new stronger varieties are transported via (cheaper) shipping containers as they can endure longer sea-freight transit times.

Similarly, variety management and development companies in the citrus and deciduous fruit industries import new varieties from around the world and commercialize plant breeders' new varieties both in South Africa and internationally. To secure the profitability of investments in breeding new varieties, which can take up to ten to sixteen years, intellectual property management companies ensure that plant breeders earn royalties and commissions for every plant sold in nurseries.

The technological ability of the local industry to develop or import improved varieties has an important impact on the structure and governance of the value chain. The development of new varieties, tightly managed by intellectual property rights, is becoming the organizing principle of the fruit value chain. Owners of protected varieties can exercise significant power in dictating to farmers the terms and conditions of production, volumes, marketing, and exports. This means that owners of protected varieties can control the entire fruit value chain of a specific variety—from production to marketing—enabling them to capture value through royalties and commissions.

For example, the citrus industry is moving towards more protected varieties for niche markets in order to control and earn higher prices through restrictions on production, which avoid market flooding. The market trend has been to move away from oranges and navels towards easy-peeling naartjies (mandarins) for which global demand is growing. These include branded mandarin varieties called ClemenGold and Tango, which are protected varieties. The plant breeder and the intellectual property management company decide on the allocation of hectares for planting protected varieties. For instance, they can stipulate that only up to 1,000 hectares of the variety can be planted in a specific growing season and once the plantings reach that number they can no longer sell the variety.

6.4.2 On-Farm Production Technologies

The increasing effects of variable rainfall and more frequent drought conditions mean that farmers need to augment plantings of improved varieties that are adaptable to local conditions, coupled with new irrigation and pest control technologies. This is critical for producing the right size and quality of fruit demanded in export markets.

For example, the Eastern Cape region—the second-largest citrus-producing region in South Africa (after Limpopo) and accounting for 26 per cent of the total 88,569 hectares under production in 2019—has experienced two prolonged droughts, in 2015/16 and 2019/20. In particular, Citrus production in the Gamtoos Valley area in the Eastern Cape, along with other agricultural production activities (such as chicory, avocados, strawberries and blueberries, vegetables, dairy, and herbs) relies entirely on the Kouga Dam for irrigation water. The dam supplies 59.9 million cubic metres of water to farmers, with each farmer having a standard water allocation of 8,000 cubic metres per annum per scheduled hectare (Gamtoos Irrigation Board, 2019). However, the dam's reduced water levels caused by the long droughts have led to water restrictions being imposed by the irrigation board and the Department of Water and Sanitation. In January 2018, with the Kouga Dam at only 9.75 per cent capacity, growers were allocated a 20 per cent water quota for the 2017/18 season. This meant that farmers could only draw 1,600 cubic metres of their normal annual water allocation of 8,000 cubic metres per scheduled hectare. In late 2018, there was good rainfall, which increased the dam-water level to 55 per cent and farmers were permitted to draw 85 per cent of their annual water allocation for the 2019/20 water year. However, in 2020, the dam's water level dropped again to below 7 per cent and growers were allocated a 20 per cent water quota, forcing growers to remove some of the newly planted citrus trees and to not plant new seedlings (Gamtoos Irrigation Board, 2019).

The pressure from the recent droughts in South Africa is forcing growers to adopt irrigation and precision-farming technologies to maintain and improve production. Firms have been adopting the use of low-flow micro and drip irrigation technologies, which are programmed and operated through mobile phones. These fertigation systems allow crops to be irrigated and fertilized at the same time and monitor the nutritional needs of a tree. These kinds of adaptation point to increasingly roundabout processes in agriculture, as it is organized through an intricate nexus of inputs, technologies, and organizational requirements. It is also clearly shaped by the related process of 'servicification' (see Lanz and Maurer, 2015) by which a rising share of value of non-service output is accounted for by service-type activities.

Alongside the water-security challenges imposed by worsening climatic conditions, the growing susceptibility of crops to pest and diseases is driving the fruit industry to expand research and technical services. These are critical for compliance with phytosanitary standards in export markets, which are the biggest constraint for fresh-fruit exports. The compliance process requires the industry to conduct research and provide specific technical and scientific information to satisfy importing countries that there are no risks of any pests and diseases. This research information is a critical tool for governments to negotiate trade agreements with other countries or market it to potential trading partners.

A number of players in the South African fruit industry are engaging in research activities. Part of the Citrus Growers' Association (CGA), Citrus Research International (CRI) conducts industry research and technical services with funding primarily from the association's levy on exported citrus. CRI has spent a significant and increasing amount of its annual income levy on research and technical services: 57 per cent of its total annual income levy of R91 million in 2019/20, compared to 53 per cent in 2018/19 (CGA, 2019 and 2020). CRI's research on diseases and integrated pest management has focused largely on false coddling moth, citrus black spot, and fruit flies, which have presented key market-access challenges for citrus fruit products. To fund the growing demand for research driven by the increasing requirements of export markets, the Minister of Agriculture, Land Reform and Rural Development approved the Citrus Growers' Association's application to increase the citrus export levy by more than 100% from 74 cents per every 15kg carton exported for 2020 to R1.64 for 2021 (CGA, 2020).[9] Additional public funding to the citrus industry includes an extension of the Sector Innovation Fund from the Department of Science and Technology, in the form of the Research for Citrus Exports programme and the Post-Harvest Innovation Programme. The Post-Harvest Innovation Programme is a public-private partnership between the Department of Science and Technology and the Fresh Produce Exporters Forum. The South African Berries Association, established in 2011, has also invested in research for the government to use in trade negotiations. That research has concentrated on insects and fungi that affect blueberries, including viruses and bacteria.

[9] www.cga.co.za (2021).

6.4.3 Post-harvest Production Technologies: Automated Sorting and Grading Equipment, and Cold Storage

The need to reduce defects and increase the quality and speed of fruit sorting to meet growing consumer demands is driving key technological improvements. Access to new sorting technologies that are more accurate than hand-grading enables producers to improve productivity and to achieve consistency in the supply of high-quality, defect-free fruit to consumers. Consistency in the quality of supply is also critical for compliance with sanitary and phytosanitary standards for market access. Investing in new sorting technologies, to raise the proportion of higher valued fruit exported, is central to firms' prospects for upgrading within fruit value chains.

Leading fresh-fruit exporters have computerized their entire systems in packhouses. Packhouses are installed with optical graders and sizers, which use a camera system that grades the fruit into different grades and classes.[10] These technologies are imported from leading manufacturers in France, the Netherlands, and New Zealand; South Africa has limited research, technical, and engineering skills to develop new sorting technology locally.

Another important determinant of success in the fruit industry is a firm's ability to install sophisticated cold-chain technologies that ensure a longer product shelf life. The adoption of these technologies has provided greater access to geographically dispersed and distant markets. This has been particularly important for delicate fruits, such as berries, that have a short shelf life and for which the slightest reduction in turnaround times will increase profits significantly (Wyman, 2018).

6.4.4 Digital Innovations for Improving Market Access

Competitive success in global agricultural trade turns on the capacity to produce and export a reliable supply of high-quality output that meets demanding sanitary and phytosanitary standard requirements. One dimension of this is that the need for improved processes of capturing, storing, and sharing information for compliance purposes has driven the adoption of innovative digital platforms in the fruit industry. One South African example is an electronic data-sharing platform for growers for issuing export phytosanitary certification.[11]

---

[10] https://www.tru-cape.com/tru-news/new-technologies-keep-tru-cape-and-its-packhouses-in-the-lead/;https://www.tru-cape.com/tru-news/new-grabouw-sorting-line-and-packhouse-uses-the-latest-global-tech-available/.

[11] https://www.citrusresourcewarehouse.org.za/home/document-home/news-articles/south-african-fruit-journal-safj/sa-fruit-journal-2016/3748-sa-fruit-journal-aug-sept-2016-cga-phytclean-update/file.

To complement and realize the benefits of the industry initiative to move to electronic certification and data-sharing systems, individual firms, particularly large producers, are implementing electronic data interchange (EDI) systems within their supply chains to integrate information in the packhouse and cold-chain facilities. This technology allows for the seamless monitoring of supply-chain processes as the system syncs the information from the packhouse and cold-storage facility and then produces comprehensive reports and documentation. Tablet devices installed with apps that use cloud storage are used to conduct audits and inspections on the farms that are necessary to acquire accreditation in export markets. Nonetheless, however sophisticated their own operations may be, firms in rural areas often run up against the wall of poor connectivity; this is addressed in section 6.5 below.

6.5 Constraints on Effective Structural Transformation in South Africa's Fruit Industry

Despite evidence of dynamism in fruit production, effective structural transformation in the South African fruit industry has been limited by widespread underinvestment in ports, water, and telecommunications infrastructure, and technical capacity.

6.5.1 Congestion and Delays at Ports

High levels of congestion and delays at South Africa's main ports have continued to pose one of the biggest challenges in the industry.[12] Machinery breakdowns caused by ageing and worn-out infrastructure frustrate operations at the ports. The additional pressures during the Covid-19 pandemic put further strain on maintenance and exposed the failure of spreaders, straddles, and mobile cranes.[13] Port congestion and delays have been particularly acute during peak seasons of major export products such as citrus. The process of moving fresh produce through South Africa's main ports can take seven to eight weeks, drastically reducing the shelf life of perishable goods (Chisoro-Dube et al., 2019). Fruit exporters have also lost money in unplanned expenditure on additional plug-ins for vessels that were delayed at the ports.[14]

---

[12] https://www.freshplaza.com/article/9123535/crisis-at-south-africa-s-harbours-affecting-citrus-exports/; https://www.freshplaza.com/article/9239660/tru-cape-searches-for-solutions-to-cape-town-port-crisis/.

[13] https://www.freshplaza.com/article/9232871/productivity-at-all-south-africa-s-port-terminals-currently-well-below-norm/.

[14] https://www.freshplaza.com/article/9123535/crisis-at-south-africa-s-harbours-affecting-citrus-exports/.

The causes of congestion have included institutional snags, port capacity, and the build-up of traffic from trucks carrying containers into and out of the ports. Although government and industry stakeholders have acknowledged the urgency of addressing congestion issues at the ports, the crisis has continued to worsen.[15] For example, in December 2019 the Department of Economic Development and Tourism, and Transnet in the Western Cape, established a task team to address a shortage of cranes, traffic bottlenecks, and sluggish logistics communications in the supply chain at the port of Cape Town, but the challenges persisted into 2020.

6.5.2   Ageing and Poorly Maintained Water Infrastructure

Similar to the challenges of ageing and worn-out infrastructure at the ports has been the historical underinvestment in water resources and the inadequate maintenance of water infrastructure. The average age of water infrastructure is thirty-nine years and there has been a poor maintenance record (Amis et al., 2017). Backlogs in investments and maintenance of water infrastructure are especially serious in rural parts of the country. The consequences have been particularly acute during drought periods.[16]

Insufficient funding from the fiscus for the Department of Water and Sanitation, which is the custodian of water resources and responsible for coordinating investments in water infrastructure, has constrained the ability of government to deliver infrastructure timeously. It has been estimated that South Africa requires at least R1.4 billion investments per annum (approximately US$85 million per annum)[17] to maintain the current water infrastructure (Amis et al., 2017).

Water management in South Africa has also been characterized by a significant lack of capacity among water professionals, many of whom have migrated to the private sector in search of better working conditions. Inadequate engineering skills in the country have exacerbated the problem (Amis, Zinyengere, and Cassim, 2017). South Africa's engineering industry ranked forty-ninth out of ninety-nine countries in the Global Engineering Capability Index in 2020; its infrastructure ranking was fortieth, behind countries including Uruguay, Chile, Greece, and Latvia; and its digital infrastructure ranking was even lower, at fifty-fourth.[18]

The backlog in infrastructure maintenance at the Kouga Dam in the Eastern Cape is one example of the effects of poor infrastructure. The Gamtoos Irrigation

---

[15] https://www.freshplaza.com/article/9239660/tru-cape-searches-for-solutions-to-cape-town-port-crisis/.

[16] https://www.cbn.co.za/news/manufacturing/financing-of-water-infrastructure-takes-centre-stage-in-south-africa/.

[17] This is based on the exchange rate as of 21 October 2020 accessed at https://www.xe.com/.

[18] For safety standards, South Africa ranked seventy-seventh: http://reports.raeng.org.uk/global-engineering-capability-review/appendix-1/.

Board manages and distributes water from Kouga Dam and the provincial Department of Water and Sanitation is responsible for maintaining the dam and water infrastructure, such as the water canal system and dam wall. However, the department has not done any maintenance on the water infrastructure since the mid-1990s. While the Gamtoos Irrigation Board stepped in to carry out some maintenance functions, it could not afford the high levels of investment required to adequately address the backlog. This means that there will have to be more investment on the part of government and more effective intervention at the technical level.

6.5.3 Inadequate Telecommunications Infrastructure

The use of irrigation and precision-farming technologies to respond to the impacts of droughts and the growing susceptibility of crops to pest and diseases imposed by climate change requires stable internet access and cell-phone connectivity. Yet in many rural areas there is poor internet and cell-phone connectivity. The problems have been exacerbated by South Africa's low levels of broadband penetration and limited access to fixed and mobile infrastructure. The high cost of investments required to roll out fixed and mobile infrastructure, particularly in rural areas, and of leasing space on existing infrastructure sites, has limited broadband penetration.

Fixed services in rural areas are vital for providing high speeds and high volumes of data at a lower cost (Hawthorne et al., 2016; Robb and Paelo, 2020). Historically, Telkom was the fixed-line monopolist in South Africa until government's decision, reflected in the 1995/6 White Paper, to adopt managed liberalization in the telecommunications sector. As part of this process, Telkom was partially privatized and was entrusted to facilitate universal broadband rollout. However, Telkom used its control of upstream infrastructure to frustrate downstream rivals and limit competition in the sector (Hawthorne et al., 2016; Robb and Paelo, 2020).

Organizations like the Perishable Produce Export Control Board (PPECB), which conducts audits for export markets and accreditations, have struggled in this context of limited connectivity. Organizations carrying out this kind of activity cannot afford downtime in connectivity because inspections need to be conducted timeously.

6.5.4 Insufficient Technical Capacity

The cumbersome process of importing seed varieties into the country and the long quarantine periods depend on various factors such as the ability of exporting countries to comply with South Africa's import requirements and the phytosanitary risk that varieties pose to the South African industry. Countries such as Spain and Chile have fast-tracked their systems for pathogen testing by accepting products tested in internationally certified laboratories, thus stealing a march on countries like South Africa, which as well as not accepting varieties tested abroad have not invested sufficiently in lab equipment or quarantine facility skills.

Limited technical capacity and know-how at the quarantine laboratories of the Department of Agriculture Land Reform and Rural Development for clearing exotic pests and diseases slows the process and leads to delayed commercial production. Plants can die in quarantine, with a high financial impact on the importer. Also, when varieties are not tested and released fast enough, there is limited time to discover whether they work in South African agroclimatic conditions and then to register the variety for plant breeders' rights, which protect the variety when it becomes commercially viable.

6.6 Conclusion

In this chapter, detail has been provided on the ways in which production for export of fresh fruit in South Africa embodies the characteristics of the industrial: fruit production is increasingly sophisticated and complex, it is organizationally and materially 'roundabout', and an increasingly intricate technical nexus is inserted between the genetic plant stock origins of fresh fruit (themselves the focus of high-tech research and development) and the point of consumption. The knowledge-intensive, productivity-enhancing processes involved in exporting fresh fruit are precisely those that economists have long identified as central to structural transformation. But the chapter has also shown how the scope and shape of structural transformation within fruit—and broader agricultural—production are shaped by a number of complex factors: national ecosystems of infrastructure and knowledge production capable of generating dynamic increasing returns (Best, 2018; Oqubay and Lin, 2020), agroclimatic conditions and climate change, the dynamics and power relations within GVCs, and domestic politics and policy.

Not only does South Africa have considerable potential for further structural change through fruit production and export, structural change that can contribute to foreign exchange earnings and employment, but also it is clear that South Africa's competitiveness in fruits requires greater prioritization and more coordinated policy attention by government. For although there has been impressive expansion in some fruits, overall South African fruit exports have failed to keep pace with other leading exporters, such as those in Latin America.

And South Africa has lost the technical lead it had earlier established in key areas like cold-storage facilities. Individual South African firms, and some industry association bodies, have invested and worked to develop capabilities and institutions to support improvements in efficiency and quality. But underlying much of the relative failure of South African fruit production overall has been the weakness of government policy. The evidence from the fruit sector suggests that the government, distracted by the political framing of a transformation agenda, has undermined fruit exports and weakened the dynamic of structural change. It has done this by underinvesting in port facilities, rural internet capacity, and water infrastructure, as well as in engineering capabilities, technical capacity, and trade negotiation. It has also failed to build the kind of patient, long-term development finance that has been critical to many other experiences of agrostructural change.

Developments in South Africa's fruit sector have important implications for other African countries in terms of development and industrialization within agriculture. South Africa's fruit story shows that industrialization and structural transformation are not limited to manufacturing but extend to many 'primary' agricultural products. Agriculture is still the mainstay of the majority of African economies with few manufacturing activities. There are therefore important lessons to be drawn from South Africa's fruit-production experiences for how other African countries might leverage agriculture for economic growth. Such growth is dependent on building industrial capabilities to harness technological changes necessary to produce high-quality fruit for high-value export markets. And the evidence, in South Africa as elsewhere, is that this requires concerted, targeted state support.

References

Amis, M., N. Zinyengere, and A. Cassim (2017). 'Exploring opportunities for domestic-local investment in water and sanitation services: challenges and constraints.' Water Research Commission. http://www.wrc.org.za/wp-content/uploads/mdocs/TT%20725–17.pdf.

Amsden, A. H. (2001). *The Rise of 'The Rest': Challenges to the West from Late-Industrializing Economies*. Oxford: Oxford University Press.

Andreoni, A. and H.-J. Chang (2016). 'Industrial policy and the future of manufacturing.' *Journal of Industrial and Business Economics* 43: 491–502.

Best, M. (2018). *How Growth Really Happens: The Making of Economic Miracles through Production, Governance, and Skills*. Princeton: Princeton University Press.

Chisoro-Dube, S., T. Paremoer, C. Jahari, and B. Kilama (2018a). 'Growth and development of the fruit value chain in Tanzania and South Africa.' CCRED Working Paper 2018/5. Johannesburg: CCRED.

Chisoro-Dube, S., R. Das Nair, and N. Landani (2019). 'Technological developments in South Africa's fruit industry and implications for market access and participation.' CCRED Working Paper 2019/5. Johannesburg: CCRED.

Chisoro-Dube, S., R. Das Nair, M. Nkhonjera, and N. Tempia (2018b). 'Structural transformation in agriculture and agroprocessing value chains.' CCRED Working Paper 2018/8. Johannesburg: CCRED.

Cimoli, M., G. Dosi, and J. E. Stiglitz (2009). *Industrial Policy and Development: The Political Economy of Capabilities Accumulation*. Initiative for Policy Dialogue Series. Oxford and Toronto: Oxford University Press.

Citrus Growers' Association of Southern Africa (CGA) (2019). 'Annual report.' https://c1e39d912d21c91dce811d6da9929ae8.cdn.ilink247.com/ClientFiles/cga/CitrusGowersAssociation/Company/Documents/CGA%20Annual%20Report%202019%20v6%20FINAL.pdf.

Citrus Growers' Association of Southern Africa (CGA) (2020). 'Annual report.' http://c1e39d912d21c91dce811d6da9929ae8.cdn.ilink247.com/ClientFiles/cga/CitrusGowersAssociation/Company/Documents/CGA%20Annual%20Report%202020e.pdf.

Cramer, C., J. Di John, and J. Sender (2018). 'Poinsettia assembly and selling emotion: high value agricultural exports in Ethiopia.' AFD Research Papers Series No. 2018–79, September. Paris: Agence Français de Développement.

Cramer, C. and J. Sender (2015). 'Agro-processing, wage employment and export revenue: opportunities for strategic intervention.' Department of Trade and Industry Working Paper. Johannesburg: TIPS.

Cramer, C. and J. Sender (2019). 'Oranges are not only fruit: the industrialization of freshness and the quality of growth.' In A. Noman, R. Kanbur, J. Stiglitz (eds), *The Quality of Growth in Africa*, 209–33. New York: Columbia University Press.

Dallas, M., S. Ponte, and T. J. Sturgeon (2018). 'A typology of power in global value chains.' Working Paper in Business and Politics No. 92. Copenhagen: Copenhagen Business School.

Food and Agriculture Organisation (FAO) of the United Nations (2017). 'The future of food and agriculture: trends and challenges.' Rome.

Gamtoos Irrigation Board (2019). 'Annual report.' https://gamtooswater.co.za/files/2019/10/GIB-Annual-Report-2019.pdf.

Gereffi, G. (1994). *The Organisation of Buyer-Driven Global Commodity Chains: How U.S. Retailers Shape Overseas Production Networks*. Westport, CT: Greenwood Press.

Gereffi, G. and K. Fernandez-Stark (2011). *Global Value Chain Analysis: A Primer*. Center on Globalization, Governance & Competitiveness (CGGC). Durham: Duke University Press.

Gereffi, G. and J. Lee (2012). 'Why the world suddenly cares about global supply chains.' *Journal of Supply Chain Management* 48(3): 24–32.

Gereffi, G. and J. Lee (2016). 'Economic and social upgrading in global value chains and industrial clusters: why governance matters.' *Journal of Business Ethics* 133(1): 25–38.

Hausmann, R., B. Cunningham, J. Matovu, R. Osire, and K. Wyett (2014). 'How should Uganda grow?' Harvard Kennedy School Faculty Research Working Paper Series No. RWP14-004. Cambridge Massachusetts, Harvard Kennedy School.

Hawthorne, R., P. Mondliwa, T. Paremoer, and G. Robb (2016). 'Competition, barriers to entry and inclusive growth: telecommunications sector study.' CCRED Working Paper 2016/2. Johannesburg: CCRED.

Humphrey, J. and H. Schmitz (2002). 'Developing country firms in the world economy: governance and upgrading in global value chains.' Regional Studies, 61/2002.

ITC Trade Map (2019). https://www.trademap.org/Index.aspx.

ITC Trade Map (2020). https://www.trademap.org/Index.aspx.

Khan, M. and S. Blankenburg (2009). 'The political economy of industrial policy in Asia and Latin America.' In M. Cimoli, G. Dosi, and J. E. Stiglitz (eds), *Industrial Policy and Development—The Political Economy of Capabilities*, 336–77. Oxford: Oxford University Press.

Kuznets, S. (1973). 'Modern economic growth: findings and reflections.' Nobel Lecture. *American Economic Review* 63: 247–58.

Lall, S. (2004). 'Reinventing industrial strategy: the role of government policy in building industrial competitiveness.' G-24 Discussion Papers 28, São Paulo, United Nations Conference on Trade and Development.

Lanz, R. and A. Maurer (2015). 'Services and global value chains: servicification of manufacturing and services networks.' *Journal of International Commerce, Economics and Policy* 6(3): 1–18.

Mijiyawa, A. G. (2017). 'The case of the manufacturing sector in Africa.' *World Development* 99: 141–59.

Nolan, P., J. Zhang, and C. Liu (2008). 'The global business revolution, the cascade effect, and the challenge for firms from developing countries.' *Cambridge Journal of Economics* 32(1): 29–47.

Oqubay, A. and J. Y. Lin (2020). *The Oxford Handbook of Industrial Hubs and Economic Development*. Oxford: Oxford University Press.

Page, J. (2014). 'Can Africa industrialise?' *Journal of African Economics* 21(2): 86–125.

Robb, G. and A. Paelo (2020). 'Competitive dynamics of telecommunications markets in South Africa, Tanzania, Zambia, and Zimbabwe.' WIDER Working Paper 2020/83. Helsinki: UNU-WIDER.

Samaniego, R. M. and J. Y. Sun (2016). 'Productivity growth and structural transformation.' *Review of Economic Dynamics* 21: 266–85, https://ink.library.smu.edu.sg/soe_research/1707.

Storm, S. (2015). 'Structural change.' *Development and Change* 46(4): 666–99.

Syrquin, M. (1988). 'Patterns of structural change.' In H. Chenery and T. N. Srinivasan (eds), *The Handbook of Development Economics*, 1:203–73. Amsterdam: North-Holland.

Wyman, O. (2018). 'Disruption in fruit and vegetable distribution.' Fruit Logistica Trend Report 2018. Berlin: Messe Berlin GmbH, https://www.oliverwyman.de/content/dam/oliverwyman/v2- de/publications/2018/Mai/Fruit_Logistica_Trend_Report_2018_Part1_2_3.pdf.

Young, A. (1928). 'Economic progress.' Economic Journal 38: 527–42.

7

Sustainability and Green Capital Accumulation

Lessons from the South African Wine Value Chain

Stefano Ponte

7.1 Introduction

In the past two decades or so, 'green capitalism', 'green growth', the 'green economy', and the 'circular economy' have become popular constructs in view of addressing climate change and other pressing environmental crises (popular books include Lovins et al., 2007; Esty and Winston, 2009; Friedman, 2009; McDonough and Braungart, 2010; Schwab, 2017). Considerations of sustainability and resilience have also been widely referred to in the context of the impact of the Covid-19 pandemic and recovery from it. Essentially, these concepts have been employed to argue that the capitalist mode of production can be leveraged to solve the pressing environmental issues that arise from its very logic. We are told that new business models, innovation, and technological progress can save the environment and still facilitate capital accumulation and everlasting growth. In other words, we are led to believe that green capitalism contains the seed of salvation.

Of course, some of the technologies and models have the potential to address pressing environmental challenges—but they almost always address the manifest-ations rather than the roots of problems, and often focus on individual models and production technologies without exploring the systemic and structural elements in which they are embedded. In other words, while green capital accumulation strategies that optimize production and resource use are helping to lower the relative energy and material intensity of production, they do not address the overall ecological limits to growth because they are based on a logic of continuous expansion (Kovel, 2007; Newell and Paterson, 2010; Higgs, 2014). To restate in slightly different terms, these relate to technological and organizational fixes which do not address the overall structural change required (Coe and Yeung, 2015).

One approach that has been often used to implementing these fixes is for lead firms in global value chains to place new environmental demands on their

Stefano Ponte, *Sustainability and Green Capital Accumulation: Lessons from the South African Wine Value Chain* In: *Structural Transformation in South Africa: The Challenges of Inclusive Industrial Development in a Middle-Income Country.* Edited by: Antonio Andreoni, Pamela Mondliwa, Simon Roberts, and Fiona Tregenna, Oxford University Press. © Oxford University Press 2021. DOI: 10.1093/oso/9780192894311.003.0007

suppliers, which come with requests for more information on supplier cost structures and operations (Ponte, 2019). In supplier jurisdictions where regulatory monitoring is poor or difficult, this can lead to pro forma compliance with buyer demands and certifications, while further limiting the actual impact on environmental sustainability. When profit margins decrease for suppliers (negatively affecting their economic sustainability), these demands can also have negative rebounding effects on social sustainability—for example, driving suppliers to cut labour costs or worsen work conditions to recoup the extra environmental costs.

This chapter highlights how sustainability and green capital accumulation go hand in hand—through the analysis of economic and environmental upgrading in the wine value chain in South Africa. These processes of accumulation are built on a structural logic that extracts value upstream from producers as they attempt to improve their environmental performance, and that leaves upstream actors with little leverage on how to (re)capture the 'environmental value' that they themselves create. The South African wine industry is widely viewed as a successful example of value chain upgrading, one that changed over the 1990s and 2000s from producing mainly bulk wine of low quality to delivering demand-driven wine styles in the basic quality segment of the industry and higher quality wines in new niches (Ponte and Ewert, 2007; Ponte and Ewert, 2009).[1] In both quality segments, upgrading has included offering certified Fairtrade, organic, and biodynamic wines, and some degree of improvement in environmental practices. Yet domestic producers' economic returns have been squeezed, while marketers and retailers in importing countries reap the benefits of economic and environmental upgrading.

The rest of this chapter discusses first the general trend of how capital accumulation has taken place along value chains on the basis of addressing (or pretending to address) environmental sustainability concerns. The chapter then moves on to the analysis of different aspects of economic and environmental upgrading in the wine value chain originating in South Africa and ending in the UK, in the context of recent dynamics that characterize the global wine value chain. Upgrading is examined through three kinds of processes: first, product, process, volume, and/or variety—including their environmental aspects; second, changing and/or adding functions; and, third, transferring capabilities between chains. In the next section, the actual economic and environmental outcomes of upgrading are discussed, with specific focus on producers. The chapter concludes with a reflection on what the case study of wine says about structural transformation in South Africa more generally.

---

[1] http://www.sawis.co.za.

7.2 Sustainability and Capital Accumulation in Global Value Chains

As competitive advantage becomes denationalized and increasingly shaped by the functioning of global value chains, new winners and losers arise within and across nations (Baldwin, 2016; Milanovic, 2016). In South Africa, inequality has often been examined in relation to the agenda of black economic empowerment (BEE) (Southall, 2007; Khagram and Rohan, 2008; Tangri and Southall, 2008; Mebratie and Bedi, 2013; Bowman, 2019; Bracking, 2019; Hamann et al., 2020; and Chapter 9) and research on production, economic development, and sustainability has paid particular attention to the specific consequences for disadvantaged groups. In this context, discussions on the sustainability of production are discussions that focus on power relations, inequality, and social, environmental, and climate justice.

Yet, in its current manifestation, 'sustainable development' (including much of the construction of the UN Sustainable Development Goals) has been stripped of its justice elements and has become 'all but synonymous with "sustained economic growth"' (Dale et al., 2016). It has embedded unfettered and apolitical technological optimism and 'sustainability consumerism'. Green capitalism is going hand in hand with green and/or blue 'grabbing' that is operated through the exploitation of land and water resources (Benjaminsen and Bryceson, 2012; Fairhead et al., 2012; Hill, 2017), a contemporary instance of accumulation by dispossession (Harvey, 2004). As capitalism metamorphoses into green capitalism, it comes along with its financial imperatives, its (im)moralities and its values, in South Africa and beyond (Bracking, 2012; Sullivan, 2013; Dempsey, 2016; Asiyanbi, 2017; Ouma et al., 2018).

Global value chain (GVC) analysis has provided important insights into how sustainability and capital accumulation interact. It does this by examining the power relations that underpin the governance of discrete 'value chains' that are explicitly governed by one or more groups of 'lead firms' (such as retailers or branded food processors) (Gereffi, 1994). Two dimensions of GVC analysis are especially relevant for the purposes of this chapter. A first dimension concerns various forms of GVC governance (Cattaneo, Gereffi, and Staritz, 2010; Gereffi, 1994; Gereffi, Humphrey, and Sturgeon, 2005; Gibbon and Ponte, 2005; Milberg and Winkler, 2013; Ponte and Gibbon, 2005; Ponte, 2014) and the different kinds of power that shape them. This literature underscores the role played by powerful corporations, especially those that exert 'buyer power' by placing large orders in their value chains (e.g. Gereffi et al., 2005) and how lead firms in GVCs are leveraging sustainability to extract more information from suppliers, strengthen power relations to their advantage, and find new venues of value creation and capture (Ponte, 2019).

A second dimension, often coupled with reflections on economic development, refers to GVC upgrading—the paths for value chain actors to add value and extract more rent, eventually moving up the value chain to more sophisticated and skill-intensive operations (Gereffi, 1999; Humphrey et al., 2004; Gereffi, 2014). Much of this literature has highlighted paths for actors to 'move up the value chain' for economic gain—identifying the sources of capabilities that facilitate access to new markets (Giuliani et al., 2005; Morrison et al., 2008) and/or how knowledge and information flow within value chains between lead firms and their suppliers (Gereffi, 1999). The research agenda on upgrading has recently moved from the examination of its economic and social aspects to the consideration of environmental concerns as well—and thus to the processes that can improve or minimize the environmental impact of GVC operations, including production, processing, distribution, consumption, and disposal or recycling (De Marchi et al., 2013; Krishnan, 2017).

Elsewhere (Ponte, 2019), it has been shown that the management of sustainability concerns has become a key element of both governance and upgrading in GVCs. Geographically, production is moving to locations that can meet basic sustainability specifications in large volumes and at low cost. Organizationally, multi-stakeholder initiatives on sustainability are playing a key role in redefining the minimum accepted standards for products. And, the need to verify sustainability compliance has led to the adoption of new technologies of measurement, verification, and trust (Busch, 2011; Freidberg, 2013; Freidberg, 2014; Fouilleux and Loconto, 2017). It has also been argued (Ponte, 2019) that the 'business case' for sustainability has by and large been solved: lead firms in global value chains not only extract sustainability value from their suppliers, especially those based in the global South, but they can also benefit from internal cost savings, supplier squeezing, reputation enhancements, and improved market capitalization. As the value of goods increasingly depends more on their intangible properties (including those related to the environment) than on their functional or economic value, sustainability management becomes a central function of corporate strategy— filtering through companies' organization, marketing, operations, and logistics.

Producers in the global South, including in South Africa, have undergone impressive upgrading trajectories. Yet they have achieved limited economic gains (Ponte, 2019). They are offering increasingly sophisticated sustainability features, often to simply keep participating in GVCs as buyers place increasing demands on them. This often leads to lower margins for producers unless productivity gains can more than compensate for higher costs. When producers do manage to receive higher prices, it is usually in the context of much larger gains that buyers obtain in the same GVC. The value created by producers through economic-cum-environmental upgrading is mostly captured by buyers. At the same time, consumers can enjoy a wide variety of special and/or 'sustainable' products that deliver a feel-good factor.

In other words, lead firms are using sustainability to appropriate surplus value from other GVC actors—often small producers based in the global South (Starosta, 2010; Quentin and Campling, 2018). This sustainability-driven supplier squeeze (Ponte, 2019) is yet another manifestation of a larger process of value extraction from suppliers that has been observed in many GVCs (Milberg and Winkler, 2013), which can lead to the adverse incorporation of suppliers (Gibbon and Ponte, 2005; Phillips, 2011) and to immiserizing growth (Kaplinsky, 2005).

7.3 Economic and Environmental Upgrading in the South African Wine Value Chain

In GVC analysis, the general term *upgrading* has been used to highlight paths for actors to 'move up the value chain' for economic gain. There are two broad orientations within this literature. A first orientation seeks to identify the *sources* of capabilities that facilitate access to new markets. Some argue that 'horizontal' flows are key, including locational and interactive knowledge built in clusters (Giuliani et al., 2005; Morrison et al., 2008). Others focus on 'vertical' relations and how knowledge and information flow within value chains between lead firms and their suppliers (Gereffi, 1999). But integrative efforts assessing which paths and aspects of upgrading originate from combinations of socio-spatial dynamics and 'learning from global buyers' have also been developed (Giuliani et al., 2005; Murphy, 2007; Gereffi and Lee, 2016; De Marchi et al., 2017).

A second orientation, the one taken in this chapter, is concerned with the nature of upgrading and its trajectories, often based on four kinds of economic upgrading (Humphrey and Schmitz, 2002, 2004, and 2006): (1) product upgrading: moving into more sophisticated products with increased unit value; (2) process upgrading: achieving a more efficient transformation of inputs into outputs through the reorganization of productive activities; (3) functional upgrading: acquiring new functions (or abandoning old ones) that increase the skill content of activities; and (4) inter-chain upgrading: applying competences acquired in one function of a chain and using them in a different sector/chain.

GVC scholars initially highlighted the importance of a 'high road' trajectory to upgrading (from process to product to functional upgrading) eventually leading to performing functions in a value chain that have more skill and knowledge content (Gereffi, 1999). Others have argued that a specific trajectory should not be an end in itself, and that attention should also be paid to what conditions can improve the position of disadvantaged actors along GVCs (e.g. smallholder producers, developing country processors, women entrepreneurs) and more generally achieve a 'better deal' for developing country-based operators (Tokatli, 2012; Glückler and Panitz, 2016a). This includes examining in detail the complex upgrading and downgrading trajectories that are emerging (Gibbon, 2001;

Gibbon and Ponte, 2005; Tokatli, 2007; Ponte and Ewert, 2009; Cattaneo et al., 2010; Mitchell and Coles, 2011; Tokatli, 2012; Hansen et al., 2014; Ponte et al., 2014; Blažek, 2015; Bernhardt and Pollak, 2016; Gereffi and Lee, 2016; Glückler and Panitz, 2016b). Recent efforts in GVC scholarship have attempted to go beyond the discussion of economic upgrading to also examine social upgrading trajectories and the interactions between the two (Barrientos et al., 2010; Gereffi and Lee, 2012; Barrientos and Visser, 2013; Coe and Hess, 2013; Milberg and Winkler, 2013; Rossi, 2013; Pegler, 2015; Bernhardt and Pollak, 2016; Gereffi and Lee, 2016).

The research agenda on upgrading in GVCs is also finally moving to the consideration of its environmental aspects (Lister et al., 2015; Poulsen et al., 2016). Environmental upgrading in the literature is seen as 'a process by which actors modify or alter production systems and practices that *result in positive (or reduce negative) environmental outcomes*' (Krishnan, 2017: 117; emphasis in the original). This emerging literature has usefully distinguished between different drivers of environmental upgrading, and between upgrading as a process vis-à-vis upgrading as an outcome (Krishnan, 2017), an effort that continues in this chapter.

7.3.1 The Global Wine Value Chain: The Global Context and Overall Trends

The global wine value chain has perhaps the most complex and sophisticated quality infrastructure in the agrofood industry. It has been going through a major process of restructuring in the past few decades—where the application, challenge, and re-interpretation of different ideas and representations of quality and sustainability have been contested and redefined in the context of the emergence of large multinational companies (Anderson, 2004) and an increasing level of concentration in the marketing of wine.

Recent trends in the geography of wine production, trade and consumption, as well as changes in the quality composition of supply and demand, have been well documented (Anderson 2004; Unwin 2005; Anderson and Nelgen 2011; Hira 2013; Gilinsky et al. 2015). These included, in the last decades of the twentieth century, a dramatic fall in production volumes and per capita consumption in traditional (so-called 'Old World') wine-making and wine-consuming countries, such as Portugal, Spain, France, and Italy; this was partly compensated by growing production and exports in 'New World' producing countries (Argentina, Chile, South Africa, New Zealand, Australia, and the USA) and by increasing consumption in the UK, the USA, and in some Asian countries. Table 7.1 shows the ranking of the top wine-producing and wine-consuming countries from 2010 to 2018. The top five producing countries by volume (Italy, France, Spain, the USA, and Argentina) in 2018 accounted for 64 per cent of global supplies. The top five consuming countries (USA, France, Italy, Germany, and China) accounted for 49 per cent of global demand (see Table 7.2).

The years 2002–7 marked a period of major growth in wine consumption. This was accompanied by a spurred interest in firms applying environmental management systems as part of a multiplication of wine offerings and the search for new differentiation strategies (Atkin et al., 2012; Gilinsky et al., 2015). As the global financial crisis hit in 2008, the wine industry suffered a dramatic downturn with global consumption starting to decline. This led to downward pressure on prices and margins, and a drop in the introduction of new wine brands and offerings, at least in the USA.[2] By the second half of the 2010s, however, the trend had reversed, and the industry's volume of consumption was back to the levels of the mid-2000s.[3]

Growing concentration led to the top four global wine merchant groups controlling almost 10 per cent of the global market in 2006, a figure that had decreased only marginally by 2012 (see Table 7.3). It is worth noting that the same top three groups, all US-based, rank at the top in both periods. In 2012, the fourth-placed company (based in Australia) was a spin-off of the wine division of Fosters into an independent company in 2011. This suggests that there has been little change in the top rankings overall. Wine retail, which was traditionally the domain of small specialist shops, is now in the hands of supermarket chains, especially in northern Europe, the UK, and the USA, but increasingly in southern Europe as well. Although there are fears of homogenization of styles and offerings in the wine market, this is still an industry that produces a phenomenal array of different products, which are sold under a combination of brand names, grape variety, sustainability certifications, and/or indications of origin (Ponte, 2009).

Many of the main wine companies, both globally and in South Africa, are to different degrees vertically integrated—they may also produce wine and may own a number of flagship estates for grape production. The general tendency, however, has been for these conglomerates to concentrate more on value-chain functions that require less capital investment, and to find an appropriate equilibrium between own production (usually for top-quality wines) and purchasing from external suppliers (Ponte and Ewert, 2009).

In relation to sustainability issues, organic certification (and Fairtrade for social issues) has been the early mover in wine, as in many other agrofood GVCs. Although the cultivation of organic grapes for winemaking is still a minor proportion of total production, it has been growing rapidly and has reached 5 per cent of the total area under production in Spain, the leading country in this field (Gilinsky et al., 2015: 42). Organic grape cultivation has also grown dramatically in New World producing countries, where producers have fewer restrictions on

---

[2] http://www.oiv.int/en/databases-and-statistics/statistics.
[3] http://www.oiv.int/en/databases-and-statistics/statistics.

Table 7.1 Top ten wine-producing countries (2010–18)

Rank (2018)		2010 mhl	2010 World share	2011 mhl	2011 World share	2012 mhl	2012 World share	2013 mhl	2013 World share	2014 mhl	2014 World share	2015 mhl	2015 World share	2016 mhl	2016 World share	2017 mhl	2017 World share	2018 mhl	2018 World share
1	Italy	48.5	18.4%	42.8	16.0%	45.6	17.7%	54	18.7%	44.2	16.3%	50	18.2%	50.9	18.9%	42.5	17.1%	54.8	18.8%
2	France	44.4	16.8%	50.8	19.0%	41.5	16.1%	42.1	14.6%	46.5	17.2%	47	17.2%	45.3	16.8%	36.3	14.6%	48.6	16.6%
3	Spain	35.4	13.4%	33.4	12.5%	31.1	12.1%	45.3	15.7%	39.5	14.6%	37.7	13.8%	39.7	14.7%	32.5	13.1%	44.4	15.2%
4	USA	20.9	7.9%	19.1	7.1%	21.7	8.4%	23.6	8.2%	23.1	8.5%	21.7	7.9%	23.7	8.8%	23.3	9.4%	23.9	8.2%
5	Argentina	16.3	6.2%	15.5	5.8%	11.8	4.6%	15	5.2%	15.2	5.6%	13.4	4.9%	9.4	3.5%	11.8	4.7%	14.5	5.0%
Top 5		165.5	62.7%	161.6	60.3%	151.7	58.8%	180	62.3%	168.5	62.2%	169.8	62.0%	169	62.6%	146.4	58.8%	186.2	63.8%
6	Chile	8.8	3.3%	10.5	3.9%	12.6	4.9%	12.8	4.4%	9.9	3.7%	12.9	4.7%	10.1	3.7%	9.5	3.8%	12.9	4.4%
7	Australia	11.4	4.3%	11.2	4.2%	12.3	4.8%	12.3	4.3%	11.9	4.4%	11.9	4.3%	13.1	4.9%	13.7	5.5%	12.9	4.4%
8	Germany			9.1	3.4%	9	3.5%	8.4	2.9%	9.2	3.4%	8.8	3.2%	9	3.3%	7.5	3.0%	10.3	3.5%
9	South Africa	9.3	3.5%	9.7	3.6%	10.6	4.1%	11	3.8%	11.5	3.8%	11.2	4.1%	10.5	3.9%	10.8	4.3%	9.5	3.3%
10	China	13	4.9%	13.2	4.9%	13.8	5.3%	11.1	3.8%	13.5	5.0%	13.3	4.9%	13.2	4.9%	11.6	4.7%	9.1	3.1%
	Russia	7.6	2.9%																
Top 10		215.6	81.7%	215.3	80.3%	210	81.4%	235.6	81.5%	224.5	82.8%	227.9	83.2%	224.9	83.3%	199.5	80.1%	240.9	82.5%
	World	264		268		258		289		271		274		270		249		292	

Source: OIV—Statistical report on world vitiviniculture (2010–19).

Table 7.2 Top ten wine-consuming countries (2010–18)

Rank (2018)		2010 mhl	2010 World share	2011 mhl	2011 World share	2012 mhl	2012 World share	2013 mhl	2013 World share	2014 mhl	2014 World share	2015 mhl	2015 World share	2016 mhl	2016 World share	2017 mhl	2017 World share	2018 mhl	2018 World share
1	USA	27.6	11.5%	28.4	11.7%	30	11.7%	30.2	12.5%	30.6	12.7%	30.9	12.7%	31.7	13.0%	32.6	13.3%	33.0	13.4%
2	France	29.3	12.2%	28.3	11.7%	28	11.5%	27.8	11.5%	27.5	11.4%	27.3	11.2%	27.1	11.1%	27.0	11.0%	26.8	10.9%
3	Italy	24.6	10.2%	23	9.5%	21.6	8.9%	20.8	8.6%	19.5	8.1%	21.4	8.8%	22.4	9.2%	22.6	9.2%	22.4	9.1%
4	Germany	20.2	8.4%	19.7	8.1%	20.3	8.3%	20.4	8.4%	20.3	8.4%	20.5	8.4%	20.2	8.3%	19.7	8.0%	20.0	8.1%
5	China	15.1	6.3%	16.3	6.7%	17.1	7.0%	16.5	6.8%	17.4	7.2%	18.1	7.4%	19.2	7.9%	19.3	7.8%	17.6	7.2%
Top 5		116.8	48.5%	115.7	47.8%	117	48.0%	115.7	47.8%	115.3	47.8%	118.2	48.6%	120.6	49.4%	121.2	49.3%	119.8	48.7%
6	UK	12.9	5.4%	12.8	5.3%	12.8	5.3%	12.7	5.2%	12.6	5.2%	12.7	5.2%	12.9	5.3%	12.7	5.2%	12.4	5.0%
7	Russia	12	5.0%	12.2	5.0%	11.3	5.08	10.4	4.3%	11.1	4.6%	10.8	4.4%	10.5	4.3%	11.1	4.5%	11.9	4.8%
8	Spain	10.9	4.5%	10	4.1%	9.9	4.1%	9.8	4.0%	9.8	1.0%	9.8	1.1%	9.9	4.1%	10.5	4.3%	10.5	4.3%
9	Argentina	9.7	4.0%	9.8	4.0%	10.1	4.1%	10.4	4.3%	9.9	4.1%	10.3	4.2%	9.4	3.9%	8.9	3.6%	8.4	3.4%
10	Australia	5.3	2.2%	5.3	2.2%	5.4	2.2%	5.4	2.2%	5.4	2.2%	5.5	2.3%	5.4	2.2%	5.9	2.4%	6.0	2.4%
Top 10		167.6	69.5%	165.8	68.5%	166.5	68.2%	164.4	67.9%	164.1	68.1%	167.3	68.8%	168.7	69.1%	170.3	69.2%	169.0	68.7%
World		241		242		244		242		241		243		244		246		246	

Source: OIV—Statistical report on world vitiviniculture (2010–19).

Table 7.3 World's top wine marketers

Rank	Company	Headquarters	World share (%)
2006			
1	Constellation Brands	USA	3.9
2	E&J Gallo Winery	USA	2.7
3	The Wine Group	USA	1.6
4	Foster's Wine Estates	Australia	1.5
Top 4			9.7
2012			
1	E&J Gallo Winery	USA	2.7
2	Constellation Brands	USA	2.2
3	The Wine Group	USA	1.6
4	Treasury Wine Estates	Australia	1.8
Top 4			8.3

Sources: Own elaboration of data from Marketline.com (for 2012) and *Impact* 37(11–12), June 1 and 15, 2007, p. 6 (for 2006).

viticulture and wine-making practices. Biodynamic production, whether certified or not, is also spreading worldwide, but remains a small niche. In France and Italy, small vineyards in traditional wine-producing regions, such as Bordeaux and Chianti, also make claims of 'reasonable' viticultural practices or the production of 'natural wines' based on the characterization that traditional local techniques are similar to those used in organic production.

New World producing countries have spurred a number of broad sustainability initiatives (Borsellino et al., 2016). Programmes for carbon-footprint minimization are also starting to be considered in the wine industry (Flint et al., 2016). Most of the current wine sustainability programmes and certifications focus on environmental issues, rather than social concerns. Exceptions are Fairtrade and some South Africa-specific initiatives—such as the Wine and Agricultural Ethical Trade Association (WIETA) and other projects attempting to address black economic empowerment issues in the wine industry (Du Toit et al., 2008).

7.3.2 The South African Wine Industry

What are the implications of this sustainability focus for economic and environmental upgrading in the South African wine industry? In order to answer this question, upgrading is broken down into three broad categories: first, improving product, process, volume, and/or variety; second, changing and/or adding functions; and third, transferring capabilities between chains (see details in Ponte, 2007; Ponte and Ewert, 2007; Ponte, 2009; Ponte and Ewert, 2009).

7.3.2.1 Upgrading through Improving Product, Process, Volume, and/or Variety—Including Environmental Aspects

Substantial upgrading took place in the South African wine industry in the broad category of improving product, process, volume, and/or variety. Environmental sustainability has been an important element of this (see Table 7.4). Throughout much of the twentieth century, the wine industry in South Africa was centred around cooperative wine cellars, which were responsible for a large proportion of total wine production. They supplied bulk wine of low quality and their farmers were dependent on cheap black labour. Although some upgrading had taken place before the formal ending of apartheid in 1994, the industry has upgraded substantially since. This was most evident in the 1990s, followed by a less steep curve in the 2000s (Ponte and Ewert, 2007 and 2009).[4]

Environmental issues have also played a role in the upgrading trajectories of the wine value chain in South Africa. These initiatives can be observed in two categories. The first category includes global, codified and standardized best practices that are embedded in sustainability certifications that include environmental content, such as the BRC Global Standard-Food and/or the IFS-Food standard. The popularity of general environmental management standards, such as ISO 14001 certification, is also on the rise (in 2005, only a handful of cellars held this certification). And exports of organic or biodynamic certified wines have also grown, albeit from a small base.[5]

7.3.2.2 Upgrading through Changing and Adding Functions

The case study of wine in South Africa suggests two key features on upgrading through changing and/or adding functions (see Table 7.4). First, wine producers-wholesalers have shed off upstream functions linked to grape and wine production. Where complete outsourcing has not been possible, value-chain operators across the board have tried to move from hands-on management systems (requiring close supervision) to more hands-off systems, with the exception of top-quality wines. Most small and medium-scale wineries rely to some degree on own-grape growing and always make their own wine. All marketers, by definition, do not grow grapes or make their own wine—they rely on contracted wineries (often producer cooperatives). But even the largest and historically most important producer-wholesalers have been moving away from grape growing on their own farms and in some cases even winemaking—thus becoming pure marketers (Ponte and Ewert, 2009). Large cooperatives (or ex-cooperatives) do not have outsourcing options because their members are grape growers. As a result, they are increasingly holding stock (and facing higher risks)

---

[4] http://www.sawis.co.za.   [5] http://www.sawis.co.za.

Table 7.4 Overview of economic and environmental upgrading trajectories in the South African wine industry

Improving product, process, volume, and/or variety	
Aspect of upgrading	General trend in South African wine industry
overall intrinsic quality	improved
proportion of bottled exports vs bulk exports	increased, but then stagnated in the 2000s
proportion of natural vs rebate/ distilling wine production	more or less the same
noble variety proportion	increased
top quality wines	number and visibility increased
proportion of wine certified under Wine of Origin Scheme	increased
product consistency	improved
economies of scale	increased (mainly in coops)
economies of scope	improved
managerial systems	improved
viticultural practices	improved
wine-making practices	improved
marketing, advertising, provision of promotional support	improving, but still a relatively weak point
sustainability certifications	increasing sales of organic and biodynamic wines
biodiversity preservation	BWI initiative promoted conservation efforts, but current status is unclear
environmental management	large proportion of operators meet IPW scheme standards
Changing and/or adding functions	
Location of functional upgrading/ downgrading	General trend in South African wine industry
in South Africa	cellars and producer-wholesalers moving away or reducing their engagement in grape-growing
	marketers moving away from winemaking
	cooperatives becoming more engaged in marketing and branding through joint ventures
	product innovation increasingly done by European/ US marketers and agents
in Europe	South African producer-wholesalers and marketers divesting from own agencies in the UK and Europe, or entering in joint ventures
	Brand ownership by South African actors decreasing
Inter-chain capability transfer	
tourism industry	mutually beneficial interactions and joint capability building
environmental sustainability	leveraged to build brand recognition and sales

Source: Author's own analysis; adapted and updated from Ponte (2007), Ponte and Ewert (2009), and Ponte (2019).

on behalf of other actors downstream in the value chain. This is a classic vertical specialization process, common in many GVCs, that in the wine sector entails many private cellars and producer-wholesalers moving away from, or reducing their engagement in, grape growing. Some of the most successful producer-wholesalers have largely abandoned even winemaking, thus divesting from holding fixed capital and becoming pure marketers (Ponte, 2007 and 2009).

Second, the few South African producer-wholesalers and marketers used to have their own agencies in the UK and Europe. They have now divested from them or have entered in joint-ventures with Europe-based branders and marketers. Many of the most successful brands of South African wine in the UK are owned or co-owned by overseas companies. These are processes of functional *downgrading* from a point of view of South African producers—yet, they have yielded positive results in terms of successfully selling their stock before the next harvest comes in (what operators call 'moving volume'). Conversely, many cooperatives and ex-cooperatives have become more engaged in direct marketing and branding through joint ventures. This is an example of functional upgrading on their part.

UK agents and marketers have also upgraded functionally. Under pressure from shorter lead times, they had to increase their control over logistics—with some importers selling to retailers with delivery executed at the warehouse in the UK instead of 'free-on-board' on the ship in Cape Town as in the past. As retailers are seeing themselves increasingly as shelf-space providers, the replenishment function now falls upon UK agents. Much product innovation, new packaging, and new presentations and styles are also generated by these agents/marketers. This does not mean that upstream learning is not taking place. Up to the early 1990s, quality in South African wine was 'producer-generated', whereas now cellars and South African marketers are able to interpret consumer market changes and react to downstream requests much more quickly and efficiently.

7.3.2.3 Upgrading through Transferring Capabilities between Chains

Wine tourism is a well-developed industry in the Western Cape, the major wine-producing region in South Africa, with a number of organized wine routes. Cape Town is part of the Great Capitals of Wine network. A good proportion of cellars are open to the public and have tasting facilities. Many have restaurants and some have hotels on-site. Scenic beauty and many flagship properties displaying Cape Dutch architecture (and some interesting contemporary architecture as well) add flavour to the 'Cape wine experience'. A large share of the revenue accruing from wine tourism comes from food sales and accommodation—the volume of wine sales at the cellar-door is not significant in absolute terms—with the exception of some flagship estates such as Vergelegen, Boschendal, or some Constantia-based cellars and farms.[6] Branding and marketing capabilities are used for promoting

---

[6] http://www.wosa.co.za/Wine-Tourism.

both wine sales and broader tourism-related income. Cellar and property visits tend to improve wine sales beyond the tasting room, and visibility in retail can bring tourists to a property as well. While for the major producer-wholesalers wine sales are far more significant than wine tourism income, their flagship properties with wine-tasting rooms, restaurants, and/or hotels continue to be important elements of their overall brand offering. South Africa is considered a sophisticated player in the global tourism industry, and can offer excellent value for money—benefiting the wine industry as well (Bruwer, 2003; Ferreira and Hunter, 2017).

7.4 Discussion: The Economic and Environmental Outcomes of Upgrading

As has been examined elsewhere (Ponte, 2019), governance in the wine GVC underwent a major transformation between 1960–90 and 1990–2018. It moved from a multipolar structure where producers, international merchants, and retailers exerted limited power on each other, to an increasingly unipolar one with retailers at the helm. These transformations in the wine GVC have led to a series of new demands placed on merchants and producers in South Africa, especially in the low-end quality segment, and the pressure to deliver wines at scale at different quality points. Within South Africa, in terms of governance, what has emerged is a value chain where the main drivers are producer–wholesalers and marketers, although their power over other actors in the South African segment of the value chain is limited by their own need to deliver volume and quality to importers and retailers in importing countries.

Producer-wholesalers and marketers are reshaping the functional division of labour within the wine value chain in South Africa, with inventory being pushed upstream (in terms of volume and duration) all the way to cooperatives and other wine producers. At the same time, large South African producer–wholesalers have moved away from branding and marketing operations in Europe to concentrate on value-chain functions within the country. Although this is a *downgrading* trajectory from a traditional GVC perspective, it has been important in terms of securing volume of purchases from other, previously competing, international merchants (Ponte and Ewert, 2009).

While sustainability demands from international marketers and retailers have been relatively limited so far, South African operators and regulators placed strategic importance in proactively profiling sustainability to secure elements of additional competitive advantage in a crowded global supply field. This led to a number of actions and initiatives to deliver environmental content, including most wine producers meeting the (relatively low) sustainability standards of the Integrated Production of Wine (IPW) scheme.

A superficial reading of these trends would suggest a successful upgrading story for South Africa's wine industry: delivery of demand-driven wine styles; volume and consistency have allowed the industry to grow in the basic quality segment of the industry, while the proliferation of higher quality wines has opened new niches. In both quality segments, South Africa has also increased its offering of certified Fairtrade, organic and biodynamic wines; wine producers are now able to comply with an increasingly demanding package of specifications expected as a given; this has in turn stimulated a further process of upgrading in the form of improved vineyard operations, wine-cellar innovation, better managerial and environmental practices, and more systematized quality management.

However, the economic *outcomes* for South African wine producers and grape growers remain problematic, as the margins for improvement have now decreased in many areas. The extras (e.g. promotional support, certifications, sustainability) that the industry delivers to obtain or even just maintain a listing with major retailers are becoming more complex and costly. Margins remain extremely low in the retail markets of the UK, Germany, and the Netherlands, and the industry has a limited presence in the more lucrative US market (Ponte, 2007 and 2009). According to a 2005 study of all South African wineries with a revenue of less than R25 million (approximately US$4 million), 36 per cent were making a loss, and of those with a revenue of R25–90 million (US$4–14 million), 25 per cent were making a loss. The average profit in small wineries was reported at R13 (US$2) per 9-litre case, against R20 (US$3.1) in Australia. Fast-forward to 2016, and the picture has become even worse, with returns to investment dropping to less than 1 per cent. VinPro data indicate that only 13 per cent of the 3,300 producers operate at sustainable income levels, 44 per cent are operating at break-even, and 40 per cent are making a loss.

The implication of these findings is that South African grape and wine producers have made substantial strides in terms of processes of economic and environmental upgrading. But this has not translated into positive *economic outcomes* in the aggregate. This suggests that while suppliers are delivering more content to buyers (including marketable environmental sustainability features), they are facing profitability challenges. At the same time, consumers—both in South Africa and in importing countries—can enjoy a variety of wine qualities at competitive prices, including those delivering sustainability features.

Comprehensive evaluations of the *environmental outcomes* of these upgrading processes and related sustainability initiatives in South Africa are not available. However, it is probably safe to assume that there have been some positive impacts in terms of biodiversity conservation, decreasing agrochemical application (when farms convert to organic or biodynamic), and better environmental stewardship of the land and water resources. At the same time, grape growing is a mono-crop cultivation method that when applied to previously natural areas destroys rather than enhances biodiversity (McEwan and Bek, 2009).

In sum, the case study of the South African wine value chain suggests that: first, sustainability is used opportunistically by global 'lead firms' for marketing, reputational enhancement, and risk management purposes; second, South African value-chain actors and institutions have invested heavily in portraying the industry and individual companies as caring for the environment, and painted this portrait along with scenic and natural beauty of the winelands in this country; although the wine GVC is becoming more unipolar and driven by retailers, South African suppliers have driven environmental sustainability proactively in view of highlighting the unique features that can provide some form of competitive advantage; and third, major economic and environmental upgrading processes in the South African wine value chain took place, but did not lead to positive economic outcomes for most domestic players, and to environmental outcomes that are likely to have been limited. Collectively, these lessons suggest a combined process of capital accumulation by lead firms, coupled with a process of supplier squeeze.

7.5 Conclusion

The case study of the wine industry in South Africa is, at a superficial level, a global value chain story of economic and environmental upgrading and of improved international competitiveness. This has included the lead firms and key institutions driving environmental sustainability as part of consumer positioning of South African wines in the global market. However, the growing concentration of the wine industry globally has come together with increased bargaining power by retailers and international merchants, which is leading to a cascade of squeezed margins upstream all the way to grape and wine suppliers and their workers. In other words, lead firms in the global wine industry are using sustainability opportunistically to shape a structurally unfavourable functional division of labour along the value chain. This is happening as the South African industry is carrying out all sorts of upgrading processes, including those related to environmental management and certification, while diverting attention from the fundamental changes required in the Cape peninsula—one of the most unequal areas in the world and one of those most at risk from the climate crisis.

References

Anderson, K. (2004). *The World's Wine Markets: Globalization at Work*. Cheltenham: Edward Elgar.

Anderson, K. and S. Nelgen (2011). *Global Wine Markets: A Statistical Compendium, 1961–2009*. Adelaide: University of Adelaide Press.

Asiyanbi, A. P. (2017). 'Financialisation in the green economy: material connections, markets-in-the-making and Foucauldian organising actions.' *Environment and Planning A* 50(3): 531–48.

Atkin, T., A. Gilinsky Jr, and S. K. Newton (2012). 'Environmental strategy: does it lead to competitive advantage in the US wine industry?' *International Journal of Wine Business Research* 24: 115–33.

Baldwin, R. (2016). *The Great Convergence: Information Technology and the New Globalization*. Cambridge, MA: Harvard University Press.

Barrientos, S., G. Gereffi, and A. Rossi (2010). 'Economic and social upgrading in global production networks: developing a framework for analysis.' *International Labor Review* 150: 319–40.

Barrientos, S. and M. Visser (2013). 'South African horticulture: opportunities and challenges for economic and social upgrading in value chains.' *Capturing the Gains Working Paper* 12. University of Manchester. Available at: http://www.capturingthegains.org/pdf/South-Africa-horticulture-final.pdf

Benjaminsen, T. A. and I. Bryceson (2012). 'Conservation, green/blue grabbing and accumulation by dispossession in Tanzania.' *Journal of Peasant Studies* 39: 335–55.

Bernhardt, T. and R. Pollak (2016). 'Economic and social upgrading dynamics in global manufacturing value chains: a comparative analysis.' *Environment and Planning A* 48: 1220–43.

Blažek, J. (2015). 'Towards a typology of repositioning strategies of GVC/GPN suppliers: the case of functional upgrading and downgrading.' *Journal of Economic Geography* 16: 849–69.

Borsellino, V., G. Migliore, M. D'Acquisto, C. P. Di Franco, A. Asciuto, and E. Schimmenti (2016). '"Green" wine through a responsible and efficient production: a case study of a sustainable Sicilian wine producer.' *Agriculture and Agricultural Science Procedia* 8: 186–92.

Bowman, A. (2019). 'Black economic empowerment policy and state-business relations in South Africa: the case of mining.' *Review of African Political Economy* 46: 223–45.

Bracking, S. (2012). 'How do investors value environmental harm/care? Private equity funds, development finance institutions and the partial financialization of nature-based industries.' *Development and Change* 43: 271–93.

Bracking, S. (2019). 'Black economic empowerment policy in Durban, e-Thekwini, South Africa: economic justice, economic fraud and "leaving money on the table".' *Review of African Political Economy* 46: 415–41.

Bruwer, J. (2003). 'South African wine routes: some perspectives on the wine tourism industry's structural dimensions and wine tourism product.' *Tourism Management* 24: 423–35.

Busch, L. (2011). *Standards: Recipes for Reality*. Cambridge, MA: MIT Press.

Cattaneo, O., G. Gereffi, and C. Staritz (2010). *Global Value Chains in a Postcrisis World: A Development Perspective*. Washington, DC: World Bank.

Coe, N. M. and M. Hess (2013). 'Global production networks, labour and development.' *Geoforum* 44: 4–9.

Coe, N. M. and H. W.-C. Yeung (2015). *Global Production Networks: Theorizing Economic Development in an Interconnected World*. Oxford: Oxford University Press.

Dallas, M. P., S. Ponte, and T. J. Sturgeon (2019). 'Power in global value chains.' *Review of International Political Economy* 26: 666–94.

Dale, G., M. V. Mathai, and J. A. P. de Oliveira (2016). *Green Growth: Ideology, Political Economy and the Alternatives*. London: Zed Books Ltd.

De Marchi, V., E. Di Maria, and G. Gereffi (2017). *Local Clusters in Global Value Chains: Linking Actors and Territories through Manufacturing and Innovation*. London: Routledge.

De Marchi, V., E. Di Maria, and S. Ponte (2013). 'The greening of global value chains: insights from the furniture industry.' *Competition & Change* 17: 299–318.

Dempsey, J. (2016). *Enterprising Nature: Economics, Markets, and Finance in Global Biodiversity Politics*. Hoboken: John Wiley & Sons.

Du Toit, A., S. Kruger, and S. Ponte (2008). 'Deracializing exploitation? "Black economic empowerment" in the South African wine industry.' *Journal of Agrarian Change* 8: 6–32.

Esty, D. and A. Winston (2009). *Green to Gold: How Smart Companies Use Environmental Strategy to Innovate, Create Value, and Build Competitive Advantage*. Hoboken: John Wiley & Sons.

Fairhead, J., M. Leach, and I. Scoones (2012). 'Green grabbing: a new appropriation of nature?' *Journal of Peasant Studies* 39: 237–61.

Ferreira, S. L. and C. A. Hunter (2017). 'Wine tourism development in South Africa: a geographical analysis.' *Tourism Geographies* 19: 676–98.

Flint, D. J., S. L. Golicic, and P. Signori (2016). *Contemporary Wine Marketing and Supply Chain Management: A Global Perspective*. London: Springer.

Fouilleux, E. and A. Loconto (2017). 'Voluntary standards, certification, and accreditation in the global organic agriculture field: a tripartite model of techno-politics.' *Agriculture and Human Values* 34: 1–14.

Freidberg, S. (2013). 'Calculating sustainability in supply chain capitalism.' *Economy and Society* 42: 571–96.

Freidberg, S. (2014). 'Footprint technopolitics.' *Geoforum* 55: 178–89.

Friedman, T. L. (2009). *Hot, Flat, and Crowded 2.0: Why We Need a Green Revolution—And How It Can Renew America*. London: Picador.

Gereffi, G. (1994). 'The organization of buyer-driven global commodity chains: how US retailers shape overseas production networks.' In G. Gereffi and M. Korzeniewicz (eds), *Commodity Chains and Global Capitalism*. London: Praeger.

Gereffi, G. (1999). 'International trade and industrial upgrading in the apparel commodity chain.' *Journal of International Economics* 48: 37–70.

Gereffi, G. (2014). 'Global value chains in a post-Washington Consensus world.' *Review of International Political Economy* 21: 9–37.

Gereffi, G., J. Humphrey, and T. Sturgeon (2005). 'The governance of global value chains.' *Review of International Political Economy* 12: 78–104.

Gereffi, G. and J. Lee (2012). 'Why the world suddenly cares about global supply chains.' *Journal of Supply Chain Management* 48: 24–32.

Gereffi, G. and J. Lee (2016). 'Economic and social upgrading in global value chains and industrial clusters: why governance matters.' *Journal of Business Ethics* 133: 25–38.

Gibbon, P. (2001). 'Upgrading primary production: a global commodity chain approach.' *World Development* 29: 345–63.

Gibbon, P. and S. Ponte (2005). *Trading Down: Africa, Value Chains, and the Global Economy*. Philadelphia: Temple University Press.

Gilinsky Jr, A., S. K. Newton, T. S. Atkin, C. Santini, A. Cavicchi, A. R. Casas, and R. Huertas (2015). 'Perceived efficacy of sustainability strategies in the US, Italian, and Spanish wine industries: a comparative study.' *International Journal of Wine Business Research* 27: 164–81.

Giuliani, E., C. Pietrobelli, and R. Rabellotti (2005). 'Upgrading in global value chains: lessons from Latin American clusters.' *World Development* 33: 549–73.

Glückler, J. and R. Panitz (2016a). 'Relational upgrading in global value networks.' *Journal of Economic Geography* 16: 1161–85.

Glückler, J. and R. Panitz (2016b). 'Relational upgrading in global value networks.' *Journal of Economic Geography* 16: 1161–85.

Hamann, R., S. Khagram, and S. Rohan (2008). 'South Africa's charter approach to post-apartheid economic transformation: collaborative governance or hardball bargaining?' *Journal of Southern African Studies* 34: 21–37.

Hansen, U. E., N. Fold, and T. Hansen (2014). 'Upgrading to lead firm position via international acquisition: learning from the global biomass power plant industry.' *Journal of Economic Geography* 16: 131–53.

Harvey, D. (2004). 'The "new" imperialism: accumulation by dispossession.' *Socialist Register* 40: 63–87.

Higgs, K. (2014). *Collision Course: Endless Growth on a Finite Planet*. Cambridge, MA: MIT Press.

Hill, A. (2017). 'Blue grabbing: reviewing marine conservation in Redang Island Marine Park, Malaysia.' *Geoforum* 79: 97–100.

Hira, A. (2013). *What Makes Clusters Competitive? Cases from the Global Wine Industry*. Montreal: McGill-Queen's Press.

Humphrey, J. and H. Schmitz (2002). 'How does insertion in global value chains affect upgrading in industrial clusters?' *Regional Studies* 36: 1017–27.

Humphrey, J., H. Schmitz, and H. Schmitz (2004). *Local Enterprises in the Global Economy: Issues of Governance and Upgrading*. Cheltenham: Edward Elgar.

Kaplinsky, R. (2005). *Globalization, Inequality, and Poverty: Between a Rock and a Hard Place*. Cambridge: Polity.

Kovel, J. (2007). *The Enemy of Nature: The End of Capitalism or the End of the World?* London: Zed Books.

Krige, H. (2005). 'Writing on the wall for haphazard finances—Deloitte benchmarking study.' *Wineland* (July).

Krishnan, A. (2017). 'Re-thinking the environmental dimensions of upgrading and embeddedness in production networks: the case of Kenyan horticulture farmers.' Phd Thesis, School of Environment, Education and Development, University of Manchester.

Lister, J., R. T. Poulsen, and S. Ponte (2015). 'Orchestrating transnational environmental governance in maritime shipping.' *Global Environmental Change* 34: 185–95.

Lovins, L. H., A. Lovins, and P. Hawken (2007). *Natural Capitalism*. New York: Little, Brown.

McDonough, W. and M. Braungart (2010). *Cradle to Cradle: Remaking the Way We Make Things*. New York: North Point Press.

McEwan, C. and D. Bek (2009). 'The political economy of alternative trade: social and environmental certification in the South African wine industry.' *Journal of Rural Studies* 25: 255–66.

Mebratie, A. D. and A. S. Bedi (2013). 'Foreign direct investment, black economic empowerment and labour productivity in South Africa.' *The Journal of International Trade & Economic Development* 22: 103–28.

Milanovic, B. (2016). *Global Inequality*. Cambridge, MA: Harvard University Press.

Milberg, W. and D. Winkler (2013). *Outsourcing Economics: Global Value Chains in Capitalist Development*. Cambridge: Cambridge University Press.

Mitchell, J. and C. Coles (2011). *Markets and Rural Poverty: Upgrading in Value Chains*. Ottawa: IDRC.

Mondliwa, P. and S. Roberts (2020). 'Black economic empowerment and barriers to entry.' In T. Vilakazi, S. Goga, and S. Roberts (eds), *Opening the South African Economy: Barriers to Entry and Competition*. Johannesburg: HSRC Press.

Morrison, A., C. Pietrobelli, and R. Rabellotti (2008). 'Global value chains and technological capabilities: a framework to study learning and innovation in developing countries.' *Oxford Development Studies* 36: 39–58.

Murphy, J. T. (2007). 'The challenge of upgrading in African industries: socio-spatial factors and the urban environment in Mwanza, Tanzania.' *World Development* 35: 1754–78.

Newell, P. and M. Paterson (2010). *Climate Capitalism: Global Warming and the Transformation of the Global Economy*. Cambridge: Cambridge University Press.

Ouma, S., L. Johnson, and P. Bigger (2018). 'Rethinking the financialization of "nature".' *Environment and Planning A: Economy and Space* 50(3): 500–11.

Pegler, L. (2015). 'Peasant inclusion in global value chains: economic upgrading but social downgrading in labour processes?' *The Journal of Peasant Studies* 42: 929–56.

Phillips, N. (2011). 'Informality, global production networks and the dynamics of "adverse incorporation".' *Global Networks* 11: 380–97.

Ponte, S. (2007). 'Governance in the value chain for South African wine.' TRALAC Working Paper 2007/9. Stellenbosch: Trade Law Centre for Southern Africa.

Ponte, S. (2009). 'Governing through quality: conventions and supply relations in the value chain for South African wine.' *Sociologia Ruralis* 49: 236–57.

Ponte, S. (2014). 'The evolutionary dynamics of biofuel value chains: from unipolar and government-driven to multipolar governance.' *Environment and Planning A* 46: 353–72.

Ponte, S. (2019). *Business, Power and Sustainability in a World of Global Value Chains.* London and New York: Zed Books.

Ponte, S. and J. Ewert (2007). *South African Wine: An Industry in Ferment.* TRALAC Working Paper 2007/8. Stellenbosch: Trade Law Centre for Southern Africa.

Ponte, S. and J. Ewert (2009). 'Which way is "up" in upgrading? Trajectories of change in the value chain for South African wine.' *World Development* 37: 1637–50.

Ponte, S. and P. Gibbon (2005). 'Quality standards, conventions and the governance of global value chains.' *Economy and Society* 34: 1–31.

Ponte, S., I. Kelling, K. S. Jespersen, and F. Kruijssen (2014). 'The blue revolution in Asia: upgrading and governance in aquaculture value chains.' *World Development* 64: 52–64.

Poulsen, R. T., S. Ponte, and J. Lister (2016). 'Buyer-driven greening? Cargo-owners and environmental upgrading in maritime shipping.' *Geoforum* 68: 57–68.

Quentin, D. and L. Campling (2018). 'Global inequality chains: integrating mechanisms of value distribution into analyses of global production.' *Global Networks* 18: 33–56.

Rossi, A. (2013). 'Does economic upgrading lead to social upgrading in global production networks? Evidence from Morocco.' *World Development* 46: 223–33.

Schmitz, H. (2004). *Local Enterprises in the Global Economy.* Cheltenham: Edward Elgar.

Schmitz, H. (2006). 'Learning and earning in global garment and footwear chains.' *The European Journal of Development Research* 18: 546–71.

Schwab, K. (2017). *The Fourth Industrial Revolution.* New York: Crown Business.

Southall, R. (2007). 'Ten propositions about black economic empowerment in South Africa.' *Review of African Political Economy* 34: 67–84.

Starosta, G. (2010). 'The outsourcing of manufacturing and the rise of giant global contractors: a Marxian approach to some recent transformations of global value chains.' *New Political Economy* 15: 543–63.

Sullivan, S. (2013). 'Banking nature? The spectacular financialisation of environmental conservation.' *Antipode* 45: 198–217.

Tangri, R. and R. Southall (2008). 'The politics of black economic empowerment in South Africa.' *Journal of Southern African Studies* 34: 699–716.

Tokatli, N. (2007). 'Networks, firms and upgrading within the blue-jeans industry: evidence from Turkey.' *Global Networks* 7: 51–68.

Tokatli, N. (2012). 'Toward a better understanding of the apparel industry: a critique of the upgrading literature.' *Journal of Economic Geography* 13: 993–1011.

Unwin, T. (2005). *Wine and the Vine: An Historical Geography of Viticulture and the Wine Trade*. London: Routledge.

8

Structural Transformation, Economic Power, and Inequality in South Africa

Sumayya Goga and Pamela Mondliwa

8.1 Introduction

South Africa is the most unequal country in the world, of those on which comparable data are collected (World Bank, 2018; Chatterjee et al., 2020; Webster et al., 2020: 8). Wealth is even more concentrated than income. In 2017, the richest 10 per cent in South Africa held 86 per cent of the total wealth (the top 1 per cent held 55 per cent), while the poorest 60 per cent held a mere 7 per cent of total wealth.[1] These levels of inequality pose challenges for South Africa's ability to effect structural transformation and achieve economic development and growth. Inequality has been shown to have a negative effect on both medium-term growth rates (Cingano, 2014) and the duration of growth spells (Berg and Ostry, 2017). This is because inequality adds to weak aggregate demand and makes politics vulnerable to elite capture, economic entrenchment, clientelism, and populism—all of which divert attention and economic resources away from the capability accumulation required for structural change and growth (Doner and Schneider, 2016).

This chapter contributes to the literature on the role that structural transformation can play in reducing inequality (other recent contributions include Doner and Schneider, 2016; Hartman et al., 2017; Baymul and Sen, 2019; Bhorat et al., 2020; Goga et al., 2020). Though much of the literature focuses on the implications of sectoral transitioning from agriculture to manufacturing and services for inequality, increasing attention is being paid to the implications for inequality of sectoral deepening and diversification within manufacturing—the focus of this chapter. Here, it is argued that the economic power of large and lead firms plays an influential role in reproducing the economic structure, which undermines the reduction of inequality. In this context economic power can be understood as control over accumulation. Within an economy, economic power is usually distributed in line with the prevailing economic structure (Behuria et al., 2017). This implies

---

[1] https://wid.world/country/south-africa/.

Sumayya Goga and Pamela Mondliwa, *Structural Transformation, Economic Power, and Inequality in South Africa* In: *Structural Transformation in South Africa: The Challenges of Inclusive Industrial Development in a Middle-Income Country.* Edited by: Antonio Andreoni, Pamela Mondliwa, Simon Roberts, and Fiona Tregenna, Oxford University Press.

that interests linked to activities that dominate a country's economic structure are able to influence policy and regulation in their favour as they are regarded as important for investment and growth (Goga et al., 2020).[2]

To shed more light on how the observed outcomes of inequality have been reproduced over time, building on Goga et al. (2020), the chapter undertakes an analysis of the role of economic power in shaping the patterns of structural transformation in South Africa. The analysis of economic power draws on insights from political settlements literature on the distribution of power in societies and how it can be leveraged to shape outcomes (Khan, 2010, 2018b, and 2018a; Behuria et al., 2017; Gray, 2018). This is complemented with insights from competition literature, which explains how market power (as a form of economic power) can be used to shape patterns of structural transformation and the distribution of surplus from consumers to producers (see for example Doyle and Stiglitz, 2014; Khan and Vaheesan, 2017; Ennis et al., 2019; Mondliwa et al., 2021). The analysis focuses on how interests in the economy have set agendas and shaped markets, policy, and regulation to maintain economic power in the hands of powerful actors linked to economic structure, to the detriment of structural transformation.

To illustrate how economic power reinforces outcomes in terms of economic structure and inequality, two case studies on two industry groupings in South Africa are analysed over the period 1994 to 2019—metals, machinery, and equipment; and chemicals-to-plastics. The metals, machinery, and equipment, and chemicals-to-plastics industry groupings are good locations from which to understand the poor outcomes in the South African economy (Chapter 1). The basic chemicals and basic metals sub-sectors accounted for 25 per cent of manufacturing output and 47 per cent of manufacturing exports in 1994, with policy in the post-democratic period seeking to leverage the relatively strong productive base in these industries for developing downstream labour-absorbing industries through strong local value chains. Upstream basic metals and basic chemicals industries are considered strategically important for industrialization since they are producers of key inputs into a number of downstream industries, including metal products and machinery, and plastics.

In section 8.2, the relationships between structural transformation, inequality, and economic power are explored. Section 8.3 briefly sketches out structural transformation outcomes in South Africa's post-apartheid period and gives an overview of selected industries. Section 8.4 analyses these outcomes using a political settlement analysis, drawing on experiences in the metals, machinery, and equipment and chemicals-to-plastics industry groupings in

---

[2] These interests are also regarded as an important source of tax contributions and financing elections.

South Africa. In section 8.5, the implications of the lack of structural change for inequality are explored.

8.2 Inequality, Structural Transformation, and Economic Power

8.2.1 Inequality and Structural Transformation

Economists' understanding of the relationship between structural transformation, growth, and inequality has evolved over time. Initially, it was understood that for developing countries the relationship between inequality and growth can be represented by an inverse-U curve, whereby economic growth initially leads to increasing levels of inequality as populations transition from agriculture (characterized as low productivity) to higher productivity sectors (Kuznets, 1955). But, as countries develop by changing the structure of their economies, larger portions of their populations move from agriculture into other sectors of the economy and their skills bases expand, incomes increase, and inequality falls. Kuznets's thesis has since been challenged in part due to changes in the industrialization trajectories of developing countries. There has been increasing incidence of countries deindustrializing prior to achieving high-income status (meaning that potential higher-income jobs are not created). Here the implication is that inequality continues to increase rather than decrease over time. Dynamics within sectors have also changed. For instance, not all activities in agriculture are low-productivity, while services activities are highly heterogenous.

The nature of structural change clearly matters and the manufacturing sector continues to be important for reducing inequality by absorbing more labour in jobs that are more productive, better paid, and offer better labour conditions. Manufacturing-driven structural transformation has been found to decrease inequality, regardless of the stage of structural transformation the country is in, while the outcomes are more nuanced for services-driven structural change (Baymul and Sen, 2020). Certainly, in many East Asian countries, the shift from agriculture to manufacturing was accompanied by reductions in inequality, thus not conforming to the inverted-U curve. For developing countries, services-driven structural change increases inequality (Baymul and Sen, 2020).

Furthermore, manufacturing has a pulling effect on other sectors, stimulating demand for more primary goods as well as services. Its strong linkages with other sectors impact on employment creation in other sectors due to indirect effects (UNIDO, 2013).[3] Both the direct and indirect employment effects suggest

---

[3] Lavopa and Szirmai (2012) suggest that every job created in manufacturing is associated with two or three jobs created outside of manufacturing (UNIDO, 2013).

reductions in inequality. Furthermore, there are multiplier effects associated with net increases in income received by workers in jobs created directly or indirectly through investment in manufacturing, which also serve to reduce inequality. However, there is heterogeneity within manufacturing and downstream diversified industries such as plastics, and machinery and equipment, have relatively higher employment multipliers (Tregenna, 2012).

There are also other spillover effects associated with an increase in manufacturing. Investment in research and development improves the prospects for innovation and technology transfers. Where this does occur, there are knowledge spillovers and productivity growth in other sectors as well (Weiss, 2013). There are thus multiple benefits associated with the stimulation of manufacturing activities: positive effects on job creation and production in manufacturing and related sectors, increases in overall demand associated with increased employment and incomes, and spillover effects related to productivity and technology in other sectors.

Inequality outcomes are also increasingly being linked to inequality of opportunities (Doyle and Stiglitz, 2014). In South Africa, this has two dimensions. First, the high barriers to entry and expansion limit the opportunities for entrants and smaller firms to successfully enter and grow businesses (Vilakazi et al., 2020). The second dimension is linked to opportunities for education and access to other basic services, which is not discussed further here. In terms of barriers to economic participation, the falling competitiveness of downstream industries as a result of strategic conduct of upstream incumbent firms (among other factors) means reduced employment opportunities for those at the bottom to earn an income. When there is a lack of competition and ineffective mechanisms to manage rents, inequality is reinforced and entrenched because barriers maintain the patterns of ownership of productive assets and control of rents in society, and therefore the distribution of income and wealth to the wealthy few (including through dividends and capital gains), while limiting opportunities for others (Khan and Vaheesan, 2017; Ennis et al., 2019). Opening up the economy and changing its structure is critical to deal with entrenched inequities.

In highly unequal societies the distinct power dynamics and political economy means insiders enjoy greater power and outsiders have less recourse for checking that power (Doner and Schneider, 2016). This dynamic is likely to keep reproducing itself unless changes are made to the mechanisms that drive it. One of these mechanisms is economic power, the impact of economic power on structural transformation is discussed in more detail below.

8.2.2 Structural Transformation and Economic Power

While there are competing ideas about how to move developing economies onto the path of structural transformation, the political economy of transformation is increasingly being recognized as important for understanding the process. This is because the political context and underlying power dynamics shape performance (Chapter 14). Those with economic power can use it to influence outcomes, even though institutions ('rules of the game') to transform the economy may exist. The role of power in explaining the effectiveness of particular institutional arrangements is thus key. It goes beyond coercive power in which one actor uses incentives or sanctions to directly compel another actor to act according to their wishes (Dahl, 1957), to more subtle exertions of power, such as covert power, which can be agenda-setting (Dallas et al., 2019).

The evolution and performance of economies are impacted by how institutions are influenced by powerful groups, both formally and informally (Di John and Putzel, 2009; Khan, 2010). If powerful groups are not satisfied with the distribution of resources through the current institutional structure, they will seek ways to change the structure (Khan, 2010), that is, to shape agendas, policy, and laws. In developing countries, informal mechanisms are often used to modify the operation of formal institutions and influence the allocation of resources (Khan, 2010). So understanding how economic development happens in a particular context requires an analysis of both a country's formal institutions and of how powerful interests shape these institutions and agendas in order to influence outcomes. It is possible to analyse who benefits from institutions and who may lose out and, therefore, will seek to block or influence institutional changes that promote development.

Institutions or policies create benefits for firms, but the configuration of power across different types of organizations (firms, and formal and informal groups in society) influences both the institutions that emerge and how these are implemented (Khan, 2018b). For instance, if a policy is developed to benefit downstream firms in a particular value chain, the ability of these firms to capture the benefits depends on the configuration of power in the value chain. Organizations constantly mobilize to change rules, reflecting ongoing changes in their relative power, and in turn, their activities further impact on their future position.

A distribution of organizational power becomes a 'political settlement' if it reproduces itself over time. This is defined as the combination of power and institutions that are mutually compatible and sustainable in terms of economic and political viability (Khan, 2010). A particular political settlement implies a balance between the expectations of different organizations based on their assessment of their relative power and what they are getting through the political and economic process.

A political settlement analysis allows an understanding of how agency is exercised—how interests are pursued in an economy by powerful groups. It allows an unpacking of development outcomes by analysing the interaction between powerful groups and the institutions that these groups seek to influence. This means that the strategies of various powerful groups in the face of institutional rules for transformation can be analysed. More generally, it enables an understanding of the nature of economic change (or the slow pace of it) in developing-country contexts like South Africa, resulting from incentives that can be shaped in different ways by ideas, formal and informal institutions, and the distribution of power.

Examining the interaction of agency and institutions through a political settlement analysis makes it possible to think more creatively about how elite incentives can be restructured for the purposes of transformation, rather than focusing on how to 'fix' institutions. This is important because transformation in developing countries tends to be successful when institutions are effective in changing behaviour. This is usually possible when outcomes are aligned with the interests of the powerful or are in the interests of those which can enforce these outcomes, given the distribution of power (Khan, 2018a). Focusing on the strategies of powerful groups allows for an exploration of how and why they intervene, how they assert agency, and how institutions fare in the face of the actions of the powerful. This, in turn, allows for better interventions for transformation that engage with the reality of the power balance in specific contexts, and with an awareness of the need to incentivize the powerful for the purposes of transformation while taking care that institutions are not captured by them.

Whether a particular political settlement persists depends on the 'holding power' of different actors, where 'holding power' is understood to be the capability of an individual or group to engage in and survive conflicts. Holding power is determined by the economic strength of organizations as well as the networks they are able to organize and mobilize (Khan, 2018c), that is, the historically rooted capacities of different groups to organize. There are four main sources of holding power: economic structure, ideology, violence rights (the threat or use of violence), and rents (Khan, 2018c; Behuria et al., 2017). Determining the holding power of different groups requires an understanding of economic structures and how rents are distributed between different groups, and the interplay between these and other factors, including ideology and the appropriation of violence rights (Behuria et al., 2017). Different sources of holding power are analysed in the political settlement analysis of the two industry groupings in section 8.4.

In the South African context, Goga et al (2020) analysed and found economic structure, rents, and ideology have to be influential in shaping outcomes (Goga et al., 2020). The case studies are analysed through these three sources of holding power.

8.3 Structural Transformation, Inequality, and the Internationalization of Key Industries in Post-apartheid South Africa

South Africa has not experienced the type of structural change that would facilitate accumulation by the poor to reduce inequality, as observed in the late

SUMAYYA GOGA AND PAMELA MONDLIWA   171

industrializers in East Asia. South Africa underwent a process of industrialization that started in the inter-war period until the mid-twentieth century, a process which created a particularly concentrated and exclusive economic structure (Freund, 2018). Though manufacturing is generally inequality-reducing, the structure of manufacturing determines the distribution of the gains (Baymul and Sen, 2019). In South Africa, where there is significant concentration in capital-intensive industries linked to minerals, this has translated into the gains from industrialization accruing to a small group of equity owners and employed citizens. From the 1980s, the country started deindustrializing, with employment losses across manufacturing. (See Chapter 11 for an analysis of South Africa's experience of premature deindustrialization.) Within manufacturing, there has been a decline in light and medium manufacturing, which are relatively more labour-absorbing, representing a structural regression (Bell et al., 2018; and Chapter 1). This has been accompanied by a dramatic rise in low-wage service employment.

The structural change dynamics observed in South Africa have exacerbated inequality in two ways. First, premature sectoral transitioning from manufacturing to services has been dominated by low-value services. A higher share of services is associated with increasing inequality in all income groups (Baymul and Sen, 2019). Second, there has been weak sectoral deepening towards higher value-added and productivity-inducing activities, particularly in manufacturing.

Sectoral deepening in South Africa has, in part, been undermined by the concentration of the economy in capital-intensive and minerals-based industries. Though industrial concentrations are important for taking advantage of economies of scale to achieve international competitiveness, it is important that, where these concentrations are fostered by the government, there are conditionalities to limit extractive rent-seeking and to promote reinvestment in capabilities and wider gains for the economy (Amsden and Singh, 1994; Khan 2010; Mondliwa and Roberts, 2018; Goga et al., 2020). South Africa has a poor record of enforcing conditionalities on state support (Mondliwa, 2018). Instead, there has been an overreliance on competition law and international competition to address the market power of domestic firms (Bell et al., 2018). For instance, while significant capabilities were developed in the upstream metals and chemicals sectors during apartheid through the creation of large firms, the government has failed to manage rents associated with these firms for the benefit of downstream, more labour-intensive manufacturing industries.

The reason for this is that large and dominant firms use their economic power to lobby for policies and regulations in their favour. This means that the economic power that arises from monopoly positions readily translates into the capture of political power that reinforces those positions (Zingales, 2017; Mondliwa and Roberts, 2018).

In South Africa, the liberalization from the 1990s benefited those firms and industries that had established capabilities at the point of opening up, largely in the industries in the upstream minerals-energy complex (Black and Hasson, 2016; Bell et al., 2018). These industries are typically capital intensive, which meant that the gains from exports tended to flow to a small group of existing equity owners and the employed. Within manufacturing, the small grouping of basic heavy industries in South Africa consisting of refineries, basic chemicals, and basic metals accounted for 19 per cent of manufacturing output and 44 per cent of manufacturing exports in 1994.[4] Given the levels of concentration in these sectors, this was effectively due to just a handful of companies. Subsequently, aside from non-ferrous metals, these industries have all grown more rapidly than manufacturing as a whole and, recorded high average rates of investment. Other diversified manufacturing sectors, including the downstream activities of manufacture of plastic and metal products generally performed more poorly than the average, with the notable exception of motor vehicles (Tregenna, 2012; Black et al., 2016; and Chapter 5).

The trade liberalization that started in the 1990s led to the expected increases in import penetration for most sectors (see also Roberts, 2000; Black and Roberts, 2009). Yet, in the upstream industries of basic chemicals, basic metals, and basic ferrous metals, the relative importance of imports in meeting domestic demand was actually lower in 2019 than in 1994 (see Chapters 3 and 4). Import penetration increased substantially for downstream plastic products, metal products and other diversified manufacturing. Machinery and equipment already had very high rates of import penetration in 1994, which increased further while exports also grew substantially.

The apartheid state's industrialization strategy had focused on heavy industry with linkages into mining and energy. Steel was a key pillar and, as a result, the basic metals industries received favourable electricity tariffs, logistics support, and investments aimed at promoting competitiveness. Machinery and structural steel were key intermediate capital inputs to mining. The main state-owned steel business Iscor was privatized in 1989 as an effective monopolist of flat steel products and the single-largest producer of long products. The development of the sector up to 1994 was thus a reflection of the priorities and power of the apartheid state (Chapter 3).

A second important pillar of the apartheid industrial strategy was petrochemicals, which was centred around Sasol, the state-owned producer of liquid fuels from coal and later natural gas. Sasol also produced fertilizer and explosives, key inputs to agriculture and mining, respectively, and a range of other intermediate industrial chemical inputs, including monomers and polymers for plastic products manufacture. Sasol was privatized in 1979.

[4] The rest of this section draws from Mondliwa et al. (2021).

In the 2000s, Iscor and Sasol both internationalized, though in quite different ways. Iscor was acquired by a major multinational (in 2001) and became part of the ArcelorMittal group (Zalk, 2017), becoming Arcelor Mittal South Africa (AMSA). Sasol outwardly internationalized with a dual listing in New York (in 2003), a major US investment (in 2014), as well as other investments and acquisitions. In contrast with Iscor, which was vertically separated around the time that it was privatized, Sasol has maintained and even increased its vertical integration upstream into its feedstocks. This involves substantial ownership of its own coal mines and the rights to gas from Mozambique, along with the pipeline infrastructure for it to be transported to Secunda in Mpumalanga, the location of its second-largest extraction refinery. It has also been able to acquire key chemical businesses from its competitors, including African Explosives and Chemical Industries ("AECI")'s polymer business, though acquisitions in the fuel industry have been blocked by the competition authorities.

The significance of these industries in the South African economy meant that they continued to receive a disproportionate share of government incentives post-apartheid. The basic metals and basic chemicals sectors continued to receive substantial support in the 1990s, including development finance, as part of the firms' steps to improve production efficiencies and be internationally competitive in liberalized markets (Roberts and Rustomjee, 2009; Zalk, 2017; Rustomjee et al., 2018). Other forms of support included generous tax allowances and favourable electricity prices (Goga et al., 2020). Iscor continued to dominate the upstream steel industry, together with Highveld Steel and Scaw Metals (which manufactured thick steel plate and structural steel products), both owned by Anglo American. Iscor and the Anglo American companies also had joint shareholdings in a number of related companies in the sector, reflecting the historically close integration of the state with big business.

8.4 Unpacking the Role Played by Lead Firms in Structural Transformation Outcomes through a Political Settlement Analysis

This section involves an analysis of the political settlement dynamics that have undermined the type of structural transformation of the South African economy that would serve to reduce inequality. This is done through two case studies: one focusing on the metals, machinery, and equipment grouping, and the other on the chemicals and plastics industry grouping. The outcomes from various perspectives are considered, as well as the various strategies used by the upstream firms to maintain power. These include how the upstream industries have extracted support in order to maintain the structure, and how upstream firms have captured rents and influenced rent management. The analysis shows that decisions and non-decisions have been heavily influenced by dominant business groupings for their benefit. Ideologies have shaped the overarching economic policies that have been pursued post-apartheid, including the unbundling and privatization of key conglomerates, while economic power has impacted on rent management. A central part of the analysis is that due to the fragmented nature of policymaking in South Africa, interests can lobby different parts of the state (see Chapters 1 and 2).

In both industries, the power players include the firms at the different levels of the value chain, various government departments, and government agencies such as development funding institutions, regulators, and labour unions. In the chemicals and plastics industry group, Sasol is the upstream firm, while in the metals, machinery and equipment grouping, the upstream firms are AMSA, Scaw Metals and Highveld. The downstream firms are plastic product convertors, and metal fabricators and machinery and equipment firms.

8.4.1 The South African Metals, Machinery, and Equipment Industry

As in many other developing economies, the steel industry in South Africa has been given special status due to the important linkages to the rest of manufacturing production. As such, it has been supported by the state with the end goal of developing the competitive downstream steel fabrication industry through competitively priced intermediary input steel (see Chapter 3 for a detailed description of the support). This has meant that every time the industry has been in trouble, the state has come to its rescue, even at the cost of developing the downstream industry that would contribute more effectively to reducing inequality.

Two critical policy decisions in the post-apartheid period, accompanied by weak conditionalities, illustrate the continued state support. First, when the steel business was unbundled in the early 2000s from the iron ore mining business, a deal was struck for iron ore to be sold to the steel business at cost plus 3 per cent. The pricing effectively created rents for the steel firm. In exchange, the government sought to negotiate a developmental price for steel to downstream local users, but these negotiations were never completed. Providing cheap steel to downstream industries was meant to bolster local manufacturing capability on the basis of the competitive advantage inherent in local mineral resources. Government entered into protracted negotiations on developmental steel prices with AMSA, but the pricing standoff dragged on for years, with the government unable to use any policy levers to steer AMSA into contributing to long-term development.[5] AMSA in fact increased the domestic prices of steel to full import-parity levels, which

---

[5] https://trudimakhaya.co.za/arcelormittal-settlement-is-new-and-tricky-territory-for-competition-authorities/.

were as much as 50–100 per cent above the prices it received for roughly half of its production, which was exported. This was despite its plants being in the lowest quartile of all plants in the world in terms of production costs at the time (Roberts, 2008; Robinson, 2016; and Chapter 3). AMSA therefore abused its access to cheap supply of iron ore by fixing import-parity prices for steel and did not show any regard for government's objective of making cheaper steel available to downstream industries to help build South Africa's manufacturing base.

The importance that was placed on the steel industry meant that it had the ear of government, and as a result the iron ore price deal was included in contracts. These rents were meant to be passed on to downstream steel users, but downstream steel users are more fragmented and less organized, and in the negotiations their interests were represented by government. Given that the government is an arena for contestations between interests, the more organized groups are more likely to succeed, and in this case, developmental steel price negotiations which were meant to benefit the downstream were never concluded. Furthermore, AMSA negotiated high-wage agreements for workers, thus 'co-opting labour', and these wage agreements were forced on already embattled downstream industry players— the prescribed minimum wage in the steel industry is at least 35 per cent higher that South Africa's second-most expensive industry.[6]

The second critical policy decision followed the global recession of 2009, when there was once more a crisis in the global steel industry.[7] At the behest of the steel producers, the government intervened in the industry, bailing out Scaw in 2012 and giving support to AMSA in 2016. Government agreed to a basket of support for AMSA, including tariffs of 10 per cent (which effectively increased to 22 per cent when safeguard measures are included) for a period of three years on all imports of hot rolled steel. The 10 per cent customs duty effectively increased the cost of steel for the downstream fabricating industry, making their products less competitive and resulting in an increase in imports of finished products (Rustomjee et al., 2018).

It has been argued that the tariff and safeguard support allowed AMSA to use the downstream industry as a buffer to protect its old ineffective steel mills, since the tariffs reduced the pressure on AMSA to upgrade its steel plants to be more effective.[8] In return, AMSA agreed that it would cease import-parity pricing and pay a settlement amount to settle a number of competition cases against it. Downstream firms expressed reservation about whether the government would be able to match AMSA's power during the detailed technical and financial negotiations around the price-basket, particularly as the rationale and detailed calculations behind the selection of the basket were not clear (Rustomjee et al., 2018).

---

[6] https://www.cbn.co.za/opinion/mittal-vs-the-downstream-steel-industry-war/.
[7] Global steel export prices dropped to ten-year lows between 2012 and 2016.
[8] https://www.cbn.co.za/opinion/mittal-vs-the-downstream-steel-industry-war/.

AMSA and the government communicated that the pricing principles would be determined by the weighted average of countries South Africa competes with but would exclude China and Russia. The exclusion of China—the world's largest steel producer—from the equation, was also questioned by stakeholders.[9] Given the past record in terms of monitoring and enforcing conditionalities, the settlement raises concerns about government's ability to ensure the implementation of the agreed pricing structure to benefit downstream steel using industries.

The policy decisions to support the upstream industry, and AMSA in particular, shed light on the distribution of power in the value chain. Before the support was given, AMSA was alleged to have been charging excessive prices (Rustomjee et al., 2018); the cartel cases showed that the steel producers including AMSA were governing the value chain to maximize value capture at steel production level. In addition, AMSA was not producing much of the grades of steel required by downstream industries. There are also relatively fewer jobs in steel production than in the beneficiation of steel by downstream industries. South Africa's industrial policy priorities suggest that the decisions taken by policymakers should have prioritized the downstream industries.

In addition to influencing policy decisions, firms are able to use other strategies to capture value. Extraction of rents by AMSA was evident from the outflows of funds from AMSA to its shareholders, even in the face of rising inefficiencies. This included substantial payments related to the Business Assistance Agreement (BAA) in 2003 and 2004 (which exclude BAA remuneration received in the form of Iscor shares), dividend outflows, and fees remitted to the parent company for 'corporate services' from 2008 and 'research and development' from 2009. In total, between 2001 and 2015 the recorded flow of funds out of AMSA to its shareholders amounted to R21.8 billion (or US$1.3 billion),[10] of which 63 per cent accrued to the ArcelorMittal global group (Zalk, 2017).

AMSA has also attempted to vertically integrate backwards by proposing a black economic empowerment (BEE) deal with Imperial Crown Trading (ICT) for mineral rights at the Sishen mine, after AMSA's mineral rights at the Sishen mine expired in 2009.[11] The deal would give it access to 21.4 per cent of South Africa's iron ore reserves. This is an example of how BEE, which was intended to redistribute wealth, has been leveraged to further entrench incumbent firm positions (see Chapter 9). The National Union of Metalworkers of South Africa (NUMSA) opposed the transaction, arguing that ICT was co-opted by AMSA in

[9] https://www.cbn.co.za/opinion/mittal-vs-the-downstream-steel-industry-war/.
[10] Rand amount converted to US dollars using exchange rate as at 28 October 2020 (R1 equivalent to $0.061).
[11] Kumba (the firm that owns the iron ore level of former SOE Iscor) and ArcelorMittal SA were co-owners of the mineral rights at the Sishen mine, holding 78.6 per cent and 21.4 per cent, respectively. Linked to these rights, Kumba supplied AMSA with iron ore at cost plus 3 per cent from the Sishen mine. Kumba cancelled the 2001 contract to supply cheap iron ore when AMSA failed to re-apply for the mining rights with the introduction of the Mineral and Petroleum Resources Development Act.

order to shore up its dominant position, and that the two companies 'colluded with each other and abused their financial muscle and political contacts to obtain mineral rights'.[12] ICT was linked to the Gupta family, a key player in the so-called state capture process during the Zuma presidency, for which investigations are on-going. After a protracted legal battle, the rights were eventually awarded to Kumba.

The issues around pricing of steel to downstream users, outflow of funds from AMSA to the Arcelor Mittal global group, and AMSA's attempt to capture the iron ore rights all show how AMSA has used its power to influence rent management and capture rents in the metals, machinery, and equipment value chain.

The economic power of the steel industry is in part derived from the market power of the steel firms. AMSA has held a dominant position in flat steel and the long steel market is oligopolistic. There have been a series of cases that have been brought to the competition authorities relating to the unilateral exertion of market power by AMSA. These include cases relating to AMSA's pricing to local customers at import-parity levels while charging substantially lower prices to export customers, as described above. In one case, a customer complained that AMSA abused its dominance by charging excessive prices at import parity for flat steel, even though a very large proportion of total production was exported and there were low input prices. The case was lost on appeal, with the Competition Appeal Court deciding that the economic value (competitive benchmark prices) needed to reflect a 'long-run competitive equilibrium'. This has been interpreted as a price necessary to reward capital investment as if made by a greenfield entrant and not considering benefits from historical state support (Roberts, 2008; Das Nair and Mondliwa, 2017).

The case highlights the implications of the state adopting a static neoclassical microeconomic framework that is biased towards allocative efficiency, and which effectively assumes that competition will arise in the absence of constraints. Such a framework does not consider the intrinsic concentration given scale economies, the incremental nature of capability building, and the role of historical state support to underpin the large investments required, which also means entrenching firms' dominant positions. In these conditions, real competition is not promoted through the instruments of competition law enforcement.

8.4.2 The South African Chemicals and Plastics Industry

The petrochemical value chain involves functions ranging from resource extraction (crude oil, coal, and natural gas) and refining through various levels of chemicals processing to produce industrial and consumer products (see

[12] https://www.politicsweb.co.za/documents/arcelormittal-bee-deal-a-looting-scheme—numsa.

Chapter 4). This discussion focuses on how the lead firm in the industry grouping can leverage its economic power to influence rent management and maintain the status quo in terms of value capture in the value chain. There is also an examination of how state support, and regulation and energy policy have shaped the power relations in the industry, as well as the implications for the sectoral deepening that is a necessary component in reducing inequality.

In many of the industries that Sasol has been operating in, it holds monopoly or near monopoly positions. However, Sasol's dominant market position has been further entrenched by various policy and regulatory decisions with weak conditionalities that undermine the productive use of rents which would have wider benefits for the economy.

First, South Africa's petrochemical complex was established around Sasol through a succession of policy levers and regulation, beginning under the apartheid state (Rustomjee, 2012; Mondliwa and Roberts, 2014; Mondliwa and Roberts, 2019; Mondliwa et al., 2020). Various conditionalities on the support were put in place, including a requirement to price chemical intermediate inputs to downstream industries at export-parity levels to support the development of the downstream industry (Mondliwa and Roberts, 2019). These conditionalities were honoured until about 2003, when Sasol was 'effectively' released from prior obligations on state support by the termination of the main mechanism for support, the Main Supply Agreement (Mondliwa and Roberts, 2014). This decision ignored the fact that state support had entrenched Sasol's market position, thus skewing power dynamics in its favour relative to its customers.

Between 1994 and 2019, various arms of government have taken policy and regulatory decisions that have facilitated the firm's further vertical integration and entrenched market power. Analyses of the negotiations of important deals and regulatory outcomes in this period point to a balance of power that tips in Sasol's favour (for detailed descriptions of the main deals see Mondliwa and Roberts, 2017 and 2019). With regards to regulation, South Africa's approach to fuel regulation has assumed away the fact that Sasol produces multiple products and that it can leverage market power across different product markets. Fuel regulation has continued to disproportionately advantage Sasol, as the Windfall Tax Task Team found (2007). This advantage has also filtered through to chemical co-products, as prices are linked to fuel prices. Although this has followed international norms, the generous price regulation has meant that downstream industries have paid higher prices for co-products and by-products, thus undermining their competitiveness (Mondliwa and Roberts, 2019). The regulated fuel price formula has also largely remained unchanged, and still contains notional transport costs from the coast to Sasol's plants in the inland region (Mondliwa and Roberts, 2019). This is effectively a transfer from consumers to Sasol.

The state has also taken decisions that have further entrenched Sasol's market power in chemical markets by supporting its vertical integration into natural gas.

A deal struck with Sasol and the South African and Mozambican governments in 2001 resulted in Sasol becoming the monopoly supplier of natural gas in South Africa.[13] This has two implications. First, an alternative firm could have used the gas to produce goods that could compete with Sasol, giving downstream firms an alternative supplier and thus improving their bargaining power. Second, the regulation of gas prices has been to Sasol's advantage: it has focused on pricing to external customers, while the bulk of the gas was converted into fuel (which was regulated) and chemical products (which were not regulated), so the customers have not received the benefits of the cheap gas (Mondliwa and Roberts, 2019).

The combined effect of these decisions has entrenched Sasol's market position, bestowing on it market power. In turn, the exertion of this market power has shaped the strategies of other value chain participants, including decisions for expansion or technological upgrading (Mondliwa et al., 2020) and its pricing strategies in particular have undermined the development of downstream industries (see Chapter 4).

Sasol's vertical integration has allowed it to leverage market power at specific points of the value chain to determine the terms of participation of other firms. For example, in polymers, Sasol has been both the monopoly supplier of the input and the competitor to Safripol in the supply of polypropylene.[14] Sasol was able to restrain Safripol's ability to expand and colluded with it in the pricing of polypropylene to downstream plastic producers (Mondliwa and Roberts, 2019). The two firms negotiated a supply agreement whereby the price of the propylene input supplied by Sasol was dependent on the price of polypropylene charged by the two producers. This had the impact of indirectly fixing the polypropylene prices in the country and resulted in prices above competitive levels for the downstream plastic products industry. This has allowed Sasol to control value capture in the value chain, skewed towards upstream activities, and resulted in a vicious cycle of low margins, and limited investment in capability upgrading for the downstream plastics industry, thus undermining competitiveness (Chapter 4).

The main mechanism for countering market power in South Africa has been competition law and import competition. In terms of competition law, the excessive pricing case against Sasol in 2014 succeeded at the Competition Tribunal but the decision was overturned by the Competition Appeal Court in 2015. The Appeal Court found that the Competition Tribunal had not allowed a sufficient return on capital. Fortunately, the South African Competition Amendment Act of 2018 (section 8(3)) includes changes to the tests for excessive pricing, including that structural characteristics of the market can now be taken

[13] The deal facilitated the construction of a pipeline from Mozambique to Sasol's plants in South Africa, access to gas from the Pande Temane fields, and low prices.

[14] Safripol (with approximately 20 per cent market share) is a polypropylene producer that competes with Sasol (with approximately 80 per cent market share) and relies on Sasol for propylene inputs. Sasol holds a 94 per cent market share in propylene. Market shares are based on capacity.

into account along with past or current advantages such as state support. Both the SCI and the AMSA case discussed above may have had different outcomes if they had been assessed through the new framing. The amendments also allow for the Minister of Trade, Industry, and Competition to make regulations regarding the calculation and determination of an excessive price.

8.5 Structural Transformation, Economic Power, and Inequality: Insights from a Micro and Meso Analysis

The chapter has examined at the industry level how power relations within and across manufacturing matter for reducing inequality. The move towards higher productivity and high value-added sub-sectors within manufacturing would allow for broad increases in income, which would reduce income inequality. In the South African context, positive structural transformation would mean a move away from minerals-related sub-sectors towards more diversified and labour-absorbing industries with enhanced employment creation, learning, and skill acquisition. The comparative industry assessment has highlighted how in South Africa, inequality has instead been reinforced by the lack of such transformation in key industry groupings.

8.5.1 Structural Transformation Means More Businesses and Jobs, and a Reduction in Inequality

Historically, structural transformation and sectoral deepening within manufacturing have led to increased employment and wages, creating the conditions for more equitable income distribution. A more diversified economy means that there are greater opportunities for people to accumulate, including through better participation of smaller firms and higher prospects of earning an income from employment. Evidence shows that the manufacturing sector has the highest indirect employment multiplier and downstream industries have relatively higher employment multipliers (Tregenna, 2012).

Historically South African industry has largely been resource-based, and this has not changed in the post-apartheid period, with little evidence of growth in broader manufacturing capabilities. The economy has displayed high levels of concentration, and instances of entry of new and dynamic businesses to rival established incumbents have been scant (Vilakazi et al., 2020). Furthermore, the shift of the economy towards sectors that employ more skilled workers and the tertiary sector (Bhorat et al., 2020) has impacted negatively on inequality outcomes. Skilled workers have attracted a high salary premium while the tertiary sector has a large vertical pay differential, with the majority of the jobs being low-paying (Mondliwa and Roberts, 2018; Bhorat et al., 2020).

At a macro level, large firms have been relatively more successful in shaping the policy agenda, as is evident in the overarching economic policies adopted. This has largely been done by their influencing the ideology that has underpinned economic policymaking. For instance, it was argued that the market-leaning policies that were implemented when apartheid ended would serve as a counterbalancing force to the apartheid government's support for large-scale capital-intensive industries and the history of poor productivity (Joffe et al., 1995; Hanival and Hirsch, 1998; Ponte et al., 2007). In particular, the expectation was that internationalization and the reduction of tariffs would spur the development of non-traditional manufactured exports—as with increased competition and a more international orientation, transnational corporations (TNCs) would invest and upgrade technology, thus improving the competitiveness of domestic industries. Even though the high levels of concentration in the economy were identified as a potential challenge for diversification, it was expected that both import competition and competition law would constrain market power (Joffe et al., 1995). However, competition law itself was shaped by the market ideologies of the time,[15] and in retrospect, it has become clear that the market policies adopted primarily served the existing participants in the economy. Despite the low growth of the economy and investment levels, profit levels have been sustained (OECD, 2013).

The outcomes described in the two industry studies, consistent with economy-wide reviews (Bell et al., 2018; Driver, 2019), demonstrate the ineffectiveness of market liberalization for engaging with the power of entrenched dominant firms. In both the metals, machinery, and equipment, and the chemicals to plastics industry groupings, the economic power of the lead firms contributed to the slow pace of sectoral deepening. This is evident in three ways. First, the lead firms in these value chains have been able to leverage market power to increase input prices for the downstream industries. The higher input prices effectively transfer value to the upstream levels where the gains are shared by a smaller group. The higher prices are detrimental for the competitiveness of the downstream industries, which can lead to poorer performance and a decline in employment. This has direct implications for inequality both in terms of incomes from wages and wealth creation from returns to equity. The abuse of this market power can also lead to a direct transfer from the poor to the rich. While some degree of market

[15] The 1995 draft paper on competition advised that competition policy should not be used to break up the conglomerates as a means of advancing black economic interests, with the implication being that BEE and the unbundling of conglomerates should be pursued separately (Michie and Padayachee, 1997). This decision and the subsequent design of the BEE system has been unsuccessful in promoting independent black-owned businesses and has not resulted in meaningful empowerment (Ponte et al., 2007).

concentration is desirable for investment and innovation purposes, market power is often associated with poor outcomes if left unchecked.

Despite its dominance in steel production, AMSA has improved neither investments, nor the range or quality of its products, while it has priced steel at import parity despite significant steel exports. The unfavourable pricing of steel, and lack of investment to improve the quality and range of products has meant that downstream businesses have not benefited from the government's support of the upstream. The internationalization and financialization of both Sasol and AMSA has also meant that much of the value created by domestic rents have been transferred out of the economy. Both Sasol and AMSA increased dividends payouts on internationalization (see Zalk (2017) for details on AMSA, and Chapter 10 for details on Sasol).

The second way in which the economic power of the lead firms has contributed to the slow pace of sectoral deepening is that the current economic structure bestows economic power on upstream firms that have been deemed 'too big to fail' in some instances. This is particularly the case in the metals, machinery, and equipment value chain, where AMSA has continued to extract rents from the state, including import tariffs. The support rendered to AMSA has come at the expense of the downstream industries, which have been identified as being critical for more inclusive development. The importance that has been placed on the steel industry in the prevailing structure has undermined the interests of the downstream firms, which are also relatively less organized to push effectively for their interests.

Third, conditionalities are critical for ensuring that rents created by state support are productive and that there are wider benefits for the economy. In both the value chains analysed, the conditionalities have either been weak or poorly enforced, making rents created susceptible to being extractive rather than productive. The case studies have further revealed that the state acts more as an arena where conflicts for value capture take place rather than a power player in itself. The interests of the lead firms have triumphed in part due to the good organization at these levels, while downstream firms have been relatively less organized and the economically excluded have relied on the government to represent their interests.

The structural regression in these value chains in South Africa has had negative implications for business and employment creation, and therefore inequality outcomes. In both value chains, there has been significant potential for employment growth within the more dynamic and robust downstream industries, including the potential for entrants to develop and thrive—which would support the reduction of both income and wealth inequality. Roberts and Nkhonjera (2019) estimated that there is potential for direct employment growth of 65,000 jobs and another 325,000[16] jobs in related activities due to multiplier effects, by

---

[16] This is significant, given that total manufacturing employment was 1.5 million in 2018 (the base year for the estimation).

increasing local machinery production by more than 50 per cent in order to regain the market share that South Africa was enjoying in the regional market in around 2010. Similarly, in plastics, Beare and colleagues (2014) estimated that the plastics industry had the potential to create another 20,000 direct jobs in South Africa. These are sizeable figures in an economy which has failed to create significant numbers of jobs. However, generating more jobs would require significant government support for existing and new firms in these downstream industries. Apart from incomes for new workers, the wealth creation for new and expanded businesses and the wider consumption effects would all contribute to a reduction in inequality.

8.5.2 The Role of the Politics behind Policies and Institutions

South Africa has developed a significant base upon which industrialization could have been better effected, leading to a reduction in inequality. Why this has not happened is indeed the question. While there have been some policies and interventions to support new and more dynamic businesses, these have had little effect on the structure of the economy and the dominance of incumbent firms. Looking at the role of political economy, and more specifically, the role of political settlements in keeping the status quo and the impact of this on the ability to accumulate and therefore on inequality, goes some way to answering it.

As the case studies show, the economic power of dominant firms like AMSA and Sasol has allowed, these firms to reinforce their dominant positions through lobbying policies and regulations in their favour. Sectoral deepening within the metals, machinery and equipment, and chemicals-to-plastics value chains policies that support capability development and technology upgrading at the downstream level, and power dynamics that support diversification of the value chain. The case studies have shown how economic power within these value chains has been leveraged to influence the kinds of policies that have been adopted, which businesses have received support, and what kinds of support, and rent management and the capturing of rents.

There has been insufficient engagement in South Africa about how to reorient large businesses that dominate the economy for the purposes of more inclusive growth. In particular, insufficient attention has been given to the underlying power dynamics and how they have influenced and continue to influence outcomes in the economy. Instruments like competition law have had muted impacts, particularly for dealing with abuse of dominance by large incumbent firms (Roberts, 2020). In part this has been due to the design of the competition law, which was itself an outcome of negotiations between large businesses, government, and labour. Focusing simply on competition law does not deal with the ability of large firms to lobby agencies of government to shape regulations in their favour; nor does it address market failures in access to finance. Re-industrialization of the economy would require an engagement with these dynamics, in order to analyse how outcomes have been and continue to be influenced.

Strategies for better inclusion would be more effective if the need for appropriate design of policies and institutions across different political settlements is better understood. Policy and institutions should be designed and implemented so that conditions that would hurt firms if they fail to deliver results can be credibly enforced. One way to do this is for policy to promise sufficient ex-post rents to give a high return for risky investments (Khan, 2018a). Furthermore, as Khan (2018a) further observes, policy prescripts should be realistic in tackling value chains individually: countries like South Africa do not have the political and institutional capacity to support development across a broad range of sectors at once, as this would require disciplining *ex ante* policy rents to a broad range of businesses in various sectors.

References

Amsden, A. and Singh, A. (1994). 'The optimal degree of competition and dynamic efficiency in Japan and Korea.' *European Economic Review* 38: 940–51.

Baymul, C. and K. Sen (2019). 'Kuznets revisited: what do we know about the relationship between structural transformation and inequality?' *Asian Development Review* 36(1): 136–67.

Baymul, C. and K. Sen (2020). 'Was Kuznets right? New evidence on the relationship between structural transformation and inequality.' *The Journal of Development Studies* 56(9): 1643–62.

Beare, M., P. Mondliwa, G. Robb, and S. Roberts (2014). 'Report for the plastics conversion industry strategy.' Research Report prepared for the Department of Trade and Industry.

Behuria, P., L. Buur, and H. Gray (2017). 'Studying political settlements in Africa.' *African Affairs* 116(464): 508–25.

Bell, J., S. Goga, P. Mondliwa, and S. Roberts (2018). 'Structural Transformation in South Africa: moving towards a smart, open economy for all.' CCRED Working Paper 9/2018. Johannesburg: CCRED.

Berg, A. G. and J. D. Ostry (2017). 'Inequality and unsustainable growth: two sides of the same coin?' *IMF Economic Review* 65(4): 792–815.

Bhorat, H., K. Lilenstein, M. Oosthuizen, and A. Thornton (2020). 'Structural transformation, inequality, and inclusive growth in South Africa.' No. wp-2020-50. World Institute for Development Economic Research (UNU-WIDER). Helsinki: UNU-WIDER.

Black, A., S. Craig, and P. Dunne (2016). 'Capital intensity, industrial policy, and employment in the South African manufacturing sector.' Working Paper 23. REDI 3x3.

Black, A. and H. Hasson (2016). 'Capital-intensive industrialisation, comparative advantage and industrial policy.' In A. Black (ed.), *Towards Employment Intensive Growth in South Africa*. Cape Town: University of Cape Town Press.

Black, A. and S. Roberts (2009). 'The evolution and impact of industrial and competition policies.' In J. Aron, B. Kahn, and G. Kingdon (eds), *South African Economic Policy under Democracy*. Oxford: Oxford University Press.

Chatterjee, A., L. Czajka, and A. Gethin (2020). 'Estimating the distribution of household wealth in South Africa.' WIDER Working Paper 2020/45. Helsinki: UNU-WIDER.

Cingano, F. (2014). 'Trends in income inequality and its impact on economic growth.' OECD Social, Employment and Migration Working Papers, no. 163. Paris: OECD Publishing.

Dahl, R. A. (1957). 'The concept of power.' *Behavioral Science* 2(3): 201–15.

Dallas, M. P., S. Ponte, and T. J. Sturgeon (2019). 'Power in global value chains.' *Review of International Political Economy* 26(4): 666–94.

Das Nair, R. and P. Mondliwa (2017). 'Excessive pricing under the spotlight: what is a competitive price?' In J. Klaaren, S. Roberts, and I. Valodia (eds), *Competition Law and Economic Regulation: Addressing Market Power in Southern Africa*. Johannesburg: Wits University Press.

Di John, J. and J. Putzel (2009). 'Political settlements.' Issues Paper.

Doner, R. F. and B. R. Schneider (2016). 'The middle-income trap: more politics than economics.' *World Politics* 68(4): 608–44.

Doyle, M. W. and J. E. Stiglitz (2014). 'Eliminating extreme inequality: a sustainable development goal, 2015–2030.' *Ethics & International Affairs* 28(1): 5–13.

Driver, C. (2019). 'Trade liberalization and South African manufacturing: looking back with data.' WIDER Working Paper 2019/30. Helsinki: UNU-WIDER.

Ennis, S. F., P. Gonzaga, and C. Pike (2019). 'Inequality: a hidden cost of market power.' *Oxford Review of Economic Policy* 35(3): 518–49.

Freund, B. (2018). *Twentieth-Century South Africa: A Developmental History*. Cambridge: Cambridge University Press.

Goga, S., P. Mondliwa, and S. Roberts (2020). 'Economic power and regulation: the political economy of metals, machinery and equipment industries in South Africa.' In D. Francis, I. Valodia, and E. Webster (eds), *Inequality Studies from the Global South*. London: Routledge.

Gray, H. (2018). *Turbulence and Order in Economic Development: Institutions and Economic Transformation in Tanzania and Vietnam*. Oxford: Oxford University Press.

Hanival, S. and A. Hirsch (1998). 'Industrial policy and programmes in South Africa.' TIPS Forum Paper, April 1998.

Hartmann, D., M. R. Guevara, C. Jara-Figueroa, M. Aristarán, and C. A. Hidalgo (2017). 'Linking economic complexity, institutions, and income inequality.' *World Development* 93: 75–93.

Joffe, A., D. Kaplan, R. Kaplinsky, and D. Lewis (1995). 'Improving manufacturing performance in South Africa.' Report of the Industrial Strategy Project. http://www.idrc.ca/EN/Resources/Publications/openebooks/4395/index.html#page_250. Accessed 15 June 2020.

Khan, L. M. and S. Vaheesan (2017). 'Market power and inequality: the antitrust counterrevolution and its discontents.' *Harvard Law and Policy Review* 11: 235.

Khan, M. H. (2010). 'Political settlements and the governance of growth-enhancing institutions.' Unpublished.

Khan, M. H. (2018a). 'Institutions and Asia's development: the role of norms and organizational power.' WIDER Working Paper 2018/132. Helsinki: UNU-WIDER.

Khan, M. H. (2018b). 'Political settlements and the analysis of institutions.' *African Affairs* 117(469): 636–55.

Khan, M. H. (2018c). 'Power, pacts and political settlements: a reply to Tim Kelsall.' *African Affairs* 117(469): 670–94.

Kuznets, S. (1955). 'Economic growth and income inequality.' *The American Economic Review* 45(1): 1–28.

Lavopa, A. and A. Szirmai (2012). 'Industrialization, employment and poverty.' UNU-MERIT Working Paper Series 2012-081. Maastricht, The Netherlands: United Nations University, Maastricht Economic and Social Research Institute on Innovation and Technology.

Michie, J. and V. Padayachee (1997). *South Africa's Transition: The Policy Agenda.* London: Dryden Press.

Mondliwa, P. (2018). 'Capabilities, diversification and market power in industrial development: a case study of South African manufacturing and the plastics industry.' MCom dissertation. Johannesburg: University of Johannesburg.

Mondliwa, P., S. Goga, and S. Roberts (2021). 'Competition, productive capabilities and structural transformation in South Africa.' *The European Journal of Development Research* 33(2): 253–74.

Mondliwa, P., S. Ponte, and S. Roberts (2020). 'Competition and power in global value chains.' *Competition and Change* online, DOI:10.1177%2F1024529420975154.

Mondliwa, P. and S. Roberts (2014). 'Excessive pricing and industrial development: the recent Competition Tribunal finding against Sasol Chemical Industries.' *New Agenda: South African Journal of Social and Economic Policy* 55: 48–51.

Mondliwa, P. and S. Roberts (2017). 'Economic benefits of Mozambique gas for Sasol and the South African government.' Working Paper 23/2017. Centre for Competition, Regulation and Economic Development. Johannesburg: University of Johannesburg.

Mondliwa, P. and S. Roberts (2018). 'Rewriting the rules governing the South African economy: a new political settlement for industrial development.' Industrial Development Think Tank Policy Brief 10, Centre for Competition, Regulation and Economic Development.

Mondliwa, P. and S. Roberts (2019). 'From a developmental to a regulatory state? Sasol and the conundrum of continued state support.' *International Review of Applied Economics* 33(1): 11–29.

Organisation for Economic Co-operation and Development (OECD) (2013). *OECD Economic Surveys: South Africa 2013*. Paris: OECD Publishing.

Ponte, S., S. Roberts, and L. Van Sittert (2007). '"Black economic empowerment": business and the state in South Africa.' *Development and Change* 38(5): 933–55.

Roberts, S. (2000). 'Understanding the effects of trade policy reform: the case of South Africa.' *South African Journal of Economics* 68(4): 270–81.

Roberts, S. (2008). 'Assessing excessive pricing: the case of flat steel in South Africa.' *Journal of Competition Law and Economics* 4: 871–91.

Roberts, S. (2020). 'Assessing the record of competition law enforcement in opening up the economy.' In T. Vilakazi, S. Goga, and S. Roberts (eds), *Opening the South African Economy: Barriers to Entry and Competition*. Cape Town: HSRC Press.

Roberts, S. and M. Nkhonjera (2019). 'Sectoral perspective for machinery and equipment.' Industrial Development Think Tank. Johannesburg.

Roberts, S. and Z. Rustomjee (2009). 'Industrial policy under democracy: apartheid's grown-up infant industries? Iscor and Sasol.' *Transformation* 71: 50–75.

Robinson, I. (2016). 'The globalization of the South African mining industry.' *Journal of the Southern African Institute of Mining and Metallurgy* 116(8): 769–75.

Rustomjee, Z. (2012). 'Witness statement in Competition Commission V Sasol Chemical Industries.' Case Number 48/Cr/Aug10 (Non-Confidential). Competition Tribunal.

Rustomjee, Z., L. Kaziboni, and I. Steuart (2018). 'Structural transformation along metals, machinery and equipment value chain—developing capabilities in the metals and machinery segments.' Industrial Development Think Tank Report. Johannesburg.

Tregenna, F. (2012). 'Sources of subsectoral growth in South Africa.' *Oxford Development Studies* 40(2): 162–89.

United Nations Industrial Development Organization (UNIDO) (2013). 'Sustaining employment growth: the role of manufacturing and structural change.' Industrial Development Report 2013. Vienna: UNIDO.

Vilakazi, T., S. Goga, and S. Roberts, eds (2020). *Opening the South African Economy: Barriers to Entry and Competition*. Cape Town: HSRC Press.

Webster, E., I. Valodia, and D. Francis (2020). 'Towards a Southern approach to inequality: inequality studies in South Africa and the global South.' In D. Francis, I. Valodia, and E. Webster (eds), *Inequality Studies from the Global South*, 1–19. Abingdon: Routledge.

Weiss, J. (2013). 'Industrial policy in the twenty-first century: challenges for the future.' In A. Szirmai, W. Naude, and L. Alcorta (eds), *Pathways to Industrialization in the Twenty-First Century: New Challenges and Emerging Paradigms*. Oxford: Oxford University Press.

World Bank. (2018). 'Overcoming poverty and inequality in South Africa: an assessment of drivers, constraints and opportunities.' Washington, DC: World Bank.

Zalk, N. (2017). 'The things we lost in the fire: the political economy of post-apartheid restructuring of the South African steel and engineering sectors.' Unpublished PhD thesis. Department of Economics, School of Oriental and African Studies, University of London.

Zingales, L. (2017). 'Towards a political theory of the firm.' *Journal of Economic Perspectives* 31(3): 113–30.

9

Black Economic Empowerment, Barriers to Entry, and Economic Transformation in South Africa

Thando Vilakazi and Teboho Bosiu

9.1 Introduction

Economic growth requires structural transformation of the economy, and growing the manufacturing sector in particular (Tregenna, 2008; McMillan and Rodrik, 2011; Felipe et al., 2012). As set out in the introductory chapters of this volume, for South Africa this means diversifying investments and economic activity away from upstream capital-intensive industries to value-added and labour-absorptive downstream industries, which have the potential to increase employment and productivity (Tregenna, 2008; Hartman et al., 2017; Baymul and Sen, 2018). Rivalry from local or foreign rivals can lead to dynamic gains in productivity and investments in improved capabilities, which are also associated with structural transformation (McMillan and Rodrik, 2011). However, the evidence in South Africa is that rivalry is restricted by high barriers to entry in key economic sectors. These are especially high for black-owned firms (Vilakazi et al., 2020).

The chapter develops the insight that racial transformation and addressing barriers to entry (generally, and for black South Africans in particular) are critical for structural transformation of the economy. It does this in three key parts. First, in section 9.2, the chapter sets the scene by drawing on the literature to show that economic inclusion and rivalry, and racial transformation of the economy, are critical for structural transformation to be achieved in South Africa. Second, in section 9.3, the evolution of South Africa's black economic empowerment (BEE) policy is assessed in terms of how it has been implemented and the challenges it has faced. This includes the shift to broad-based black economic empowerment (BBBEE).

Third, in section 9.4 the chapter presents a case study of the South African government's black industrialists scheme (BIS) as an important development and alternative to the approach adopted with BBBEE. The BIS is an industrial policy

Thando Vilakazi and Teboho Bosiu, *Black Economic Empowerment, Barriers to Entry, and Economic Transformation in South Africa* In: *Structural Transformation in South Africa: The Challenges of Inclusive Industrial Development in a Middle-Income Country*. Edited by: Antonio Andreoni, Pamela Mondliwa, Simon Roberts, and Fiona Tregenna, Oxford University Press. © Oxford University Press 2021. DOI: 10.1093/oso/9780192894311.003.0009

tool focused on targeted funding and non-financial support of 'black industrialists' (BIs) involved in value-adding manufacturing activities. Although it is relatively soon after its implementation in 2016, evidence from a survey of applicants to the programme demonstrates its strong potential for enhancing both the structural and racial transformation of the economy. The scheme's design and intended focus is specifically on fostering competitive black-owned companies in the manufacturing sector.

9.2 Setting the Scene: Why Inclusion and Black Economic Empowerment Matter for Structural Transformation

Drawing from the existing literature this section sets out the ways in which rivalry and inclusion are important parts of the process of structural transformation, with specific reference to South Africa. The key point is that the inclusion of black people is critical for structural transformation to take place.

9.2.1 Rivalry and Inclusion Matter for Structural Transformation

The competitive process can drive economic efficiency and higher productivity. Rivalry between businesses is important as it enlists firms to intensify effort and create new products and business models to improve their own offering, and ensures a sharper focus on businesses finding ways of deriving productive and dynamic efficiencies (Roberts, 2010). While markets are inherently imperfect, forms of competitive discipline arising from the threat of entry, regulations, or exposure to foreign competition and international export markets can ensure that firms retain the economic incentive to improve their competitiveness, even in concentrated industries (Amsden, 1989; Singh, 2002; Roberts, 2010; McMillan and Rodrik, 2011). The gains from competition are therefore dynamic and linked to investments in capabilities, technological upgrading, and shifts to the production of more complex products.

In South Africa, however, investment and growth in productivity have been hampered by high levels of concentration and barriers to entry (Vilakazi et al., 2020). In some cases, the exercise of market power upstream, which is reinforced by government policies that effectively protect incumbency, can mean that competition and investment in adjacent markets are stifled (Mondliwa and Roberts, 2019). In addition, international competition and openness have not served to stimulate rivalry and discipline the market power of large local businesses, and the economy remains highly concentrated (see Bell et al., 2018; Bell and Goga, 2020; Goga et al., 2020). Notwithstanding the enforcement of competition law, there is a growing evidence base that shows that substantial barriers to the entry and growth of rivals remain, which prevent them from effectively contesting the market and undermining the economic rents being earned by incumbents (Vilakazi et al., 2020).

While large firms are important for realizing economies of scale and scope and making necessary investments for upgrading, they need rivals to spur them on to do so. A lack of an optimal degree of competition to discipline market power enhances inequality, in that concentration forms the basis of rents, wealth, and the returns from ownership of assets and resources for the rich in societies (Baker and Salop, 2015; Ennis et al., 2019). Barriers to entry and market power are therefore directly and indirectly linked with inequality (Chapter 8).

The implications are that improving productivity and competition requires a strong role for industrial policies that are aligned with effective BEE policies. Such policies are important to stimulate the entry of new rivals at sufficient scale and with capabilities to contest markets with established rivals, as part of driving structural transformation of the economy. Equity and efficiency do not necessarily pull in opposite directions, as had come to be understood from classic welfare economics (Atkinson, 2015: 246). Here, rather, it is suggested that the objectives of increasing participation and rivalry, while promoting productive growth and structural transformation, can go hand in hand. Indeed, rivalry from different sources is a key component in driving improvements in productivity and driving structural change.

Moreover, inequality undermines social cohesion (Atkinson, 2015). In South Africa, this is especially the case given that inequality in wealth and income occurs along racial lines—more than 90 per cent of the population are black (Stats SA, 2020), but ownership of economic assets and wealth is skewed heavily towards white South Africans (Chatterjee et al., 2020). Furthermore, recent evidence shows that while barriers to entry are high in general, they are especially high for black businesspeople. This serves to reinforce the lack of dynamism in the economy and the high levels of economic concentration and control by leading white-owned firms (Vilakazi et al., 2020; Vilakazi and Ponte, 2020; Bosiu et al., 2020). As such, the political economy of inclusion and affirmative action in South Africa is inseparable from economic policymaking and market outcomes.

9.2.2 Racial Transformation of the Economy Is Necessary for Structural Transformation

The emphasis on racial transformation as part of economic policymaking in South Africa is similar to the context of affirmative action and indigenization policies in other countries addressing a colonial legacy, such as Malaysia. In fact, it is not that different from many policies in other countries that are designed to improve the economic position of marginalized groups, including South Africa's apartheid-era policies for the empowerment of Afrikaners in the mid-1900s (Terreblanche, 2002; Gqubule, 2006; MacDonald, 2006; Von Holdt, 2019). Experiences with affirmative action, in particular, are well documented in the literature (see, for example, Gqubule, 2006; Lee, 2015). These are not canvassed in this chapter, except to note that in Malaysia, affirmative action policies contributed to the economic upliftment of the marginalized majority Bumiputera population, particularly in the education sector. However, as in South Africa, there remain concerns about rent-seeking, fronting, and lack of transformation in the ownership of wealth (Lee, 2015). This is not surprising as economic policies to achieve empowerment of economically marginalized groups are necessarily deeply politicized.

Economic exclusion and its social consequences and drivers speak to the sustainability and stability of a country's political settlement (Gqubule, 2006; Lee, 2015; Khan, 2017; and Chapter 14). As such, in the South African context for structural transformation of the economy to be sustained it will depend on the ability to ensure that the pattern of growth and diversification of the economy is inclusive in terms of its racial dynamics. At the simplest level, opening up markets for new and/or black-owned firms and forging a black capitalist elite has been critical for sustaining and stabilizing the political settlement (Hirsch, 2005; MacDonald, 2006; Von Holdt, 2019; Mondliwa and Roberts, 2020). It can also lead to potentially better economic outcomes arising from more economic dynamism and contestation (Vilakazi et al., 2020)—both of which can have a positive impact on structural transformation. In addition, the path of structural change needs to enable large-scale inclusion of the black majority through emphasis on more diversified industries and the steering of investments in the economy towards labour-absorptive sectors, which also tend to have lower barriers to entry.

This brief overview of the interlinkages between inclusion, racial transformation, and structural transformation shows that policies focused on each of these areas are closely related and mutually reinforcing. Building on this framework, the following section analyses the challenges with the approach taken with BBBEE, and provides insights into its inability, to-date, to address specific barriers to entry and expansion.

9.3 The Evolution and Challenges of Black Economic Empowerment and Fostering Meaningful Black Participation in the Economy: An Overview

Black economic empowerment (BEE) was defined by the South African government in 2003 as 'an integrated and coherent socioeconomic process that directly contributes to the economic transformation of South Africa and brings about significant increases in the number of black people who manage, own and control the country's economy, as well as significant decreases in income inequalities' (DTI, 2003).[1] At the heart of BEE philosophy was an ambition to foster an economy in which black South Africans, who had been previously marginalized by apartheid government policies from long before the 1990s (Terreblanche, 2002), were able to participate 'meaningfully' in all aspects of economic life, including as owners of capital.

BEE policy became one part of a wider nexus of policies to drive socioeconomic transformation in terms of land ownership, public procurement, employment conditions, and skills and training (DTI, 2003). Of all these, BEE policy was undoubtedly important for driving racial transformation of the economy—not least because it targeted widespread changes in ownership within existing, largely white-owned businesses. Other policies, such as those relating to skills development, were arguably less direct in terms of their symbolic and political impact.

As such, expectations of BEE were high and there has been extensive scrutiny of its outcomes. A rich body of literature, which is only selectively drawn on here, has reviewed BEE and the government's incremental policy shifts over time towards a more 'broad-based' conception of empowerment (BEECom, 2001; Hirsch, 2005; Gqubule, 2006; Freund, 2007; Ponte et al., 2007; Southall, 2007; Hamann et al., 2008; Tangri and Southall, 2008; Sartorius and Botha, 2008; Patel and Graham, 2012; Mebratie and Bedi, 2013; Bracking, 2019; and Mondliwa and Roberts, 2020).

9.3.1   1994–2003: No Mandatory Compliance

Despite the widespread recognition among ruling, political, and business elites that black inclusion needed to be achieved as part of the settlement reached leading up to and after the democratic transition in 1994, there was surprisingly little specificity in policy about how this would be done (Hirsch, 2005). Various large businesses took the lead from as early as 1993 in structuring partnerships with black businesspeople, some connected with the ruling party, to sell equity stakes in established white businesses to consortia of black businesses and businesspeople. A notable transaction was by Sanlam, one of the largest conglomerate insurance and financial services groups, which sold 10 per cent of Metropolitan Life to a black-owned consortium called Methold, which was later renamed as New Africa Investments Limited (Gqubule, 2006). Many similar initiatives were concluded in the 1990s. These became known as 'BEE deals',

---

[1] In the BBBEE Act of 2013, black people are defined as Africans, Coloureds, and Indians who are citizens of South Africa by birth or descent; or who became citizens by naturalization in different defined parameters.

which denoted the transactions through which BEE firms and consortia would acquire stakes in existing firms as BEE partners.

The manner in which this process evolved in the 1990s revealed a number of fundamental issues that would require government attention. First, it was obvious that white businesses were offloading many non-core business assets to black empowerment partners, in highly leveraged empowerment transactions. This put the consortia into extremely indebted positions and exposed them to volatility in economic conditions in sectors such as mining, which meant that their returns from the deals were neither stable nor significant (Ponte et al., 2007; Southall, 2007; Tangri and Southall, 2008; Patel and Graham, 2012). In addition, the overseas listings of some of the major conglomerate groups meant pressure from overseas shareholders to focus on more clearly identified areas of 'core business' (Chabane et al., 2006; Ponte et al., 2007; and Chapter 10). One way of doing this was to sell non-core assets to the black business groups, claiming credit for being engaged in empowerment transactions, while at the same time organizing finance for these groups at full commercial rates (Ponte et al., 2007; Mondliwa and Roberts, 2020).

Second, there were almost no black businesses that had access to significant capital to make investments. This meant that only a few black individuals and their companies emerged as leading black partners for various deals, including some that were clearly linked to the ruling party (Gqubule, 2006; Southall, 2007). Arguably, businesses also targeted partnerships with these connected businesspeople because it meant that they could leverage these links to lobby for favourable policies in particular economic sectors.

Third, there was no legal compulsion for white businesses to consider deals or other strategies for including black businesspeople, because there was no clear policy or mandatory compliance with BEE. This was in spite of the fact that legislation had been developed for the formalization of transformation in other areas, such as, employment equity, a land rights process, and black inclusion through preferential procurement (DTI, 2003).

A report released by the BEE Commission, which had been set up in 1998 under the auspices of the Black Business Council, was submitted to President Mbeki in 2001. It highlighted in detail the range of concerns about the manner in which transformation had taken place since the democratic transition. These included disenchantment with the fact that there was no policy direction, no formal voice for black business, the fact that white businesses had led the BEE agenda on their own terms, and that transformation had been narrowly defined (BEECom, 2001).

In some sectors, established businesses tried to anticipate the changes that would come, and address the biggest concerns by agreeing to sector charters— arguably to head off more aggressive policy interventions by government to drive transformation at the sectoral level. The first two sector charters were in the liquid fuels and petroleum value chains, and in mining (Bowman, 2019). Both included voluntary commitments by firms to broaden the scope of empowerment initiatives from a focus on ownership transfers to black inclusion in management and company value chains and structures (Hirsch, 2005; Gqubule, 2006). Notably, these early charters were in regulated sectors where government had relatively strong leverage in terms of how it could use sector regulations to drive more radical reforms (Ponte et al., 2007; Bowman, 2019).

9.3.2 2003–19: Formal BEE Legislation and Successive Amendments

The Broad-Based Black Economic Empowerment (BBBEE) Act of 2003 represented an important change. After 2003, most empowerment transactions or BEE deals became more broad-based, in line with the Act. This was a significant development from the early forms of black empowerment of the 1990s (Hirsch, 2005; Gqubule, 2006).

In response to some of these core criticisms of the manner in which empowerment had evolved since 1994, particularly the view that BEE had only benefited a few, the notion of black empowerment in the BBBEE Act was expanded beyond what was effectively a focus on ownership in the 1990s, to include seven dimensions of empowerment (BEECom, 2001; DTI, 2003).[2] The government strategy that was published by the Department of Trade, Industry, and Competition (DTIC) in 2003 emerged partly as a result of the BEE Commission's findings, which were endorsed by the president, and set in motion a process of formalizing and codifying empowerment (DTI, 2003). There was also an attempt to consolidate BBBEE through the issuing of Codes of Good Practice to provide the basis for a generic scorecard against which firms' empowerment credentials would be measured when they competed for government contracts (Gqubule, 2006; Southall, 2007; Tangri and Southall, 2008). Importantly, however, compliance with these new provisions was not compulsory and there were no legal penalties on firms for failing to comply.

Even after the first BEE legislation was enacted in 2003, there was arguably limited commitment from the private sector to implement it. Many companies, particularly those not reliant on government contracts or licences, have failed to meet BEE requirements for various reasons, including the lack of an economic incentive to do so (Tangri and Southall, 2008; Mondliwa and Roberts, 2020). This has been recognized in the subsequent reviews of progress with BEE by the BBBEE Commission and others (BBBEE Commission, 2017a). In addition, the

---

[2] The seven areas were human resource development, employment equity, enterprise development, preferential procurement, as well as investment, ownership and control of enterprises, and economic assets.

model of equity acquisitions by black business and groups has failed because many of those acquisitions were based on loans that left real economic control and returns in the hands of the established corporations (Southall, 2007; Tangri and Southall, 2008; Mondliwa and Roberts, 2020).

Large proportions of the private sector were also being excluded from having to comply with BEE, in different ways. While this may be justifiable as a reason for not wanting to disadvantage smaller entities with disproportionate compliance obligations, it did mean that only some firms had to bear the costs and responsibilities of putting in place transformation programmes. The practice from the early 2000s was that companies with relatively small annual turnovers did not have to comply with any of the BEE requirements (Tangri and Southall, 2008; BBBEE Commission, 2017a); and medium-sized companies could initially choose four from the seven (previously five from seven) scorecard components to comply with (Tangri and Southall, 2008). Larger companies could pick up points for spending on corporate social investment schemes such as rural development and social upliftment initiatives, which may have been helpful to society in general terms (such as supporting youth education schemes) but were often unrelated to the core business of the enterprise. This implied less of a need on the part of white-owned businesses to focus on incorporating black businesses or individuals into their value chains and management structures (Bracking, 2019).

The above concerns were some of the reasons for the 2013 BBBEE Amendment Act. The amendments focused on strengthening enforcement and the monitoring and evaluation of BEE across the board. This was in response to the very poor record of compliance by companies since 2003 (RSA, 2014). A new component was to make all measurement categories compulsory from 2016, with only some accommodations for qualifying small enterprises (Bracking, 2019). The BBBEE Amendment Act of 2013 also led to the establishment of a BBBEE Commission, and strengthened reporting obligations for South African companies and those listed on the Johannesburg Stock Exchange (JSE) (Bracking, 2019). The 2014 amendments to the BBBEE Codes of Good Practice changed the system from seven to five elements: ownership; management control, which combined the previous employment equity and management control elements; skills development; socioeconomic development; and enterprise and supplier development, which combined the previous enterprise development and preferential procurement elements. Importantly, the amendments included minimum targets of a 40 per cent score on ownership, skills development, and enterprise and supplier development, which were identified as priority elements (RSA, 2013).

The changes also increased the credit for and weighting of black ownership from 20 to 25 points in public procurement considerations, introduced a formal definition of fronting and criminal sanctions for it, and increased the weighting of accreditation for efforts to encourage training and black representation in the supply chain in the area of enterprise and supplier development (Bracking, 2019). These changes reflected a greater emphasis on driving compliance and targeting the inclusion of black businesses in value chains. This was undoubtedly a response to shifts in the political settlement and increased agitation within the ruling party under President Zuma for more 'radical' and extensive transformation of the economy—a key tenet of which was economic inclusion of black South Africans (Von Holdt, 2019).

The amendments also gave expression to the need to confront the problematic and cynical culture of compliance—or non-compliance—that had developed. Some white-owned firms blatantly entered into 'fronting' deals to skirt regulations. A common practice was for black business partners to be brought in as 'nameplate' partners to win contracts and create the perception of compliance, thus undermining the spirit of broad-based transformation. To counter this, the amended legislation included a new and specific definition and penalty for fronting. The amended legislation also sought to encourage compliance by introducing the 'once-empowered, always-empowered' provision, which meant that formerly white-owned companies were allowed to retain their empowerment credentials even after their black shareholders had sold their shares, including to white investors (BBBEE Commission, 2017b). While it made it easier for BEE groups to raise finance, it was a potentially problematic shift, however, because it meant that businesses in key economic sectors such as mining and finance—which no doubt lobbied for the changes—would not have the incentive to seek out new BEE partnerships once previous BEE partners had exited. It meant prior gains made through previous BEE deals could be eroded (Gqubule, 2018).

While the amended legislation did lead to a wider participation of black businesses in the economy, its effects were not at the structural level. The challenge posed by the BEE policy agenda was that in its essence it was an attempt to engender a fundamentally interventionist and redistributive social programme—in the form of black economic empowerment—in a wider economic policy context that was fundamentally neoliberal and market-oriented, and in which the control of capital was highly concentrated (Ponte et al., 2007; Southall, 2007; Patel and Graham, 2012). As others have analysed in this volume and elsewhere, this was a very conflicted policy approach, one underpinned by orthodox macroeconomic policy and liberalized trade. There was no clear strategy for how to deal with the legacy of entrenched economic concentration, the power of large firms, high barriers to entry, and the challenge of developing new black industrialists and firms (Chabane et al., 2006; Hamann et al., 2008; Bell et al., 2018).

9.3.3 Despite Changes to BEE Legislation and Policy, Fundamental Problems Persist

9.3.3.1 Persistently High Barriers to Entry and Other Constraints
While the changes to BBBEE policy were significant, a number of the key issues addressed in 2013 were very similar to the concerns raised in 2001 by the BEE

Commission initiated by the Black Business Council. This suggests that only limited progress had been made on the ground. A key problem that persists, up to 2020, is that throughout the economy there is still insufficient focus on the need to address the barriers that inhibit entry in general, and that of black-owned firms in particular. Barriers faced by black businesses are especially high. This is because access to markets and capital for black businesses is made more difficult by exclusion from well-established business networks and value chains, there are reputation and trust issues vis-à-vis white-owned businesses, and there is a history of skewed ownership of productive resources, which means that many black businesspeople struggle to find collateral when applying for business loans (Bosiu et al., 2020; Vilakazi et al., 2020).

As an illustration of the lack of the necessary complementary measures, requiring existing companies to procure from black-owned businesses assumes that these black suppliers both exist and that they have grown enough to be able to supply large firms. And, where they do exist, the BBBEE approach assumes that they are given a fair chance in bidding for contracts with existing firms, or that they are connected to networks that enable them to integrate into value chains and that they are given the opportunity and support to overcome barriers and grow (das Nair et al., 2018; das Nair and Landani, 2020). This is in fact not the case in many value chains analysed in recent research (Bosiu et al., 2020; Vilakazi et al., 2020).

This form of BBBEE also had the major—and probably unintended—consequence that by including black capitalists in the ownership and management of existing large businesses the position of entrenched incumbents has only been reinforced. Aligning the economic incentives of the emerging black middle class with those of the existing capitalists has made it far less likely that black capitalists will agitate for more extensive reforms to address the entrenched racial skewing of capital ownership. Calling for a change to the structure of markets and the need to address concentration more directly would not serve the interests of the large firms from which black businesspeople, elites, and the emerging middle class have been benefiting. The black partners have shared the incentive to protect the established rents of the insiders (Vilakazi and Ponte, 2020).

The BBBEE policy has, therefore, not gone nearly far enough in addressing the complex ways in which outsiders are excluded from economic participation. The principal and mutually reinforcing barriers include lack of access to finance, difficulties integrating into existing value chains, lack of access to inputs, and limited access to key routes to market and large-scale patient finance to enable growth and the achievement of scale economies. These and other constraints are discussed below:

9.3.3.2 Problems with Access to Funding
Foremost among these barriers is the lack of a comprehensive system of industrial financing with provision of adequate 'patient' capital to allow for the time it takes

firms to build capabilities and make large-scale investments. While there is an established network of government development finance institutions (DFIs), their activities have largely been uncoordinated and are not aligned with a central objective of driving structural transformation. In the post-apartheid period in general, the reorientation of government's industrial development initiatives have not successfully supported more diversified industrial activities (Goga et al., 2019).

Funding for the development of downstream linkages has remained relatively weak, despite stated government objectives of increasing beneficiation, strengthening local value chains, and supporting more labour-intensive (and downstream) activities (Maia et al., 2005; Bell et al., 2018). This has been perpetuated by a commercial banking and private equity sector whose lending and investments have been directed at private consumption, household credit, and short-term portfolio interests, rather than at productive fixed investments in the real economy (Bosiu et al., 2017; and Chapter 10). Importantly, black-owned businesses in particular continue to report challenges with access to finance and a problem with DFI institutions that do not steer a proportional share of capital towards black businesses (IDC, 2003 and 2015; Goga et al., 2019; Bosiu et al., 2020; Vilakazi et al., 2020).

9.3.3.3 Poor Coordination of Economic Policy

A further problem is that industrial policy, and competition and empowerment policies have not worked effectively together to address other barriers to entry and racial transformation. For example, it appears that the issue of improving access to routes to market for challenger firms has not been addressed directly by the different policies. This has been acknowledged by the ministry responsible for trade and industry (Bosiu et al., 2020). In practice, these gaps in policy coordination and implementation have effectively meant that laws not specifically intended to effect transformation, such as competition law, have rightly or wrongly been viewed as primary tools for promoting transformation. Competition policy (as opposed to the narrower enforcement of competition law) is an important potential tool to remove strategic barriers preventing black business participation as competitors, as contemplated in the definition of BEE policy discussed earlier. With the 2018 amendments to the Competition Act, greater participation by smaller enterprises and businesses owned by black people, in particular, is also now included in specific provisions relating to anticompetitive conduct.

9.3.3.4 Problems with Gaining Access to Value Chains in Crucial Sectors

There has also not been recognition in policies of the complexity of entering certain value chains in key, labour-absorptive sectors. For example, in order to survive and then compete with established, vertically integrated firms, successful entry into the agroprocessing sector requires finance, skills, and achieving scale economies in activities such as processing and distribution (Bagopi et al., 2016; Nkhonjera, 2020). While incumbent firms have been penalized for engaging in anticompetitive practices in agroprocessing that further raised barriers to entry and limited participation (Mncube, 2014; Nkhonjera, 2020), this needs to be complemented by appropriate measures to support effective entry.

Emerging firms also face challenges in terms of accessing retail shelf space and routes to market, despite the expansion of retail supplier development programmes that have historically been token corporate social investment schemes (das Nair et al., 2018; Chisoro-Dube and das Nair, 2020; das Nair and Landani, 2020). This is a challenge that still confronts black industrialists, in particular, because of the lack of established networks and a proven track record with existing white-owned businesses (Bosiu et al., 2020).

The size of investments required to establish competitive challenger firms is significant, and entry has been difficult in many value chains, even for firms that do have established links with sizeable holding companies (Nkhonjera, 2020). Large-scale entrants have found it difficult to build market share in tightly held sectors (Chisoro-Dube and das Nair, 2020; Nhundu and Makhaya, 2020; Robb, 2020). In many cases, there are difficulties with building a brand and overcoming network effects, first-mover advantages, and high switching costs. However, they also reflect the effective lobbying by insiders for regulations that protect their positions (Nhundu and Makhaya, 2020; Vilakazi and Ponte, 2020). This is in addition to the restrictions that incumbents can impose in relation to the accessing of routes to market and key infrastructure (Paelo et al., 2017; Chisoro-Dube and das Nair, 2020; Mondliwa, 2020; Robb, 2020).

All this shows that the structure of markets and the racial composition of ownership and control has not changed significantly over time, despite the many iterations and amendments to empowerment policies and legislation. Clearly a more focused intervention is needed.

9.4 Rethinking Empowerment towards Structural Transformation in South Africa: New Evidence from the Black Industrialists Scheme

The case study of the black industrialists scheme (BIS) offers key insights into how the failures of BEE policy can be addressed through a sector-oriented strategy for inclusion, which also has a focus on the structural transformation of the economy.[3]

Diversifying the economy in terms of productive activities and control of resources by black South Africans clearly requires new thinking about policies for increasing black participation. The discussion in section 9.2 suggests that a

---

[3] The discussion in this section draws substantially from an underlying working paper (Bosiu et al., 2020). See also DTI (2015).

comprehensive policy approach to achieving structural transformation needs to be closely linked with industrial and competition policies to address barriers that can undermine structural change. This is reinforced by the experience of BEE in practice reviewed in section 9.3, which has highlighted the lack of a policy focus in the early years, ineffective enforcement, low levels of compliance once legislation has been in place, and the lack of coordination with other critical policy areas.

The focus of the BIS, launched in 2016, has been on firms in the manufacturing sector with a high potential to contribute to structural change, including through investments in diversified and medium-technology production activities. Another of its features is its aim to address important barriers related to finance and access to markets, which, as has been argued, are key determinants of effective participation of black-owned businesses. In this section the BIS's design and key outcomes are evaluated, followed by a discussion of the cross-cutting implications of key policy gaps for barriers to entry.

9.4.1 Key Features of the Black Industrialists Scheme

The rationale of the BIS is that the development of the manufacturing sector through the production of higher-value products, creating employment, and broadening black participation within it, is critical for establishing a new economic growth trajectory for South Africa (NCOP, 2016). Early discussions around the BIS began in the mid-2000s, although the BIS policy was only launched publicly in February 2016. Importantly, at the core of the rationale for the programme is an evolution in the strategy for BEE (without displacing BBBEE laws), as reflected in the parliamentary summary of the inputs of the Director General of the Department of Trade, Industry, and Competition (DTIC, formerly DTI), Lionel October:

> [T]he first step for the DTI had been to transform existing enterprises to assist the black majority in entering the market. This was the rationale behind the first phase of BEE policies, which stipulated that companies must be BEE compliant, having certain levels of black ownership, management, and procurement... [the BIS] targeted businesses that already had black ownership and management. In other words it was a secondary project, a second phase... to help black businesses expand their market penetration or enter new markets.
>
> (NCOP, 2016)

This reference suggests a recognition by the government that, since its inception in 2003, the BBBEE policy had not sufficiently addressed certain aspects of barriers to entry. The BIS can thus be seen as a progression in policy—and with the potential to catalyse structural transformation in targeted industries, tied into broader economic objectives. Indeed, the design of the BIS programme points to an important shift in the understanding of barriers and what it takes to build challenger firms beyond the scorecard parameters of BBBEE.

The two main tools used to achieve the objectives of the BIS programme are the provision of access to capital, and access to markets. Access to markets is to be facilitated through state-owned companies, and progressively through private-sector channels. In practice, the scheme aims to assist so-called 'black industrialists' (BIs) through providing concessional funding (grant plus debt) through a central office which sources funding from the Industrial Development Corporation (IDC), South Africa's primary DFI, and provincial DFIs. The BIS targets enterprises operating in industries that fall within the DTIC's priority manufacturing sectors noted in the Industrial Policy Action Plan (IPAP).

The IPAP is the primary industrial policy implementation strategy in South Africa (arising from the National Industrial Policy Framework of 2007), updated through various iterations with a particularly strong sectoral focus (DTI, 2015; NCOP, 2016). This is a critical aspect as it means that black industrialist support is directly linked to the strategy to grow South Africa's manufacturing sector as part of long-term growth. A key difference with BBBEE is that the BBBEE policy necessarily applies a generic code system and criteria across all economic sectors and cannot be adapted to issues that may be specific to certain sectors or industries.

Qualifying BIs are defined as those entities in which the black owners hold more than 50 per cent of the shares in the firm that operates within a focus sector of the IPAP. The BIs need to demonstrate a medium- to long-term commitment to the firm, exercise operational control, bear personal risk in the venture as the primary entrepreneur, and be involved in driving the strategy and day-to-day running of the firm. The very specific characterization of the qualifying industrialists appears to respond to a key criticism of BBBEE, namely that many black shareholders (and managers), even in broad-based arrangements, were not exposed to key operational aspects of the existing businesses in which they became owners and so could not gain the skills and experience relevant for building new enterprises in the medium and long term.

The two broad qualifying criteria—the scale of the project and the potential contribution to the economy—suggest the prioritization of large-scale projects that have the potential to impact on competitive dynamics in markets and create substantial employment.[4] In terms of substantial scale, the specific project for which funding is being sought must require a minimum investment of R30 million (US$1.8 million, in 2020). The DTIC then provides a cost-sharing grant

---

[4] Smaller projects and companies are, in principle, catered for through other programmes of the DTIC and/or those of other government agencies.

of between 30 per cent and 50 per cent of the required investment for the project, up to a cap of R50 million (US$3 million). The contribution to the economy is based on eight equally weighted criteria in terms of the expected contribution to: employment (securing, retaining, or increasing direct jobs); market share (securing new business or increasing existing operations); quality improvement (reducing relative prices and/or increasing the quality of products offered); green technology and resource-efficiency improvements; localization (increasing local production activities, diversification, and exports); improving the regional spread of production (in rural areas or regions with unemployment higher than 25 per cent); personal risk (demonstrating own financial and/or non-financial contribution to the business); and empowerment credentials (BBBEE scores) (DTI, 2015).

The criteria have therefore been designed to reward and incentivize certain behaviours that are aligned with a range of socioeconomic and manufacturing-specific objectives. The amount of the government contribution is based on the combined performance of the applicant in relation to black ownership (with more being desirable) and on the economic benefit criteria. However, it is a significant concern that these criteria have only applied at the pre-qualification stage, and firms are not required to report on their performance against them, once they are on the programme. This means that there are no repercussions if the firms do not achieve any of the objectives claimed in the application stage.

Overall, a total of 135 enterprises had been supported under the scheme since its commencement in 2016 to the time of the survey in May 2019, with a substantial combined value of approved project disbursements (DTIC and co-funder funds combined) of approximately R12 billion (US$700 million) (Bosiu et al., 2020).[5] The potential impact of the programme is therefore significant.

9.4.2 The Survey of the Black Industrialists Scheme

9.4.2.1 The Aim and Design of the Survey
The analysis of the outcomes of the BIS involved an online, anonymized survey administered in May 2019 (for full details refer to Bosiu et al., 2020). The survey gathered data on the businesses and their performance, including under the economic benefit criteria, and their experience with difference stages of application and disbursement processes at the DTIC as well as other DFIs or private funders as comparators. There were thirty-nine respondents, which included both applicants and beneficiary firms of the programme since its inception in 2016—out of 255 applicants or beneficiary firms (Bosiu et al., 2020). At the time of the survey, there were 135 beneficiaries, at different stages of the

---

[5] By comparison, South African public sector institutions spent approximately R250 billion on fixed assets in 2018. See Statistics South Africa website: http://www.statssa.gov.za/?p=12,705.

programme cycle between approval and claims and disbursement. The survey was accompanied by verification workshops and in-depth interviews with selected firms as well as with the DTIC as the responsible ministry, and various other state- and private-sector agencies responsible for the provision of financial and non-financial support to small and medium-sized firms in South Africa. This combination of engagements served to test and strengthen the robustness of the findings.

9.4.2.2 Key Findings of the Survey: Has the BIS Contributed to Inclusive Structural Transformation?

The focus here is on aspects relating to the programme's potential to drive an inclusive form of structural transformation in the terms discussed in sections 9.2 and 9.3 above. Further details can be found in Bosiu et al. (2020).

The majority of the investments made by the BIS beneficiaries have been expansionary capital investments in diversified manufacturing, which suggest that the programme has contributed to catalysing investments in new productive assets in the economy. These investments occurred at a time in South Africa when private and public gross fixed capital formation was stagnant (Bosiu et al., 2017; Bell et al., 2018). Given their particular emphasis on diversified manufacturing activities, this meant that they contributed incrementally to structural change. Although the businesses of BIs are relatively small compared with large South African businesses (such as those listed on the JSE), the survey found that these businesses have invested in relatively large projects, in line with the BIS objectives, ranging up to R390 million (US$23 million, 2020) in value.

The BIS cost-sharing grant offers support in three main categories of interventions: capital investment, investment support, and business development. Of total investment allocations for approved BIs that responded to the survey, matched against data from the DTIC database, 97 per cent (R2.9 billion, US$177 million, 2020) of actual and projected disbursements by the DTIC and the co-funders were committed to capital investments. Indeed, 80 per cent of these funds were earmarked for investments in machinery and equipment, implying that firms were expected to invest in productive assets that would improve production capacity, scope, and capabilities. The majority of firms responding confirmed that their output had increased since approval to the BIS, in many cases due to the project for which they had applied to the BIS.

Generally, these are also large investments relative to those supported under other government programmes and some private-sector schemes. This targeting of the programme is especially significant because it implies a focus on firms that have already overcome the initial stages of testing and learning involved in the building of organization capabilities and have sufficient scale and scope to compete as effective rivals in the markets in which they operate. This includes shifting to more sophisticated activities and stimulating rivals to do the same as part of the competitive process.

There is also significant diversity in the manufacturing activities in which the firms surveyed are involved, and many of them have operations in 'rural' locations, although this is not a strong feature in the data. Specifically, based on self-classification by the firms under the IPAP focus areas, fifteen of the thirty-nine respondents operated in chemicals, pharmaceuticals, and plastics, followed by agroprocessing, and clean technology and energy. Other activities included: manufacturing of wiring and electrical components; electrical and digital devices; food additives, preservatives, food processing; household consumables; and clothing and textiles products. These are generally activities which entail medium-technology manufacturing processes, and, importantly, are also labour-absorptive, which means ultimately shifting the employment of labour to higher value-added activities in the economy.

In response to questions on whether they had made improvements under each of the eight economic benefit criteria, many companies responded with detailed descriptions of specific technologies acquired and indications of the savings made in some cases (with 63 per cent of respondents reporting and describing some form of improvement). Firms also reported improved product quality, advancing product development, and achieving cost efficiencies which are important in terms of upgrading production processes and the potential to be competitive in international markets. In terms of employment, the respondents reported an increase of almost two thousand jobs when comparing their employment levels at the time of their first application to the BIS up to the time of the survey in 2019. Many of these were jobs in operational activities (rather than technical) involving large proportions of youth and women employees (Bosiu et al., 2020).

In addition to the competitiveness improvements noted above, nearly three-quarters of firms increased sourcing from local and/or black-owned firms, indicating local linkages. However, more than 80 per cent of the primary input materials are still imported from China and the USA, followed by Europe and India, which means there may be opportunities to increase local supply linkages over time.

The evaluation of the survey points to the importance of targeted industrial policy interventions which require effective levers and support, while also placing strong conditions on firms in terms of expected outcomes from funding grants. In this regard, the DTIC does not require firms in the BIS to report on the above outcomes at all, except if they are applying for additional funding. While this is potentially problematic, the risk of funds being squandered or used in unproduct-ive ways is partly mitigated by the fact that the BIS operates on a claims-based system, which requires firms to first make the investments they have committed to in their applications (using own or external funding), before they can claim for a refund under the scheme. The claims-based system also means that the BIS effect-ively 'rewards' existing projects and entrepreneurs that have been able to commit some of their own or borrowed funding for the projects already. The challenge, of course, is that many black-owned businesses have reported significant difficulties with sourcing funds, including for working capital requirements. In this regard, the DTIC has created a joint funding forum with private sector funders and DFIs to work closely with the DTIC on the BIS applications.

The insights gained from the programme at a relatively early stage in its life suggest that the BIS has a significant potential contribution to driving structural transformation, not least through investments in improved capabilities. Overall, it is clear that the provision of finance and the accompanying non-financial support is critical, and that this is best done through targeted programmes that build the capabilities of potential (medium-sized) challenger firms in the manufacturing sector, in particular.

9.5 Conclusion

The precarious and shifting balance in South Africa's political settlement necessitates a rethinking about how to achieve structural transformation and economic inclusion. In this chapter it has been argued that these objectives must go together. As a political and social necessity, structural transformation of the economy must account for the politics *and* economics of the exclusion of black individuals and enterprises from participating in the mainstream economy.

Black economic empowerment and opening up the economy to entrants and more competition generally are essential for the process of structural transformation in South Africa. A crucial point to highlight is that inclusion and rivalry need to be substantive for there to be productivity-enhancing effects. This means that entrants and emerging firms need to be able to compete as effective rivals in the economy to stimulate dynamic efficiencies through the competitive process— pointing in turn to the importance of addressing barriers to entry and expansion that are even higher for black-owned businesses. The competitive pressure that new rivals can bring contributes to dynamic gains to the economy in terms of investments, diversification, and upgrading to improve competitiveness. These are all critical factors in the process of structural transformation.

The BBBEE policies have been an important and necessary first step towards achieving economic inclusion, but they have not gone far enough or provided the right incentives for incumbent interests and black capitalists to drive structural change. They certainly have not addressed the structural and strategic barriers discussed in the chapter which prevent smaller and black-owned firms from expanding; nor have the different strategies focused in any way on competition and building effective rivals. Development finance has not provided the expected thrust for driving inclusion and structural transformation, and BEE deals have created a false sense of inclusion.

In this context, the BIS marks an important shift in the thinking about the role of industrial policy that is integrated with BEE in driving inclusion and competition. The main insights are that the provision of finance and the accompanying non-financial support is critical, and that this is best done through targeted programmes that build the capabilities of potential (medium-sized) challenger firms in the manufacturing sector, in particular. The early-stage survey of the performance of firms under this programme shows that the scheme has had a catalytic effect in terms of stimulating relatively large investments by industrialists, as well as driving improvements in their production capabilities, cost efficiencies, and product development. The programme has, however, not been successful in improving access to markets and into established value chains. This is the function of a lack of a coherent and coordinated strategy within South Africa's industrial, sector regulation, and competition policy space to systemically address barriers of this nature. The potential benefits of developing such a strategy for driving structural transformation of the economy are significant, requiring extensive further research to inform policymaking that must avoid the pitfalls of previous approaches.

The impact of the programme in driving inclusion and structural transformation is therefore likely to be more significant if there is more focus on opening up access to markets through procurement by government and private-sector entities. This is because there has not been a systemic approach to understanding and targeting specific barriers faced by black-owned firms, such as lack of access to markets.

The lack of focus on specific barriers such as finance in the BBBEE and industrial policies has meant that other areas of policy, such as competition law, have become viewed as the primary tools for transformation, despite their limited legal remit. A more integrated and comprehensive approach, involving different agencies and private-sector bodies is required. Such an integrated approach is also necessary for dealing with some of the administrative challenges raised by the firms surveyed, particularly with respect to delays in disbursements and the lack of coordination between agencies of government.

It is clear that while the BIS presents a number of challenges to address, it also offers a great deal to build on for it to become an effective tool to drive a process of inclusive structural transformation. Early indications are that the programme has promoted diversification, employment creation, entry and expansion, and investments in improved capabilities, which are all essential for structural change.

References

Amsden, A. (1989). *Asia's Next Giant: South Korea and Late Industrialization*. New York: Oxford University Press.

Atkinson, A. B. (2015). *Inequality: What Can Be Done?* London: Harvard University Press.

Bagopi, E., E. Chokwe, P. Halse, J. Hausiku, M. Humavindu, W. Kalapula, and S. Roberts (2016). 'Competition, agro-processing and regional development: the case of poultry in South Africa, Botswana, Namibia and Zambia.' In S. Roberts (ed.), *Competition in Africa: Insights from Key Industries*, 66–101. Cape Town: HSRC Press.

Baker, J. B. and S. C. Salop (2015). 'Antitrust, competition policy, and inequality.' *The Georgetown Law Journal Online* 104(1): 1–28.

Baymul, C. and K. Sen (2018). 'Was Kuznets right? New evidence on the relationship between structural transformation and inequality.' Global Development Institute Working Paper Series 272018. Manchester: GDI, The University of Manchester.

BBBEE Commission (2017a). 'National state of transformation and trend analysis.' National Report, https://bbbeecommission.co.za/wp-content/uploads/2017/05/B-BBEE-Commission-National-State-of-Transformation-and-Trend-Analysis-National-Report-Booklet.pdf.

BBBEE Commission (2017b). 'The "once empowered, always empowered" has no place in a transforming South Africa.' The Whistle Newsletter, 2nd edn, https://bbbeecommission.co.za/wp-content/uploads/2017/01/The-Whistle_2nd-Edition-2017.pdf.

Bell, J. and S. Goga (2020). 'Key competition challenges in the South African economy: large firms, concentration and lack of dynamism.' In T. Vilakazi, S. Goga, and S. Roberts (eds), *Opening the South African Economy: Barriers to Entry and Competition*, 11–23. Cape Town: HSRC Press.

Bell, J., S. Goga, P. Mondliwa, and S. Roberts (2018). 'Towards a smart, open economy for all.' *New Agenda: South African Journal of Social and Economic Policy* 70: 6–11.

Black Economic Empowerment Commission (BEECom) (2001). 'Report.' Johannesburg: Skotaville Press, http://www.kznhealth.gov.za/TED/commission.pdf. Accessed 12 October 2020.

Bosiu, T., N. Nhundu, A. Paelo, M. O. Thosago, and T. Vilakazi (2017). 'Growth and strategies of large and lead firms: top 50 JSE firms.' Working Paper No. 2017/17. Centre for Competition, Regulation and Economic Development. Johannesburg: CCRED.

Bosiu, T., G. Nsomba, and T. Vilakazi (2020). 'South Africa's black industrialists scheme: evaluating programme design, performance and outcomes.' CCRED Working Paper No. 1/2020. Johannesburg: CCRED. https://static1.squarespace.com/static/52246331e4b0a46e5f1b8ce5/t/5eaa7589b0caa85f5c4d4234/1588229526930/CCRED+Report_BIS+Economic+Evaluation_CCRED+Working+Paper+1-2020.pdf. Accessed 3 July 2020.

Bowman, A. (2019). 'Black economic empowerment policy and state-business relations in South Africa: the case of mining.' *Review of African Political Economy* 46(160): 223–45.

Bracking, S. (2019). 'Black economic empowerment policy in Durban, eThekwini, South Africa: economic justice, economic fraud and "leaving money on the table".' *Review of African Political Economy* 46(161): 415–41.

Chabane, N., A. Goldstein and S. Roberts (2006). 'The changing face and strategies of big business in South Africa: more than a decade of political democracy.' *Industrial and Corporate Change* 15(3): 549–77.

Chatterjee, A., L. Czajka and A. Gethin (2020). 'Estimating the distribution of household wealth in South Africa.' Southern Centre for Inequality Studies Working Paper 3, https://www.wits.ac.za/scis/publications/working-papers/. Accessed 22 September 2020.

Chisoro-Dube, S. and R. das Nair (2020). 'Confronting entry barriers in South Africa's grocery retail sector.' In T. Vilakazi, S. Goga, and S. Roberts (eds), *Opening the South African Economy: Barriers to Entry and Competition*, 57–74. Cape Town: HSRC Press.

das Nair, R., S. Chisoro and F. Ziba (2018). 'The implications for suppliers of the spread of supermarkets in southern Africa.' *Development Southern Africa* 35(3): 334–50.

das Nair, R. and N. Landani (2020). 'New approaches to supermarket supplier development programmes in Southern Africa.' *Development Southern Africa* online, DOI:10.1080/0376835X.2020.1780565.

Department of Trade and Industry (DTI) (2003). 'South Africa's economic transformation: a strategy for broad based black economic empowerment.' http://www.thedtic.gov.za/wp-content/uploads/bee-strategy.pdf. Accessed 12 October 2020.

Department of Trade and Industry (DTI) (2015). 'Black industrialists policy.' http://www.thedtic.gov.za/financial-and-non-financial-support/incentives/black-industrialists-scheme-bis/. accessed 18 September 2020.

Ennis, S., P. Gonzago, and C. Pike (2019). 'Inequality: a hidden cost of market power.' *Oxford Review of Economic Policy* 35(3): 518–49.

Felipe, J., U. Kumar, A. Abdon, and M. Bacate (2012). 'Product complexity and economic development.' *Structural Change and Economic Dynamics* 23: 36–68.

Freund, B. (2007). 'South Africa: the end of apartheid and the emergence of the "BEE Elite".' *Review of African Political Economy* 34(114): 661–78.

Goga, S., T. Bosiu, and J. Bell (2019). 'Linking IDC finance to structural transformation and inclusivity in post-apartheid South Africa.' *Development Southern Africa* 36(6): 821–38.

Goga, S., P. Mondliwa, and S. Roberts (2020). 'Economic power and regulation: the political economy of metals, machinery and equipment industries in South Africa.' In D. Francis, I. Valodia, and E. Webster (eds), *Inequality Studies from the Global South*, 75–98. London: Routledge.

Gqubule, D. (2006). *Making Mistakes, Righting Wrongs: Insights into Black Economic Empowerment*. Johannesburg: Jonathan Ball Publishers.

Gqubule, D. (2018). 'New sectoral charters threaten transformation and empowerment.' *BEE News*, 4 December 2018, https://www.bee.co.za/post/2018/12/04/opinion-duma-gqubule-new-sectoral-charters-threaten-transformation-and-empowerment. Accessed 12 October 2020.

Hamann, R., S. Khagram, and S. Rohan (2008). 'South Africa's charter approach to post-apartheid economic transformation: collaborative governance or hardball bargaining?' *Journal of Southern African Studies* 34(1): 21–37.

Hirsch, A. (2005). *Season of Hope: Economic Reform under Mandela and Mbeki.* Scotsville: University of KwaZulu-Natal Press.

Industrial Development Corporation (IDC) (2003). 'Industrial Development Corporation annual report.' Available on request.

Industrial Development Corporation (IDC) (2015). 'Industrial Development Corporation annual report.' https://www.idc.co.za/about-the-idc/financial-results.html.

Khan, M. H. (2017). 'Political settlements and the analysis of institutions.' *African Affairs* 117(469): 636–55.

Lee, H. (2015). 'Affirmative action in Malaysia and South Africa: contrasting structures, continuing pursuits.' *Journal of Asian and African Studies* 50(5): 615–34.

MacDonald, M. (2006). *Why Race Matters in South Africa.* Scotsville: University of KwaZulu-Natal Press.

Maia, J., L. Mondi, and S. Roberts (2005). 'Industrial development and industrial finance in Brazil and South Africa: a comparative assessment.' Trade and Industrial Policy Strategies Annual Forum.

McMillan, M. and D. Rodrik (2011). 'Globalization, structural change and productivity growth.' No. w17143. Cambridge, MA: National Bureau of Economic Research.

Mebratie, A. D. and A. S. Bedi (2013). 'Foreign direct investment, black economic empowerment and labour productivity in South Africa.' *The Journal of International Trade and Economic Development* 22(1): 103–28.

Mncube, L. (2014). 'The South African wheat flour cartel: overcharges at the mill.' *Journal of Industry, Competition and Trade* 14: 487–509.

Mondliwa, P. (2020). 'Barriers to entry in concentrated industries: a case study of Soweto Gold.' In T. Vilakazi, S. Goga, and S. Roberts (eds), *Opening the South African Economy: Barriers to Entry and Competition*, 43–55. Cape Town: HSRC Press.

Mondliwa, P. and S. Roberts (2019). 'From a developmental to a regulatory state? Sasol and the conundrum of continued state support.' *International Review of Applied Economics* 33(1): 11–29.

Mondliwa, P. and S. Roberts (2020). 'Black economic empowerment and barriers to entry.' In T. Vilakazi, S. Goga, and S. Roberts (eds), *Opening the South African Economy: Barriers to Entry and Competition*, 215–30. Cape Town: HSRC Press.

National Council of Provinces (NCOP) (2016). 'Black industrialists policy: Department of Trade and Industry briefing.' Trade and International Relations Committee. 24 February 2016, https://pmg.org.za/committee-meeting/22065/. Accessed 3 July 2020.

Nhundu, N. and G. Makhaya (2020). 'Competition, barriers to entry and inclusive growth in retail banking: Capitec case study.' In T. Vilakazi, S. Goga, and S. Roberts (eds), *Opening the South African Economy: Barriers to Entry and Competition*, 143–62. Johannesburg: HSRC Press.

Nkhonjera, M. 'Entry challenges in vertically integrated industries: insights from three agro-processing value chains in South Africa.' In T. Vilakazi, S. Goga, and S. Roberts (eds), *Opening the South African Economy: Barriers to Entry and Competition*, 27–42. Johannesburg: HSRC Press.

Paelo, A., G. Robb, and T. Vilakazi. (2017). 'Competition and incumbency in South Africa's liquid fuel value chain.' In J. Klaaren, S. Roberts, and I. Valodia (eds), *Competition Law and Economic Regulation: Addressing Market Power in Southern Africa*, 172–88. Johannesburg: WITS University Press.

Patel, L. and L. Graham (2012). 'How broad-based is broad-based black economic empowerment?' *Development Southern Africa* 29(2): 193–207.

Ponte, S., S. Roberts, and L. Van Sittert (2007). '"Black economic empowerment", business and the state in South Africa.' *Development and Change* 38(5): 933–55.

Republic of South Africa (RSA) (2013). 'Government gazette notice No. 36928.' 11 October 2013, https://bbbeecommission.co.za/wp-content/uploads/2017/12/Phase-1-36928_11-10_TradeIndCV01_3a.pdf. Accessed 29 October 2020.

Republic of South Africa (RSA) (2014). 'Minister Rob Davies on enactment of Broad-Based Black Economic Empowerment Amendment Bill.' Media statement, 30 January, https://www.gov.za/president-jacob-zuma-signs-broad-based-black-economic-empowerment-amendment-bill-2013-law. Accessed 29 October 2020.

Robb, G. (2020). 'Bridging the digital divide in South Africa: case studies in incumbency versus competition.' In T. Vilakazi, S. Goga, and S. Roberts (eds), *Opening the South African Economy: Barriers to Entry and Competition*, 125–42. Johannesburg: HSRC Press.

Roberts, S. (2010). 'Competition policy, competitive rivalry and a developmental state in South Africa.' In O. Edigheji (ed.), *Constructing a Democratic Developmental State in South Africa: Potentials and Challenges*, 222–37. Cape Town: HSRC Press.

Roberts, S. (2020). 'Assessing the record of competition law enforcement in opening up the economy.' In T. Vilakazi, S. Goga, and S. Roberts (eds), *Opening the South African Economy: Barriers to Entry and Competition*, 179–98. Johannesburg: HSRC Press.

Sartorius, K. and G. Botha (2008). 'Black economic empowerment ownership initiatives: a Johannesburg Stock Exchange perspective.' *Development Southern Africa* 25(4): 437–53.

Singh, A. (2002). 'Competition and competition policy in emerging markets: international and developmental dimensions.' G-24 Discussion Paper Series, Issue 18.

Southall, R. (2007). 'Ten propositions about black economic empowerment in South Africa.' *Review of African Political Economy* 34(111): 67–84.

Stats SA (Statistics South Africa) (2020). 'Statistical release P.0302: mid-year population estimates.' http://www.statssa.gov.za/publications/P0302/P03022020.pdf. Accessed 18 September 2020.

Tangri, R. and R. Southall (2008). 'The politics of black economic empowerment in South Africa.' *Journal of Southern African Studies* 34(3): 699–716.

Terreblanche, S. (2002). *A History of Inequality in South Africa, 1652–2002*. Scotsville: University of KwaZulu-Natal Press.

Tregenna, F. (2008). 'Characterising deindustrialisation: an analysis of changes in manufacturing employment and output internationally.' *Cambridge Journal of Economics* 33(3): 433–66.

Vilakazi, T. and S. Ponte (2020). 'The political economy of competition, regulation and transformation: black economic empowerment (BEE) and quota allocations in South African industrial fisheries.' Joint working paper of the Centre for Competition, Regulation and Economic Development (University of Johannesburg) and the Centre for Business and Development Studies (Copenhagen Business School).

Vilakazi, T., S. Goga, and S. Roberts, eds (2020). *Opening the South African Economy: Barriers to Entry and Competition*. Cape Town: HSRC Press.

Von Holdt, K. (2019). 'The political economy of corruption: elite-formation, factions and violence.' Working Paper 10, Society, Work and Politics Institute. Johannesburg: University of Witwatersrand.

10

Profitability without Investment

How Financialization Undermines Structural Transformation in South Africa

Antonio Andreoni, Nishal Robb, and Sophie van Huellen

10.1 Introduction

Sustained investment in productive capabilities and fixed-capital formation is a key driver of inclusive and sustainable structural transformation. Both historically and compared to other middle-income countries, South Africa has performed poorly in terms of sustaining domestic-productive investments. This failing has coexisted with the development of a stock market with the second-highest level of capitalization over gross domestic product (GDP) in the world (a record retained since 2013, and second only to Hong Kong), and high levels of profitability across several economic sectors. This means that, despite the deepening of financial markets and persistently high profits, investments have not materialized.

In this chapter, this apparent paradox is unpacked through the presentation of new evidence on the specific ways in which financialization of non-financial corporations (NFCs) in South Africa has resulted in low investment performances. Aggregate evidence of the coexistence of high profitability, deep financial markets, and sluggish productive investment is provided. This is borne out further by the focus on two large, publicly listed corporations operating across different economic sectors—Sasol in heavy manufacturing industry, and Shoprite in supermarket retail. Built on an analysis of company financial statements, the case studies identify a number of shifts in firm behaviour and corporate strategy between 2000 and 2019, particularly in regard to sources and uses of funds.

The analysis shows that firms have increasingly financed operations, capital expenditure, and distributions to shareholders with debt. The US dollar-denominated share of this debt has grown rapidly in the period studied, exposing firms to increased exchange and interest rate risk in a volatile global macroeconomic environment. Distributions to shareholders, driven by dividends rather than share repurchases, have also risen markedly over the same period—with growing repayments to creditors further augmenting the flow of resources away from productive reinvestment and toward financial markets.

Antonio Andreoni, Nishal Robb, and Sophie van Huellen, *Profitability without Investment: How Financialization Undermines Structural Transformation in South Africa* In: *Structural Transformation in South Africa: The Challenges of Inclusive Industrial Development in a Middle-Income Country.* Edited by: Antonio Andreoni, Pamela Mondliwa, Simon Roberts, and Fiona Tregenna, Oxford University Press. © Oxford University Press 2021. DOI: 10.1093/oso/9780192894311.003.0010

These dynamics are attributed in part to South Africa's subordinate position in a global economic hierarchy encompassing currencies, value chains, and financial markets, and which imposes profound limitations on the development strategies and policy space available to low and middle-income countries. An exploration of these dynamics helps to identify the scale and complexity of the challenges facing attempts to resist the influence of financialization, and to pursue growth paths premised on redressing a growing imbalance between financial and non-financial sectors through redirecting resources away from finance and towards productive investment.

For the rest of the chapter, section 10.2 introduces the literature on the role of finance in structural transformation and the ways in which financialization hampers sustained productive investments. Building on, and extending, a specific stream of research focusing on the tension between financialization and innovation within NFCs (Lazonick and O'Sullivan, 2000; Lazonick, 2014), a number of financialization factors and dynamics which are specific to companies in middle-income countries are identified. Section 10.3 focuses on the South African case, and presents new historical evidence on a selected number of financialization indicators for publicly listed NFCs. Section 10.4 presents the two case studies and an in-depth investigation into several factors driving the financialization of NFCs across companies in South Africa and, potentially, other middle-income countries. Section 10.5 concludes and reflects on the implications for industrial policy.

10.2 Structural Transformation, Finance, and Investments: Why Financialization Matters

The processes of countries' structural transformation are complex, involving changes in multiple dimensions. By directing and sustaining strategic investments in productive capabilities, finance can play a critical role in driving structural transformation (Samargandi et al., 2015). The experience of early industrializers (and successful late industrializers) points to the fact that reinvestment of profits generated within business enterprises is a major source of finance, alongside financial institutions. By retaining profits and reinvesting them strategically in the development of productive capabilities, collective learning, and technologies, business enterprises can develop managerial and organizational capabilities that allow them to exploit economies of scale and diversification opportunities (Penrose, 1959; Lazonick, 1990).

Economies of scale, of scope, and innovation are not only key drivers of growth—they are also key generators of large profits. In order to be (and remain) innovative, business enterprises need to exercise strategic control over the financial resources they are able to generate as an organization (Lazonick and

O'Sullivan, 2000; Lazonick, 2010). They also need to make sure that long-term cycles of learning and innovation are properly funded over time, and against uncertainty. Commitment of financial resources under uncertainty is central for sustaining productive capabilities development and accumulation, and steering them towards innovation, from both company and country perspectives (Chang and Andreoni, 2020).

However, business enterprises can become financialized—that is, the nexus between finance, investment, and structural transformation can break. Financialization happens because, to quote Epstein's (2005: 3) definition of financialization, with the 'increasing role of financial motives, financial markets, financial actors, and financial institutions in the operation of the domestic and international economies', resources generated in the real economy are diverted from productive investments towards the expansion of the financial sector. Middle-income countries are fully exposed to global financial systems and financialization dynamics, while at the same time large segments of their economies are structurally and institutionally underdeveloped, and thus exposed to unproductive financial systems development. After each of these points is addressed, the discussion turns to how they play out in the specific context of middle-income countries like South Africa.

10.2.1 Theoretical Perspectives on Financialization

Financialization is a global phenomenon, although it impacts different countries in specific and interdependent ways (Chang and Andreoni, 2020). Across middle-income economies, financialization diverts finance from those productive investments needed to sustain industrialization efforts and infrastructure development. It also undermines technological catch-up and reduces returns to workers for their key contribution to value creation within business enterprises. Indeed, by undermining productive structural transformation, financialization also has a direct and indirect distributional impact on the demand and employment side, ultimately impacting the rise of domestic effective demand. Finally, given that financial markets are global and business enterprises are transnational, there are plenty of transmission mechanisms through which financialization in one country (or company) affects the other country (or company, especially those operating along the same sectoral value chain).

In the decade since the global financial crisis, much of the popular discourse on financialization has focused on financial 'innovations' such as credit default swaps (CDS) and derivatives, and their roles in precipitating the crisis. However, there was already extensive scholarship on financialization from a range of perspectives before the crisis. This body of literature has discussed financialization at multiple levels—from analysis of household assets and liabilities, and the changing behaviour of NFCs, to its influence on financial systems at a national and international level; and from multiple angles, including social provision by states, shifts in the international division of labour, class formation, and international monetary architecture (see Krippner (2005) for a review of the pre-crisis literature).

Marxist political economists and post-Keynesian scholars, in particular, have developed theories of financialization from a macro perspective, mainly focusing on the ways in which financialization operates across sectors and across classes within a macroeconomic framework (see e.g. Fine, 2013; Lapavitsas, 2013). Lapavitsas (2013), for example, focuses on the different 'set[s] of social mechanisms that systematically convert temporarily idle funds into money capital available for lending' (2013: 118). From this perspective, financialization is embodied in changing relations between and within sectors in the last three decades or so of the twentieth century—with firms, banks, households, and the state in advanced economies representing the key sectors. As NFCs developed the financial intermediation capabilities required to trade in financial markets and pursue financial profits, their relations with and reliance on banks weakened over time. In turn, banks sought new streams of profit in direct lending to households and increased financial intermediation services. At the same time, states' withdrawal from social provision—pensions, housing, education, and healthcare key among these—combined with changing patterns of bank lending to draw ordinary households more deeply into the financial system than ever before (Lapavitsas, 2013: 2–4). The core argument here is that financialization is, in the final analysis, antithetical to real accumulation. Financialization results in increasing appropriation of value by the financial system at the expense of the 'real' or productive economy, and ultimately exposes households and whole economies to new forms of vulnerability.

A different stream of research has focused on the ways in which financialization of NFCs has historically emerged out of specific institutional changes in corporate governance regimes (Lazonick and O'Sullivan, 2000; Lazonick, 2014) and has shaped and spread along global value chains (GVCs) (Baud and Durand, 2011; Milberg and Winkler, 2013; Auvray and Rabinovich, 2019). Starting in the 1980s, with the increasing globalization of financial markets and fragmentation of production, the refocusing of multinational corporations (MNCs) on core businesses and the increasing power of global institutional investors, corporate strategies shifted from the old logic of 'retaining and investing' to one of 'downsizing and distribution'. The affirmation of what came to be called 'shareholder value maximization' ideology—a new hegemonic principle of corporate governance—is considered to be the main mechanism underpinning corporate financialization.[1]

---

[1] See also Froud et al. (2006) on the link between financialization and changes in corporate governance, with a focus on three iconic NFCs—i.e. GlaxoSmithKline, Ford, and General Electric.

The shareholder value maximization (SVM) perspective was built on 'residual claimant' theories of the firm. These proposed that only a firm's owners or shareholders truly take a risk in investing in it, as they are only guaranteed a return on their investment if the firm turns a profit (the 'residual' to which they have claim). The interests of other stakeholders—workers, managers, and creditors—are contractually enforceable, and are thus not always perfectly aligned with profit maximization. Shareholders are therefore seen as having the most powerful incentives to ensure the efficiency of the firm, maximizing profits and their own returns, which they are best placed to allocate to further reinvestment in the firm or to other private ends. SVM ideology maps this argument onto society as a whole: because shareholders' incentives lead them to maximize profits at firm-level, shareholders' returns ought to be maximized in general, allowing them to allocate those returns to further profit-maximizing activities, thus maximizing utility at an overall social level (Alchian and Demsetz, 1972; Jensen and Meckling, 1976). This amounts to the simple idea that what is best for the owners of shares is best for society as a whole.

Lazonick (2014) has challenged this perspective, arguing that shareholders in the context of contemporary financial markets ought not to be considered 'investors' in the traditional sense. This is because they tend not to make consistent investments of their resources in a given firm and they have the ability to sell off their shares in a way that means their 'investments' are rarely subject to major risk. In contrast, it is employees, taxpayers, and governments who make regular investments of time and resources in firms, and tend to be the ones to pay the price when risks transform into genuine crisis. According to Lazonick, SVM is the key justification and corporate governance principle behind the financialization of NFCs, and has contributed powerfully to the inability of the USA, for example, to achieve inclusive and innovative growth. For Lazonick, the combination of increasing distribution of 'excess cash' to shareholders and financial markets through dividends and share repurchases, and the growth of stock-based compensation for executives, has broken the finance–investment nexus that had driven growth in the US economy from the second world war until the 1970s.

10.2.2 Financialization of Non-financial Corporations in Middle-Income Countries: Towards a Micro-level Perspective

While most scholarship on financialization has focused on advanced economies, since the early 2000s, several contributions have explored the transmission mechanisms of financialization between advanced ('core') and developing ('peripheral') economies. In this context, Powell (2013) advances a theory of 'subordinate financialization', according to which financialization across emerging markets and developing economies (EMDEs) is driven by a combination of power dynamics inherent in the global financial architecture. These result in macroeconomic and financial system vulnerabilities for EMDEs. Powell argues that EMDEs are experiencing financialization, 'but in a distinctive form which has been shaped by imperial relations in the current world market conjuncture' (2013: 144).

Powell proposes several hypotheses about the likely features of subordinate financialization in EMDEs in the context of this particular conjuncture. First, as a consequence of the subordinate position of EMDE states and their currencies in the international financial system, financial liberalization is likely to undermine investment, especially in productive activity. Second, international private capital flows, driven by monetary conditions in advanced economies and increasing in volume and volatility, expose EMDEs to financial crisis. This imposes costly risk-management strategies for policymakers in EMDEs, negatively affecting credit conditions and rates of fixed investment. Third, leading NFCs in EMDEs are likely to become increasingly reliant on market-based finance, generating volatility in national financial systems, especially where foreign currency-denominated debt is taken on by NFCs. Fourth, banks are likely to turn towards global capital markets, creating new vulnerabilities by opening the domestic banking sector to external factors with potentially negative macroeconomic consequences. Finally, households are likely to become financialized in terms of both assets and liabilities. Bonizzi et al. (2019: 10) argue that these vulnerabilities in developing economies 'may serve to cement or even deepen their subordi-nation in the global hierarchy of nations'; the subordinate financialization perspective is thus grounded in the exploration of fundamentally hierarchical and extractive relations between core and peripheral economies (see also Bonizzi, 2013).

The subordinate financialization literature introduces important insights into the specific financialization mechanisms operating at the macro and financial system levels across middle-income countries and other peripheral countries. A number of these specific mechanisms reflect micro-level financialization processes within NFCs, which will be different from those highlighted in NFCs based in advanced economies like the USA.[2] To advance a micro-level perspec-tive that shows the specific forms of tension between financialization and invest-ments across NFCs in middle-income countries, three clusters of issues are discussed: heterogeneity between different sectors and different segments of the GVC with respect to the rentieristic nature of activities; pull factors, such as asymmetries along GVCs, foreign ownership, and dependence on international

---

[2] For instance, taking the cases of Apple Inc. and Foxconn International Holdings (FIH) as exam-ples, Froud et al. (2014) find different—though still interdependent, because of their being in the same GVC—financialization processes within the companies and broader outcomes for their respective countries.

finance; and inducement factors, such as cheap credit, and the need to meet shareholders' expectation and mitigate the risk of hostile takeovers.

There are six major interlinked factors related to these issues. First, financialization is heterogenous across sectors. This is because profitability margins, industry organizations along value chains, and competition are different across sectors. Extractive sectors, for example, tend to offer high profitability margins, especially when beneficiation activities are limited. Once initial fixed investments are in place, the financial stream from these activities can be extremely high and relatively stable (depending on commodity cycles). Similarly, in the energy sector, prices are largely determined by financing costs more than production costs. Mineral and non-mineral rents can be easily extracted in the form of royalties and often in a situation of limited competition or monopoly (see Bowman (2018), on South African platinum mining). Competition is critical in determining the extent to which companies need (or not) to reinvest to retain their dominant position.

Second, even within the same sector, financialization can take different forms, depending on the business enterprises' positioning along the value chain. The reason is that opportunities for rents are disproportionately distributed along sectoral value chains, especially when NFCs do not face major competitive pressures. Hence the value chain structure matters in shaping specific forms of financialization, especially across middle-income countries. In upstream sectors producing industrial materials such as chemicals or steel, the scale-efficiency of the investment is very high—also relative to the domestic demand. As a result, very few players can operate or control the sector—and in the case of a monopoly price regime, only one. In downstream industries such as retail and distribution, by controlling access to final markets, NFCs can also extract significant extra profits by simply applying large price mark-ups. This dominant position gives businesses the opportunity to extract rents along the entire value chain of buyers. The lack of competition does not provide any compulsion for reinvestment, and companies' extra profits can be easily targeted by predatory value extractors in both the domestic and international markets.

Third, business enterprises in low and middle-income countries tend to be squeezed along their GVCs, given the 'endogenous asymmetries' characterizing modern GVC structures (Milberg and Winkler, 2013; Chang and Andreoni, 2020). The endogenous asymmetries allow for international companies to extract extra profits generated in the host economies and use them to respond to short-term financialization pressures from international shareholders. As a result of these asymmetries, profitability margins of new productive investments in low and middle-income countries can be limited. Companies' strategic response—especially in manufacturing industries—could be to move away from long-term productive capabilities development towards trade intermediation and service activities. In effect, this is functional downgrading. This is particularly the case in the absence of effectively enforced industrial and trade policies, as business enterprises are squeezed along the value chain and in the international market by established business enterprises (Auvray and Rabinovich, 2019; Ponte et al., 2019; and Chapter 12).

Fourth, business enterprises' ownership structures matter. Foreign ownership—especially by institutional investors—might expose companies in low and middle-income countries to powerful extractive forces and pressures to extract financial resources and capture rents. Bonizzi (2017) points out that institutional investors, largely based in high-income economies, collectively owned the equivalent of 60 per cent of global GDP in 2014. From a political economy point of view, the lack of a mature class of industrial capitalists with interests embedded in the domestic economy, impacts negatively on the financial commitment of business enterprises. In a number of middle-income countries like South Africa, the privatization of state-owned enterprises (SOE) has opened the door to a number of major international institutional investors, including pension funds, and an accompanying shift in corporate governance strategies. Their interest in a sustained flow of dividends can affect the long-term financial commitment of resources in productive investments.

Fifth, business enterprises in middle-income countries rely on international financial markets for access to cheap credit and foreign exchange needed for operational purposes, exposing them to high levels of exchange and interest rate risks. Subordination in the international financial system means NFCs in middle-income countries turn to high-income countries' capital markets to source capital at competitive rates and to gain access to foreign exchange needed to settle import bills. US dollar-denominated debt positions expose middle-income country NFCs to two types of vulnerabilities: a currency mismatch between income generating activities and debt servicing costs, aggravated by exchange rate volatility; and a policy risk as the sustainability of the US dollar-denominated debt position is at the mercy of a foreign central bank (primarily the US Federal Reserve), which sets policy rates with no regard for the fate of foreign companies. This double vulnerability requires middle-income country NFCs to engage in costly financial risk management activities or suffer from sudden and substantial losses if the risk is not managed effectively.

Sixth, business enterprises in middle-income countries rely to a large extent on foreign capital for liquidity of domestic capital and equity markets. In order to keep foreign investors happy, these enterprises have to offer high risk-adjusted returns to compensate for the higher risk associated with their subordinate position. At the same time, enterprises must fend off potential hostile takeovers by keeping their share price high through offering large shareholder pay-outs, either via dividends or share buy-backs.

Moreover, depending on a country's particular sectoral composition and patterns of industrialization and deindustrialization (see Chapter 11), the combination of these sector-specific factors will magnify the impact of financialization on the economy as financialization dynamics reinforce each other. For example, as highlighted in Fine and Rustomjee (1996), it can be expected that an economy like South Africa's, which has traditionally developed around the 'minerals energy complex' (MEC), will be dominated by several of the sector-specific financialization dynamics highlighted above.

10.3 Signs of Financialization and the Broken Profit–Investment Nexus

By the early 1990s, South Africa already had a relatively well-developed and influential financial sector, characterized by a strong banking system and sophisticated capital markets (Isaacs and Kaltenbrunner, 2018). By the early 2000s, the country's first democratic government had made a formal commitment to a conventional macroeconomic policy framework targeted at low inflation and debt. Integration into global financial markets on this basis was explicitly aimed at attracting capital inflows from abroad, and incentivizing domestic investment by exposing leading domestic firms to the discipline of international competition (Mondliwa and Roberts, 2019; Ndikumana et al., 2020). However, despite South Africa's strict adherence to Washington Consensus policies, its growth strategy has largely failed—evident in the persistently high levels of poverty, inequality, and unemployment (Rodrik, 2006; Bosiu et al., 2017). Chronically weak investment combined with relatively rapid trade and capital account liberalization has driven a post-apartheid economic restructuring of which manufacturing industries have been a major casualty, eliciting diagnoses of 'premature de-industrialization' (Bosiu et al., 2017). An overwhelmingly non-selective, supply-side approach to industrial policy during liberalization has failed to support industries in need of more controlled exposure to international competition, and contributed to major manufacturing job losses and the shedding of entire industries (Roberts, 2007; Zalk, 2014; Andreoni and Tregenna, 2020).

Figure 10.1a shows how market capitalization of listed South African NFCs has increased steadily, while fixed capital formation has plateaued and been declining since 2008. Using the two-digit standard industrial classification (SIC) code, Figure 10.1b distinguishes between mining and energy sectors (ME), which have been studied extensively in the financialization literature on South Africa (Fine and Rustomjee, 1996; Karwowski, 2015; Isaacs, 2017; Ashman et al., 2012),[3] and other sectors. Figure 10.1b shows a declining trend in fixed capital investment in

---

[3] ME sectors here are simply combining the mining and quarrying, and electricity, gas, and water supply sectors. This does not correspond to the MEC, originally confined around six conglomerate groups, which serves as an analytical unit, not an industry classification.

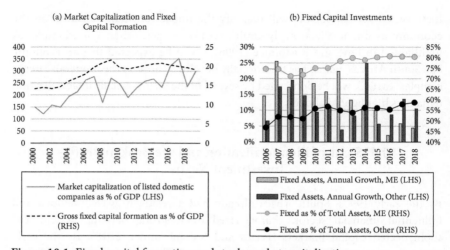

Figure 10.1 Fixed capital formation and stock market capitalization

Source: (a) Statistics South Africa, Annual Financial Statistics Survey (authors' calculations). (b) South African Reserve Bank and World Federation of Exchanges database via The World Bank Data (authors' calculations).

the ME sectors since the global financial crisis, and a similar trend for other sectors, initially. A reversal of the trend is identified from 2014, driven by a construction boom paired with a rapid expansion of the financial services sector.

These trends develop alongside high profitability and increasing shareholder payouts with some sectoral differences. Figure 10.2 shows annual profitability as net-profits as a percentage of turnover, and total dividends paid to shareholders as a percentage of net-profits, for the ME sectors (Figure 10.2a), and for the remaining sectors (Figure 10.2b). The most noteworthy observations are that the profitability of the ME sectors varies with global commodity cycles (demonstrating sectoral specificities), that ME sectors' dividend payments continue even in times of negative net-profits, and that dividend payments increase steadily for other sectors while profit margins remained relatively flat after the GFC. Interestingly, the spike in 2016 in Figure 10.2b is due to a steep increase in dividends paid by the financial services sector. The financial services sector is now the largest provider of dividends before manufacturing and exceeding the ME sectors (the largest providers in the early 2000s) by far, showing a remarkable expansion in both profits and size over the past two decades.

10.3.1 Factors Contributing to South Africa's Failure to Achieve Structural Transformation

The post-apartheid state's weakness vis-à-vis powerful factions of domestic capital, in particular the MEC, is critical in understanding South Africa's failure

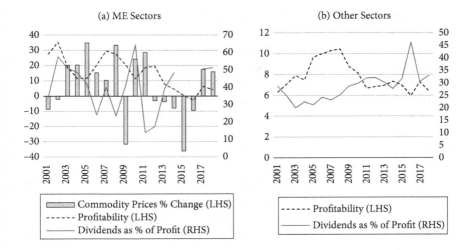

Figure 10.2 Profitability and dividend payments

Notes: Dividends as % of profits in (a) are interrupted for 2015 and 2016 as profits turned negative, while dividend payments were maintained throughout. Profitability is measured as net-profits as a % of turnover.

Source: Statistics South Africa, Annual Financial Statistics Survey (authors' calculations).

to achieve structural transformation (Fine and Rustomjee, 1996). Rather than strategically utilizing the high profitability of dominant upstream firms to strengthen production, consumption, and technological linkages with manufacturing industries in particular, the nature of the political settlement has allowed these firms to entrench their access to rents and their influence on policy (Roberts and Rustomjee, 2009; Zalk, 2014 and 2017; and Chapter 14).

Changing sentiment in international financial markets was a key driver of the post-1994 unbundling of the powerful, diversified conglomerate groups that constituted the MEC into separate entities focused on specific industries. Shares in diversified conglomerates had tended to trade at a discount in international markets due to the challenges posed by diversified holdings for market valuation methods and 'transparency' for shareholders (Bowman, 2018: 395), and unbundling proceeded rapidly (Mohamed, 2009).[4] Largely unencumbered by strategic oversight, regulation, or industrial policy on the part of the government, this process had extremely destructive consequences for industrial capabilities in some cases (see Chapter 2).

---

[4] It should be noted, however, that conglomerate unbundling has not resulted in more competitive markets—see Chabane et al. (2006). Industries considered to be highly concentrated include ICT, energy, financial services, food and agroprocessing, infrastructure and construction, intermediate industrial products, mining, pharmaceuticals, and transport.

Following the post-apartheid government's commitment to liberalization, exchange controls were gradually eliminated, a number of large corporates were allowed to list on foreign stock exchanges (notionally to raise capital for domestic investment), capital markets deepened substantially, and South African banks internationalized their operations and investments. Non-resident market capitalization as a percentage of total market capitalization has increased substantially since the early 2000s, both in equity, driven by robust liquidity and profitability, and debt, reflecting a sizeable carry trade attracted by high bond yields related to persistent current account deficits, and significant levels of offshore trading of rand-denominated assets (Isaacs and Kaltenbrunner, 2018). This trend has been accompanied by an increase in market-based credit relative to bank-based credit.[5] These developments are in line with a general trend across low and middle-income countries, which has ignited growing concern about new vulnerabilities and the phenomenon of subordinate financialization in these economies.

These developments have resulted in key domestic prices—exchange rates, interest rates, and asset and property prices—becoming increasingly delinked from domestic conditions, and driven instead by financial conditions in high-income economies and the decisions of large institutional investors.[6] Further, the changing demands of the global financial system on firms hoping to attract international investment have reinforced tendencies toward financialization in the domestic political economy. This is evident in increased payouts to shareholders in the post-apartheid period, driven by international investors' demands for competitive rates of return to shareholders. The distribution of profits to financial markets depletes NFCs' most efficient source of finance for expanded investment, entrenching an extractive and dependent relation between financial system and profitable enterprise.

South Africa's integration into the global financial system has been accompanied by shifts in the country's corporate governance framework, and the role of corporate governance in relation to financialization. The processes of liberalization, internationalization, and de-conglomeration came with a formal shift from a 'management-controlled, "social club" approach', dominated by family, cultural, and other informal networks, towards an Anglo-American[7] corporate governance model centred around the principle of maximizing shareholder value (see Padayachee, 2013 and 2017). Aspects of the former 'social club' dispensation

---

[5] However, bank-based credit remains the dominating source of credit, covering almost 90 per cent of total credit to non-financial corporations in 2019 according to BIS Statistics.

[6] These relations also act as a transmission channel for crisis in other parts of the world; exchange rate and bond yield movements in the context of the Covid-19 crisis reflect this starkly.

[7] In the sense of the countries, not the company.

remain in place, however, and a remarkably consistent flow of corporate scandals and collapses has spanned across twenty-five years and four editions of the King codes, which set out corporate governance requirements with which all the companies listed on the Johannesburg Stock Exchange (JSE), banks, financial institutions, and SOEs must comply. Despite this, the World Bank and the Institute for International Finance 'have rated South Africa among the top countries in terms of corporate best practice, and King 2 was seen as a benchmark worldwide' (Padayachee, 2013: 268).

While the evidence on levels of actual compliance with corporate governance regulations and principles is mixed, the impact of the shareholder value maximization aspect of the post-apartheid shift is clear. This is reflected materially in rising shareholder payouts, but also in the institutional and regulatory environment that has facilitated increasing distribution of profits to financial markets. Provisions allowing companies (and, critically, their subsidiaries) to repurchase their own shares were introduced in 1999, followed by further rounds of deregulation, resulting in relatively lax requirements on authorization, announcements, and reporting.

Wesson (2015), whose research on repurchases in the South African context is unparalleled, notes that the South African regulatory environment is unique in its approach to repurchases. First, subsidiaries of a parent company can purchase parent company shares up to 10 per cent of the total. Repurchases in the 2000–9 period were mainly driven by subsidiary repurchases since these were taxed at a lower rate than direct repurchases and dividends until 2012 (Wesson, 2015). Changes to the tax system introduced in 2012 reduced taxation on dividends in an effort to increase the country's attractiveness to international investors (Nyere and Wesson, 2019). In addition, the stock exchange listing requirements state that a firm is only required to declare a repurchase once cumulative repurchases surpass 3 per cent of total shares. Due to ambiguity in these regulations, however, many firms interpret the rule to mean that they need only announce repurchases once these have surpassed 3 per cent in a single year, rather than 3 per cent cumulatively over multiple years (Wesson, 2015).

As a result, unlike in the USA, UK, France, Hong Kong, and most other countries with much stricter repurchase announcement requirements, in South Africa it is impossible to track the full extent of a company's repurchasing activity in real time unless they are also listed on overseas exchanges (Wesson et al., 2015). Scrutiny of these regulatory lacunae has increased following a number of high-profile accounting scandals in leading South African firms, some of which have destroyed billions of Rands in value. However, decisive action on the part of the government or the JSE is lacking, and enforcement capacity remains weak (Crotty, 2019).

10.4 Financialization of Non-financial Corporations: Sasol and Shoprite, a Comparative Case Study Analysis

It is worthwhile recapping the six major interlinked factors set out in section 10.2: (1) sectoral heterogeneity (at firm, industry, and value chain levels); (2) value chain positioning and opportunities for rents; (3) financialization pressures on firms due to endogenous asymmetries in GVCs; (4) ownership structure, especially in regard to foreign institutional investors; (5) risks associated with reliance on international financial markets for relatively cheap credit and foreign exchange needs; and (6) the impact on domestic enterprises of the need to provide foreign investors with high risk-adjusted returns due to middle-income countries' subordinate position in global financial hierarchies.

This section examines how these factors play out in two JSE-listed South African firms located in different sectors and value chain positions: Sasol, an upstream producer of fuels, specialty chemicals and other primary inputs, and Shoprite, the country's leading supermarket chain.

10.4.1 The Story of Sasol

Sasol was established in 1950 as the South African Coal, Oil, and Gas Corporation Ltd, a SOE. Privatized in the 1980s, Sasol is now a fullyfledged multinational company, employing over 30,000 people across thirty-two countries. Initially an energy producer specializing in coal-to-liquid (CTL) fuel production, Sasol later diversified into other synthetic fuels and industrial chemicals, a strategy the firm intensified in the post-1994 democratic era in anticipation of lower profits from its energy-producing assets (Mondliwa and Roberts, 2019; and Chapter 4). This strategy proved successful, with Sasol coming to dominate the South African market across a range of specialized industrial chemicals, including polymers, explosives, waxes, and fertilizers, and forming part of a small group of highly vertically integrated firms that dominate the value chain from import, refinement, and production, to distribution and retail (Paelo et al., 2014).

Having secured its position in South Africa in the early years of the post-1994 dispensation, Sasol looked abroad in the 2000s. The firm listed on the New York Stock Exchange in 2003, and allocated significant capital expenditure to a series of overseas projects in Malaysia (2000), Mozambique (2000), Qatar (2003), China (2006/7), India (2008), Uzbekistan (2009), and a series of extremely large investments from 2011 onwards in North America (especially in Canada) (Sasol, 2012; Mondliwa and Roberts, 2019; and Chapter 2).

The fuel and chemicals industries in which Sasol operates are highly strategic due to their economic impact on consumers and downstream industries (Paelo et al., 2014). Mondliwa and Roberts (2019) among others have shown that Sasol has benefited from significant state support throughout the post-apartheid era via a number of channels. Direct support has included subsidies, large shareholdings by state development finance institutions, and other supportive industrial policy measures; indirect support has largely taken place through ineffective efforts to discipline and reallocate monopoly rents accruing to the set of dominant firms to which Sasol belongs (Davie, 2005; Zalk, 2014: 330; DTI, 2018). Efforts by the government to use regulation and competition policy to influence Sasol in ways that benefit downstream manufacturing and the economy more broadly have not only failed, but in some cases have been in direct conflict with other industrial policy measures and stated national strategies for growing the industrial base (Mondliwa and Roberts, 2019).

10.4.2 The Story of Shoprite

Like Sasol, Shoprite is a dominant player in an important strategic sector—food retail. Not only have Shoprite, its subsidiaries, and a small handful of major competitors maintained a firm grip on the South African market in spite of the entrance of new firms, they have extended their reach into a number of other countries on the continent. This expansion and search for new markets, aided by a strategy of differentiated brand offerings for different income groupings, has been identified as Shoprite's key growth strategy (das Nair and Chisoro-Dube, 2017: 9).

Shoprite retains a market share of at least 30 per cent in South Africa. This has been due in part to a series of key acquisitions, including, famously, the acquisition of the OK Bazaars chain for R1—less than $5 at the time (Jones, 1997). Shoprite's dominance is also due, in part, to large investments in an advanced retail and distribution infrastructure, including its own logistics fleet, and sophisticated information management systems (das Nair and Chisoro-Dube, 2015 and 2017). It is the only supermarket chain in the JSE's top fifty firms, with the third-highest revenues and the third-highest number of employees (almost 150,000) on the exchange (Bosiu et al., 2017; Thomson-Reuters, 2019).

As a large employer and a dominant lead firm in an industry with a direct impact on households and a range of other non-financial sectors, Shoprite's impact on the broader economy is significant. das Nair and Chisoro-Dube (2015) argue that more competition in the industry would be beneficial for households and suppliers, and describe a range of barriers to entry in the markets Shoprite operates in. These include prohibitive initial investment costs, and the time and 'patient' finance needed for the development of key capabilities, as well as a set of 'strategic barriers' essentially to do with anticompetitive practices by dominant firms (2015: 17). das Nair and Chisoro-Dube (2017) also note that, as lead firms in their supply chains, dominant supermarkets like Shoprite are able to exert huge pressure on suppliers, primarily through demanding lower costs, larger quantities, and higher standards. Lastly, Shoprite has also benefited from substantial state support over the years, in the form of significant state ownership of equity, employment subsidies, and minimal penalties for anticompetitive behaviours (see Chapter 8).

10.4.3 The Symptoms of Financialization in Both Firms

Both Sasol and Shoprite show a number of symptoms of financialization. These reflect the spread of what Lazonick has referred to as 'the American disease'—the extraction of profits or 'excess cash' out of firms and into financial markets via dividend payments, share repurchases, and payments to creditors. However, in these two cases the disease manifests differently than in Lazonick's work in the US context, with growing shareholder distributions driven by dividends rather than share repurchases (see Figure 10.3).

Figure 10.3 compares shareholder distributions from 2000–9 with those from 2010–19. Data for the earlier period are drawn from Wesson's (2015) database for dividends and repurchases, while figures for the more recent period have been constructed from company financial statements and the Thomson-Reuters Eikon database.

It is clear that both firms have significantly increased their total distributions to shareholders (TDS), with Shoprite increasing TDS to a greater degree than Sasol. This shows that, in terms of the extent of their financialization, non-ME sectors may be in a process of 'catching up' with ME sectors. Perhaps most interestingly, dividends have driven the increase in total distributions, while growth in repurchases has been less significant in the latter period, even declining in Sasol's case. This pattern resembles that observed by Andreoni et al. (2020) in the UK and broader European context, in contrast with the USA.

Clear shifts in strategy in relation to sources of funds are also observed in the latter period, with both firms financing capital expenditure, acquisitions, and shareholder distributions increasingly with debt (see Figure 10.4).

Two points can be made about Sasol's sources of funds in the last twenty years or so. First, the funds Sasol raises from equity are extremely small in comparison with funds raised from sales revenues and from debt. The highest total raised from equity in a single year was equivalent to around US$750,000 in 2013, while in that same year around US$1.4bn was raised in debt alone. This evidence seems to confirm Lazonick's (2008) proposition that the primary function of the modern stock market is not to provide resources to firms, but to extract from them.

The second point is that debt has increased rapidly from around 2012, in a context of first stagnating and then rapidly declining net income as oil prices

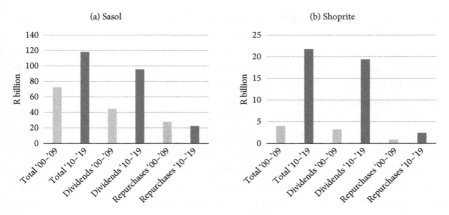

Figure 10.3 Composition of distributions to shareholders, 2000–9 vs. 2010–19
Source: Wesson (2015); company annual financial statements and Thomson-Reuters Eikon database.

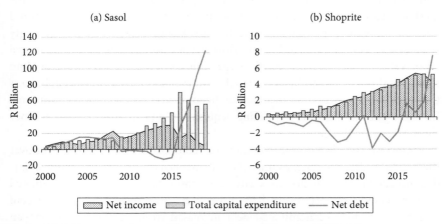

Figure 10.4 Sources and uses of funds in Sasol and Shoprite (2000–19)
Source: Company annual financial statements and Thomson-Reuters Eikon database.

collapsed toward the end of 2014. These outcomes reflect a major strategic shift from 2011 onwards, led by the firm's first 'outsider' CEO—a former FluorCorp executive, David Constable. A key outcome of this shift was that the company started to pivot away from major new investments in South Africa and other international operations in favour of new US-based 'megaprojects', the viability of which depended to a large extent on the maintenance of relatively high oil prices. Another related outcome was that it reorganized its corporate structure, organization, and culture in line with what Lazonick and others have described as a 'downsize and distribute' model of corporate governance. In the case of Sasol this took the form of thousands of retrenchments, divestment from 'non-core' downstream operations, rapid increases in stock-based executive remuneration, and larger distributions to shareholders.

Related both to Sasol's strategic pivot towards North America and loose monetary conditions in the USA, the currency composition and overall level of Sasol's debt has changed drastically since 2011. Dollar-denominated debt surpassed rand-denominated debt in 2015 and has grown rapidly since, approaching the equivalent of R130bn in 2019, more than ten times its 2013 level. Sasol's exposure to exchange rate risk, escalated by delays in the construction of key dollar-generating assets has clearly intensified sharply in recent years. Over the same period, a major decoupling has taken place between where Sasol generates its profits—overwhelmingly and consistently in South Africa through the period studied here—and where it invests these profits, with capital expenditure in South Africa stagnating as investment in the USA took precedence from 2011 onwards.

Analysis of Shoprite's sources of funds indicates a similar escalation in the proportion of debt to net income, with net debt increasingly volatile from 2008 and growing rapidly from 2012 onwards. Shoprite has not experienced the same level of decline in net income as Sasol, but net incomes stagnated in 2017–18 and fell by a worrying 18 per cent from 2018 to 2019. Shoprite reported a large equity issue in 2017, to the value of R4.6bn. However, a close examination of its annual reports shows that this represented a large-scale conversion of debt securities into shares, and ought not to be considered as new funds raised from shareholders (Shoprite, 2012). These securities had been issued in 2012, to institutional investors only, as a means of funding acquisitions and to 'shore up the balance sheet' (News24, 2012).

While available data on the evolution and composition of Shoprite's debt over the period studied are poor, its financial statements have reported growing dollar-denominated debt from 2015 onwards. These show that while rand-denominated debt increased from R110m to R134m between 2015 and 2018 (a 22 per cent increase), US dollar-denominated debt increased from R249m to R6.9bn—an increase of almost 2,700 per cent (Shoprite, 2016 and 2018). Such a rapid escalation in the firm's foreign debt is concerning. Further, unlike Sasol (despite its present difficulties), Shoprite has acquired no assets that generate US dollars or any other 'hard currency', and it appears to have no plans to develop any. It is also worth noting that large portions of Shoprite's borrowings have come from branches of international banks based in tax havens including Mauritius and the Isle of Man.

Shoprite's 2018 Integrated Annual Report acknowledges exchange rate volatility and shortages of hard currency as high-risk concerns that 'continue to create major obstacles' for the firm (p. 25). Shoprite's key risk mitigation strategy is to increase investments in US treasury bills (short-term, low-yield debt obligations). This reflects one of the key concerns of the subordinate financialization perspective, as the strategy generates increased net flows of capital from EMDEs to advanced economies (see Lapavitsas, 2013; Powell, 2013). As Akyuz (2018) argues, these dynamics entrench EMDE current account deficits as EMDE holdings of low-yielding foreign assets increase alongside relatively high-yielding foreign liabilities.

Another component of Shoprite's risk mitigation strategy is that the firm instructs its subsidiaries to pay out its 'excess' cash to the parent company to pay back short-term debt (Shoprite Integrated Annual Report 2018: 25). This is made possible because Shoprite exercises control over a buyer-driven value chain. As a result of this power, resources that could be ploughed back into productive reinvestment, spread more equitably in less oligopolistic markets, or used to raise low wages and improve poor working conditions, are instead being paid out to Shoprite's creditors and are lost to the continent entirely.

Building on Wesson's (2015) finding that share repurchases in South Africa tend to be conducted via subsidiaries, it is argued here that these trends suggest increasing extraction of value out of productive assets and into financial markets.

10.4.4 Key Finding: Corporate Strategies Are Driven by the Availability of International Capital

The evidence presented above supports one of the key arguments of subordinate financialization scholars: that changes in NFCs' corporate strategy—particularly regarding capital structure and investment patterns—have not been driven by operating characteristics, as theorized in orthodox economics, but by the availability of international capital to EMDE firms in an era of global financial liberalization (Powell, 2013).

The core findings illustrate an increase in financial activity relative to productive activity, indicated by an increasing reallocation of precious firm resources away from productive investment and toward financial interests, paying high returns to property in shareholdings and to creditors. It is also clear that while companies operating in different sectors and stages of the value chain are all affected by financialization, there is heterogeneity in the ways in which financialization operates across NFCs. So, to the extent that financialization can manifest differently, it also hampers structural transformation in different ways.

10.5 Conclusions

Over the last two decades, financialization in South Africa has been driven by the joint effect of the distribution of power in the domestic political economy and the nature of South Africa's integration with global finance. These two factors have mutually reinforced each other and deprived the economy of the precious resources needed to spur investment-led structural transformation. Specifically, it has been shown how financialization has undermined the translation of profits into domestic investment, reducing its capacity to drive structural transformation.

Post-apartheid liberalization and internationalization coincided with a global conjuncture in which private capital flows and underlying economic performance have become increasingly delinked. This has, in combination with increased international investment and trading in South African equity, debt, and currency markets, contributed to increased financial vulnerability and extraction of profits from South African firms.

The prevailing economic policy framework and the additional measures taken to buffer the economy from crisis have essentially socialized the costs of these developments, while the benefits accrue to international investors, domestic finance capital, speculative asset traders, and wealthy beneficiaries of asset price inflation. Safeguarding macroeconomic stability via inflation targeting and reserve accumulation has entrenched high interest rates and reliance on short-term inflows. As South Africa started to reconnect with international financial markets, NFCs were put under extreme pressure to conform with contemporary corporate strategies and to align with the international demand for shareholder value maximization. This realignment is at the expense of productive reinvestment of profits in general, and especially in South Africa where they are generated.

As shown in the two case studies in section 10.4, studies of financialization in middle-income countries can benefit a great deal from a firm-level analysis. This allows for the recognition of a range of heterogeneities at the firm, industry, and value chain level, an evaluation of how value chain positioning impacts the creation and extraction of rents, and the analysis of common financialization pressures faced by NFCs in spite of their differences. Sasol and Shoprite, lead firms operating in different sectors and value chain positions, clearly illustrate this. Both firms show symptoms of financialization, increasing their distributions to shareholders markedly in the period under study, with the composition of this increase driven by dividends rather than share repurchases. Despite their differing operating characteristics, the analysis of the firms' sources and uses of funds shows that both have increasingly financed their investments, operations, and even shareholder distributions with debt, much of which has been denominated in US dollars. This has exposed both firms to significant risks given that the bulk of their profits are generated in Rands, and is an especially troubling development for Shoprite in light of its apparent lack of dollar-generating assets. The strategies employed to mitigate these risks reflect power dynamics underlying South Africa's financialization on two levels: the acquisition of low-yielding, dollar-denominated 'safe haven' assets to hedge against currency risk reflects the country's subordinate position in the global hierarchy of currencies and financial markets; and the extraction of profits from subsidiaries to finance dramatically increased debt reflects the power of lead firms' value chain position and market dominance.

These processes have further empowered domestic capital vis-à-vis the state, which has enacted forms of deregulation that further entrench financialization and appears to retain relatively little leverage to induce large domestic firms to invest in accordance with a strategic national growth path.

While enabled by changes in corporate governance, financialization is entrenched within a broader political economy context in South Africa, and in South Africa's relations with the rest of the world. Given the complex firm-level processes of financialization revealed by the case study analysis, a more detailed framework capable of unveiling heterogeneous processes of financialization is called for. Without such deep dives into specific company trajectories, corporate governance reforms alongside competition and industrial policy for structural transformation cannot be effective.

References

Akyuz, Y. (2018). 'External balance sheets of emerging economies: low-yielding assets, high-yielding liabilities.' Political Economy Research Institute: Working Paper no. 476.

Alchian, A. and H. Demsetz (1972). 'Production, information costs, and economic organization.' *The American Economic Review* 62(5): 777–95.

Andreoni, A., M. Hopkins, and W. Lazonick (2020). 'Governing financialisation: a UK industrial strategy to retain and reinvest.' GoFinPro Working Paper 4, forthcoming.

Andreoni, A. and F. Tregenna (2020). 'Escaping the middle income technology trap.' *Structural Change and Economic Dynamics* 54: 324–40.

Ashman, S., B. Fine, and S. Newman (2012). 'Systems of accumulation and the evolving MEC.' In B. Fine, J. Saraswati, and D. Tavasci (eds), *Beyond the Developmental State: Industrial Policy into the 21st Century*. London: Pluto.

Auvray, T. and J. Rabinovich (2019). 'The financialization-offshoring nexus and the capital accumulation of U.S. nonfinancial firms.' *Cambridge Journal of Economics* 43(5): 1183–1218.

Baud, C., and C. Durand (2011). 'Financialization, globalization and the making of profits by leading retailers.' *Socio-Economic Review* 10(2): 241–66.

Bonizzi, B. (2013). 'Financialization in developing and emerging countries.' *International Journal of Political Economy* 42(4): 83–107.

Bonizzi, B. (2017). 'An alternative post-Keynesian framework for understanding capital flows to emerging markets.' *Journal of Economic Issues* 15(1): 137–62.

Bonizzi, B., A. Kaltenbrunner, and J. Powell (2019). 'Subordinate financialization in emerging capitalist economies.' Greenwich Papers in Political Economy. University of Greenwich, Greenwich Political Economy Research Centre.

Bosiu, T., N. Nhundu, A. Paelo, M. O. Thosago, and T. Vilakazi (2017). 'Growth and strategies of large and leading firms—top 50 firms on the Johannesburg Stock Exchange.' Centre for Competition, Regulation and Economic Development, Working Paper 17. Johannesburg: CCRED.

Bowman, A. (2018). 'Financialization and the extractive industries: the case of South African platinum mining.' *Competition and Change* 22(4): 388–412.

Chabane, N., A. Goldstein, and S. Roberts (2006). 'The changing face and strategies of big business in South Africa: more than a decade of political democracy.' *Industrial and Corporate Change* 15(3): 549–77.

Chang, H.-J. and A. Andreoni (2020). 'Industrial policy in the 21st century.' *Development and Change* 51(2): 324–51.

Crotty, A. (2019). 'Shareholders have a right to know.' *Business Day*, https://www.businesslive.co.za/fm/opinion/boardroom-tails/2019-08-08-ann-crotty-shareholders-have-a-right-to-know/.

das Nair, S. and S. Chisoro-Dube (2015). 'Competition, barriers to entry and inclusive growth: case study on fruit and veg city.' CCRED Working Paper. Johannesburg: CCRED.

das Nair, S. and S. Chisoro-Dube (2017). 'Growth and Strategies of Large, Lead Firms—Supermarkets.' CCRED Working Paper. Johannesburg: CCRED.

Davie, K. (2005). 'Government's R6bn gift to Sasol.' *The Mail and Guardian*, https://mg.co.za/article/2005-09-23-governments-r6bn-gift-to-sasol.

Department of Trade and Industry (DTI) (2018). 'Industrial policy action plan 2018/19–2020/21.' Pretoria: DTI.

Epstein, G. A. (2005). *Financialization and the World Economy*. Cheltenham: Edward Elgar.

Fine, B. (2013). 'Financialization from a Marxist perspective.' *International Journal of Political Economy* 42(4): 47–66.

Fine, B. and Z. Rustomjee (1996). *The Political Economy of South Africa: From Minerals-Energy Complex to Industrialisation*. London: C. Hurst & Co.

Froud, J., S. Johal, A. Leaver, and K. Williams (2016) *Financialization and Strategy: Narrative and Numbers*. London: Routledge.

Isaacs, G. (2017). 'Financialization in post-apartheid South Africa.' PhD thesis. London: SOAS, University of London.

Isaacs, G. and A. Kaltenbrunner (2018). 'Financialization and liberalization: South Africa's new forms of external vulnerability.' *Competition and Change* 22(4): 437–63.

Jensen, M. C. and W. H. Meckling (1976). 'Theory of the firm: managerial behavior, agency costs and ownership structure.' *Journal of Financial Economics* 3(4): 305–60.

Karwowski, E. (2015). 'The finance-mining nexus in South Africa: how mining companies use the South African equity market to speculate.' *Journal of the Southern African Studies* 41(1): 9–28.

Krippner, G. R. (2005). 'The financialization of the American economy.' *Socio-Economic Review* 3: 173–208.

Lapavitsas, C. (2013). 'Profiting without producing: how finance exploits us all.' London: Verso.

Lazonick, W. (1990). 'Competitive advantage on the shop floor.' Cambridge, MA: Harvard University Press.

Lazonick, W. (2008). 'The quest for shareholder value: stock repurchases in the US economy.' *Louvain Economic Review* 74(4): 479–540.

Lazonick, W. (2010). 'Innovative business models and varieties of capitalism: financialization of the U.S.' *Business History Review* 84: 675–702.

Lazonick, W. (2014). 'Profits without prosperity.' *Harvard Business Review* (September): 46–55.

Lazonick, W. and M. O'Sullivan (2000). 'Maximising shareholder value: a new ideology for corporate governance.' *Economy & Society* 29: 13–35.

Milberg, W. and D. Winkler (2013). 'Financialization and the dynamics of offshoring.' In *Outsourcing Economics: Global Value Chains in Capitalist Development*, 210–37. Cambridge: Cambridge University Press.

Mohamed, S. (2009). 'Financialization, the minerals energy complex and South African labour.' Global Labour University Conference. Tata Institute for Social Sciences, Mumbai, India.

Mondliwa, P. and S. Roberts (2019). 'From a developmental to a regulatory state? Sasol and the conundrum of continued state support.' *International Review of Applied Economics* 33(1): 11–29.

News24 (2012). 'Shoprite shares dive on expansion plans.' Fin24, https://www.fin24.com/Companies/Retail/Shoprite-shares-dive-on-expansion-plans-20120322.

Ndikumana, L., K. Naidoo, and A. Aboobaker (2020). 'Capital flight from South Africa: a case study.' PERI Working Paper 516. University of Massachusetts-Amherst.

Nyere, L. and N. Wesson (2019). 'Factors influencing dividend payout decisions: evidence from South Africa.' *South African Journal of Business Management* 50(1): 1–16.

Padayachee, V. (2013). 'Corporate governance in South Africa: from "old boys club" to "Ubuntu"?' *Transformation: Critical Perspectives on Southern Africa* 81/2: 260–90.

Padayachee, V. (2017). 'King IV is here: corporate governance in South Africa revisited.' *New Agenda* 66: 17–21.

Paelo, A., G. Robb, and T. Vilakazi (2014). 'Study on barriers to entry in liquid fuel distribution in South Africa.' CCRED Working Paper 13. Johannesburg: CCRED.

Penrose, E. (1959). *The Theory of the Growth of the Firm*. Oxford: Oxford University Press.

Ponte, S., G. Gereffi, and G. Raj-Rechert (2019). *Handbook of Global Value Chains*. Cheltenham and Northampton, MA: Edward Elgar.

Powell, J. (2013). 'Subordinate financialization: a study of Mexico and its non-financial corporations.' PhD dissertation. London: SOAS University of London.

Roberts, S. (2007). 'Patterns of industrial performance in South Africa in the first decade of democracy: the continued influence of minerals-based activities.' *Transformation: Critical Perspectives on Southern Africa* 65: 4–35.

Roberts, S. and Z. Rustomjee (2009). 'Industrial policy under democracy: apartheid's grown-up infant industries? Iscor and Sasol.' *Transformation: Critical Perspectives on Southern Africa* 71: 50–75.

Rodrik, D. (2006). 'Understanding South Africa's economic puzzles.' NBER Working Paper.

Samargandi, N., J. Fidrmuc, and S. Gosh (2015). 'Is the relationship between financial development and economic growth monotonic? Evidence from a sample of middle-income countries.' *World Development* 68: 66–81.

Wesson, N. (2015). 'An empirical model of choice between share repurchases and dividends for companies in selected JSE-listed sectors.' PhD thesis. Stellenbosch: University of Stellenbosch.

Wesson, N., B. W. Bruwer, and W. D. Hamman (2015). 'Share repurchases and dividend payout behaviour: the South African experience.' *South African Journal of Business Management* 46(3): 43–54.

Zalk, N. (2014). 'Industrial policy in a harsh climate: the case of South Africa.' In J. M. Salazar-Xirinachs, I. Nubler, and R. Kozul-Wright (eds), *Transforming Economies: Making Industrial Policy Work for Growth, Jobs and Development.* Geneva: ILO.

Zalk, N. (2017). 'Things we lost in the fire: the political economy of post-apartheid restructuring of the South African steel and engineering sectors.' PhD thesis. London: SOAS University of London.

Data sources

Sasol. Annual financial statements (2004–19).

Sasol. Integrated annual reports (2004–19).

Sasol. Prospectus for issue of debt securities, filed with United States Securities and Exchange Commission (2012, 2018), https://www.sec.gov/Archives/edgar/data/314590/000104746912010234/a2211472z424b5.htm and https://sec.report/Document/0001104659-18-057884.

Shoprite. Annual financial statements (2003–19).

Shoprite. Integrated annual reports (2003–19).

South African Reserve Bank. Online statistical query system, https://www.resbank.co.za/Research/Statistics/Pages/OnlineDownloadFacility.aspx.

Statistics South Africa. Annual financial statistics survey, http://www.statssa.gov.za/?page_id=1866&PPN=P0021&SCH=7681.

Statistics South Africa. Statistical release P3043: manufacturing: utilisation of production capacity by large enterprises. Pretoria: Statistics South Africa, http://www.statssa.gov.za/?page_id=1866&PPN=P3043&SCH=7729.

Thomson-Reuters Eikon database. Accessed via SOAS University of London subscription.

11

The Middle-Income Trap and Premature Deindustrialization in South Africa

Antonio Andreoni and Fiona Tregenna

11.1 Introduction

The South African economy has been stagnant over an extended period of time, going back to the apartheid era. This is manifest in the lack of structural transformation and in weak economic growth. Even with the unique characteristics of the South African economy, it shares commonalities with some other middle-income countries and can be considered as an example of an economy stuck in the 'middle income trap'. It has remained in middle-income status over a long period of time, without approaching a transition towards high-income status. Growth has been stagnant, with little improvement in average living standards. At a structural level, the economy has not undergone the kind of structural transformation that could form the basis for a shift towards a superior growth path.

Premature deindustrialization (Palma, 2005 and 2008; Tregenna 2009, 2015, 2016a and 2016b; Rodrik, 2016) is among the key factors locking many middle-income countries in a trap of stagnant growth and thwarting their catching-up with advanced economies. When premature, deindustrialization is likely to have more severe consequences for growth than deindustrialization in advanced economies, as discussed further below. South Africa arguably started to deindustrialize in the early 1980s; by 2020 it was still at relatively low levels of income per capita and shares of manufacturing in gross domestic product (GDP) and total employment (see Chapter 2).

Beyond falling in the middle-income trap in general, with many of the features of premature deindustrialization, a further impediment to South Africa's economic progress has been that the country can also be understood to have been stuck in a 'middle income technology trap'. Andreoni and Tregenna (2020: 324) introduce this idea, conceptualized as 'specific structural and institutional configurations that are not conducive to increasing domestic value addition and

Antonio Andreoni and Fiona Tregenna, *The Middle-Income Trap and Premature Deindustrialization in South Africa*
In: *Structural Transformation in South Africa: The Challenges of Inclusive Industrial Development in a Middle-Income Country.*
Edited by: Antonio Andreoni, Pamela Mondliwa, Simon Roberts, and Fiona Tregenna, Oxford University Press.
© Oxford University Press 2021. DOI: 10.1093/oso/9780192894311.003.0011

to sustained industrial and technological upgrading'. This is reflected in the lack of crucial industrial and technological upgrading that could enable new development trajectories, with severe consequences for industrial development and economic growth. The middle-income technology trap is thus closely linked with the concept of premature deindustrialization.

The middle-income technology trap can contribute to premature deindustrialization, as the failure to upgrade manufacturing and move to more technology-intensive industries can exacerbate the poor performance of manufacturing. Premature deindustrialization, in turn, can contribute to countries being stuck in a middle-income trap. Linking the middle-income technology trap and premature deindustrialization presents the possibility of a vicious cycle of weak techno-logical and broader industrial upgrading, deindustrialization, lack of structural transformation, and poor economic growth.

This diagnosis brings to the fore the importance of industrial policies in supporting industrial development and structural transformation, in particular in promoting technological upgrading throughout manufacturing and a shift towards more technology-intensive manufacturing activities. The effectiveness of industrial policy in addressing premature deindustrialization in middle-income countries critically depends on the specific features of the industrial system. Indeed, countries that are traditionally classified in the group of middle-income countries are highly heterogeneous with respect to their premature deindustrialization experiences.

This chapter analyses structural change, the middle-income trap, and premature deindustrialization in South Africa, in the context of the specific industrialization challenges faced by middle-income countries today. It provides global and regional evidence for the different premature deindustrialization trajectories that countries have followed. Throughout the chapter, reference is made to three selected middle-income countries as comparator cases: Brazil, China, and Malaysia. Whereas South Africa previously (up until 1972) had the highest income per capita of these countries, by 2020 it had the lowest. The four countries have followed very different policies, with diverse outcomes in structural transformation and growth. While there are some commonalities among them, these marked differences draw attention to the profound deficiencies in South Africa's policy choices and economic outcomes.

Section 11.2 discusses the issue of the 'middle-income trap' and the challenges that middle-income countries face in industrializing during the current period. Section 11.3 presents an empirical analysis of selected global evidence on the phenomenon of premature deindustrialization, situating South Africa in an international comparative perspective. Section 11.4 briefly discusses industrial policy implications for middle-income countries, and section 11.5 concludes.

11.2 The Middle-Income Trap, the Middle-Income Technology Trap, and Industrialization Challenges

11.2.1 The Middle-Income Trap

As a stylized fact, many middle-income economies have experienced stagnant economic growth and have struggled to transition to high-income status. In some cases, this manifests as a slowdown in growth after an earlier period of more rapid growth that took them from low- to middle-income status. The notion of a 'middle-income trap' has been used to refer broadly to the problem of a failure of middle-income countries catching up with advanced economies and transitioning to upper-income status.[1] Many middle-income countries have experienced stagnant growth (in both absolute and relative terms) over a long period of time, and being 'trapped' in an apparent low-growth equilibrium.

It is worth noting that the middle-income trap is not a confinement from which countries have no hope of escape. Between 1994 (the year of South Africa's democratization) and 2019, nine countries that had been classified as lower-middle-income transitioned to high-income status; seven of these nine countries were East European. In addition, over this period, a diverse group of twenty-two countries moved from upper-middle-income to high-income status, including Chile, Greece, Hungary, Uruguay, and Saudi Arabia. This indicates that there is a degree of mobility, and that some countries have moved ahead while South Africa has remained stuck in middle-income status. South Africa was one of nine countries classified as middle-income in both 1994 and 2019, with others including Brazil, Argentina, Malaysia, and Mexico. Of course, within these countries that remained in middle-income status during this period, some (such as Malaysia) followed a catching-up trajectory while others (including South Africa) fell further behind, as discussed further below. Eight low-income and thirty-five lower-middle income countries moved to upper-middle-income status between 1994 and 2019, a number of these overtaking South Africa in income per capita.

Of course, these income categories are based only on income levels (specifically, gross national income (GNI) per capita in US$), and do not reflect the deeper structural features that are associated with the concept of a middle-income trap. Nonetheless, these observations do point on the one hand to the stagnation of some countries (including South Africa) in middle-income status, while on

---

[1] For recent literature on the middle-income trap, see for instance Gill and Kharas, 2007; Arias and Wen (2015); Wade (2016); Felipe et al. (2017); Kang and Paus (2020); Klingler-Vidra and Wade (2020); Lebdioui et al. (2020); and Paus (2020).

the other hand others have been able to attain sustained high growth rates and transition to high-income status, some of these overtaking South Africa in the process.[2]

Various explanations have been advanced for the apparent prevalence and persistence of the middle-income trap (see Wade, 2016). One focuses on productivity, and specifically the failure of middle-income countries to sustain rates of labour productivity growth above those of advanced economies (see, for example, Lin, 2017). Other authors such as Lee (2013) draws attention to middle-income countries being squeezed between, on the one hand, countries with lower wages and that have been successful as large-scale exporters, and on the other hand, more technologically advanced economies.

If the idea is embraced that manufacturing industries play a critical role in boosting productivity, value addition, and technological change, premature deindustrialization could be another factor responsible for the phenomenon of the middle-income trap. Countries can be considered to experience premature deindustrialization when the level of GDP per capita and/or the shares of manufacturing in total employment and GDP at which deindustrialization sets in are lower than is typically the case internationally.

11.2.2 South Africa: Stuck in the Middle

According to various indicators of industrial competitiveness, South Africa is stuck in the middle-income countries segment, and has shown signs of an ongoing process of premature deindustrialization. Over several decades, the annual growth rate of the manufacturing sector has slowed down dramatically, thereby affecting the absolute manufacturing value addition produced in the country. As a result of this premature deindustrialization process, if South Africa's export performances are benchmarked against those of other middle-income countries, gross export value is shown to increase after 2000, but at a much slower pace than major comparator countries.[3]

Figure 11.1 compares the evolution of South Africa's GDP per capita with that of the three comparator middle-income countries that are referenced throughout this chapter: Brazil, China, and Malaysia. Each of the four countries' GDP per capita is shown relative to that of the USA over the period 1960–2019, showing the extent to which they are catching up or falling behind.

---

[2] See Felipe et al. (2017) for a systematic analysis of countries' historical transitions between income categories; they argue that the evidence suggests that there is no generalized phenomenon of a middle-income trap.

[3] Chapter 2 provides a comprehensive overview of relevant empirical trends in the South African manufacturing sector, demonstrating the lack of structural transformation and deindustrialization.

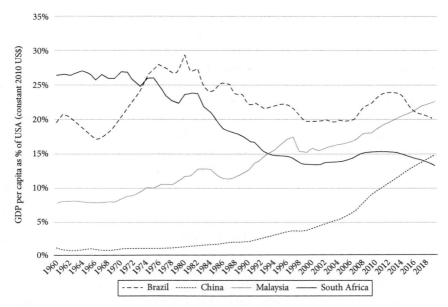

Figure 11.1 South Africa and comparator countries: % of US GDP per capita 1960–2019
Source: World Bank World Development Indicators (WB WDI).

Until 1972, South Africa had the highest level of GDP per capita in the group, after which it was overtaken by Brazil. South Africa was then overtaken by Malaysia in 1993 and China in 2018, leaving it with the lowest income level among these four countries. South Africa's income per capita remained at a little over a quarter of that of the USA until the mid-1970s, but this ratio fell dramatically during the 1990s and 2000s. There was modest growth in South Africa during the 2000s, which saw some catching-up with the US benchmark. However, this ratio has fallen again from 2011 onwards. Thus, over an extended period of time, instead of catching up, South Africa fell further behind, with a GDP per capita just 13 per cent of that of the US in 2019.

Figure 11.1 also illustrates the contrasting fortunes of the three comparator countries, all of which are currently classified as middle-income economies. Brazil experienced rapid catching-up from 1966 to 1980, reaching almost 30 per cent of US income per capita; it then experienced a short period of catching-up during the Lula presidency and the early years of the Dilma presidency, before again falling behind the USA as well as being overtaken by Malaysia in 2016. Malaysia and China are pre-eminent examples of sustained catching-up. China's GDP per capita rose from just 1 per cent of that of the USA to 15 per cent over the period shown. While these are both classified as middle-income countries at the time of writing, neither has been stuck in a middle-income trap.

It is true that virtually all countries would show up poorly when benchmarked against China's long-run growth miracle. Yet South Africa performed poorly when compared not just against the three comparator countries and the benchmark of the US as shown here, but against all relevant country groupings and aggregates.

This underscores the long-term structural deficiencies of South Africa's economy and growth trajectory, and the extent to which it is has remained stuck in its middle-income position and in fact has fallen down the global rankings in GDP per capita. Even during the period of relatively rapid economic growth in the 2000s, there was a failure of structural transformation in the South African economy.

11.2.3 Structural Challenges: The Middle-Income Technology Trap

Andreoni and Tregenna (2020) identify three specific structural factors associated with the middle-income trap: breaking into globally concentrated industrial production; linking up with global value chains (GVCs) while also linking back with local production systems; and keeping pace with technological change. The combined impact of these three structural challenges is what they call the 'middle-income technology trap'. Indeed, capturing this set of factors and observing how they unfold in different countries along different structural trajectories constitutes a key step in designing appropriate industrial policy for middle-income countries.

11.2.3.1 The Challenges of Breaking into Globally Concentrated Manufacturing Production

First, global industrial production generally remains highly concentrated, with world manufacturing value added shares being captured by a few mature and emerging economies. This is despite a small number of countries (especially in East Asia) having managed to meaningfully expand and upgrade their industrial production. In this context of the global industrial landscape, South Africa has faced a fundamental challenge in increasing its domestic value added (DVA) in manufacturing industries and exported products. Simply put, manufacturing DVA indicates the extent to which a country adds value in manufacturing, excluding the value of imported intermediate inputs. In South Africa, the net DVA declined among all major manufacturing subsectors between 1995 and 2008 (Figure 11.2). Some recovery was registered after 2008, for example in the machinery and equipment industries (see Chapter 13).

11.2.3.2 The Challenge of Linking Up with GVCs While Linking Back with Local Production Systems

A second challenge identified by Andreoni and Tregenna (2020) is that of 'linking up' through productive integration in GVCs, while also 'linking back' with the

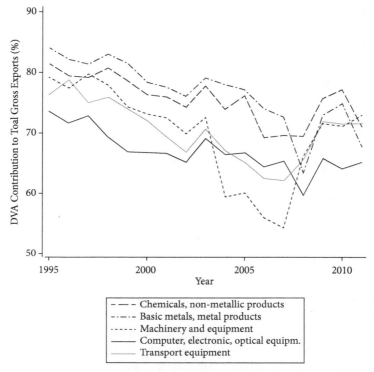

Figure 11.2 Domestic value-added content of South African exports by major manufacturing sub-sectors

Source: Authors, based on TIVA.

local production system. It is important that countries develop their industrial capabilities and maximize the potential benefits of forward integration into GVCs.[4] Between 1990 and 2010, African countries experienced limited gains from GVC integration and declining forward integration (and DVA) in international trade. Much of Africa's participation in GVCs has developed in upstream production (backward integration), with declining downstream integration. South Africa has seen an increase in backward integration, measured in this context as the share of foreign value added in exports, from 17 per cent in 1995 to 30 per cent in 2011 (Figure 11.3).

Middle-income countries like South Africa typically struggle to move into the more complex, technologically sophisticated, and profitable segments of GVCs, which can contribute to their often remaining stuck in a middle-income technology trap, and a middle-income trap more broadly. Where middle-income countries' engagement with RVCs or GVCs is predominantly in low value-added production, this brings the risk of disarticulation with the domestic manufacturing

---

[4] See Chapter 13 for more discussion on GVCs, in particular around upgrading and integration.

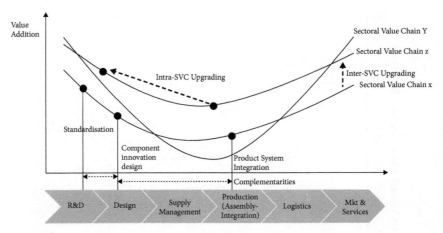

Figure 11.3 Capturing high-value niches and the need for multiple sets of complementary capabilities
Source: Andreoni (2019).

sector and a hollowing out of domestic industrial capabilities. This points to the importance of 'linking back' with domestic production systems, in a way that fosters structural transformation. GVC upgrading involves transitioning to more profitable and/or technologically advanced economic niches within GVCs. To do so, firms require multiple sets of capabilities that are relevant to various stages of value chains (Figure 11.3).

Intersectoral upgrading is becoming increasingly important, given that modern, high-value manufacturing activities require cross-cutting capabilities and technology systems. Technology systems such as biotechnologies, advanced materials, microelectronics, and automation are required in a range of manufacturing activities (Chapter 12). These complementary sets of capabilities are thus important for innovation and technological upgrading—both intra- and inter-sectoral upgrading—and hence to enable new development trajectories.

11.2.3.3 The Challenge of Keeping Pace with Technological Change

A third challenge is that of 'keeping pace' with technological change and innovation (Andreoni and Tregenna, 2020). Technological change at the innovation frontier—the so-called fourth industrial revolution—has increasingly been recognized by lower- and middle-income countries as a critical competitive factor for GVC upgrading and a leapfrogging opportunity.

'Key technology systems' are particularly important in keeping pace with technological change, especially in the current global industrial landscape. The European Commission (2009), for example, identified the following list of technology systems as key enablers of innovation and structural change in the global economy: micro- and nano-electronics and nanotechnology, photonics,

Table 11.1 South Africa and comparator countries: R&D and technology indicators

	Brazil	China	Malaysia	South Africa
Total R&D personnel per million inhabitants	2,917	3,824	3,835	1,327
Total R&D personnel per thousand total employment	6.3	7.0	8.3	4.6
Gross domestic expenditure on R&D as a percentage of GDP	1.3	2.1	1.4	0.8
Gross domestic expenditure on R&D per capita (current PPP$)	194	320	405	108
Scientific and technical journal articles	60,148	528,263	23,661	13,009
Patent applications, residents	4,980	1,393,815	1,116	657
High-technology exports (% of manufactured exports)	13.0	31.4	52.8	5.3

Note: Each variable is shown for the most recent year for which data are available for all four countries; years and data sources as follows: both R&D personnel measures are for 2014 and from UNESCO; both R&D expenditure measures are for 2014 and from UNESCO; all other measures are for 2018 and from the World Bank World Development Indicators (WB WDI).

industrial biotechnology, advanced materials, and advanced manufacturing systems. These key enabling technologies (KETs) are transversal, in that they are utilized across multiple sectors and supply chains. They are also embedded, playing an important function in integrated technology systems. Key technology systems have the potential to be quality-enhancing, productivity-enhancing, and strategic. All of these characteristics render key technology systems important in technological upgrading and for avoiding a middle-income technology trap.

Regarding the challenge of keeping pace with these technologies, Table 11.1 compares South Africa with Brazil, China, and Malaysia for some key research and development (R&D) and technology indicators. The comparisons show South Africa ranked as the worst in all seven of these measures. For instance, South Africa had approximately one-third of the R&D personnel per million inhabitants as did both China and Malaysia, and also spent far less on R&D (both as a percentage of GDP and per capita) than the three comparator countries. As an indication of technological intensity, South Africa had by far the lowest share of high-technology exports in total manufactured exports. South Africa is clearly a laggard in both the 'inputs' to technological upgrading and the 'outcomes' in technological intensity and, as seen earlier, economic growth. Insofar as 'keeping pace' is important in avoiding a middle-income trap, these comparisons do not bode well for South Africa's prospects of catching up.

Furthermore, recognizing the role of 'key technology systems' draws attention to the fact that there are important functions and activities relating to these technological capabilities which are not necessarily located in individual manu-facturing firms. For instance, these activities could be in separate engineering, design, and research institutions and businesses, which may be classified within the services sector. While sector categories remain relevant, the blurring between sectoral divisions and the growing integration between sectors needs to be recognized (Andreoni and Chang, 2017; Cramer and Tregenna, 2020). This also affects apparent trends in manufacturing employment and output shares. While manufacturing employment share may have remained steady or even fallen in countries that have successfully developed these capabilities, the manufacturing share is nevertheless higher than predicted, as in the cases of China and Malaysia for instance.

Apparent deindustrialization, based on aggregate trends in manufacturing output or employment, can obscure different dynamics in the composition of manufacturing, in productivity (Tregenna, 2009 and 2013), the extent of outsourcing to the services sector (Tregenna, 2010), and, of particular relevance here, the role of 'key technology systems'. Structural transformation involves not just change in the overall sectoral composition of the economy, but also a shift towards activities with the scope for higher cumulative productivity increases. Key technology systems have important roles to play in this, irrespective of the sectors within which these activities may be formally classified.

Middle-income countries such as South Africa run the risk of undermining the 'technological preconditions' that have to be met in order to capture value opportunities from technological change. For example, to make investments in ICT and digital solutions valuable, investments in the production capacity and hardware and organizational capabilities must be in place. In particular, the integration of digital technologies and networks with robotics and autonomous systems requires investments in key technology sub-systems and components, including automation and m2m (machine-to-machine) technologies, embedded software, sensors and human interfaces, and augmented reality. These emerging technologies are expected to reshape the industrial plant of the future, making processes faster and more responsive, while reshaping the nature of jobs and skills (see Chapter 12).

11.3 Premature Deindustrialization: South Africa from an International Comparative Perspective

This triple set of structural challenges faced by middle-income countries, as synthesized in the idea of a 'middle-income technology trap', highlights the existence of potential reinforcing mechanisms and cumulative vicious cycles undermining structural transformation.[5] Specifically, breaking into the global

---

[5] The literature on circular and cumulative causation initiated by Allyin Young and later developed by several structuralist and development scholars, including Gunnar Myrdal and Nicholas Kaldor, has emphasized the risks of cumulativeness and circularity in structural dynamics. While these properties can be responsible for virtuous expansionary cycles of increasing returns, they can also turn into negative cycles and a low-level equilibrium trap. For a review, see Toner, 1999.

economy, linking up while linking back, and keeping pace with technological change are in themselves interlinked challenges. But they are also intertwined and reinforced by the cumulative structural dynamics of industrialization or deindustrialization. If a country falls behind in its industrialization pathway, and it shows signs of premature deindustrialization, the triple set of structural challenges discussed above becomes progressively more constraining. With a reduction in a country's industrial base, its opportunities for DVA shrinks, and its companies will find it increasingly difficult to 'link back'. Furthermore, investments in technological upgrading and innovation will be limited by reduced expansionary dynamics and scale across manufacturing industries. These domestic dynamics of manufacturing and technological contraction will also be reflected in a reduced international competitiveness and potential growth in import penetration. It is then unsurprising that many countries that are stuck in a middle-income technology trap have also undergone a process of deindustrialization, in particular premature deindustrialization.

Having explored the structural challenges facing middle-income countries, the discussion turns to a closer exploration of deindustrialization. Deindustrialization trends across countries are empirically analysed, the patterns and dynamics of deindustrialization internationally—in particular premature deindustrialization—are explored, and South Africa is located in the context of these trends.

The first step is an estimation of the relationship between countries' GDP per capita and their shares of manufacturing in total employment. This simple regression analysis enables the identification of the level of GDP per capita and share of manufacturing in total employment associated with the 'turning point' at which the share of manufacturing levels off and begins to decline. Second, is the characterization of country experiences based on countries' changes in share of manufacturing in total employment, and on whether their actual share of manufacturing in total employment is higher or lower than the regression analysis would predict. Countries are categorized based on these two dimensions. Finally, combining this with data on countries' 2015 level of GDP per capita and manufacturing employment share makes it possible to identify potential premature deindustrializers among middle-income economies. Throughout, particular attention is drawn to the case of South Africa, while also making reference to the three comparator countries.

11.3.1 The 'Inverted-U' Pattern of Industrialization and Deindustrialization

This part of the study begins with an analysis of the relationship between GDP per capita and the share of manufacturing in total employment. This step of the method follows Rowthorn (1994), Palma (2005 and 2008), Tregenna (2015), and

Tregenna and Andreoni (2020). Rowthorn (1994) identifies an inverted-U relationship between countries. That is, at higher levels of GDP per capita, the share of manufacturing in total employment typically rises, up to a turning point associated with a particular level of GDP per capita and share of manufacturing employment, after which manufacturing accounts for a declining share of total employment. Naturally, this is a stylized pattern based on data for many countries, and countries will inevitably have either a higher or lower actual employment share than would be predicted, based on the regression analysis.

The share of manufacturing employment in total employment is estimated as a function of GDP per capita and GDP per capita squared (all in natural logs). The inclusion of the squared term takes account of the expected non-linear relationship between the explanatory and independent variables.[6] The final sample comprises 148 countries, with excellent coverage across regions and across levels of development.[7]

The results confirm the expected inverted-U relationship between GDP per capita and manufacturing share of employment. This simple regression yields an estimated turning point for 2015 of approximately $17 000 (2015 current US$). This level of GDP per capita corresponds (in this regression) to a 12 per cent share of manufacturing in total employment. The curve is shown in Figure 11.4, which also shows the turning point of the regression—the level of GDP per capita and associated share of manufacturing in total employment at which the latter levels off and subsequently begins to decline.

11.3.2   Characterizing Country Patterns

Next, countries are categorized based on two dimensions. First, whether their actual share of manufacturing in total employment in 2015 was higher or lower than would be 'predicted' based on their level of GDP per capita in 2015 and the estimated coefficients from the regression (that is, the sign of the residual term for each country). This dimension gives a sense of which countries may be 'under-industrialized' given their level of GDP per capita. Where this is positive, a country falls above the curve in Figure 11.4, and conversely where this is negative. Second, whether they experienced an increase or decrease in the share of

---

[6] Data on GDP per capita and population are from the United Nations (UN) Main National Accounts database (UNMNA), available at https://unstats.un.org/unsd/snaama/Introduction.asp (UNMNA). GDP data are in current US$. Data on manufacturing share of employment are taken from the International Labour Organisation (ILO) ILOSTAT database, available at http://www.ilo.org/ilostat/faces/ilostat-home/home?_adf.ctrl-state=97dmq1had_4%26_afrLoop=410,550,119,330,777#.
[7] The initial sample includes 181 countries for which data are available on all variables for both 2005 and 2015. All countries with a population below one million people are excluded from the sample. This excludes from the analysis small island nations and other small countries, which may follow atypical development paths that can distort the analysis. A further three countries identified as outliers are also excluded.

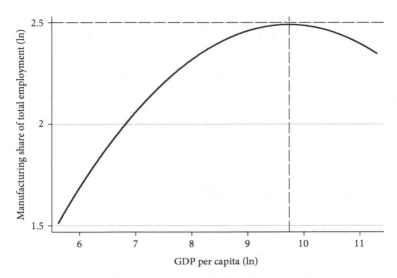

Figure 11.4 Estimated relationship between GDP per capita and manufacturing share of employment, 2015
Note: Dashed lines indicate the turning point of the relationship.

manufacturing in their total employment between 2005 and 2015. This second dimension indicates which countries can be considered (simply on the basis of sectoral employment shares) to have deindustrialized during this period. Taken together, these two dimensions allow for the tentative classification of countries into four broad categories, depicted schematically in the four quadrants of Figure 11.5.

It must be emphasized that this analysis is exploratory and indicative, rather than definitive.[8] It is thus only suggestive of which countries might be considered as deindustrializers, and especially as premature deindustrializers.

Quadrant I includes countries in which the share of manufacturing employment is higher than expected in 2015, and in which this share grew between 2005 and 2015. Based on this analysis, these countries do not raise a concern in terms of deindustrialization. Countries in Quadrant 4 are also growing their share of manufacturing in total employment, which in 2015 remained below their 'expected' values. Thus, even though these countries might be regarded as

---

[8] Reasons for circumspection include: that this is just one approach to conceptualizing and measuring premature deindustrialization; the inclusion of estimated values in the ILOSTAT database; limitations of the econometric methodology and specification (including the non-inclusion of explanatory variables other than GDP per capita and its squared term); the narrow range of the predicted values of manufacturing share of total employment; measurement of deindustrialization only in terms of employment shares and not also shares in GDP; and sensitivity to the specific years used in the analysis. Furthermore, to reach more definitive conclusions, individual country-level analysis would be needed, taking into account country-specific dynamics.

QUADRANT II	QUADRANT I
Countries in which: Share of manufacturing in total employment decreased (2005–2015) and Share of manufacturing in total employment is higher than predicted (2015)	Countries in which: Share of manufacturing in total employment increased (2005–2015) and Share of manufacturing in total employment is higher than predicted (2015)

x-axis: change in share of manufacturing in country's employment, 2005–2015

QUADRANT III	QUADRANT IV
Countries in which: Share of manufacturing in total employment decreased (2005–2015) and Share of manufacturing in total employment is lower than predicted (2015)	Countries in which: Share of manufacturing in total employment increased (2005–2015) and Share of manufacturing in total employment is lower than predicted (2015)

Figure 11.5 Characterization of international trends in deindustrialization

'under-industrialized', they show evidence of industrializing during this decade (2005–15).

Countries falling in Quadrants II and III can be characterized as possible deindustrializers, in that their share of manufacturing in total employment fell between 2005 and 2015. Yet, in the case of Quadrant II countries, their manufacturing employment share in 2015 still remained above their 'expected' level.

From the standpoint of structural change and concerns around the impact of deindustrialization on growth, it is the countries falling in Quadrant III that potentially raise more significant concerns. In these countries, the share of manufacturing in employment fell over the period 2005–15 as well as being lower than expected (based on cross-country regressions) in 2015. Rather than catching up to their 'expected' level of industrialization, this group of countries fell further behind. Furthermore, some of these countries had a higher than expected level of industrialization in 2005, but fell below the curve by 2015.

South Africa falls in Quadrant III—the category of greatest potential concern in terms of deindustrialization. Between 2005 and 2015, the share of manufacturing in South Africa's total employment fell from 13.9 per cent to 11.2 per cent (based on the ILOSTAT data). Worth noting is that this is in fact only slightly below the expected value for 2015 based on South Africa's GDP per capita and international patterns of widespread deindustrialization; that is, South Africa's share is actually close to its predicted value.

In contrast with South Africa, the three comparator countries—Brazil, China, and Malaysia—all fall in Quadrant II. Like South Africa, their share of manufacturing in total employment declined between 2005 and 2015. Yet, unlike the case of South Africa, their share of manufacturing in total employment remained higher than predicted in 2015. A key factor in this difference is that these three comparator countries began the period of analysis at relatively higher shares of manufacturing in total employment, for their levels of income per capita, than in the case of South Africa.

Key statistics for South Africa, Brazil, China, and Malaysia are shown in Table 11.2. South Africa had the lowest share of manufacturing in total employment in both 2005 and 2015. Moreover, as discussed, it is the only one among this cohort of countries to have a lower than predicted share of manufacturing in total employment in 2015 (albeit only very slightly lower than predicted). Brazil's actual share is only slightly higher than its predicted share, while in China and Malaysia the actual shares were well above predicted shares, indicating the high levels of industrialization in the latter two countries.

11.3.3 Identifying Possible Premature Deindustrializers

Next, Quadrant III countries are further divided into those that might be regarded as possible premature deindustrializers. Possible premature deindustrializers for 2015 are identified as those countries in which: (1) the share of manufacturing in

Table 11.2 South Africa and comparator countries

	Actual share of manuf. in total employment 2005 (%)	Actual share of manuf. in total employment 2015 (%)	Difference btw actual & predicted share of manuf. in total employment 2015 (%)
South Africa	13.9	11.2	−0.1
Brazil	14.2	12.5	0.7
China	23.6	17.6	5.9
Malaysia	19.8	16.5	4.6

total employment fell between 2005 and 2015; (2) the share of manufacturing in total employment in 2015 was less than would be expected based on their GDP per capita (i.e. they fell below the curve shown in Figure 11.4; and (3) their GDP per capita in 2015 was below the level of GDP per capita associated with the turning point in the relationship based on the pattern found across countries (i.e. they fell to the left of the turning point shown in Figure 11.4). As such, this set of countries excludes those in Quadrant III with levels of GDP per capita above the income turning point (i.e. advanced economies that are deindustrializing). This part of the analysis thus introduces a third dimension (to the left or right of the income turning point), to identify the (potential) premature aspect of the deindustrialization experiences internationally.

From this, middle-income countries that emerge as possible premature deindustrializers are listed in Table 11.3. This excludes low-income (e.g. Zimbabwe) and high-income (e.g. Chile) countries that also fit the criteria of possible premature deindustrializers.

11.4 The Role of Industrial Policy in Avoiding the Middle-Income Trap

This section is a brief reflection on some industrial policy implications (industrial policy for structural transformation is more fully discussed in Chapter 15). Industrial policy is crucial for avoiding a middle-income technology trap in general and a middle-income technology trap in particular, for avoiding or reversing premature deindustrialization, and of course more broadly for structural transformation. Table 11.4 provides a list of industrial policy instruments, organized around five key policy areas, namely: building production, technological, and organizational capabilities; innovation and technological change; linking up while linking back into GVC and industrial restructuring; demand and trade; and industrial finance.

These areas have been selected as they match the critical challenges that countries in the middle-income status present, which might also relate to their premature deindustrialization. A number of policy instruments are effective tools in addressing more than one policy area. The table also shows the extent to which the selected comparator countries—Brazil, China, and Malaysia—have adopted these instruments (for a discussion of the historical trajectories in industrial policymaking across these countries, see Andreoni and Tregenna, 2018; and Andreoni and Tregenna, 2020).

As discussed in Andreoni (2016), the identification of a mix of policy instruments is only the first step. Indeed, these instruments must be aligned, coordinated, and synchronized over time. Andreoni (2016) conceptualizes an

Table 11.3 Possible middle-income premature deindustrializers, 2005–15

Country	Income group	Region
Albania	Upper-middle	Europe and Central Asia
Angola	Upper-middle	Sub-Saharan Africa
Armenia	Lower-middle	Europe and Central Asia
Botswana	Upper-middle	Sub-Saharan Africa
Cameroon	Lower-middle	Sub-Saharan Africa
Costa Rica	Upper-middle	Latin America and the Caribbean
Cuba	Upper-middle	Latin America and the Caribbean
Dominican Republic	Upper-middle	Latin America and the Caribbean
Ecuador	Upper-middle	Latin America and the Caribbean
Georgia	Upper-middle	Europe and Central Asia
Ghana	Lower-middle	Sub-Saharan Africa
Iraq	Upper-middle	Middle East and North Africa
Jamaica	Upper-middle	Latin America and the Caribbean
Kazakhstan	Upper-middle	Europe and Central Asia
Kyrgyzstan	Lower-middle	Europe and Central Asia
Mauritania	Lower-middle	Sub-Saharan Africa
Namibia	Upper-middle	Sub-Saharan Africa
Panama	Upper-middle	Latin America and the Caribbean
Peru	Upper-middle	Latin America and the Caribbean
Philippines	Lower-middle	East Asia and Pacific
South Africa	**Upper-middle**	**Sub-Saharan Africa**
Tajikistan	Lower-middle	Europe and Central Asia

Note: Countries listed in alphabetical order. Income and regional group classifications based on World Bank classification; income groups use 2015 classification (see https://datahelpdesk.worldbank.org/knowledgebase/articles/906519-world-bank-country-and-lending-groups).

Source: The authors.

industry policy matrix with three main axes. First, the 'industrial policy governance model', referring to the level at which policies are implemented (regional/state, national/federal, or in some cases supranational). Second, 'industrial policy targets and areas', in terms of the cluster of objectives addressed by each industrial policy instrument (for example, instruments aimed at the 'innovation and technology infrastructure' policy area). Third, 'industrial policy levels of intervention', in respect of how selective each industrial policy instrument is. While some policy instruments are sector-specific or even firm-specific, others are applicable to manufacturing as a whole and others are macroeconomic in nature (although even these economy-wide measures will typically have uneven effects across sectors).

Combinations of industrial policy measures can be directed at a common objective, or they can be used to manage trade-offs between competing objectives. The success of any individual industrial policy measure will be conditional on how it is coordinated with other measures affecting the same firm, sector, or value chain. This underscores the importance of coordination between industrial policy

Table 11.4 An industrial policy toolbox for middle-income countries

Areas	Critical challenges for middle-income countries		Policy instruments	Brazil	China	Malaysia	South Africa
1	Building capabilities	1.1	Skills policy	X	XXX	XX	X
		1.2	Technology and extension services via intermediate institutions	XXX	XXX	XX	X
		1.3 & 2.1	Matching grants and targeted subsidies for investment	XX	XXX	XX	XXX
2	Innovation and technological change	2.2	Public-private partnerships and consortia with universities	XX	XXX	XX	XXX
		2.3	Joint ventures with multinational corporations	XX	XXX	XX	XX
3	Linking up while linking back into GVCs and industrial restructuring	3.1	Strategic mergers and acquisitions, and recession cartels	X	XXX	X	X
		3.2	Competition policy	X	XX	X	XX
		3.3	FDI incentives	X	XXX	XX	X
		3.4	Local content policy	XXX	XXX	XX	XX
		3.5	SMEs targeted investments	X	XX	X	X
		3.6	Cluster policy	X	XX	X	X
		3.7	Special economic zones	X	XXX	XX	X
4	Demand and trade	4.1	Export promotion zones	X	XXX	XXX	X
		4.2	Export cartels	X	XXX	X	X
		4.3	Selective trade policy	XX	XXX	XX	X
		4.4	Public procurement	XX	XXX	X	X

5	Industrial finance					
	5.1	Export finance services	X	XXX	X	X
	5.2	Development banks	XXX	XXX	XX	X
	5.3	Sector-specific development banks	X	XXX	X	X
	5.4	Hybrid finance solutions combining grants, loans, subsidies	XX	XXX	XX	X
	5.5	Direct investment policy and SOEs	XXX	XXX	XX	XX

Source: Authors, based on Andreoni, 2016; Andreoni and Tregenna, 2018; Andreoni and Tregenna, 2020; UNIDO, 2020.

and other domains—such as macroeconomic policy, innovation and technology policy, labour market policies, trade policy, infrastructure policy, and so on—in setting countries on a path of avoiding or escaping a middle-income trap and avoiding or reversing premature deindustrialization.

Andreoni and Tregenna (2020) point to three important policy issues with regard to a middle-income technology trap and a middle-income trap in general. First, while there are substantial opportunities for upgrading in value chains, this requires significant industrial policy support, including in key technological and product services. Second, it is important that firms and countries deepen their productive and technological capabilities to support innovation and upgrading. Third, countries need to both 'link up' and 'link back' through the development and integration of their local production systems, including through technological upgrading.

While industrial policies must inevitably have a particular focus on the manufacturing sector, they also need to apply to other sectors and to the ways in which sectors are interconnected. As shown here, South Africa lags behind comparator countries in R&D and technological intensity, which are especially important for avoiding a middle-income technology trap and for structural transformation more broadly. This points to the critical importance of policies specifically designed to support R&D, innovation, and technological upgrading as integral aspects of industrial development.

There is a great deal of heterogeneity among middle-income economies, including between South Africa and the three comparator countries referenced here—Brazil, China, and Malaysia. This includes differences in their industrial policies and in their innovation and technology performance. While all four countries show evidence of having deindustrialized, the analysis presented here draws attention to the difference between the trajectories in South Africa and the other three countries. South Africa presents as a failure of structural transformation, while Malaysia and China represent exemplars of structural transformation in middle-income countries. Unsurprisingly, these four middle-income countries had dramatically differing fortunes in economic growth.

11.5 Concluding Remarks

This chapter assesses the development and industrialization challenges facing South Africa as a middle-income country—and moreover, as a country that is arguably caught in a middle-income trap. South Africa can also be understood as being in a middle-income technology trap, failing in the technological upgrading necessary for structural transformation and catching-up. 'Stuck in the middle', South Africa—alongside a number of middle-income countries—has been unable to break out of its middle-income status. On the contrary, South Africa has been falling behind frontier economies and falling down global GDP rankings over a long period of time. Far from catching up with advanced economies, other countries are catching up with and overtaking South Africa, including some countries that were previously in the low-income group.

South Africa's poor growth performance has been concomitant with its failure to take forward its industrialization and to upgrade the structure of its economy. It has not successfully come to terms with the challenges of breaking into the global concentration of industrial production, linking up and back, and keeping pace with technological change. Unsurprisingly, the long-term deindustrialization trend has not been halted or reversed. This analysis of the global evidence on premature deindustrialization benchmarks South Africa's structural position and trajectory in the global context. The share of manufacturing in total employment in South Africa in 2015 is shown to have fallen over the preceding decade as well as being (slightly) below the share that would be predicted based on international patterns.

Adding to the concern about the quantitative share is the composition of South Africa's manufacturing sector and exports. With some exceptions, the profile of South African manufacturing production and exports does not show the desirable patterns of structural transformation, which would include growth in domestic value added, movement up the value chain, and increasing focus on products that show potential for cumulative productivity increases and are demand-dynamic. South Africa is also lagging in terms of innovation and in the development and application of KETs that would enable the country to become competitive in the manufacture of complex products and to gain from the opportunities associated with the fourth industrial revolution.

Reversing premature deindustrialization in South Africa will depend on the coordination of a feasible set of integrated interventions that reinforce each other. In particular, strategic forward integration and upgrading in GVCs is a complex process, as it entails both linking domestic players to foreign companies and markets, while at the same time building local supply chains of producers.

As discussed above, a variety of industrial policy tools are available. Different combinations of tools are relevant to particular country contexts. The heterogeneity among the four comparator countries and among middle-income countries overall also highlights the need for dynamic and flexible industrial policies that are well suited to individual countries' particular political economies and other relevant characteristics. At the same time, clear lessons are apparent from the diversity of industrialization and growth experiences and outcomes over a period of time.

Industrialization remains important for technological change, structural transformation, and avoiding or escaping a middle-income trap. These goals also require upgrading and compositional changes within manufacturing. Furthermore, there are significant opportunities for value addition within other sectors and at the interfaces between manufacturing and other sectors, and at the intersection of different technology systems. Certain services activities are closely linked with manufacturing and are critical to the competitiveness of manufacturing, technological upgrading within manufacturing, (re)industrialization, and structural transformation. In addition to their importance to manufacturing, some services activities (as well as some activities in other non-manufacturing sectors) provide opportunities for cumulative productivity increases and growth-pulling, and thus require industrial policy-type support. Bold industrial policy, and coordination between industrial policy and other policy areas, are crucial for shaping a new industrial ecosystem in South Africa and in helping the country escape the middle-income trap.

References

Andreoni, A. (2016). 'Varieties of industrial policy: models, packages and transformation cycles.' In A. Noman and J. Stiglitz (eds), *Efficiency, Finance and Varieties of Industrial Policy*, 245–305. New York: Columbia University Press.

Andreoni, A. (2019). 'A generalized linkage approach to local production systems development in the era of global value chains, with special reference to Africa.' In A. Noman and J. Stiglitz (eds), *Quality of Growth in Africa*, 264–94. New York: Columbia University Press.

Andreoni, A. and H.-J. Chang (2017). 'Industrial policy and the future of manufacturing.' *Journal of Industrial and Business Economics* 43(4): 491–502.

Andreoni, A. and F. Tregenna (2018). 'Stuck in the middle: premature industrialisation and industrial policy.' CCRED Working Paper 11/2018. Johannesburg: CCRED.

Andreoni, A. and F. Tregenna (2020). 'Escaping the middle-income technology trap: a comparative analysis of industrial policies in China, Brazil and South Africa.' *Structural Change and Economic Dynamics* 54: 324–40.

Arias, M. A. and Y. Wen (2015). 'Trapped: few developing countries can climb the economic ladder or stay there.' Federal Reserve Bank of St. Louis. *The Regional Economist*, October.

Cramer, C. and F. Tregenna (2020). 'Heterodox approaches to industrial policy, the shifting boundaries of the industrial, and the implications for industrial hubs.' in J. Y. Lin and A. Oqubay (eds), *The Oxford Handbook of Industrial Hubs and Economic Eevelopment*, 40–63. Oxford: Oxford University Press.

European Commission (2009). 'Preparing for our future: developing a common strategy for key enabling technologies in the EU.' European Commission Communication COM(2009) 512/3.

Felipe, J., U. Kumar, and R. Galope (2017). 'Middle-income transitions: trap or myth?' *Journal of the Asia Pacific Economy* 22(3): 429–53.

Gill, I. and H. Kharas (2007). *An East Asian Renaissance*. Washington, DC: World Bank.

Kang, N. and E. Paus (2020). 'The political economy of the middle income trap: the challenges of advancing innovation capabilities in Latin America, Asia and beyond.' *The Journal of Development Studies* 56(4): 651–6.

Klingler-Vidra, R. and R. Wade (2020). 'Science and technology policies and the middle-income trap: lessons from Vietnam.' *The Journal of Development Studies* 56(4):717–31.

Lebdioui, A., K. Lee, and C. Pietrobelli (2020). 'Local-foreign technology interface, resource-based development, and industrial policy: how Chile and Malaysia are escaping the middle-income trap.' *The Journal of Technology Transfer* (2020), DOI:10.1007/s10961-020-09808-3.

Lee, K. (2013). *Schumpeterian Analysis of Economic Catch-Up: Knowledge, Path-Creation and Middle-Income Trap*. Cambridge: Cambridge University Press.

Lin, J. Y. (2017). 'Industrial policies for avoiding the middle-income trap: a new structural economics perspective.' *Journal of Chinese Economic and Business Studies* 15(1): 5–18.

Palma, J. G. (2005). 'Four sources of "deindustrialisation" and a new concept of the "Dutch disease".' in J. A. Ocampo (ed.), *Beyond Reforms: Structural Dynamics and Macroeconomic Vulnerability*. New York: Stanford University Press and World Bank.

Palma, J. G. (2008). 'Deindustrialisation, premature deindustrialisation, and the Dutch disease.' In L. E. Blume and S. N. Durlauf (eds), *The New Palgrave: A Dictionary of Economics*, 2nd edn, 401–10. Basingstoke: Palgrave Macmillan.

Paus, E. (2020). 'Innovation strategies matter: Latin America's middle-income trap meets China and globalisation.' *The Journal of Development Studies* 56(4): 657–79.

Rowthorn, R. (1994). 'Korea at the cross-roads.' Working Paper No. 11. Cambridge: Centre for Business Research.

Toner, P. (1999). *Main Currents in Circular and Cumulative Causation Theory*. Basingstoke: Palgrave MacMillan.

Tregenna, F. (2009). 'Characterising deindustrialisation: an analysis of changes in manufacturing employment and output internationally.' *Cambridge Journal of Economics* 33(3): 433–66.

Tregenna, F. (2010). 'How significant is intersectoral outsourcing of employment in South Africa?' *Industrial and Corporate Change* 19(5): 1427–57.

Tregenna, F. (2013). 'Deindustrialization and reindustrialization.' In A. Szirmai, W. Naudé, and L. Alcorta (eds), *Pathways to Industrialization in the 21st Century: New Challenges and Emerging Paradigms*, 76–101. Oxford: Oxford University Press.

Tregenna, F. (2015). 'Deindustrialisation, structural change and sustainable economic growth.' Inclusive and Sustainable Industrial Development Working Paper Series, Working Paper 02|2015. United Nations Industrial Development Organization.

Tregenna, F. (2016a). 'Deindustrialisation and premature deindustrialization.' In J. Ghosh, R. Kattel, and E. Reinert (eds), *Elgar Handbook of Alternative Theories of Economic Development*. Cheltenham: Edward Elgar.

Tregenna, F. (2016b). 'Deindustrialisation: an issue for both developed and developing countries.' In J. Weiss and M. Tribe (eds), *Handbook on Industry and Development*, 97–115. Abingdon: Routledge.

Tregenna, F. and A. Andreoni (2020). 'Deindustrialisation reconsidered: structural shifts and sectoral heterogeneity.' Working Paper Series (IIPP WP 2020–06). UCL Institute for Innovation and Public Purpose, https://www.ucl.ac.uk/bartlett/public-purpose/wp2020-06.

Wade, R. (2016). 'Industrial policy in response to the middle income trap and the third wave of the digital revolution.' *Global Policy* 7(4): 469–80.

UNIDO (2020). *Industrialisation as the Driver of Sustained Prosperity*. Vienna: UNIDO.

12

Digitalization, Industrialization, and Skills Development

Opportunities and Challenges for Middle-Income Countries

Antonio Andreoni, Justin Barnes, Anthony Black, and Timothy Sturgeon

12.1 Introduction

The world economy is undergoing a period of structural and technological transformation, driven by the increasing digitalization of economic activity. Digitalization is influencing innovation, production, trade, consumption, and a host of business processes, though to what degree is an empirical question that will yield different answers across industries and geographies. Part of this transition, sometimes described as the 'fourth industrial revolution' (variously referred to as Industry 4.0 and 4IR) relates to the digitalization of production. The key technologies are at different stages of maturity; they include advanced robotics and factory automation, data from mobile, and ubiquitous internet connectivity (variously referred to as the internet of things, IoT, and industrial internet of things, IIoT), cloud computing, big data analytics, machine learning, and artificial intelligence (AI). Associated with this technological transition is the development of new 'platform' business models and modes of value creation (Schwab, 2016; World Bank, 2016; UNCTAD, 2018; UNIDO, 2019; Andreoni and Roberts, 2020; Sturgeon, 2021).

The technologies and business models emerging in this 'digital economy' have already disrupted traditional industries and created entirely new ones, such as social media. Aside from these dramatic developments, ongoing digitalization is raising concerns about the dislocation and job losses that might result from technologies such as robotics and artificial intelligence. Since many of the relevant technologies are skill-biased, the ability of developing countries to compete in traditionally labour-intensive industries that have supported their industrialization may be undermined (Ford, 2015; Hallward-Driemeier and Nayyar, 2018; Rodrik, 2018; Clifton et al., 2020).

Antonio Andreoni, Justin Barnes, Anthony Black, and Timothy Sturgeon, *Digitalization, Industrialization, and Skills Development: Opportunities and Challenges for Middle-Income Countries* In: *Structural Transformation in South Africa: The Challenges of Inclusive Industrial Development in a Middle-Income Country*. Edited by: Antonio Andreoni, Pamela Mondliwa, Simon Roberts, and Fiona Tregenna, Oxford University Press. © Oxford University Press 2021.
DOI: 10.1093/oso/9780192894311.003.0012

Digitalization is being experienced differentially across the globe, reflecting the range of opportunities it offers as well as the challenges specific countries face in investing in and successfully adopting advanced technologies. In South Africa, digitalization is occurring in an economy that has prematurely deindustrialized and where the digital capability gap in terms of infrastructure and skills is wide. Like many resource-dependent economies, the country has failed to fully diversify and move to higher productivity and more complex activities (Bell et al., 2018; Andreoni and Tregenna, 2020; and Chapter 11). Unemployment remains at extremely high levels, while societal inequality continues unabated.

Despite this, South Africa has islands of excellence in which firms are embracing the opportunities provided by digitalization to achieve greater efficiency, process innovation, and supply-chain integration. These examples point to what is possible, while at the same time revealing gaps and shortcomings. Both the potential and shortcomings are evident across firms (in terms of investment rates) and public institutions (in terms of services and policies). The development of digital skills in cross-cutting fields such as data science and software engineering, and complementary services, will clearly be of heightened importance.

This chapter examines the opportunities and challenges of digital industrialization in middle-income countries, mainly through the lens of South Africa. In doing so, the chapter advances a framework for understanding digitalization and how it can be harnessed as part of a broader structural transformation. This framework includes the identification of key transversal enablers, including digital skills, data connectivity, supplier and quality assurance management, investment in productive capabilities for digitalization, and the development of appropriate public policies and regulations. The emphasis is on locating the digitalization challenge at both the firm and broader societal levels. In this way a digital industrial policy for South Africa can act as a *catalyst* for more inclusive and sustainable industrial growth.

The rest of the chapter is comprised of four sections. Section 12.2 introduces the key transversal technologies and business models driving structural transformation in the digitalization context. Against this backdrop, section 12.3 discusses the South African digitalization experience and highlights challenges faced by middle-income countries as they seek to benefit from digitalization, especially in the areas of digital skills. Section 12.4 provides a set of digitalization policy principles and identifies key industrial policy and associated institutional priorities to support the successful transition of the South African economy as it embraces digitalization. Section 12.5 concludes.

12.2 The New Digital Economy: Transversal Technologies and Business Models

Digitalization brings together a range of new and established technologies, including robotics, sensors, machine learning, and IoT, all of which are transversal in that they have applications across and along sectoral value chains. Table 12.1 provides a summary of the main transversal technologies underpinning the new digital economy.

These technologies are enabling major economic changes, albeit unevenly. Changes can be incremental (e.g. improving output quality or maintenance predictability in a single machine) or disruptive (e.g. fundamentally changing the way products and services are created and delivered). The combined impact of these changes has the potential to yield manufacturing systems that respond in real time to conditions in the factory, supply-chain disruptions, and changes in demand.

Though digitalization is most often discussed in the context of manufacturing (the 'smart factory'), changes are also occurring in agriculture (such as 'precision farming'), and in mining or construction (such as autonomous vehicles and machinery). Precision farming, for example, combines high-resolution satellite or drone imagery to tailor the application of irrigation or fertilizer and monitor crop health metre by metre across the field (Chapter 6). Similarly, real-time 3-D modelling of construction sites and mines using photogrammetry collected from drones or small aircraft can allow earth-moving equipment to function without human operators.

Table 12.1 Transversal technologies in the digital economy, with key features

Transversal technologies	Key features
1. Advanced manufacturing: learning machinery; networked and autonomous factory automation systems	• Digital simulation, augmentation, and virtual reality • Rising functionality in entry-level machinery and software (e.g. low cost 3-D printers, drones, robots) • Ubiquitous monitoring and measurement of processes (sensors), connected factories and supply chains
2. New mobile and internet-connected data sources	• Industry (IIoT) and consumer (IoT) connected products and services, sensors, clickstreams, location data, etc.
3. Cloud computing	• Storage, SaaS, mobile access and constant updating of software and systems
4. Big data analysis	• Huge data storage, with sample sizes that can lead to robust results, new insights, and high fault tolerance
5. Artificial intelligence (AI)	• Machine learning, prediction, self-maintenance, regulation, and replication, autonomous visual recognition

Source: Authors.

12.2.1 The Main Features and Technologies of the Digital Economy

The collection of vast volumes of data is a key feature of digitalization. For example, data can be collected through sensors during production, when a product or service is in use, and from online search and purchasing activities by consumers. When aggregated, this 'big data' can be analysed and fed into to machine-learning algorithms, making it possible for firms to gain novel insights into production processes, supply chains, and consumer behaviour. This is often referred to as the internet of things (IoT), and in industrial settings as an industrial IoT (or IIoT). IoT-enabled digital systems make use of cloud storage, big data analytics, and, increasingly, artificial intelligence, each running on a nested set of platforms, as depicted in Figure 12.1. Digitalization enables a dynamic cycle of continuously improved efficiency that is increasingly being driven by the rapid advance of machine learning (a form of artificial intelligence).

The more members or users in a production system or platform, the more data are collated and the greater its value in respect of data aggregation and analysis—i.e. 'network effect'. However, network effects can give rise to high levels of concentration and potential abuse of market power, such as barriers to entry for smaller and independent competitors attempting to enter the market, in the absence of an appropriate regulatory and policy framework. Data are becoming

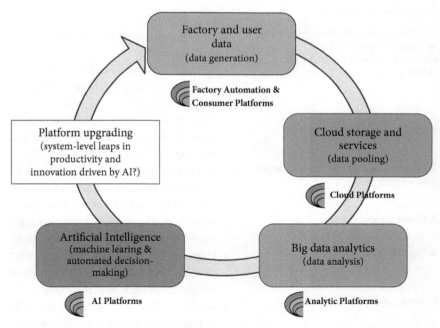

Figure 12.1 Data flow across key transversal technologies in the digital economy
Source: Sturgeon, 2021.

an asset and the ownership and control of data of dominant platforms an important determinant of power relations in value chains and markets (Andreoni and Roberts, 2020). This is more likely to be the case in the digital systems underlying consumer services (e.g. ride hailing and e-commerce) because consumer needs tend to be similar. In these cases, the influx of digital services can be very rapid and disruptive. In industrial and producer services industries user needs tend to be more complex and variable, and this appears to be dampening network effects in these sectors.

12.2.2 Digitalization of Production Technologies in Manufacturing

In industry, digitalization can improve a range of business processes through the convergence of existing technologies such as ICT and enterprise-level manufacturing software and systems (Box 12.1) with newer technology such as sensors and then connecting this IoT to 'the cloud' where it can be analysed and acted upon, as shown in Figure 12.1. Thus, through retrofitting existing equipment as a transition towards fully blown advanced digital manufacturing, incremental improvements are possible.

Advanced digital technologies can enable greater coordination efficiencies, condition monitoring, and process optimization, both within firms and along supply chains. Indeed, when firms can exchange information across various business functions, monitor processes in real time, and track operational performance at the level of individual products, data are produced that can allow machines and

---

Box 12.1 Enterprise-level manufacturing software and systems

Enterprise resource planning (ERP) refers to an integrated suite of compatible and interlinked software applications that cover a range of core business processes, such as finance, human resources (HR), distribution, manufacturing, purchasing, services, and supply-chain management.

Manufacturing execution systems (MES) are computerized systems used in manufacturing to track and document the transformation of raw materials to finished goods. They provide visibility into the performance of individual lines and workstations, often delivering analysis to management in easy to read 'dashboards' in real time.

Product lifecycle management (PLM) is a product-level information management system that can track and collect data about a product throughout its entire lifecycle, from ideation, design, and manufacture through service and disposal.

other resources to be allocated more efficiently, problems and bottlenecks to be identified more quickly, processes optimized, and defects reduced. Manufacturing execution systems (MES) for example, can deliver a kind of radical transparency that can disrupt long-standing routines for the better (Box 12.1). If mismanaged, however, they can create a climate of fear and resentment, both at the level of operators and line managers.

Digital technologies can manifest in demand changes (such as the emergence of autonomous vehicles), entirely new processes of design and production (3-D printing), increasing automation of production technologies, entirely new sales and marketing models (channel access, pricing, and packaging), and the emergence of alternative business models (for example, the rise of the sharing economy). Still, in manufacturing, the variability of requirements and the importance of physical manipulation limits the easy scalability of digital systems, resulting in more incremental adoption, and creating opportunities for the implementation of industrial policies aimed at fostering spillovers.

In product design, the combination of automated design software, additive manufacturing, and breakthroughs in material science have significantly reduced the time it takes to develop prototypes and produce tooling (Ferraz et al., 2019; Andreoni et al., 2021). Additive manufacturing, in particular, presents an opportunity to 'leapfrog' in the area of tooling. Though additive manufacturing is mostly used for pre-production activities, for example, producing design prototypes, it is increasingly being used for production and post-production activities. Because parts are produced in high-mix, low-volume production environments, additive manufacturing can be well suited for aircraft, shipbuilding, and after-market (replacement) vehicle parts. The benefits of 3-D printing have been well proven in terms of process and product upgrading, including product development through rapid prototyping, and reduction in tooling costs, material waste, supply-chain costs, and lead times to market. Still, a few firms are experimenting with connecting 3-D printers in 'swarms' to produce at higher volumes, which has the potential to disrupt the organization of value chains (Rehnberg and Ponte, 2018).

If additive manufacturing has opened up new possibilities for design, prototyping, and customization, large-scale manufacturing production has been undergoing a different set of changes with high potential for an increasing degree of automation. Automated systems are increasingly multi-purpose and multi-tasking (reprogrammable on the fly), and are networked, to aggregate data from production. However, the high costs of such systems are beyond the reach of the medium- and small-volume producers that might benefit the most from their flexibility. Indeed, the adoption of industrial robots internationally has been mainly concentrated in a few industries, especially automotive (accounting for 40 per cent of the total), computers and electronic equipment, electrical equipment, appliances and components, rubber, plastics and chemicals, and industrial machinery (Andreoni and Anzolin, 2019).

12.2.3 The Digital Economy and Innovative Business Models

The digital economy is not only about machinery and software—it operates according to a particular set of distinct business models. The following are the three most important ones.

Open innovation refers to the pre-competitive pooling of R&D activities and design criteria, either through consortia, or though the voluntary 'crowdsourcing' efforts of engineers and technologists interested in creating free resources for their technical communities. For example, nearly all the world's major computer programming languages, such as Python, are open sourced and free. Like modularity, open innovation helps firms 'vertically specialize', that is, develop a strategic focus on a specific bundle of competencies, while still providing customers with a rich set of fully functional products and solutions. Open innovations are by definition widely available, including to firms and researchers in South Africa.

Modularity describes a business model based on interchangeability, where subcomponents can be added or subtracted without redesigning entire systems. On the factory floor, different subassemblies with shared interfaces can be substituted in the assembly of larger products. In product design off-the-shelf or lightly customized modular components can be designed-in as elements of larger systems. By defining and publishing the application programming interface (API) for third parties to create platform-compatible applications, platform owners can provide access to, and collect fees from, thousands of compatible applications, deepening network effects. This is evident at both the consumer (e.g. software for PCs and mobile handsets) and industrial levels (cloud computing applications). Indeed, the digital economy can be seen as a set of nested platforms, each with multiple sub-systems and applications operating on the principle of modularity, which, viewed in aggregate can be characterized by 'deep modularity' (Sturgeon, 2021).

Platforms provide services for networks of users. There are typically different groups of users such as those using the platform to sell (for example, hotel bookings) and those looking to find and purchase goods and services, who typically use it for free. The platform owners can charge fees from both parties across this 'two-sided' market, generate revenue from third parties (such as advertisers), channel consumers to the platform's preferred services, and benefit from aggregating user data, both for analysis that improves services (see Figure 12.1) and for sale to others. Once established, network effects make it very difficult for later entrants. This is one reason that regulating, and even breaking up, dominant platforms has become a policy priority in many jurisdictions (UNIDO, 2019).

These three business models are integrated in advanced manufacturing systems. These systems are mainly comprised of modular components and machinery, and benefit from, or are even based on, inputs from open innovation. They can act as platforms upon which third-party complementors can offer specific fixtures and tools. Cloud computing services are then used to integrate production and design data, with the cloud itself operating as a platform upon which additional modules, such as data analytics and AI services, can be developed and distributed.

12.2.4 Digital Technologies and Global Value Chains

The recent wave of technological change and the emergence of new business models has been taking place in the context of globalization and the fragmentation of production systems in global value chains (GVCs). In goods production, this is reflected in the rising share of international trade in complex intermediate goods. Because of the technical specificity of inputs, this type of trade requires 'explicit coordination', typically carried out by large and internationalized corporations (Gereffi et al., 2005). While participation in GVCs can provide firms in developing economies with opportunities, incentives, and tools to upgrade capabilities, create employment, and support more inclusive growth, the emerging evidence is that GVCs have tended to benefit narrow segments of the industrial base (often the foreign-invested part), deepening polarization of income and wealth distribution (UNCTAD, 2018). There is indeed increasing evidence of 'thin industrialization', characterized in part by specialization in low-value-added segments of the value chain (Whittaker et al., 2020; and Chapter 13).

As *digital* GVCs become more important, the effects of global-scale technology platforms and the business models that underpin them also need to be considered. One possibility is that less-developed economies might experience rising technological dependency and further isolation and exclusion from high-value segments of these fast-moving and sometimes oligopolistic platform-based digital value chains. Another is that multinational firms operating in these countries are adding another layer to the digital divide by deploying state-of-the art technologies ahead of local enterprises. On the other hand, advanced digital technologies hold great promise for increasing productivity; creating opportunities for local firms to learn by customizing, adapting, and integrating global technologies; and may be providing powerful new tools for accelerating innovation as well (Andreoni and Roberts, 2020; Sturgeon, 2021).

12.3 Digitalizing South Africa: Opportunities and Challenges for a Middle-Income Country

Overall, the deployment of digital production technologies in South Africa has been mixed. Islands of successful digitalization have emerged and firms have captured some of the digital dividends associated with improved design, customization, and reduction in costs and entry barriers. Specifically, some lead firms have begun to leverage customer data to improve products and services. For example, firms in the construction, agriculture, and mining vehicles industry have been monitoring the conditions of vehicles on a real-time basis for an extended period,[1] while the mineral processing industry is using digitalization together with machine learning for condition monitoring and predictive maintenance.[2] As a result of these technological changes, a lead mineral processing machinery manufacturer interviewed for this study reduced its product development times from six to eight weeks to two to three days.[3] This is important for industries demanding a high degree of customization and where speed to market is crucial for competitiveness. Some firms have already made substantial investments in additive manufacturing, but there has been slow uptake of robotics, although it varies greatly by industry.[4] For example, in addition to automotive, the large lead firms in the food processing industry have adopted robotics in their packaging lines, which has allowed for more precision and flexibility.[5] Here, robots are substituting low-skilled labour.

While advanced digital technologies offer a wide range of opportunities for re-industrialization and inclusive growth in middle-income countries like South Africa, their limited diffusion points to challenges for both firms, public institutions, and government. The research and industry dialogues undertaken as part of this study provide a rich tapestry of digital transformation evidence across key South African value chains. They highlight a tension between firms grappling with potentially existential technology-induced value chain shifts (e.g. the emergence of autonomous vehicles, and ride-hailing applications)[6] to the efficiency-seeking digital disruptions that are likely to significantly shift the position of firms within value chains (e.g. the adoption of digital technologies that enhance services, products, and processes). Somewhere in the middle of this spectrum are new technology developments, particularly those adopted by multinational corporations (MNCs) and leading local firms, which will require suppliers and service providers across the value chain to invest in digitalization capabilities to maintain their position within value chains. In all cases, firms wanting to digitalize clearly need to operate in a digitally enabled environment that is equipped with appropriate digital skills and infrastructures. This is essential for South Africa to benefit from applications such as AI-based machine learning, virtual reality digital twinning, and additive manufacturing that are rapidly transforming businesses in developed economies.

[1] Automotive industry dialogue, 25 October 2018.
[2] DIPF policy brief 1 and Machinery dialogue, 11 October 2018.   [3] DIPF policy brief 1.
[4] Of the four hundred firms that responded to 'The Mobile Corporation in South Africa' survey, only 6 per cent indicated they were using robotics while 13.4 per cent indicated using big data and machine learning, 13.6 per cent virtual reality, and 33.9 per cent IoT.
[5] DIPF policy brief 4.   [6] See for example Arbib and Seba (2017).

12.3.1 The Inherent Tensions and Challenges
in the Adoption of Digitalization

While South African industrialists have been aware of the potential for digital disruption in the value chains within which they operate, uncertainty about the extent of the emerging disruptions (its speed, scale, and scope) has often resulted in a reluctance to make new investments. The risks and rewards associated with embracing new digital technologies have not seemed to be sufficiently understood to support more aggressive investment in these technologies, which partly explains the continued dominance of traditional industrial processes, products, and service models. Some firms have been experimenting with new technologies in narrow areas, and some have been achieving good results, which could inspire more wide-scale use and adoption.

Key cross-cutting themes and challenges fall into four main categories:

1. the extent to which digital disruptions are likely to be efficiency-enabling as opposed to only value-chain disrupting;
2. the extent to which digital disruption will impact economic activity in the purely digital space as opposed to the cyber-physical space;
3. the extent to which entirely new value-chain models develop; and
4. the extent to which digital disruption will shift the structure of GVCs, and the role of lead multinational firms in organizing their global activities.

It is also important to understand how these cross-cutting issues dynamically interact with industry- and sector-specific digitalization drivers and constraints.

Efficiency-Enabling versus Value-Chain Disrupting
The transition to digitally enabled firm-level business models is likely to incorporate both major and minor adjustments, and it is critical that these are both understood. If not, South Africa is likely to end up with a divide between universities and government operating and promoting digitally disruptive technologies on the one hand, and firms operating in the realm of more subtle incorporation of digitalization technologies to enhance competitiveness.

An example of dramatic digital disruption within value chains is the advent of autonomous electric vehicles. This would inevitably cause upheaval not just in automotive manufacturing and vehicle consumption, but across the entire automotive ecosystem. This includes at the level of energy supply and the broader transport sector, and the South African automotive industry would undoubtedly be affected. South Africa's leading articulated dump truck manufacturer, Bell Equipment, has started to explore the development of fully autonomous vehicles.

At the opposite end of the spectrum, many of the positive examples of digital progression in South Africa are less dramatic, encompassing efficiency-enabling interventions. These include improving the effectiveness of cold chain management within the agriculture-food processing value chain using IoT (see Chapter 6), improving machine reliability through the application of machine learning, or supplying fashion retail markets with more desirable products on the basis of IoT-enabled data analytics and supply-chain coordination. For example, Atlantis Foundries, which manufactures commercial vehicle engine blocks for several major international engine brands, is an excellent case of the application of AI to predict sub-surface defects. Its use here has reduced internal scrap and rework rates by up to 90 per cent.

Digital Disruption across the Cyber-Physical Space

The extent of digital disruption is linked to how digitalization transverses the purely cyber versus the cyber-physical and mainly physical value chains. For example, digital books or games that can be downloaded are primarily digital transactions (although recognizing that a physical product is ultimately required to read or play). Cyber-physical products are items such as household appliances, electronic goods, or vehicles, where an increasing amount of digital technology is embodied within these products. Finally, there are also primarily physical products or services which may be significantly augmented by digitalization in future but that will remain primarily physical activities.

Seen through this lens, certain value chains are likely to be more disrupted than others. Firms have recognized the extent to which these disruptions would be appropriate for their business. For example, having tested several innovations across the business, one of South Africa's leading clothing retailers has taken a relatively cautious view on 'digital disruption'. Its advances into e-commerce have not yielded the anticipated results, although the group is seen as a leader in this space in South Africa. The focus of its digitalization effort has, therefore, increasingly been on big data analytics to enhance marketing and supply-chain strategies in response to rapidly changing consumer preferences and the need to improve on customer experiences.

In mineral-processing machinery, digitalization enables machinery manufacturers in partnership with engineers to provide mines with a total cost of the processing service. Systems and processes are customized to specific mines, the wear of parts is tracked, enabling optimal replacement, and performance is monitored across plants. While the firms are moving to selling this as a service, competitive capabilities still involve embodying knowledge in the physical products being manufactured. The lead firms have been increasingly employing additive manufacturing and simulation in design and product development to optimize the mineral processing solutions being supplied (Chapter 3).

The Potential for New Value Chain Models

A critical consideration that emerges in respect of all the industries studied is the extent to which new value-chain models will evolve because of digitalization. The role of machines will likely increase (displacing the centrality of human-to-human interaction), platforms will take a greater share of economic activity from products (pay-for-use displacing merchandise transactions), trade will become more embodied by data rather than goods, and market intelligence will shift from tightly controlled company cores to the 'digital crowd' (McAfee and Brynjolfsson, 2017). These changes can fundamentally alter how GVCs function and are organized. And there is great risk that power is concentrated among platform leaders and the places in the world from where dominant platforms are emanating.

The primary challenge that South African industrialists face is not only the need to understand individual digital technologies and the individual business-model shifts they enable, but rather how the technologies and associated business-model shifts combine in the value chains within which their firms operate. For example, rapidly advancing automotive telemetry, which effectively plugs vehicles into the IoT, while also allowing vehicles to 'see' their immediate environment through advanced sensor technology, could provide the basis for the development of autonomous vehicles. This might change the components and materials cars are made of. Even more fundamentally, the technical dimensions of the autonomous vehicles may become superfluous to the passenger, such that vehicle ownership no longer remains important.

Global Value Chains, SMMEs, and Policy Challenges

A final set of critical cross-cutting considerations relates to the position of South African firms within complex GVCs. Many larger South African-based manufacturers are subsidiaries of MNCs, operate under licence to MNCs, or are independent but supply MNCs. These firms often have limited agency regarding the technologies they use and the products or services they offer, as these are prescribed by lead firms and parent organizations. For many South African firms, the only scope for embracing new digital technologies is in process improvements that fall into their ambit of control. For the balance of opportunities, the South African firms are ultimately dependent on how the lead firm in their GVC embraces the new digital technologies and then 'trickles these down' through their global networks. In these arrangements it would be very difficult for South African technology providers to gain entry.

On other hand, digitalization can also facilitate GVC fragmentation. For example, in the automotive industry, a key issue is the diffusion of new technologies beyond the better-positioned first-tier suppliers to the second and third tier. Increasing the share of local content in domestically assembled vehicles is a key objective of the recently developed South African Automotive Masterplan (Chapter 5; see also Barnes et al., 2017). This in turn, can facilitate the expansion of opportunities for independent SMMEs.

The use of new technologies is opening up space for innovation. In clothing, textiles, and footwear, for example, advances in digital fit software combined with rapidly advancing additive manufacturing technologies, such as vat polymerization, will have a significant impact not only on product development but all the functional areas of the value chain, from design to prototyping, and ultimately volume production. With this technology, it is possible to go directly from computer-aided design of a shoe, to the sharing of that design to anywhere in the world, to the printing of the shoe last on an additive printer; and for the upper part to then be prototyped, with the sole being also printed on an additive printer.

These inherent tensions place the South African industrial ecosystem at something of a crossroads. Will digitalization result in further consolidation of GVCs and the continued growth and dominance of MNCs as lead firms, or will it facilitate GVC fragmentation, and the expansion of opportunities for independent SMMEs? The central point of this analysis is that there is ample space for policy intervention in the digital economy. The challenge is intervening in a way that allows South African industry to move down the technology adoption curve, innovate, and avoid being trapped in low value-added segments of digital GVCs. This has proven difficult in goods-producing GVCs. Whether the road will be easier or harder in digital GVCs remains to be seen.

The Interplay between Cross-Sectoral and Industry-Specific Factors

The dynamic interplay between cross-cutting and value chain-specific digitalization issues is one of the most striking aspects of this analysis. This suggests that forms of cross-cutting support, such as skills development, need to be combined with industry-specific responses to digitalization as embedded in sector strategies.

In food value chains it appears that changing market and regulatory conditions, particularly concerns around food safety, are the key drivers of digitalization. In fresh fruit, while there is huge potential to grow exports and employment with the application of digitalization, export market access and related standards are a major obstacle. Blockchain technology and radio frequency identification (RFID) tags are causing some disruption in the food industry by addressing the core challenges around transparency and traceability along the value chain. For example, a local grower and producer of citrus fruits, Katlego Sitrus, is exporting fruit with stickers which have a quick-response barcode that consumers can scan to know the provenance of the product (Chapter 6).

The ability to absorb new digital technologies depends in part on the factor-cost profiles that dominate activities within specific value-chain linkages. For example, where labour costs represent a small proportion of total production costs, and are comparatively cheap internationally, the incentive to invest in new digital technologies is greatly reduced. While the introduction of AI-enabled robotics is growing rapidly in automotive assembly plants located within high labour-cost, developed economies, the most advanced automotive plant in South Africa still has no co-bots, despite its sister plant operating with dozens of them. Similarly, the South African clothing and footwear industries, which have low comparative labour costs, only have automation in key capital-intensive nodal points, like materials cutting and plant performance monitoring. All assembly activity is still being undertaken manually.

In mining machinery, the growing regional market in Southern Africa provides an important base from which locally based firms have been able to build capabilities. The advantages of proximity and location-specific knowledge require partnerships with the engineering procurement and construction management firms which lead mine design. The firms must simultaneously learn from global developments and provide regional solutions in, for example, predictive maintenance which requires reliable data transfer (Chapter 3).

In those value chains where data are the main source of value, especially in consumer applications, concentration in digital platforms and control of data have played a key role. Data often provide platform owners with their power and associated commercial value in areas such as search, ride hailing, performance monitoring and management, e-commerce, and social media (McAfee and Brynjolfsson, 2017; Polson and Scott, 2018; Singh, 2018; UNCTAD, 2018; Andreoni and Roberts, 2020). There are also important implications for international trade. The USA has pushed for multilateral commitments (the so-called 'Digital 2 Dozen') which would prevent measures that support local businesses in competing with currently dominant platform owners, such as a prohibition on customs duties for digital products.

12.4 Basic and Intermediate Capabilities, Digital Skills, and Infrastructure

In South Africa and other middle-income countries, a number of structural issues can hinder the adoption of advanced digital technologies by firms that are not MNCs or internationally competitive. The lack of basic and intermediate digital capabilities—digital skills in particular—and enabling infrastructural capabilities undermines domestic firms' technology efforts, specifically their absorption of digital technologies, their integration into existing production systems, and their retrofitting (Ferraz et al., 2019; UNIDO, 2019).

As discussed in section 12.1, the fact that 4IR technologies build on and co-exist with 3IR technologies means that firms will have to equip themselves with a broad array of capabilities and skills from both 3IR and 4IR. Indeed, to the extent that it is possible, for a company it would not make any sense to try to develop advanced capabilities in data analytics, for example, if the same company is still struggling to effectively deploy basic ICT; similarly, data cannot be harvested if the firms' production technologies have no sensors and, thus, connectivity. Similarly, IoT would not be feasible without the development of coding skills and standardization capabilities, as well as access to reliable connectivity infrastructure. As a further example, the introduction of robot cells and the effective use of robots for the execution of various tasks such as handling, welding, etc. implies that firms have effectively arranged the production flow and supply logistics and that robots can be fed with intermediate components (e.g. from forming presses) in time in a fully controlled environment and without any disruption. These production conditions are very difficult (and costly) to meet in firms operating in countries with limited access to high-quality electricity supply and connectivity. Moreover, the lack of well-trained operation management and engineering skills tend also to pre-empt the introduction of such digital production technologies and processes, as does the higher level of complexity involved in installing and running them effectively. As several respondents in the study indicated, it makes no sense to automate a substandard process (Andreoni and Anzolin, 2019).

These examples suggest that basic and intermediate capabilities are in fact preconditions for meaningful and effective engagement with more advanced digital capabilities. These capabilities are critical for creating the micro-efficiency and reliability conditions required to deploy new digital production technologies effectively. They also support the learning journey of technology absorption and adaptation, which should result in the retrofitting of the legacy production systems. These pre-conditions essentially set a threshold for the viability of more advanced digital capability, which many firms in middle-income countries find difficult to get past (Andreoni and Anzolin, 2019).

Firms in advanced countries are better positioned to capture 4IR opportunities, exactly because they have spent decades absorbing, deploying, and improving 3IR technologies. Some are also platform owners. Generally, firms in mature industrial economies have more easily overcome the digital capability threshold and can focus more directly on developing and putting to use the more advanced capabilities and skills of digital production technologies. Not only are these firms better positioned to incrementally integrate 4IR technologies and rethink their organizational models, they also operate in industrial ecosystems in which firms—while equipped with different capabilities—have been integrated in supply chains for a long time. As an example, it is easier for an original equipment manufacturer (OEM) in a developed country to introduce a new digital production technology, as its local suppliers operate with similar software and hardware systems, and are aligned in terms of their production standards and enabled by the same connectivity infrastructure.

These conditions are often not in place in developing countries, nor in peripheral regions in advanced countries. Given the dualistic structure of the industrial system in developing countries, a few major large firms and international OEMs operate as production islands in a sea of often disorganized, semi-formal, and small-scale business operations. This is a major 'structural' obstacle to the diffusion of 4IR technologies, especially those that are intrinsically based on networked systems and data.

12.4.1 The Institutional Challenge of Developing Digital Skills

Digitalization exacerbates the already-significant skills development challenges in several ways. Emerging technologies call for a new set of digital skills profiles— for example programming skills, web and application development skills, digital design, data management, visualization, and analytics—which build on advanced literacy, numeracy, and ICT skills. And given that digital technologies draw on and integrate different science and technology fields in new ways, traditional training often does not prepare for the use of integrated technologies. The need for training in the deployment of mechatronics, or design of digital platform interfaces integrating hardware, software, and connectivity solutions raises the digital capability threshold significantly (Andreoni et al., 2021).

Another important skills-related challenge faced by South Africa and other middle-income countries is institutional in nature. Specifically, the challenge for training institutions, technical colleges, and universities to develop and embed appropriate skills in the new and existing workforce is a big one. While there are some cases of excellent training provision in South Africa, overall the insufficient funding in the education infrastructure, in particular the necessary laboratories, tools, and machinery to develop industry- and productive task-specific skills has been a major constraint. This underfunding has also limited the much-needed curriculum development and upgrading of teachers' competencies in fast-evolving technology fields. This has often resulted in training institutions dishing out certificates rather than developing appropriate skills, and working in isolation, removed from the productive sector they are supposed to be working with.

Even when curricula have been updated and efforts have been put in place to provide high-quality formal training, lack of on-the-job training and work-integrated learning means that graduates are not sufficiently prepared to work in an industrial environment. Often the lack of these programmes is due to the limited number of qualified firms which can employ and train the workforce, and again provide funding to support costly training programmes. The challenges of skills provision are thus intertwined with the structural features of the productive economy, replicating its dualistic structure and reflecting the lack of a diffused ecosystem of competitive firms—in this case firms that are able to train youths effectively and to provide technology-rich employment prospects.

Skills challenges are not only technological, but equally operational and organizational. Given that new digital technologies are largely not plug and play, many require production system retrofitting and operational integration. Consequently, business enterprises require experienced mid-level technicians and directors of operations able to choose appropriate digital solutions, redesign and monitor processes, and address cyber-security and data infrastructure issues, alongside assuring overall organizational performance. These digital skills can be difficult to find as they comprise several tacit knowledge elements and experience-based competencies. A lack of domestic firms that actively promote the development of this experience means that a limited number of experienced people are available in general.

12.4.2 The Need for a Coherent Digital Industrial Policy in South Africa and Other Middle-Income Countries

The South African economy is at an important juncture. To benefit from the technological advances of digitalization, South African-based businesses need to address the tensions highlighted above and fill the digital capability gap related to skills and infrastructure. Most advanced digital technology will not be invented in South Africa, but its implementation—especially in a manufacturing environment—typically requires a non-trivial level of adaptation and integration, and provides a strong foundation for the development of local capabilities (Sturgeon, 2021). The challenge is to engage with global technology ecosystems, and to leverage them. There should be a fostering of *spillovers* from technology investments that can support a virtuous cycle of technology and capability development in the broader economy. At the same time, for local industrial and technology ecosystems to emerge, a broader social support system is needed, as well as policies to ensure the socially inclusive structural transformation of the South African economy.

Maximizing the benefits of the digital economy requires new approaches and analytical frameworks that are robust enough to accommodate technological dynamism and uncertainty. These frameworks should capture the changing reality of production systems and products, *and* their underlying technology platforms and organizational models—i.e. the *industrial ecosystem* (Andreoni, 2018 and 2020). New industrial policy principles should also reflect the need for more strategic coordination among (and within) public and private sectors; better targeting and policy alignment; and the introduction of both cross-sectoral interventions and industry-specific digital industrial policy.

The cross-sectoral interventions should focus on those opportunities and challenges faced by different firms across industries, especially those related to broader foundational capabilities, such as basic and transversal digital skills, and digital and manufacturing extension services; those related to technology infrastructure, such as digital software licensing, connectivity, and data quality and affordability; and those related to broader financing, investment, and regulatory conditions in the country.

The measures covering sectoral value-chains should address industry structure, including position and links to GVCs. There also needs to be a focus on the different needs and conditions of firms, in particular, the specific types of digital skills, digital technology infrastructures and services, challenges and barriers to

278 DIGITALIZATION, INDUSTRIALIZATION, AND SKILLS DEVELOPMENT

linkages development, competition conditions and value capture, and sectoral regulatory frameworks and incentives, including procurement and market regulations.

Not all industries, nor the value chains in which they are located, will be affected in the same way, so there needs to be careful prioritization. The following list of seven priorities has been identified as appropriate to the South African business experience.

Priority 1: Improved Cost, Speed, and Reliability of ICT Infrastructure (Bandwidth)

South Africa has an expensive, comparatively slow, and unreliable ICT infrastructure and industrialists deem this to be a major limitation to the adoption of more advanced digital technologies. Potential value-chain efficiencies that are likely to be gained from digitalization, enabling data analysis, and tracking of performance across plants and markets, are undermined by poor connectivity. AI-enabled machine learning systems, which are particularly data intensive, appear compromised due to this limitation, especially for SMMEs that do not have the resources to invest in bespoke infrastructure, such as microwave links. The key requirement is to release spectrum for improved connectivity and exploit 'edge computing' to bypass poor connectivity.

Priority 2: Digital Skills Policy

Embracing new digital technologies in South Africa is comparatively expensive for firms because of the substantial skills gap. This requires both scaled-up skills development programmes and the attraction of skilled immigrants in key areas. These include:

- Increasing incentives for cross-cutting skills development in software engineering, programming, data science, and related ICT skills, both in respect of on-the-job training and higher education.
- The establishment of a priority skills list for essential industrial activities in digitalization, machine learning and Artificial Intelligence, CAD/CAM technologies, and the management of MES/ERP/PLM systems. The list needs to direct public digital skills expenditure and should be updated annually in recognition of the rapidly moving digital skills frontier.
- The development of sector-specific digital skills in partnership with private sector industry associations and Sector Education and Training Authorities (SETAs).
- The reform of incentives and organizational structures within technical and vocational education and training (TVET) institutions to incentivize firm-driven training beyond narrow certification-driven training. More private sector involvement is essential to create a closer alignment between

rapidly changing sector requirements and TVET skills programmes.[7] Incentivizing internships is a major opportunity in this regard.
- The linking of digital skills policy to broader technology policy to provide less resourced firms with complementary public support in training, technology absorption and associated organizational development.

Priority 3: Digital Technology Policy

The systematic restructuring of technology policy and institutions is required in four areas: digital technology absorption, standards development and dissemination, system integration, and scaling. One such opportunity is the development (or conversion) of technology centres, science councils (e.g. the Council of Scientific & Industrial Research (CSIR)), incubators, and university units into a coordinated network of 'technology intermediary institutions' organized around the main digital technology platforms and supporting technology absorption, integration, and deployment. Public-private initiatives such as the Mandela Mining Precinct offer considerable potential (Chapter 3).

The key elements of each are:

- *Technology absorption*: This requires the provision of manufacturing and digital extension services (including organizational and operational systems), demonstration projects, beta factories, access to data and infra-technology (metrology, standards), and access to additive manufacturing.
- *Standards development and dissemination*: This would be enabled through the provision of standardization services and data, infra-technologies, testing, and certification facilities.
- *System integration*: This includes retrofitting services and legacy system integration into digital platforms, rapid prototyping facilities, and virtual design.
- *Technology scaling*: This necessitates codification and dissemination of successful technology solutions and the provision of scaling-up facilities such as accelerators for digital start-ups and SMMEs.

Incentivizing firms to incorporate digital technologies in their business models is also a key requirement, and yet the evidence from the industry case studies suggests that South Africa's R&D tax-based incentives define the opportunity so narrowly that most firms do not qualify for support. This is an important legacy consideration that is likely to exist in many middle-income economies. For example, the South African government's tax-based incentive defines what constitutes R&D, but then notes numerous exclusions. These include market research,

---

[7] An example is the Mercedes-Benz Learning Academy in East London.

market testing, or sales promotion; administration, financing, compliance, and similar overheads; and routine testing, analysis, information collection, and quality control in the normal course of business. This definition precludes data-intensive technologies. It is important that R&D incentives support both efficiency-seeking and business-model innovation in the emerging digital space.

Priority 4: Financing and Investment
Digitalization requires investment in upgraded capital equipment and human capital. In addition, there are working capital consequences when firms shift to providing end-to-end service solutions for customers as opposed to selling products. For example, South African mining machinery manufacturers are contracting with mines to deliver processed tonnes of ore rather than the supply of machinery. This has balance sheet consequences for firms, with concomitant changes to financing requirements. Development finance institutions, such as the Industrial Development Corporation (IDC), have a lead role to play in offering the appropriate financing required. Without a comprehensive understanding of disruptive new digital business models by the industrial financing institutions themselves, such support is unlikely.

Priority 5: Linkages to Development Policy
As a country with generally weak industrial supply chains, particularly with regard to the role of SMMEs, digitalization offers a major opportunity to promote the adoption of supply-chain tools (such as ERP and MES) for better supply-chain integration. Supporting second- and third-tier firms in accessing affordable digital technology licences or creating alternative models to reduce the licencing burden is crucial. The creation of a 'Catalogue of Digital SMME Suppliers' via an open and competitive digital market platform to match specific technology and production services demand and supply along and across industry value chains could be enormously valuable to SMMEs. De-risking SMME investments in new technologies and products using combined technology services and hybrid financing models (such as matching grants and pre-commercial procurement) could also support the inclusion of these firms within South Africa's industrial value chains.

Priority 6: Economic Regulation, Competition Policy, and Data
Digitalization sometimes entails the convergence of platforms and networks across the telecommunications, finance, retail, and logistics spheres. In such instances there are substantial scale and first-mover advantages. Where there are local demand specificities, domestic platforms can rival multinational platforms, as is evident in South African e-commerce. In the industrial sector, the specificities of products, process, and business models mean that digital products and platforms tend to remain more fragmented, a characteristic that provides

opportunities for the involvement of local technology vendors and system integrators. Evidence suggests that smart and flexible regulatory frameworks need to ensure that dominant platforms cannot abuse their position to undermine local rivals.

South Africa's regulatory bodies, as for most other middle-income countries, are still organized as if digitalization is not under way. There need to be appropriate regulatory and competition rules for digital platforms, including addressing data privacy and ownership, which draw on international experience, such as the measures taken recently by the EU and India to ensure a level playing field for local businesses in e-commerce and online search activities. In this regard, the 2018 amendments to the South African Competition Act have introduced provisions relating to buyer power and they do strengthen rules relating to price discrimination. However, guidelines regarding their application still need to be set.

Priority 7: Trade and Tax Policies

Middle-income countries like South Africa should be working with other countries at the WTO to resist the push by the global technology giants for digital transactions to be exempt from tariffs. The advance of digital technologies potentially weakens the position of industrializing countries as international firms can bypass import duties, local taxes, and other domestic regulations. For example, additive manufacturing may simply require the transfer of code from a data cloud to a locally based 3-D printing machine and the transfer of the code is free of import tariffs (and other taxes such as VAT and ad valorem excise taxes) or adherence to regulations relating to the safety or health properties of the end product.[8]

A key question, then, is how the South African government plans to tax imported digital products and services to enable and protect local productive activity? In principle, digital technologies do not necessarily represent a threat; they can be used to better protect the domestic market and consumers. For example, clothing, textile, and footwear products entering South Africa could be required to have radio frequency identification (RFID) tags that prove their provenance, such as where they were manufactured, and at what price they were exported from the country in which they were produced.

12.4.3   Silos Need to Give Way to an All-Encompassing Policy and Governance Framework

The effectiveness of sectoral and cross-sectoral interventions across key policy priority areas will depend on the extent to which the government is able to align

---

[8] See also the work on base erosion and profit shifting by the OECD, and the tax challenges arising from digitalization (http://www.oecd.org/tax/beps/).

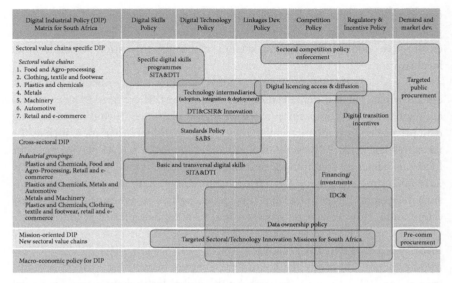

Figure 12.2 Digital industrial policy for South Africa
Source: Authors.

interventions and develop a governance framework that cuts through policy silos (Andreoni, 2016). This is a challenge facing all countries, but in resource-constrained middle-income economies such as South Africa it is more acute. This is because breaking out of policy silos is both a matter of what and how policy interventions are designed as well as what and how resources are allocated and governed. Figure 12.2 presents a potential digital industrial policy matrix for South Africa. It attempts to integrate the different key policy priorities that have been highlighted and to locate these within the specific South African context.

12.5 Concluding Remarks

The development of digital industrial policy in middle-income economies such as South Africa is an emerging field. The evidence presented in this chapter suggests that policy should aim at shaping a new industrial ecosystem in which the opportunities and challenges of new digital industrial technologies are fully seized. This means identifying and targeting areas within and across sectors in which the deployment of digital technologies allows firms to: improve products and their digital content, adapt product and system functionalities to accommodate digital transformation; move towards higher value product segments; diversify products and activities by deploying digital industrial technologies transversally across industry value chains; increase productivity via process upgrading along the value chain and the local production system; link up with other domestic and international firms; diversify market access; and develop industrial competitiveness in new global industries by leveraging domestically available resources.

While policy design and the governance framework are critical, the effective implementation and enforcement of any digital industrial policy will depend on enhanced government capacity and more effective cooperation with the private sector. Overall, digital industrialization will raise potential trade-offs and new conflicts in the economy, for example with respect to employment and new skills requirements. Given the challenges faced by SMMEs, there is a concern that digital technologies will exacerbate the existing divide between large and small firms to the detriment of the much-needed re-industrialization. Digital industrial policy must therefore actively govern these processes to ensure the digital industrial dividend is distributed across different types of firms, their employees, and broader society. This challenge is certainly not unique to South Africa. Other middle-income economies are facing the same difficulties in respect of their own industrial policy frameworks, and will need to similarly define how to incorporate digital disruption within their existing suite of policy instruments.

References

Andreoni, A. (2016). 'Varieties of industrial policy: models, packages and transformation cycles.' In A. Noman and J. Stiglitz (eds), *Efficiency, Finance and Varieties of Industrial Policy*, 245–305. New York: Columbia University Press.

Andreoni, A. (2018). 'The architecture and dynamics of industrial ecosystems: diversification and innovative industrial renewal in Emilia Romagna.' *Cambridge Journal of Economics* 42(6): 1613–42.

Andreoni, A. (2020). 'Technical change, the shifting terrain of the "industrial" and digital industrial policy.' In A. Oqubay, C. Cramer, H.-J. Chang, and R. Kozul-Wright (eds), *The Oxford Handbook of Industrial Policy*, 369–93. Oxford: Oxford University Press.

Andreoni, A. and G. Anzolin (2019). 'A revolution in the making? Challenges and opportunities of digital production technologies for developing countries.' Background Paper for the UNIDO Industrial Development Report 2020: Industrializing in the Digital Age. Vienna: UNIDO.

Andreoni, A. and F. Tregenna (2020). 'Escaping the middle-income technology trap: a comparative analysis of industrial policies in China, Brazil and South Africa.' *Structural Change and Economic Dynamics* 54: 324–40.

Andreoni, A. and S. Roberts (2020). 'Governing data and digital platforms in middle-income countries: regulations, competition and industrial policies, with sectoral case studies from South Africa.' Digital Pathways at Oxford Paper no. 5. Oxford.

Andreoni, A., H.-J. Chang, and M. Labrunie (2021). 'Natura non facit saltus.' *European Journal of Development Research* 33: 330–70.

Arbib, J. and T. Seba (2017). 'Rethinking transportation 2020–2030: the disruption of transportation and the collapse of the internal combustion vehicle and oil industries.' RethinkX, May.

Barnes, J., A. Black, and K. Techakanont (2017). 'Industrial policy, multinational strategy, and domestic capability: a comparative analysis of the development of South Africa's and Thailand's automotive industry.' *European Journal of Development Research* 29: 37–53.

Bell, J., S. Goga, P. Mondliwa, and S. Roberts (2018). 'Structural transformation in South Africa: moving towards a smart open economic for all.' CCRED Working Paper 2018/19. Johannesburg: CCRED.

Clifton, J., A. Glasmeier, and M. Gray (2020). 'When machines think for us: the consequences for work and place.' *Cambridge Journal of Regions, Economy and Society* 13(1): 3–23.

Ferraz, J. C., D. Kupfer, J. Torracca, and J. N. P. Britto (2019). 'Snapshots of a state of flux: how Brazilian industrial firms differ in the adoption of digital technologies and policy implications.' *Journal of Economic Policy Reform* 23(4): 390–407, DOI:1 0.1080/17487870.2019.1578651.

Ford, M. (2015). *Rise of the Robots: Technology and the Threat of a Jobless Future*. New York: Basic Books.

Gereffi, G., J. Humphreym, and T. Sturgeon (2005). 'The governance of global value chains.' *Review of International Political Economy* 12(1): 78–104.

Hallward-Driemeier, M. and G. Nayyar (2018). *Trouble in the Making? The Future of Manufacturing-Led Development*. Washington, DC: World Bank.

McAfee, A. and E. Brynjolfsson (2017). *Machine, Platform, Crowd*. New York: W.W. Norton & Company.

Polson, N. and J. Scott (2018). *AIQ: How Artificial Intelligence Works and How We Can Harness Its Power for a Better World*. London: Bantam Press.

Rehnberg, M. and S. Ponte (2018). 'From smiling to smirking? 3D printing, upgrading and the restructuring of global value chains.' *Global Networks* 18(1): 57–80, DOI:10.1111/glob.12166.

Rodrik, D. (2018). 'New technologies, global value chains, and the developing economies.' CESifo Working Paper 7307. Munich: CESifo.

Schwab, K. (2016). 'The future of jobs.' World Economic Forum report, https://www.weforum.org/reports/the-future-of-jobs.

Singh, P. J. (2018). 'Digital industrialisation in developing countries.' Commonwealth Secretariat.

Sturgeon, T. (2021). 'Upgrading strategies for the digital economy.' *Global Strategy Journal* 11(1): 34–57, published on-line 7 November 2019, DOI:10.1002/gsj.1364.

UNCTAD (2018). 'Trade and development report 2018: power, platforms and the free trade delusion.' United Nations publication, Sales No. E.18.II.D.7. New York and Geneva: UNCTAD.

UNIDO (2019). 'Industrializing in the digital age.' Industrial development report. Vienna: UNIDO.

Whittaker, D. H., T. Sturgeon, T. Okita, and T. Zhu (2020). *Compressed Development*. Oxford: Oxford University Press.

World Bank (2016). 'Digital dividends.' World development report. Washington, DC: World Bank.

Digital Industrial Policy Briefs

DIPF Brief 1: L. Kaziboni, M. Nkhonjera, S. Roberts. 'Machinery, equipment and electronic control systems: leading reindustrialisation in Southern Africa.'

DIPF Brief 2: J. Barnes. 'Repositioning the future of the South African automotive industry.'

DIPF Brief 3: S. Chisoro-Dube and R. das Nair. 'Technological developments and the "industrialisation of freshness" in fresh fruit supply.'

DIPF Brief 4: J. Barnes and L. Higginson. 'Practical implications for the South African food processing industry.'

DIPF Brief 5: J. Barnes and J. White. 'Repositioning the future of the South African chemicals industry.'

DIPF Brief 6: S. Goga and A. Paelo. 'An e-commerce revolution in retail?'

DIPF Brief 7: R. Stewart. 'Repositioning the future of the South African clothing and textile industries.'

DIPF Brief 8: J. Barnes and M. Ndlovu. 'Digital disruptions in the yellow metals industry—the role for government response'.

DIPF Brief 9: J. Stuart and A. Black. 'The Cape Town software development cluster.'

DIPF Brief 10: P. Mondliwa and L. Monaco. 'Digital transformation of the plastic products factory.'

DIPF Brief 11: A. Black. 'Managing the transition to electric vehicle technology.'

13

Global Value Chains, 'In-Out-In' Industrialization, and the Global Patterns of Sectoral Value Addition

Antonio Andreoni, Keun Lee, and Sofia Torreggiani

13.1 Introduction

Since the diffusion of the putting-out system among early European industrializers and, more recently, the emergence of regional and global value chains (RVCs and GVCs) among late industrializers, production-chain development has always played a key role in shaping countries' structural transformation. Although GVCs already existed in the 1960s when countries like South Korea and Taiwan were starting to industrialize, since the 1990s there has been a palpable leap in the scale and scope of the internationalization of production. This is reflected in the large volume of flows in intermediate goods, which in 2018 represented almost half of world goods traded (about US$8.3 trillion) (UNCTAD, 2019), and in the substantial increase in the geographical breadth, length, and depth of production chains. Several global changes have also made the expansion of RVCs and GVCs possible: falling transport costs and advances in technology enabling more interconnectedness via ICTs; cost-reduction opportunities associated with offshoring labour-intensive manufacturing processes; and the increasing trade and investment liberalizations (Nolan, 2001; Milberg and Winkler, 2013; Gereffi, 2014; Neilson et al., 2014; Kaplinsky and Morris, 2015).

While GVCs have remained a regional phenomenon to a certain extent, or limited to 'Factory North America', 'Factory Europe', or 'Factory Asia' (Baldwin and Lopez-Gonzalez, 2015), since the mid-1990s Latin American and, to a lesser extent, African countries have also started to show increasing inter- as well intra-regional integration. GVC integration, however, has followed very different pathways and led to very different industrial upgrading outcomes. In this chapter, the factors and dynamics that have determined this variety of GVC integration pathways and the related industrialization outcomes are analysed. This is done through the presentation of new evidence on the patterns of sectoral value chain addition that have been recorded across middle-income countries in the years

Antonio Andreoni, Keun Lee, and Sofia Torreggiani, *Global Value Chains, 'In-Out-In' Industrialization, and the Global Patterns of Sectoral Value Addition* In: *Structural Transformation in South Africa: The Challenges of Inclusive Industrial Development in a Middle-Income Country.* Edited by: Antonio Andreoni, Pamela Mondliwa, Simon Roberts, and Fiona Tregenna, Oxford University Press. © Oxford University Press 2021. DOI: 10.1093/oso/9780192894311.003.0013

1995–2011, with a particular focus on South Africa. Capturing the ways in which different sectors have contributed to domestic value addition (DVA) makes it possible to identify several stylized facts around 'late-late industrialization'. Building on this historical analysis, the discussion ends with a reflection on possible future scenarios arising from the Covid-19 crisis.

Section 13.2 starts with a review of emerging theoretical perspectives and hypotheses around factors and dynamics leading to different GVC integration pathways and related industrialization outcomes. While joining GVCs might represent a learning opportunity and open up a development pathway, there is a risk for firms—and countries as a whole—of being stuck in low value-added activities with little scope for progressing to higher tiers in the value chains. More accessible parts of the value chain are associated with limited linkages and little possibility for knowledge spillovers in the wider economy, which might result in 'thin industrialization' (Gereffi, 2014) and 'enclave effects' (Gallagher and Zarsky, 2007; Plank and Staritz, 2013). The existence of some of these factors and dynamics points to the importance of pursuing a strategic integration with GVCs. This means an integration which evolves both sequentially and in parallel with the development of local value chains and ecosystems. Industrial policy is key in integrating these two processes.

Building on these theoretical perspectives, section 13.3 involves a review of the empirical evidence on the variety of GVC integration pathways across different countries, and provides new country- and sector-level evidence of the so called 'in-out-in' industrialization hypothesis formulated by Lee et al. (2018) and the detour strategies suggested in Lee (2019). The analysis advances to a focus on two success stories of GVC integration—South Korea and China—and a study of the ways in which different economic sectors have contributed to a sustained increase in DVA at the country level. The chapter empirically documents how successful catching up has been associated with an 'in-out-in' industrialization process of GVC integration, where countries first 'couple' by entering GVCs in low value-added segments, then 'decouple' by building domestic supply chains and upgrading existing local capabilities, and finally 'recouple' by performing high value-addition activities in GVCs.

In section 13.4, this country and sectoral analysis is developed to identify emerging patterns across middle-income countries, with a particular focus on the South African case. The 'in-out-in' industrialization hypothesis is tested and several stylized facts are noted and discussed, as South Africa's sectoral GVC participation dynamics are benchmarked against those of Central and Latin American and South East Asian economies. The key finding is that, in relation to increasing DVA, today's middle-income countries have experienced different fortunes at the sectoral and country level.

Section 13.5 concludes, reflecting on possible future scenarios arising in the post-Covid-19 international context and the emergence of potential new industrialization models. For developing and emerging economies, reduced opportunities for export-led industrialization suggest the importance of diversifying their production base by leveraging existing domestic markets and creating new ones through procurement policies, and backward and forward integration. The development opportunities offered to emerging countries like South Africa through their endowments in natural resources are revisited as potential sources of innovation and diversification.

13.2 Global Value-Chain Integration and the Development of Local Ecosystems: Theoretical Perspectives

From a structural transformation standpoint, integration in GVCs offers both new opportunities and challenges for low- and middle-income countries (LMICs) like South Africa. GVCs might represent an attainable first step towards integration into regional and global markets and industrialization, while diversifying and upgrading in specific tasks and new products. Rather than having to develop an entire product, countries can specialize in specific tasks or components of a multitude of value chains, starting at the relatively accessible bottom. Through the exposure to learning processes, technology transfer, and informational flows, these countries might then benefit from knowledge spillovers and start upgrading within GVCs. The notion of upgrading represents a central concept in the GVC framework, originally defined by Gereffi (1999) as 'the process of improving the ability of a firm or an economy to move to more profitable and/or technologically sophisticated capital and skill-intensive economic niches'. This notion has been extended to the now widely accepted four-fold categorization of upgrading typologies as product, process, functional, and intersectoral upgrading (Kaplinsky and Morris, 2001; Humphrey and Schmitz, 2002). This taxonomy conceives of the movement towards higher value creation in terms of the successful adoption of new processes, the development of new products, the functional reconfiguration of who does what along the entire chain, and the entry into completely new industries.

With respect to functional upgrading in particular, the three stages of OEM-ODM-OBM have often been the key framework of understanding (Hobday, 2003). Original equipment manufacturing (OEM) is the first step in catching up among East Asian manufacturers; own design manufacturing (ODM) is the second step, where manufacturers can depart from simple jobs, such as assembling, and begin involvement in production design; and own brand manufacturing (OBM) is the last step, whereby these manufacturers perform all functions of production, design, marketing, channel management, and research and development (R&D)

independently. According to Hobday (2003), firms in East Asian countries followed a transitional path from OEM to ODM, and then to OBM. This transition is not simply limited to companies, as it also involves the development of different sets of backward and forward linkages in the domestic ecosystem (Andreoni, 2019; Andreoni and Tregenna, 2020).[1] However, the transition from one mode to the next is not easy, especially in the transition to OBM, because this step involves several risks, including counterattacks from flagship firms in existing GVCs or incumbents. This is noted in Lee et al. (2015) in the case of the South Korean SMEs trying OBM, and in Navas-Aleman (2011) in the case of the footwear and furniture sectors in Brazil. Both cases show that this stage can be prolonged by a slowdown, which may even lead to a decline in sales or market share, and even to a possible crisis for firms attempting this functional upgrading.

13.2.1 Global Value-Chain Integration: Challenges for Upgrading

When evaluating the potential opportunities as well as challenges associated with GVC integration, six main factors and dynamics should be considered (see Lee and Mathews, 2012; Andreoni, 2019; Andreoni and Tregenna, 2020).

First, transnational corporations (TNCs) leading regional and global value chains are extremely powerful organizations. Their power relies on the creation of entry barriers in the forms of patents, quality standards, and copyrights and trademarks, as well as their control over technologies, including data and digital platforms (see Chapter 12). TNCs also orchestrate global chains of suppliers and, through their localization and related buying and pricing strategies, have the power to include companies (or not). In the South African mining equipment industry, for example, sourcing decisions are controlled by a limited number of TNCs (Andreoni and Torreggiani, 2020; and Chapter 3). Other practices have been documented across several countries. For instance, in the case of consumer goods, former vendor companies (brand owners) often stop giving OEM orders to destroy the company that has begun to sell their competing brands (Lee et al., 2015). In the case of capital goods, incumbent companies suddenly charge predatory prices in the market once they realize that latecomer firms have become successful in developing their products, which poses the threat of competition against products of the incumbent. In certain cases, the incumbent reacts by filing lawsuits against the latecomers, and claiming that the latter has copied its

---

[1] In structural economics, backward linkages refer to the relationship involving a firm buying intermediate inputs from another firm in an upstream industry. Forward linkages refer to the relationship between a firm selling intermediate inputs to another firm in a downstream industry. Hence, each firm establishes linkages with upstream and downstream firms along several sectoral value chains (in some cases also with consumers of final goods). These linkages constitute the input-output production matrix of an economy.

products. In other cases, small supplier firms have had trouble with the client firm over selling prices and delivery time, among others, which has sometimes led to a sudden halt in purchasing orders from the client firm.

Second, the sectoral value chains that firms in developing and emerging economies tend to be integrated with (or the GVC stages they perform) are not those with high-value opportunities or margins for manufacturing development. Within the African context, for example, GVC integration has mainly involved upstream resource-based sectors. While there are some encouraging cases of successful integration in sectoral value chains—such as the flower and leather industry in Ethiopia (Cramer et al., 2020), and the fruit industry in South Africa (Chapter 6)—without developing a number of key manufacturing industries delivering production technologies for the other sectoral value chains, these will not be able to transform these economies and trigger cumulative processes of intersectoral learning (Andreoni, 2018; and Chapter 1).

Third, from a learning perspective, there are risks in committing scarce resources in specific assets to perform relatively unsophisticated activities such as basic processing or assembling. This can lead to a situation of 'production lock-in' when firms remain stuck in a certain low-value activity, followed by potential 'value-chain de-linking' once more price-competitive firms or new quality standards emerge (Kaplinsky and Morris, 2015). As a result of these processes, industrial systems in developing economies in the early stages of economic transformation are generally characterized by foreign-owned companies that establish few backward and forward linkages with local suppliers, and processors generally lacking the capabilities to perform activities other than basic assembling. Existing small enterprises lack the scale and skills to provide reliable intermediate products, as well as the resources to invest in technological upgrading. Particularly problematic therefore is the lack of medium-sized manufacturing firms that can do those things—the so-called 'missing middle' phenomenon.

Fourth, care is needed when interpreting upgrading trajectories with respect to the well-known 'smile curve', originally developed by Acer's CEO Stan Shih to describe the position of Taiwan in the electronics value chain (Shih, 1996). This is partly because of the risks of 'production lock-in' or 'value-chain de-linking' discussed above. The smile curve, indeed, illustrates the decomposition of value of a given product into the underlying stages (tasks) of production. According to the traditional, partly simplistic, interpretation of the smile curve theory, in order to upgrade their position, firms and countries should seek to move to tasks at the extreme ends of the curve, typically those that extract a higher share of the overall value. However, this view ignores the fact that multidimensional upgrading—for example, functional, process, product, and intersectoral upgrading—goes beyond existing firms specializing only in a limited and isolated sets of tasks. In order to capture 'high value niche' opportunities along the value chain through task specialization, companies often have to develop multiple sets of complementary production capabilities that cut across many stages of the value chain.[2]

Fifth, discussions on GVC integration tend to focus narrowly on 'vertical linkages' along the value chain, while missing the important role of cross-sectoral 'horizontal linkages' among different firms at each node of the value chain. As shown by the South Korean firms' experience, leveraging a bigger piece of the pie from global profit critically requires building and upgrading local chains for value and knowledge creation (Lee et al., 2018). More in general, export-led industrialization and successful GVC integration in several East Asian countries has advanced hand in hand with the development of horizontal cross-sectoral linkages in the domestic economy, and the resulting incremental DVA in trade (Chang, 2010).

Finally, when considering opportunities and risks associated with GVC integration, it is crucial to address context-specific political economy dynamics and issues related to ownership. Firms across developing countries tend to be adversely affected by the existing distribution of organizational power in both the public and private sectors—namely, the countries' 'political settlement' (Khan, 2010; Whitfield et al., 2015; Behuria et al., 2017; Andreoni, 2019). Given a certain political economy context, participation in GVCs might lead to entrenching power even more upstream and consolidate an incentive structure that is biased towards importers more than producers.

The fight for independence from leading firms in the GVC is a key political economy process.[3] Latecomer firms from the South certainly have the option of not fighting and remaining dependent on a single TNC or a few. This strategy may lead to stable growth for a while. However, in the longer term the outcomes are often uncertain as new late entrant firms emerge from the next-tier countries offering lower wages and costs (Lee and Mathews, 2012). The limitations of these dependent catch-up strategies are shown in the case of other countries reported in previous studies (Rasiah, 2006; Van Dijk and Bell, 2007). In the case of South Africa, for example, the emergence of competitive suppliers in China and other East Asian countries has resulted in increasing import penetration over the last two decades. Import penetration, especially from China, has also increasingly shifted from low- to medium-tech products. This has crowded out several South

---

[2] In today's advanced economies' industrial ecosystems (Andreoni and Lazonick, 2020) such as the Emilia Romagna region in Italy (Andreoni, 2018), these complementary capabilities have been developed along different cycles of industrial transformation and renewal of vertically integrated firms, supported by a dense network of local specialized suppliers and contractors.
[3] This recognition is to some degree in contrast with several studies in GVC literature that have tended to concentrate on collaborations between the flagship firms in the West and firms in the South (Ernst and Kim, 2002).

African companies, especially those that were not investing in developing their capabilities (Torreggiani and Andreoni, 2019).

In terms of ownership of value created in the GVC, upgrading from OEM to ODM and finally to OBM is a key process for creating more value locally and obtaining a certain degree of independence from the flagship firms in the existing GVC. Another important factor is for firms to eventually aim to have some form of local ownership, as building independently would be difficult (Amsden and Chu, 2003). Although Taiwan has been more dependent on foreign MNCs than South Korea, it did eventually create locally owned big businesses, thus raising its status to a high-income economy. Lee et al. (2013) confirm that having or not having a certain number of big businesses is an important benchmark for a middle-income country's ability to get out of the middle-income trap (Chapter 11), and that both South Korea and Taiwan have created a critical number of global big businesses relative to the size of their economy.[4]

13.2.2 'In-Out-In' Industrialization and Local-Production System Development

On the basis of the discussion on the challenges of upgrading, the following hypothesis is formulated: while at the initial stage of structural transformation more integration into the GVC is desirable for learning from foreign sources of knowledge, functional and sectoral upgrading requires a second stage in which domestic companies seek a form of separation and independence from the existing foreign-dominated GVCs. Then, in a third stage, after building their own local value chains, latecomer firms and economies might have to seek more opening and integration. This dynamic sequence or detour of 'in-out-in again' would generate a non-linear curve in terms of the degree of participation in the GVC, as measured by share of foreign value added (FVA) in gross exports of an economy.

Lee (2013) shows that the first phase of participating in the GVC is to obtain operational knowledge or skills in the mode of 'learning by doing' participating in the arrangement of OEM or foreign direct investments (FDI). The intermediate stage of separation, which would require building capabilities in designing, R&D, and marketing, will be illustrated in the following section (13.3). Here, drawing on Lee et al. (2015) learning at different stages is discussed in detail. The last phase of re-increasing GVC participation tends to emerge when the firms would often become internationalized in production, facing rising domestic wages, and

---

[4] By the early 2010s, Taiwan had eight companies included in Global Fortune 500 class companies and South Korea had thirteen such companies, whereas South Africa has zero number of such big businesses (Lee, 2019: table 2.2).

relocating their factories to lower-wage sites. This is exemplified in the next section by stories of South Korean firms, which included SMEs and big businesses. The 'catch-up cycle' theory (Lee and Malerba, 2017) thus acknowledges the possibility and reality that latecomer firms and industries which learn from the GVC led by firms from advanced industrial nations may take the leadership of sectors by creating their own value chains.

Thus, as is done in Lee et al. (2018), it is hypothesized here that the trend of the FVA would increase initially (during the low- and lower-middle-income stages), then decline at the upper-middle income stage as firms try to create more local value added, relying less on the GVC, and finally increase again at the high-income stage, with enhanced innovation capabilities and internationalization. This non-linear perspective considers that while more integration into the GVC is desirable at the initial stage, upgrading at the later stage requires that the latecomer firms and industries try to effect a temporary separation from the existing foreign dominated GVC, although these firms might have to look for more openings to integrate once more in the GVC after upgrading.

Throughout this 'in-out-in' industrialization process, successful catch-up also results in the development of a local production ecosystem. Indeed, several authors have recently started to recognize the urgent need for increasingly integrated frameworks that analyse how GVCs and local clusters are connected through a variety of globalization processes (Gereffi and Lee, 2016; De Marchi et al., 2018). Building on Hirschmann (1977), Andreoni (2019) highlights the need to understand production transformation from a multi-linkages perspective, with a focus on both the regional and global value chains, as well as—and more critically—the system of interdependencies in the domestic economy, referred to as the 'local production system' (LPS). This is defined as the structural configuration of multiple types of linkages in a given economy—meaning production, technological, consumption, and fiscal linkages.

Production linkages are further classified into backward (or upstream) linkages and forward (or downstream) linkages. Backward linkages correspond to the growth stimuli to sectors that provide the inputs required by a particular production activity. For instance, setting up a steel plant would stimulate the demand for steel scrap, coal, and other similar goods. Forward linkages represent the inducement to start new activities employing the output supplied by a particular production activity. An example here is the expansion of the steel industry, which would encourage the emergence of sectors employing steel as their basic input, such as machine tools.

Related to the development of production linkages, technological linkages represent potential factors that encourage or discourage both productive opportunities and technology adoption. More specifically, input-output tables—matrices of inter-industrial flows of goods and services produced domestically—provide a faithful representation of the backward and forward linkages connecting different sectors.

Technological linkages on the other hand capture the underlying direct and indirect transfer of technological capabilities within and across sectoral value chains. These technological relations are extremely important as they provide the main channels through which intersectoral learning may occur.

With specific reference to the case of countries dependent on resource extraction and primary industries, 'consumption linkage' and 'fiscal linkage' are two further concepts of linkages to be considered. Consumption linkages reflect the process by which the new incomes of the primary resource producers, in a first stage, lead to the importing of consumer goods and, later, to their replacement by domestic production in the agricultural, industrial, and service sectors. Fiscal linkages emerge when resource rents are deployed to fund public investments and to develop production in unrelated sectors.

Linkages and their context-specific structural configuration are responsible for a number of both incentive and constraining mechanisms, and are critical for understanding production transformation and, eventually, how to achieve quality of growth. Production, consumption, and, especially, technological linkages can induce learning and diversification dynamics, improvements in process efficiency, and scaling-up, as well as enhancing product quality, standards, and functionalities. The lack of these linkages might undermine the possibility of implementing scale-efficient investment, as well as result in production-related interlocking bottlenecks within and across value chains. Indeed, investment bottlenecks upstream might make it unprofitable to invest downstream in the sectoral value chain, while the lack of technological linkages might frustrate technological upgrading in sectors relying on manufacturing production technologies (such as agriculture and mining).

13.3 A Variety of Global Value Chain Integration and the 'In-Out-In' Industrialization Pathways in South Korea and China: Some Stylized Facts

Integration into GVCs has followed a variety of pathways across regions and countries. Among Asian late industrializers, Lee and Mathews (2012) and Lee (2013) find cases in South Korea and Taiwan of successful upgrading, with South Korea moving into high-end segments in the same industry and Taiwan moving into new higher value-added sectors (so called 'double upgrading'). These countries managed to escape the middle-income trap precisely because they were able to achieve a double upgrading, that is, increase their DVA in manufacturing, while matching a rise in domestic wages. Rising wages played a key role in shifting from low value-added activities towards higher value-added activities within and across industries. In contrast, Giuliani et al. (2005) observe that GVC integration has very rarely resulted in functional and intersectoral upgrading in Latin America.

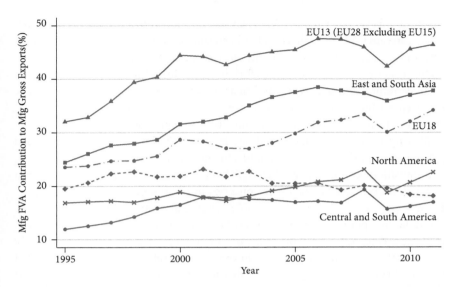

Figure 13.1 Backward participation in manufacturing GVCs by macro-regions, 1995–2011

Note: Mfg is the abbreviation for 'manufacturing'.

Source: Authors' own elaboration based on the OECD-TiVA dataset (2016 version).

Drawing on the OECD-TiVA database,[5] Figure 13.1 reports trends in backward participation in GVCs in total manufacturing, proxied by the FVA content of gross exports, by macro-regions. The main stylized fact is that all macro-regions have experienced an increase in their backward participation in manufacturing GVCs. The lowest rates of participation are reported by Central and South American economies and by countries belonging to the Rest of the World group, which also include the sub-Saharan African countries (excluding South Africa).

Disaggregated data for sub-Saharan African countries are not available in the OECD-TiVA database (with the only exception of South Africa). However, employing alternative sources, the literature has shown a set of stylized facts. As reported by Foster-McGregor et al. (2015) using data from the UNCTAD-EORA database, while the value of world imports has more than doubled during the 2000s, with intermediate goods making up 65 per cent of world imports in 2011,

---

[5] For the purpose of this historical analysis, the 2016 edition of the OECD-TiVA dataset (covering sixty-four economies and thirty-four industries over seventeen years, from 1995 to 2011) was selected. It was chosen over the more recent 2018 edition (covering sixty-four economies and thirty-six industries over eleven years, from 2005 to 2015). Unfortunately, the two databases cannot be combined as they are based on different versions of System of National Accounts (SNA). The 2020 version of the OECD-TiVA dataset, covering the period 1995 to 2018, will contribute significantly to improve understanding of the long-term dynamics of countries' GVC participation across different industries. However, this updated dataset had not yet been published at the time that this chapter was submitted for publication.

much of Africa's participation in GVCs has developed in upstream production. This upstream GVC specialization has been coupled with a declining downstream integration since 1995. Moreover, in all African countries the increase in value addition across manufacturing sectors has remained limited, while industries such as mining and quarrying, and financial intermediation are those that have experienced the largest increases in domestic value added alongside transport, wholesale trade, and utilities (Andreoni, 2019; Amendolagine et al., 2020).

Moving to a country-level analysis, Figure 13.2 shows trends in backward participation in GVCs in total manufacturing for the most important emerging and transition economies for which OECD-TiVA data are available. South Africa is benchmarked against the other countries in the respective regional groups— Latin America, South East Asia, and Eastern European transition economies. These figures point to a third stylized fact: that middle-income countries and transition economies face the difficulty of moving into more technologically sophisticated segments of GVCs. Focusing on the production of low value-added parts and components might exacerbate the risk of 'de-linking domestically' and the hollowing out of the domestic manufacturing sector. Under these conditions a combination of weak productivity growth and rising labour costs, or the emergence of alternative lower-cost locations, might lead to declining profitability, disengagement by the lead firm, and a further weakening of domestic productive capacity. In some cases, these dynamics might result in premature de-industrialization (see chapter 11).

For countries such as Mexico, the globalization of production has not resulted in greater long-term domestic investments, capital accumulation, DVA, and international value capture (see Giuliani et al., 2005; Pietrobelli and Rabellotti, 2011 for a broader discussion on GVC integration and upgrading in Latin America). An example is the 1990s FDI-led expansion of the high-technology sector in the Mexican state of Jalisco, analysed by Gallagher and Zarsky (2007). They find that the benefits of the investment flows were largely limited to the Jaliscan 'enclave', and that foreign investments 'crowded out' domestic ones, resulting in minimal net gains. Large IT TNCs from the USA with operations in Jalisco also imported 98 per cent of inputs, with the result that the domestic manufacturers that supplied Mexico's high-tech firms before the foreign penetration declined by 80 per cent. The causes of these disappointing performances lie in the barriers to entry for domestic firms, combined with policies favouring foreign over domestic investment, and inadequate R&D spending by both the government and firms.

A study by Plank and Staritz (2013) similarly reveals that the potential positive effects from TNCs' investment in the electronics sector in Hungary and Romania, as reflected in the relevance of local linkages and knowledge spillovers, have remained extremely low. Figure 13.2 shows that these countries correspond to the already high level of the GVC participation, higher than that of Mexico. Despite

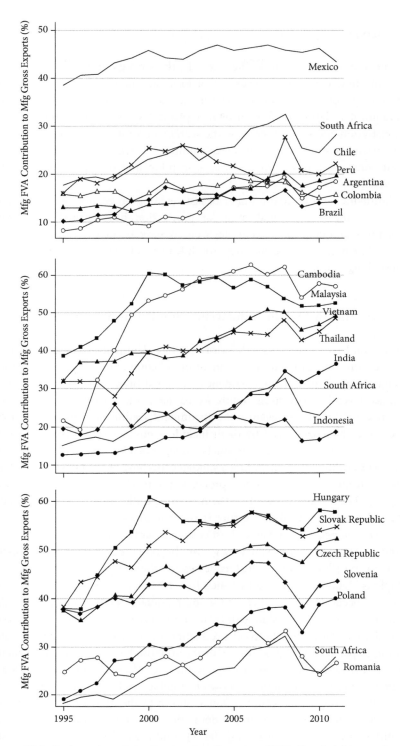

Figure 13.2 Backward participation in manufacturing GVCs, South Africa, and selected emerging and transition economies, 1995–2011

Note: Mfg is the abbreviation for 'manufacturing'.

Source: Authors' own elaboration based on the OECD-TiVA dataset (2016 version).

this, the authors argue that on the one side, the strategic interest of TNCs may have not allowed for an involvement of local suppliers that went beyond the provision of non-core products and services, and, on the other side, that the geographical isolation of foreign-owned plants has constrained the potential demonstration effects. Furthermore, the scarcity of local business actors in some industries in Central Eastern European countries, heavily dominated by foreign-owned companies, has prevented the absorption and the spread of potential spillovers.

Admittedly, for a limited number of fast catching-up economies, particularly from Asia, the internationalization of production has resulted in concrete opportunities for entering in technology-based markets and capturing value from advanced manufacturing technology. South Korea and China are perhaps the two most striking examples.

13.3.1 The 'In-Out-In' Industrialization Pathways in South Korea

Research on latecomer SMEs in South Korea has identified several cases of risky but successful transition from dependent or subcontracting original equipment manufacturing firms into independent or original brand manufacturing firms. Whereas several SMEs from South Korea have successfully increased their respective market shares against the incumbent leading brands in the global market, the challenges faced by them include a number of diverse factors: the marketing capability to sell products independently; interferences by the incumbent leading firms, including a sudden cancelling of the OEM orders; legal cases of dispute over intellectual property rights (IPRs); and price wars or dumping (Lee et al., 2018). For them, firm-specific, often tacit, knowledge (obtained mostly by trial and error) is recognized as an important source of distinctive competences and an ex post entry barrier (Lee et al., 2015).

South Korean success in achieving growth beyond the middle-income trap has been made possible mainly by big businesses' functional upgrading. A remarkable example is Hyundai Motors, established in 1968 as an assembler for Ford. With the aim of becoming an independent brand manufacturer, the company decided to end its business relationship with Ford, and in 1975 started to produce its own branded cars, Pony, with licensed production of the Mitsubishi engine. Later, after the 20 per cent equity-holding Mitsubishi refused to transfer to Hyundai the know-how to design and produce engines, the South Korean company decided to pursue the option of developing its own technology independently. This eventually resulted in upgrading within GVCs, as shown by the decreasing trend in FVA (or, alternatively, by the increasing of domestic value-added) in the 1980s and by the mid-1990s (Lee et al., 2018: 432, fig. 1). And then after upgrading domestic capabilities, the South Korean industries have actively been re-coupled with the

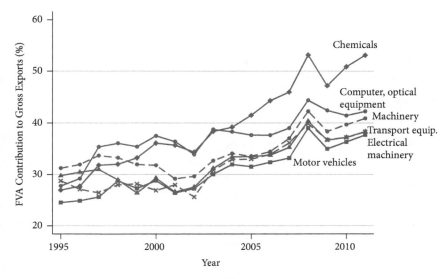

Figure 13.3 The 'in-again' phase in South Korea: backward integration in medium-high-tech sectoral value chains
Source: Authors' own elaboration based on the OECD-TiVA dataset (2016 version).

GVC. This is shown by the increasing trend of the backward GVC participation in a number of medium-high-tech sectors since the late 1990s, in Figure 13.3.

13.3.2 The 'In-Out-In' Industrialization Pathways in China

With a time lag of almost two decades, there is evidence that China followed a similar integration pattern to South Korea. In fact, as shown in Lee et al. (2018: 434, fig. 3) the backward integration of China in GVCs in total economy has been declining since the early 2000s, reflecting increasing DVA in manufacturing exports. However, total manufacturing trends hide very important sub-trends. Relevant structural change has in fact occurred over the last two decades, with China transitioning from being predominantly an exporter of textiles to an exporter of high-tech products, such as non-electrical machinery and equipment, ICT, and electronics. Across nearly all manufacturing sub-sectors this structural transformation has been paralleled, starting from the early 2000s, by a significant increase in the DVA content of China's exports. This possibly reflects an increased specialization in higher value-added activities, greater participation in domestic value chains by upstream intermediate suppliers, or a mix of the two. In 1995, for example, around three-quarters of the total value of ICT exports represented foreign content, but by 2011 this had dropped to just over half; similar large declines were evident in other high-tech sectors, such as electrical machinery and

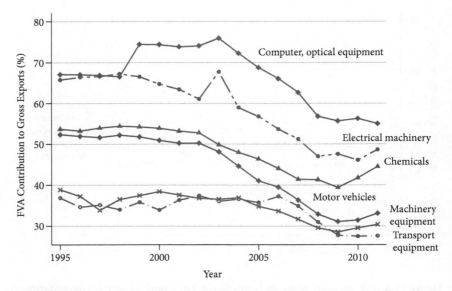

Figure 13.4 The 'out' phase in China: backward integration in medium-high-tech sectoral value chains
Source: Authors' own elaboration based on the OECD-TiVA dataset (2016 version).

transport equipment (see Figure 13.4). As an example of this transition, in 2002 China became the largest producer of machine tools and in 2012, consumed four times the number of machine tools of the USA, whose share of global production of machine tools declined from 20.4 per cent per cent in 1980 to 5.3 per cent in 2012 (Andreoni and Gregory, 2013).

13.3.3 Factors Contributing to the Successes in South Korea and China

These kinds of success stories are built on a variety of factors. Overall, in East Asia these involved strategic state intervention through the use of targeted credit and export subsides, strict conditions on inward FDI, and import protection to expand output, productivity, and export competitiveness, exports, and economic growth (Amsden, 1989; Milberg and Winkler, 2013; Andreoni and Chang, 2019; Chang and Andreoni, 2020). In China specifically, the key success factors were the domestic market dimension, the strategic use of industrial policies placing limits on FDI flows, and the targeted use of Special Economic Zones for the development of domestic industry. In all these cases, the main stylized fact is that increasing DVA resulted from a transient decoupling from foreign-dominated GVCs and the creation of horizontal cross-sectoral linkages in the domestic economy.

13.4 Global Patterns of Sectoral Value Addition: A Focus on Middle-Income Countries and South Africa

The industrialization experience in South Korea and China described above supports the argument that these countries' engagement with GVCs followed an 'in-out-in industrialization' pathway. This strategic and dynamic engagement with GVCs has resulted from two parallel structural dynamics whose rate of expansion has been different in the three stages of 'in', 'out', and 'in again' industrialization, as shown in Table 13.1 for China.[6]

In the 'in' phase, the rate of growth of FVA has been higher than that of DVA. This suggests that in this phase, countries tend to prioritize the engagement with GVC and the access to global market demand. In the 'out' phase, however, the rate of growth of DVA has been increasing more strongly than the rate of growth of FVA. This means that in the 'out' phase, countries focus their efforts on substituting some imported intermediate goods with domestic produce (Kee and Tang, 2016) and in increasing the value content of existing intermediate and final goods produced domestically. Both processes are made possible by an expansion of domestic supply-chain linkages. The last phase—'in again'—is one in which the rate of growth of FVA and DVA seems to balance out. In this phase countries benefit from cumulative dynamics of trade capacity and domestic production expansion.

The three sets of dynamics described for each phase of 'in-out-in again' industrialization are not sector neutral. Indeed, Figures 13.3 and 13.4 have already shown how in South Korea and China different sectors followed different pathways, suggesting that within the overall 'in-out-in again' industrialization pathway there are structurally heterogenous dynamics. This can be due to sub-sector-specific conditions, like the product characteristics (the value content of the product, for example), and also technology, the degree of modularity, and

Table 13.1 Drivers of 'in-out-in' industrialization, China

Phases	in	out	in-again
	1995–2003	2004–8	2008–11
Average growth rate FVA	0.196	0.274	0.157
Average growth rate DVA	0.157	0.397	0.143

Source: Authors' own elaboration based on the OECD-TiVA dataset (2016 version).

[6] From a methodological point of view, differently from Lee et al. (2018), here the focus is on the 'expansionary structural dynamics', hence the ratio of foreign value added (FVA) in gross exports over gross exports. There is also a comparison of the rates of growth in domestic value added (DVA) in gross exports and FVA in gross exports to capture the distinctive dynamics of participation in GVCs.

business and organizational models of production. Analysis of sectoral patterns becomes necessary because the overall or aggregate pattern of backward GVC participation (or the level of FVA) is affected by the degree of international integration and the industrial structure. So, a country with a high weight of the primary sectors would have a low level of FVA (Lee et al., 2018). Global market development and global political economy factors such as trade policy play important roles as well, as they determine the scope for value-chain development both globally and regionally. These sectoral dynamics are also interdependent as all these sectors are linked by production linkages—the expansionary dynamics of one sector can pull investments and value-added expansionary dynamics into other sectors.

The evidence presented in Figure 13.2 has already shown how middle-income countries and transition economies have not yet managed to complete—or even start in some cases—their 'in' phase, and have overall struggled to shift from an acceleration in the FVA expansionary dynamics to a more than proportional acceleration in the DVA expansionary dynamic. While their manufacturing industry as a whole is struggling to build its domestic production ecosystem, these challenges manifest differently in specific manufacturing sub-sectors. Figure 13.5 presents sub-sectoral evidence (with a focus on selected medium- and high-tech sectors only) for two regional groups (Central and Latin American countries, and South East Asian countries) and benchmarks South Africa's sectoral value-addition performances against them.

If South Africa is benchmarked against middle-income countries across Latin America and South East Asia (excluding China), a very different picture of the sectoral value chain patterns of integration emerges. On average, the backward participation of middle-income Latin American countries across all the selected medium- and high-tech sectors does not go above 40 per cent. In two sectors, at least, South Africa is consistently more integrated than Latin American countries (i.e. chemical products, and machinery and equipment; see Chapters 3 and 4 for a discussion of these sectoral value chains). However, if South Africa is compared with South East Asian countries, the picture changes dramatically. It is clear that South Africa is less integrated than South East Asian countries across all sectors, and that the levels of FVA are significantly lower. Overall backward integration in manufacturing is above 40 per cent for all South East Asian countries, with country peaks in the chemicals, machinery, and motor vehicle sectors above 60 per cent of FVA.

The sectoral value-addition patterns for South Africa shown in Figure 13.5 suggest a somewhat unusual situation. Contrary to other middle-income countries, which find it particularly difficult to move from an 'in' to an 'out' phase, South Africa has even struggled with engaging in the 'in' phase of increasing backward integration into GVCs. In particular, the level of backward integration

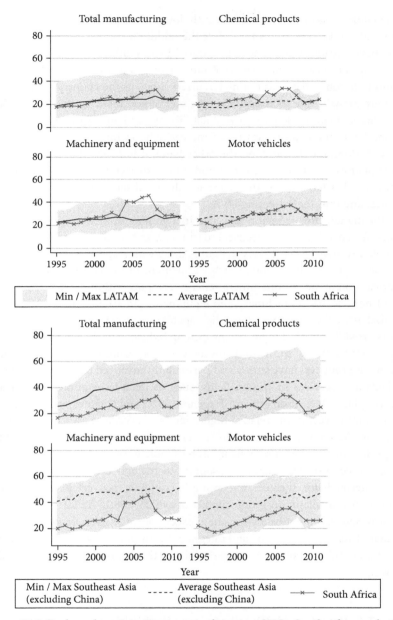

Figure 13.5 Backward participation in manufacturing GVCs: South Africa and other middle-income countries

Notes: Y-axis: FVA contribution to gross exports (%); the LATAM group includes Argentina, Brazil, Chile, Colombia, Costa Rica, Mexico, and Peru; the South East Asia group includes Cambodia, India, Indonesia, Malaysia, Thailand, and Vietnam.

Source: Authors' own elaboration based on the OECD-TiVA dataset (2016 version).

in the country has remained significantly lower than in SEA economies in the 1990s and 2000s. This means that while the middle-income countries in the SEA group have already started integrating into GVCs, South Africa has been slow in linking up into GVCs, similarly to a number of countries in Latin America. In addition, the 'out' phase has not materialized either, as the country's dependence on international trade increased after the end of apartheid in 1994, with China becoming its main trade partner in 2008 (Torreggiani and Andreoni, 2019). On the one hand, the country has relied increasingly on imports of final goods to satisfy its domestic demand; on the other hand, it has served as a gateway and export platform for foreign investors and traders to access the rest of the African continent. This has limited the scope for the localization of high value-added activities and thus for increasing DVA.

In the manufacturing sector, as well as in a number of medium- and high-tech sectors like chemicals, non-electrical machinery, and equipment and automotive, the higher relative levels of DVA in South Africa with respect to South East Asian countries is due to the country's rich endowment in mineral resources and the historical dominance of the mineral-energy complex within its economy. In the case of non-electrical machinery and equipment, this trend is mainly driven by the existence of very strong domestic capabilities in certain specific advanced sectors providing critical inputs to the mining industry (i.e. backward integration from manufacturing to natural resources). For example, domestic mining equipment producers have strong and particularly advanced capacities in offering products and services in certain fields, such as deep-level mining and related areas (Kaplan, 2012; Andreoni and Tregenna, 2020; and Chapter 3). In the case of the automotive sector, the relative higher levels of DVA along such value chains are mainly driven by the country's use of its natural resources endowment and by the specific intermediate products it has been able to produce based on that (i.e. forward integration from natural resources to manufacturing—see Chapter 5). These intermediates include, for example, catalytic converters, which make extensive use of platinum-group metals of which South Africa is the world's largest producer. Notwithstanding these exceptions, the overall failure of South Africa to diversify its economy and integrate the 'in' phase in the 1990s and 2000s has dramatically delayed its progress along the 'in-out-in' industrialization pathway.

13.5 Post-Covid-19: What Next? Rethinking Global Value Chains and Industrialization Models

The recent global pandemic has accelerated a contraction in international trade, already fuelled by rising geopolitical tensions between major regional blocks— the USA, China, and the EU. This has led to a sharp drop in global FDI, with particular reference to inflows into developing countries. As reported by UNCTAD (2020a), total world trade fell by 5 per cent in the first quarter of 2020. The organization's estimates also point to a 27 per cent drop for the second quarter of the year and to an overall annual decline of 20 per cent. The most affected sectors in terms of trade contraction in the first quarter of the year have been textiles and apparel, office machinery, automotive, energy, chemicals, non-electrical machinery and equipment, and precision instruments. To date, the agri-food sector has been the least volatile. With specific reference to developing countries, preliminary data for April 2020 suggest that South Asian and Middle Eastern countries have experienced the sharpest trade downturns, registering declines up to 40 per cent. As far as FDI is concerned, estimates from UNCTAD (2020b) expect global FDI flows to contract between 30 per cent and 40 per cent in 2020/1. Among the most affected sectors will be the consumer cyclical industries, such as airlines, hotels, restaurants, and leisure, as well as the manufacturing and energy sectors. According to the International Monetary Fund (IMF) (2020), from the beginning of the Covid-19 crisis until late March 2020, developing countries also experienced the largest capital outflow ever recorded, with investors removing US$83 billion from emerging economies.

Disruptive changes in the length, location, and governance structure of GVCs following the Covid-19 crisis have given rise to additional structural transformation challenges. But the crisis has also presented new opportunities for pursuing more inclusive and sustainable pathways of development and industrial catch-up (UNCTAD, 2020c). In particular, reduced opportunities for export- and FDI-led industrialization due to the reshoring of production and new trade regimes suggest the importance of imagining alternative industrialization models. These could provide frameworks for countries to diversify their production base by leveraging existing domestic markets and creating new ones through forward and backward integration.

Within this context, developing countries might consider with renewed interest the development possibilities offered by their natural resource endowments. This is in line with a relatively new strand of the innovation literature that departs from the 'natural resource curse' hypothesis. It shows how natural resource industries might provide emerging economies with a platform for progressively increasing downstream value addition (see Lebdioui et al. (2020) for Chile and Malaysia; Andreoni and Tregenna (2020) for Brazil; Andreoni and Torreggiani (2020) for South Africa; and see Chapter 3 on mining and Chapter 6 on fruit). It also suggests opportunities for these industries to engage and upgrade in backward and forward knowledge-intensive and higher value-added activities. Such sectoral cases also show how industrial policy has been particularly important in achieving greater degrees of linkage development, competitiveness, and technological sophistication in these natural resource industries, and in related upstream and downstream sectors.

In light of the current and expected trade disruption, South Africa's rich mineral deposits as well as the country's proximity to other equally resource-rich economies in sub-Saharan Africa might open up important opportunities for both upstream and downstream integration, as well as value addition through industrial and technological innovation. Two scenarios are elaborated: one related to backward-linked (upstream) industries, focusing on the case of mining equipment; the other in relation to forward-linked (downstream) industries, focusing on the automotive sector.

The impact of the Covid-19 crisis across different geographies has put new pressure on traditional mining global supply-chain structures, which are concentrated around a few equipment vendors from the USA, Europe, Japan, and China. According to a recent exploratory analysis conducted by international professional services organizations (Ernst & Young, 2020), mining companies are actively exploring alternative and broader sources of supply to reduce reliance on a small number of overseas vendors. On the one hand, this will open up opportunities for local or regional companies with the right level of technology and production capabilities to enter into such value chains. On the other hand, foreign multinationals supplying mining equipment and other critical inputs to mining houses might decide to progressively relocate part of their production activities closer to their clients' operations, through subsidiaries or collaborative partnerships with local companies. The South African mining equipment sector is well positioned to seize both these opportunities in the domestic and regional mining markets. Obviously, strategic industrial policy actions will be needed to put conditions in place to attract and retain productive investments, and to help domestic mining equipment producers in their attempt to enter supply chains led by major mining companies. In this respect, an institutional effort is urgently needed to reform local content and procurement policies in the South African mining sector, and to establish an efficient and affordable support system for export development of domestic equipment suppliers (see Andreoni and Torreggiani, 2020; and Chapter 3).

The pandemic hit the automotive sector at a time of dramatic technological change and industry organization restructuring globally. Climate change has made decoupling growth from fossil fuels and, thus, the use of cleaner energy sources of mobility a key priority for sustainable structural transformation. Technological solutions so far have mainly relied on alternative energy sources, in particular electric and hydrogen-based technologies. These technologies have created new global demand for natural resources such as lithium for the production of batteries, and platinum-group metal resources for the global fuel cell market. While countries endowed with lithium like Chile can look at that natural resource as a driver to attract investment in domestic production of batteries for automotive, a country like South Africa could leverage its large platinum-group metal resources to develop forward linkages in a number of emerging and innovative sectors, and become an exporter of value-added technologies based on its natural resources (platinum being the main catalyst in fuel cells). Fuel cells can be deployed in portable power generation, stationary power generation, and power for transportation (DMR, 2013). These technologies find applications across various domestic, regional, and global value chains and could be used as a way of anchoring new transformative investments in South Africa.

The two scenarios sketched above for the mining equipment and automotive industries show how sectoral value chains constantly change in their geographical breadth, length, and depth, especially as a result of major crises. And that these changes brought about by the unprecedented pandemic crisis will have a long-lasting structural impact on the sector-specific processes of value creation, capture, and distribution across countries and companies.

This chapter has shown how structural transformation has been dramatically affected by these global value-chain dynamics, especially since the 1990s. Building on several data and country cases, a number of theoretical arguments and stylized facts across a variety of middle-income country experiences have been reviewed and systematized. In spite of this variety, it has been noted how a specific type of strategic and sequential engagement with GVCs—'in-out-in-again'—is a major success factor in catching up processes underpinning structural transformation. Specifically, the analysis of the 'in-out-in-again' model of strategic integration into GVCs has been developed by extending the analyses to include South Korea and China—and in each case going below the broader sector level to show heterogeneous patterns of sub-sectoral value addition. The experiences in these countries and the wider macro-regions have then been used as benchmarks for assessing the South African case.

The new evidence shows how South Africa has been particularly slow in the 'in' phase of GVC integration, and that the 'out' phase has been limited even in those sectoral value chains with the highest potential. Moreover, domestic value addition has been mainly driven by high-value natural resource exports, more than high-value manufactured products. Several chapters in this volume have analysed the mix of production, technological, institutional, and political economy contextual factors which have hampered structural transformation in South Africa. All these factors are intrinsically related to the GVC integration pathway followed by this country, and are likely to remain so even in the post-pandemic scenario. In this sense, the South African experience is a paradigmatic example of the challenges posed by a GVC-shaped industrial landscape. The extent to which South Africa might become an example of strategic restructuring of production chains in the post-pandemic phase will dramatically depend on its industrial policy approach to local production system development and domestic value addition.

References

Amendolagine, V., A. F. Presbitero, R. Rabellotti, and M. Sanfilippo (2020). 'Local sourcing in developing countries: the role of foreign investments and global value chains.' *World Development* 113(C): 73–88.

Amsden, A. H. (1989) *Asia's Next Giant: South Korea and Late Industrialization.* Oxford: Oxford University Press.

Amsden, A. H. and W. W. Chu (2003). *Beyond Late Development Taiwan's Upgrading Policies.* Cambridge, MA: MIT Press.

Andreoni, A. (2018). 'The architecture and dynamics of industrial ecosystems. diversification and innovative industrial renewal in mature economies.' *Cambridge Journal of Economics* 42(6): 1313–42.

Andreoni, A. (2019). 'A generalized linkage approach to local production systems development in the era of global value chains with special reference to Africa.' In A. Noman and J. Stiglitz (eds), *Quality of Growth in Africa*, 264–94. New York: Columbia University Press.

Andreoni, A. and M. Gregory (2013). 'Why and how does manufacturing still matter: old rationales, new realities.' *Revue d'Economie Industrielle* 144(4): 17–54.

Andreoni, A. and H.-J. Chang (2019). 'The political economy of industrial policy: structural interdependencies, policy alignment and conflict management.' *Structural Change and Economic Dynamics* 48: 136–50.

Andreoni, A. and W. Lazonick (2020). 'Local ecosystems and social conditions of innovative enterprise.' In A. Oqubay and J. Y. Lin (eds), *The Oxford Handbook of Industrial Hubs and Economic Development*, 77–97. Oxford: Oxford University Press.

Andreoni, A. and F. Tregenna (2020). 'Escaping the middle-income technology trap: a comparative analysis of industrial policies in China, Brazil and South Africa.' *Structural Change and Economic Dynamics* 54: 324–40.

Andreoni A. and S. Torreggiani (2020). 'Mining equipment industry in South Africa: global context, industrial ecosystem and pathways for feasible sectoral reforms.' CCRED Working Paper Series, 2020/3. Johannesburg: CCRED.

Baldwin, R. and J. Lopez-Gonzalez (2015). 'Supply-chain trade: a portrait of global patterns and several testable hypothesis.' *The World Economy* 38(11): 1682–1721.

Behuria, P., L. Buur, and H. Gray (2017). 'Studying political settlements in Africa.' *African Affairs* 116(464): 508–25.

Chang, H. J. (2010). 'Industrial policy: can we go beyond an unproductive debate?' In J. Y. Lin and B. Pleskovic (eds), *Lessons from East Asia and the Global Financial Crisis.* Seoul: ABCDE, Annual World Bank Conference on Development Economics.

Chang, H. J. and A. Andreoni (2020). 'Industrial policy in the 21st century.' *Development and Change* 51(2): 324–51.

Cramer, C., J. Sender, and A. Oqubay (2020). *African Economic Development: Evidence, Theory, Policy.* Oxford: Oxford University Press.

De Marchi, V., E. Di Maria, and G. Gereffi (2018). *Local Clusters in Global Value Chains*. London and New York: Routledge.

DMR (2013). 'Fuel cells and the future role of South Africa through its platinum resources.' Report R99/2013, Department of Mineral Resources, South Africa.

Ernst, D. and L. Kim (2002). 'Global production networks, knowledge diffusion and local capability formation.' *Research Policy* 31(8/9): 1417–29.

Ernst & Young (2020). 'Covid-19: how mining companies can build more resilient supply chains.' E&Y Mining & Metals.

Foster-McGregor, N., F. Kaulich, and R. Stehrer (2015). 'Global value chains in Africa.' UNU-MERIT Working Paper 24. Maastricht: MERIT.

Gallagher, K. P. and L. Zarsky (2007). *The Enclave Economy: Foreign Investment and Sustainable Development in Mexico's Silicon Valley*. Cambridge, MA: MIT Press.

Gereffi, G. (1999). 'International trade and industrial upgrading in the apparel commodity chain.' *Journal of International Economics* 48(1): 37–70.

Gereffi, G. (2014). 'Global value chains in a post-Washington Consensus world.' *Review of International Political Economy* 21(1): 9–37.

Gereffi, G. and J. Lee (2016). 'Economic and social upgrading in global value chains and industrial clusters: why governance matters.' *Journal of Business Ethics* 133: 25–38.

Giuliani, E., C. Pietrobelli, and R. Rabellotti (2005). 'Upgrading in global value chains: lessons from Latin American clusters.' *World Development* 33(4): 459–573.

Hirschman, A. O. (1977). 'A generalised linkage approach to development, with special reference to staples.' *Economic Development and Cultural Change* 25(Supplement): 67–98.

Hobday, M. (2003). 'Innovation in Asian industrialization: a Gerschenkronian perspective.' *Oxford Development Studies* 31(3): 293–314.

Humphrey, J. and H. Schmitz (2002). 'How does insertion in global value chains affect upgrading in industrial clusters.' *Regional Studies* 36(9): 1017–27.

IMF (2020). 'IMF Managing Director Kristalina Georgieva's statement following a G20 ministerial call on the coronavirus emergency.' Press Release No. 20/98 (23 March 2020). Washington, DC: IMF.

Kaplan, D. (2012). 'South African mining equipment and specialist services: Technological capacity, export performance and policy.' *Resources Policy* 37(4): 425–33.

Kaplinsky, R. and M. Morris (2001). *A Handbook for Value Chain Research*. Ottawa: International Development Research Centre.

Kaplinsky, R. and M. Morris (2015). 'Thinning and thickening: productive sector policies in the era of global value chains.' *European Journal of Development Research* 28(4): 1–21.

Kee, H. L. and H. Tang (2016). 'Domestic value added in exports: theory and firm evidence from China.' *American Economic Review* 106(6): 1402–36.

Khan, M. H. (2010). 'Political settlements and the governance of growth-enhancing institutions.' Mimeo. London: SOAS University of London.

Lebdioui, A., K. Lee, and C. Pietrobelli (2020). 'Local-foreign technology interface, resource-based development, and industrial policy: how Chile and Malaysia are escaping the middle income trap.' *Journal of Technology Transfer*. DOI: 10.1007/s10961-020-09808-3.

Lee, K. (2013). *Schumpeterian Analysis of Economic Catch-Up: Knowledge, Path-Creation, and the Middle-Income Trap*. London: Cambridge University Press.

Lee, K. (2019). *The Art of Economic Catch-Up: Barriers, Detours and Leapfrogging in Innovation Systems*. Cambridge: Cambridge University Press.

Lee, K., B. Kim, Y. Park, and E. Sanidas (2013). 'Big businesses and economic growth: identifying a binding constraint for growth with country panel analysis.' *Journal of Comparative Economics* 41(2): 561–82.

Lee, K. and F. Malerba (2017). 'Catch-up cycles and changes in industrial leadership: windows of opportunity and responses by firms and countries in the evolution of sectoral systems,' *Research Policy* 46(2): 338–51.

Lee, K. and J. A. Mathews (2012). 'Firms in Korea and Taiwan: upgrading in the same industry and entries into new industries for sustained catch-up.' In E. Amann and J. Cantwell (eds), *Innovative Firms in Emerging Economies*. Oxford: Oxford University Press.

Lee, K., J. Song, and J. Kwak (2015). 'An exploratory study on the transition from OEM to OBM.' *Industry and Innovation* 22(5): 423–42.

Lee, K., M. Szapiro, and Z. Mao (2018). 'From global value chains (GVC) to innovation systems for local value chains and knowledge creation.' *The European Journal of Development Research* 30(3): 424–41.

Milberg, W. and D. Winkler (2013). *Outsourcing Economics: Global Value Chains in Capitalist Development*. Cambridge: Cambridge University Press.

Navas-Aleman, L. (2011). 'The impact of operating in multiple value chains for upgrading: the case of the Brazilian furniture and footwear industries.' *World Development* 39(8): 1386–97.

Neilson, J., B. Pritchard, and H. Wai-chung Yeung (2014). 'Global value chains and global production networks in the changing international political economy: an introduction.' *Review of International Political Economy* 21(1): 1–8.

Nolan, P. (2001). *China and the Global Economy: National Champions, Industrial Policy, and the Big Business Revolution*. New York: Palgrave.

Pietrobelli, C. and R. Rabellotti (2011). 'Global value chains meet innovation systems: are there learning opportunities for developing countries?' *World Development* 39: 1261–9.

Plank, L. and C. Staritz (2013). '"Precarious upgrading" in electronics global production networks in Central and Eastern Europe: the cases of Hungary and Romania.' 2 May. DOI: 10.2139/ssrn.2259671 (accessed on 30 July 2020).

Rasiah, R. (2006). 'Ownership, technological intensities, and economic performance in South Africa.' *International Journal of Technology Management* 36(1/2/3): 166–89.

Shih, S. (1996). 'Me-too is not my style: challenge difficulties, break through bottlenecks, create values.' Taipei: The Acer Foundation.

Torreggiani, S. and A. Andreoni (2019). 'Dancing with dragons: Chinese import penetration and the performances of manufacturing firms in South Africa.' WIDER Working Paper 63/2019, UNU-WIDER, DOI: 10.35188/UNU-WIDER/.

UNCTAD (2019). 'Key statistics and trends in international trade.' Geneva: UNCTAD.

UNCTAD (2020a). 'Global trade update (11 June 2020).' Geneva: UNCTAD.

UNCTAD (2020b). 'Impact of the Covid-19 pandemic on global FDI and GVCs.' Global Investment Trends Monitor No. 35 (Special Issue March 2020). Geneva: UNCTAD.

UNCTAD (2020c). 'World investment report 2020: international production beyond the pandemic.' New York and Geneva: United Nations.

Van Dijk, M. and M. Bell (2007). 'Rapid growth with limited learning: industrial policy and Indonesia's pulp and paper industry.' *Oxford Development Studies* 35(2): 149–69.

Whitfield, L., O. Therkildsen, L. Burr, and S. A. Mett (2015). *The Politics of Industrial Policy in Africa.* Cambridge: Cambridge University Press.

14

The Political Economy of Structural Transformation

Political Settlements and Industrial Policy in South Africa

Pamela Mondliwa and Simon Roberts

14.1 Introduction

Despite multiple policy interventions, South Africa has not made significant progress in achieving growth-enhancing structural transformation over the period 1994 to 2019. In terms of sectoral transitioning, the economy has prematurely deindustrialized, with manufacturing's contribution to gross domestic product (GDP) declining from 21 per cent in 1994 to 12 per cent in 2019 in favour of services (Chapter 11). The increase in the contribution of services to GDP over the period 1994 to 2019 has been accompanied by the increasing importance of lower-value, lower-productivity services overall (Chapter 1). At the same time, the growth of financial services has not been accompanied by significant growth in employment in the sector, nor by higher levels of savings and investment in the real economy.

Within manufacturing, growth in value added has continued to be biased towards mineral- and resource-based industries that were at the industrial core of the economy in 1994, reflecting limited sectoral deepening (Chapter 2). The slow progress of transformation of the industrial structure is reflected in South Africa's undiversified exports. Mineral and resource-based industries continue to dominate the export basket—accounting for approximately 60 per cent of merchandise exports in 2019—and South Africa is thus missing out on the gains from international integration in improved competitiveness and 'learning through exporting' in diversified manufacturing industries (Bell et al., 2018).

The failure to achieve growth-enhancing structural transformation has also had implications for socioeconomic outcomes, including increasing unemployment, worsening inequality (Chapter 8), and limited success in increasing participation by the previously disadvantaged black population (Chapter 9).

So why has South Africa had such a poor record, particularly as the economic-policy objectives of successive African National Congress (ANC) governments

Pamela Mondliwa and Simon Roberts, *The Political Economy of Structural Transformation: Political Settlements and Industrial Policy in South Africa* In: *Structural Transformation in South Africa: The Challenges of Inclusive Industrial Development in a Middle-Income Country.* Edited by: Antonio Andreoni, Pamela Mondliwa, Simon Roberts, and Fiona Tregenna, Oxford University Press. © Oxford University Press 2021. DOI: 10.1093/oso/9780192894311.003.0014

under democracy have been to change the structure of the economy to more diversified and labour-absorbing industries? To answer this question, it is necessary to understand the power of different interests and how they have influenced policy choices, design, and implementation (Khan and Jomo, 2000; Khan and Blankenburg, 2009; Gray, 2018).

As a salient case study on structural transformation and economic development, the South African experience offers key lessons for middle-income countries more generally. The analysis draws on the contributions in this book, reflecting on the differences and similarities observed in the detailed industry studies, including the coalitions of interests that underpin the outcomes. This is complemented by engagement with the contestation of interests at the macro level and how these conflicts influence both industrial and broader economic policies.

Section 14.2 starts with a discussion of the political settlements framework and how it assists in understanding different trajectories of industrial development. Section 14.3 then presents the observed patterns of structural change in selected industries, drawing on the in-depth industry chapters, and considers how the liberalization of the economy and the configuration of economic power influenced these patterns. Section 14.4 reflects on the shifting coalitions of interests that have underpinned the policy agendas under former presidents Mandela, Mbeki, Motlanthe and Zuma. Section 14.5 concludes the analysis by drawing out the main observations regarding South Africa's evolving political settlement, its influence on industrial development, and the wider lessons for other middle-income countries.

14.2 Political Settlements and Industrial Development

The success or failure of structural transformation, in terms of processes of production upgrading, necessarily depends on changes in the distribution and configuration of power among different organizations, that is, in the 'political settlement' (Khan, 2018). A given settlement depends on the distribution of power within countries and, for industrial development, whether the ruling coalition supports the design and implementation of policies with incentives for, and conditions on, firms to ensure high levels of investment and effort in learning and technological upgrading (Khan, 2018).

As such, successful industrial production relies on the ability of the state to create and manage rents, which are important for technological learning, which is necessary for driving structural change. The political settlements framework is a useful lens through which to examine how states' capabilities to manage these rents, including monitoring and disciplining rent recipients to ensure productive investment for growth, are influenced by the distribution of power within a society (Gray, 2018).

The political settlements framework emerged as a critique of New Institutional Economics (NIE), which focused on the adoption of institutions that enforce the rule of law, a democratic political election system, low levels of corruption, transparency of the state, and limited restrictions on the private sector, which ultimately became the 'good governance agenda' (Gray, 2019). However, the NIE struggled to explain huge differences in the development trajectories of countries despite them adopting this good governance agenda (Khan, 2018). The political settlements framework assesses how regimes work in practice and explains that the economic outcomes of an institutional dispensation is heavily reliant on the distribution of power in the environment in which they operate (Khan 2018, Gray 2019).

For example, let us consider the relationship between competition and economic development. NIE emphasizes competition with liberalized markets and independent institutions as the primary requirement for economic development and moving countries to what North et al. (2009) term 'open access orders'. However, this supposes that competition simply arises in the absence of obstacles, and fails to recognize the need to address entrenched inequality and economic power (Makhaya and Roberts, 2013). And, it does not properly explain the underlying power arrangements and configuration of interests that shapes markets and influence a given institutional configuration and framing of laws (Khan, 2010).

The new institutionalism also does not engage with the 'path-dependent' nature of development—meaning that firms which have developed productive strengths are able to re-invest, further develop capabilities, and grow their businesses. Thus, inclusion requires productive rents to induce investments in capabilities outside the initial industrial core to support structural change. NIE is primarily focused on static efficiency rather than the dynamic efficiency that is necessary for long term growth.

By comparison, in the political settlements framework, rents are pivotal in shaping the structural change required for economic development and power is held in both formal and informal institutions (Khan, 2018; Gray, 2018). The implication is that political settlements analysis entails a broader mapping of groups that hold power in society, including the elite and non-elite (Behuria et al., 2017). It is necessary to consider how powerful elites organize through formal and informal institutions, especially during development transitions, to sustain economic benefits for groups that would otherwise have lost out (Khan, 2010). The organizations which are formed are thus the mechanism through which social and political stability is maintained, helping to generate distributions of economic benefits in line with distributions of power.

The approach to political settlements adopted in this chapter draws on the contributions of Khan (2010 and 2018), together with developments by Behuria et al. (2017), and Gray (2013, 2018, and 2019). These contributions all note the importance of 'holding power', which refers to the capacity to engage and survive conflicts—in other words, the ability to inflict costs and absorb costs inflicted by opposing groups (Behuria et al. 2017). The sources of holding power include economic structure, violence rights, rents and ideology (Behuria et al., 2017; Gray, 2018).

The following section looks at some of the industry experiences in the context of the political economy and political settlement dynamics described above.

14.3 Structural Transformation in South Africa: A Review of Industry Experiences

The political settlements underlying South Africa's structural change dynamics can be observed by reflecting on the conflicts over value capture in the industrial groupings that form the core of the economy, which have been analysed from different perspectives in the book. These include metals and machinery, chemicals and plastic products, food and beverages,[1] fruit, and automotive industries (Bell et al., 2018; and Chapter 1).

The ongoing better performance of upstream resource-based industries compared with the more diversified downstream sub-sectors, into which these resource-based basic products are inputs, is reflected in the studies of metals and machinery, and chemicals and plastic products (Chapters 3 and 4). The two industry groupings show common features and interesting contrasts. Importantly, both show the failure to diversify and build stronger capabilities. Indeed, there has been a hollowing out of capabilities as the downstream more diversified parts of the value chains have performed far more poorly than the upstream resource-based basic metals, refineries, and chemicals parts of the chain.

Within each industry, however, there are pointers to the potential for growth. For example, there are segments within the machinery and equipment sub-sector linked to meeting the specialist requirements of different types of mining operations, in which South Africa has developed world-leading capabilities. While there have been such niches of advanced capabilities, the country failed to build on these capabilities through supporting broader local clusters. In the plastic products industry, for the period from 1994 to 2002 during which tariffs

---

[1] As there is no separate chapter on food and beverages, see Bell et al. (2018) for background research on this sub-sector.

were liberalized, the local firms competed effectively with imports and grew output and employment. Crucially, during this period the monopoly input supplier, Sasol, was constrained in its pricing to local customers. This changed as the regulatory regime altered, and Sasol's[2] strategy towards the local value chain moved to maximize prices (Mondliwa and Roberts, 2019).

Various forms of continued support for the upstream basic metals and chemicals sub-sectors have contributed to the outcomes. This is a puzzling question from the political economy perspective: why have capital-intensive resource-based industries continued to receive so much attention and different forms of support, while downstream, labour-absorbing, industries have in most cases not been supported by effective strategies for building capabilities? Part of the answer lies in what has been the dominant paradigm of economic policy in general, part lies in the challenges of competitiveness in these sub-sectors within the global context, and part lies in the ongoing influence of the large upstream firms, which are well entrenched and effective at lobbying.

Different factors have driven the performance of the automotive and the food industries. These are both large industries in South Africa, accounting for 7.2 per cent and 14.8 per cent of manufacturing value added respectively in 2019.[3] The automotive sector has been assisted by a targeted industrial policy, which has evolved through a series of phases (Chapter 5). Outside of resource-based sectors, it has recorded by far the best growth in manufacturing, yet the capabilities remain shallow and focused at the assembly level. The automotive industry has continued to run a significant trade deficit, while the record in growing local content has been relatively poor. South Africa has not developed the capabilities of more sophisticated automotive hubs in countries such as Thailand and Mexico. The automotive industry reflects a skewed arrangement that favours the original equipment manufacturers (OEMs). The successful lobbying of the large OEMs for ongoing support is one factor explaining the outcomes observed in South Africa. This is perhaps unsurprising as the threat of the loss of high-profile jobs in unionized factories has had a greater influence than the potential employment that could be generated by better policy support.

The food and beverage industries consist of a range of value chains extending from agriculture and agroprocessing to retail. The industries include some success stories, notably the rapid growth of fresh fruit production based on export markets (Chapter 6), and wine exports (Chapter 7). During apartheid, in the agriculture to food value chains there had been extensive regulation and support for cooperatives in processing, such as milling and dairy. The widespread

---

[2] Sasol is the upstream supplier of chemical inputs including polymers used to produce plastic products.
[3] This only counts the narrowly defined sub-sectors and not the related areas, such as automotive components classified under other sub-sectors, and agricultural production and packaging in the case of food.

liberalization of markets in the 1990s brought far-reaching restructuring with large employment losses in many segments. In this changing context, the cooperatives became privately owned with many acquired by multinational conglomerate groupings.

The fresh-fruit industry has emerged as a strong export generator and has built considerable capabilities to export fruit into international markets. A key factor in its success is coordination along the value chain to deliver higher-value products to meet the preferences of export markets. This has combined the farming of new varieties requiring advanced capabilities with the appropriate logistics and marketing operations to place the products on supermarket shelves. The successes have resulted from effective producer strategies, in the absence of a targeted government strategy, though there have been some attempts to rectify this.[4] South Africa has realized the 'industrialization of freshness' in important fruit groupings, while in other groupings the industry has not achieved the coordination and long-term investments required (Chapter 6).

14.3.1 South Africa Has an Open Economy but There Have Been Signs of Structural Regression

With the liberalization of the economy starting in the 1990s, South Africa has become extremely open and internationalized in terms of trade, capital flows, and ownership. While these changes brought far-reaching restructuring in industry, the changes have not resulted in diversification or sustained higher levels of investment (see also Black and Roberts, 2009). The experience points to the challenges of managing international integration to ensure that the linkages are built into local production systems (Chapter 13).

In terms of international trade, the liberalization in the 1990s heralded much higher levels of exports and imports (Chapter 1; and Figure 14.1). Over the period 1994–2002 the real exchange rate had weakened, as was appropriate under reduced protection. While import penetration increased so did the ratio of merchandise exports to GDP, from 18 per cent in 1994 to 25 per cent in 2000, opening up a trade surplus. This included increased exports in diversified manufacturing industries including machinery and equipment and motor vehicles (see Chapters 3 and 5). In these and other manufacturing sub-sectors, imports also grew substantially.

From 2002, however, the strengthening exchange rate underpinned by the focus on inflation targeting meant imports increased strongly, to reach 27 per cent of gross domestic expenditure (GDE) in 2008 (Figure 14.1). As reflected in the

---

[4] This seemed to be changing, when in 2019 a process began for developing a master plan to support fruit alongside other selected agricultural products.

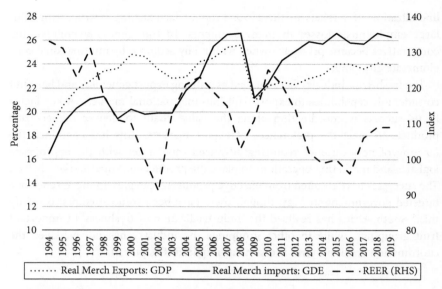

Figure 14.1 Trade and the real effective exchange rate
Note: the real effective exchange rate is indexed at 2015 = 100.
Source: South African Reserve Bank data.

industry studies, these increased imports were largely of diversified manufactured products and undermined local producers who could not compete with cheap imports. The increase in imports in fact exceeded the higher earnings from minerals exports and the country went into a trade deficit during the international resources boom to 2008. The end of the boom saw much poorer export earnings, while the hollowing-out of diversified productive capabilities meant a widening trade deficit once again from 2011.

Instead of the hoped-for export-led growth, the far-reaching liberalization and international integration led South Africa to prematurely deindustrialize, with the contribution of manufacturing to GDP declining from 21 per cent in 1994 to 12 per cent in 2019.[5] Moreover, within manufacturing, the structural change has in fact been regressive in nature, as growth in value added has continued to be biased towards mineral and resource-based sub-sectors (Chapters 1 and 2). The share of diversified manufacturing (including metal products, plastic products, and food and beverages) in total manufacturing value added in fact declined between 1994 and 2019 (Chapter 1). There has been a decrease in manufacturing employment across the board, but the largest losses have been borne by exactly those diversified manufacturing industries where strong growth would create jobs, both directly and in related industries. As noted above and in Chapters 1 to 6,

---

[5] Statistics South Africa (2019). Statistical Release P0441 Gross domestic product Quarter 4, 2019, https://www.statssa.gov.za/publications/P0441/P04414thQuarter2019.pdf.

there have been 'islands' of strong export capabilities in manufacturing, such as in mining machinery, but these have not been built upon to be replicated in other parts of the economy.

Its openness to the global economy has further meant that South Africa has been exposed to global commodity price volatility. This is evident in the huge swings in steel prices (Chapter 3). The effects of downturns have been for the local producer to lobby for support, while in years of high prices the profits have been taken out of the business.

South Africa's liberalization of capital flows has seen large volumes of portfolio and foreign direct investment (FDI) inflows and outflows (Figure 14.2). As South African companies such as SABMiller and Naspers have become part of huge transnational corporations (TNCs), the capitalization of the Johannesburg Stock Exchange (JSE) has increased to an equivalent of more than 300 per cent of the country's gross domestic product (GDP). This has not meant higher levels of fixed investment in South Africa, however. Capital account liberalization has also allowed South African corporations to move capital abroad on a grand scale, both legally and illegally (see Ashman et al., 2011).

The rise in portfolio and FDI inflows has been matched by an increase in foreign ownership of the JSE. Measured in terms of control of companies listed on the JSE by their capitalization, foreign ownership increased from 4 per cent in

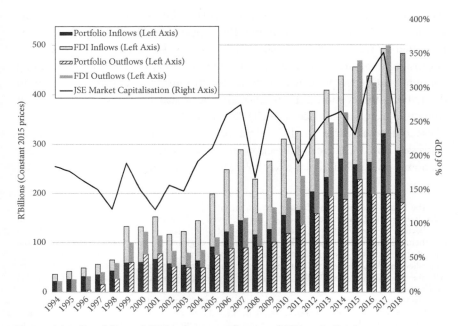

Figure 14.2 Portfolio and FDI inflows, outflows, and JSE capitalization
Source: Authors' calculations using South African Reserve Bank data.

the late 1990s to 25 per cent in 2018.[6] The significance of TNCs in South Africa's economy is in line with global trends, which show individual corporations controlling resources (at least in monetary terms) and having security, intelligence, and public relations operations larger than many states, as well as significant lobbying capabilities, such as through donations to political campaigns (Zingales, 2017; UNCTAD, 2018).[7]

The international ownership of key businesses in South Africa has in some industries been part of a deliberate government strategy. In the case of basic steel, the government strategy was for Iscor to have an international steel equity partner to enable access to technology and investment (Chapter 4).[8] Ultimately, the company became absorbed into ArcelorMittal, the largest steel transnational corporation in the world. The local business became peripheral to the parent, given the relatively small domestic demand and low levels of growth, and the parent company did not invest in the R&D in the South African business required for learning higher-tier capabilities. The weakening of historical cost advantages meant it was vulnerable to commodity price swings, while subject to transfer pricing and profit shifting by the parent company, and weakening local linkages and technology collaboration (see also Lee, 2015).

14.3.2 Key Insights from the Industry Experiences

Political settlements are stable when the distribution of rents is in line with the distribution of power in the economy. This suggests that powerful groups can be identified by studying the patterns of rents or benefits of economic policy. The key insight to be drawn from the discussion of industry experiences is the strong continuity of better performance by upstream industries and poor progress in diversifying the economy. There have also been sustained high profit levels in some sub-sectors of services (OECD, 2013; World Bank, 2018; and Chapter 2). These outcomes point to the weight of path dependency that needs to be addressed for a change in direction, in which industrial policy and broader economic policy should play a key role. However, the degree of success or failure

---

[6] The largest South African conglomerates, led by Anglo American and Richemont/Rembrandt (now Remgro) had always been internationalized, even while being identified as South African, in part because of their origins and in part because of their response to economic sanctions during apartheid. However, these were still family-controlled conglomerate groups with a very substantial part of their business based in South Africa (Chabane et al., 2006). Remgro has remained family-controlled and Anglo American has unbundled; the huge growth in foreign ownership was boosted by AB Inbev's acquisition of SABMiller (the biggest listed company in recent years in terms of its market capitalization).

[7] The significance of large global corporations is not new of course (Zingales, 2017).

[8] Iscor was the state-owned and vertically integrated steel producer with interests in iron ore and steel production. When it was privatized, it was split into Kumba Iron Ore and Arcelor Mittal South Africa ("AMSA").

in effecting this change is dependent on the extent to which the powerful interests or groups support this diversification. Three important observations from the industry experience can be made. These are discussed briefly below and are developed further in the discussion on the evolving political settlement underpinning South Africa's industrial development, in section 14.4.

First, the patterns of performance were reinforced by the adoption of the liberalization policy paradigm, which mainly benefited the established large and competitive firms in the economy. The analysis of the evolving political settlement must engage with the extent to which different organizations influenced the policy decisions taken, as well as the underlying ideological conflicts in the policies that were adopted. The ideology and dominant policy paradigms have implications for policy choices and influence the relative holding power of different groups (Gray, 2018). In this regard, free market economic orthodoxy, together with the liberalization agenda, have privileged the interests of existing capitalists at the expense of a model to support the entry and growth of challenger firms that would bring greater economic dynamism.

Second, the industry experiences point to the continued government support of the large incumbents, despite the industrial policies apparently being aimed at improving productive capabilities and investing in the diversification of certain industries. Our [?] analysis examines the economic power of large firms and the extent to which these firms have influenced the evolution of the political settlement. This is based on the assumptions that industrial support creates rents and the distribution of these rents has largely followed the existing economic structure; and the prevailing economic structure reflects a country's economic history, including the construction of markets and the main participants, as well as the large incumbent businesses.

Third, the lack of industrial diversification also reflects the problems with coordination across policy areas that include energy, minerals, and infrastructure. Understanding the underlying factors in the poor policy coordination is important, particularly if this failing is a result of conflicts of interests—as appears to have been the case.

It is important to understand the makeup of the main groups or interests that have been engaged in conflicts over policies, rents, and policy coordination. These are essentially established businesses, previously excluded black capitalists and black entrepreneurs, industry associations, trade unions, and the government and its constituencies. Many of the established businesses have also had interests in extractive industries with favourable dispensations governing inputs, energy, and infrastructure provision, and in which profits did not necessarily depend on investment in upgrading capabilities. The previously excluded black capitalists have been fragmented into two main groups, the black elites that often had ties with the ruling political party, and independent black entrepreneurs. Industry associations have provided important platforms for engaging on policy and have generally been made up of different combinations of entrenched firms, black capitalists, black entrepreneurs, and entrepreneurs more generally. The trade unions representing workers have focused on the interests of the existing workforce, meaning that these have been largely aligned with the existing economic structure, and chiefly focused on worker issues within this context. The unemployed and market entrants have not been sufficiently organized to counteract the influence of entrenched firms on economic policy, and government has been the arena where conflicts of interests play out rather than a strong voice for the former groups. What is evident is that the interplay between these groups has been dynamic and fluid: in certain periods, some have managed to organize their power better and control rents, while in other periods different groups have been more successful.

14.4 The Evolution of the Political Settlement and Economic Policy for Industrial Development

South Africa's democratic economic policy can be assessed in three phases that roughly coincide with the presidential tenure of Presidents Nelson Mandela (May 1994 to June 1999), Thabo Mbeki (June 1999 to September 2008), and Jacob Zuma (May 2009 to February 2018). The period under President Cyril Ramaphosa (from February 2018 and continuing at the time of writing) is too short to properly assess, while President Kgalema Motlanthe (September 2008 to May 2009) was an interim president for less than a year. As the chapter is concerned with structural change, the analysis considers the distribution of rents or flow of income between the initial industrial core (as at 1994) and more diversified and labour-absorbing industries. This section also considers broader economic policy beyond industrial policy, as the rent management systems of a country are strongly influenced by ideological commitments and dominant policy paradigms (Gray, 2018).

14.4.1 The 1994 Compromises: A Political Settlement to End Apartheid

The compromises reached in 1994 meant that the economic structure was left intact, in effect continuing to protect white ownership of wealth and privileged employment positions of the existing workforce for at least five years in exchange for improvements in labour rights. The compromises were premised on the growth that was expected on the part of established businesses. The major changes adopted were the liberalization of trade and capital flows, the deregulation of agricultural markets, and moves towards privatization. These choices effectively de-prioritized redistribution and inclusion.

The compromises reflected the relative power of big business interests. Business had invested heavily in influencing the economic policy-thinking for the democratic era. This included engaging with all the stakeholders leading up to and during the Convention for a Democratic South Africa (CODESA) negotiations in 1991, providing technical support and data for scenario-planning exercises, punting a market-friendly environment that informed both the ANC and the National Party in the coalition 'Government of National Unity' (Padayachee and Van Niekerk, 2019). The holding power that was leveraged was a combination of ideology and economic structure. Big business was at the helm of the country's industrial core and this placed it in a privileged position, as it was understood that without businesses' support, the economy would underperform. Big business's position was further buttressed by the appointment of former banker Chris Liebenberg as the Finance Minister of democratic South Africa, following the resignation of Derek Keys, who was also a businessman. Chris Stals, who had close ties with the existing business establishment, was retained as governor of the Reserve Bank. Big business, recognizing the potential power of black entrepreneurs, initiated the principles and practice of black economic empowerment (BEE), with its emphasis on ownership transfers to influential individuals (linked to the ANC), to secure buy-in for orthodox reforms, particularly capital account liberalization (Zalk, 2016). These BEE deals started long before the actual legislation came into effect, and as such, served to significantly shape it.

Big business sought to mould institutions and set the rules of the game, to protect their interests over time. This continuity that has been observed over the democratic period confirms that the structure of power in the 1990s has effectively shaped the institutions in its favour.

In the period from 1994 to 1999, there was no overarching industrial policy. The Industrial Strategy Project (ISP), which guided microeconomic policy in the period mischaracterized South Africa's economic challenge as having a high degree of industrial diversification from import substitution along with inefficiencies associated with protection from imports (Joffe et al., 1995: 45). As a result, the policy recommendations focused on facilitating specialization with three elements: fostering the role of market incentives, strengthening underlying capabilities in human resources and technology, and providing an appropriate institutional environment to facilitate industrial restructuring (Joffe et al., 1995: 45). This was very much aligned with the orthodox economic ideology that prevailed at the time, where emphasis was placed on fixing the fundamentals and allowing market forces to do the rest, rather than adopting targeted industrial policy to shape the development path.

The high levels of concentration and lack of competition in many sub-sectors were acknowledged as a challenge for a growing economy (Joffe et al., 1995). However, the Competition Act of 1998, which was negotiated by government, labour, and business, emphasized market efficiency and did not directly tackle the extreme concentration of control by dominant firms in many markets. The issues of inclusion specified in the preamble of the Act were only really given effect in mergers and acquisitions in the form of a public interest provision. As such, it was a reflection of the balance of power between the key constituencies and the strength of big business in particular (see Roberts, 2000: 124–42 for a detailed description of the negotiations). Many of the firms in the big business grouping were already dominant in the markets in which they operated and thus were more concerned about the implications of abuse of dominance provisions rather than merger regulation. The choices made mattered for structural transformation, as the strategic conduct of incumbents can raise entry barriers, exclude smaller businesses, and undermine capability development and diversification (Mondliwa et al., 2020; Mondliwa et al., 2021).

The 'holding power' of big business in the negotiations reflected the fact that government at the time of the legislation was very concerned about investment levels in the economy, which, given the economic structure, depended in large part on the decisions of big businesses. Indeed, the implicit threat of not investing if the commercial environment was not 'friendly' or conducive to 'business certainty' played a part in determining the outcomes of the negotiations. This was reflected in the significant changes made between the government's initial draft and the final provisions (Roberts, 2000: 138). As a result, even though the Competition Act acknowledges the objective of wealth redistribution, the orthodox provisions meant to deal with abuse of a dominant position have proven to be limited (Roberts, 2020).[9]

At the same time, macroeconomic policy emphasized 'stability' and cutting the fiscal deficit, with monetary policy attempting to target the money supply to control inflation. This was despite alternatives that were on the table, including the 'framework for macroeconomic policy in South Africa' put forward by the ANC's Macroeconomic Research Group (MERG). The MERG framework emphasized an initial public investment-led approach for the 1990s and sustained growth in 2000s underpinned by supply-side industrial policy interventions to alter the development trajectory (MERG, 1993). The rejection of the MERG proposals by President Mandela and Deputy President Mbeki followed the critique by the white business community which labelled them as 'macroeconomic populism' (Gumede, 2007). The final negotiated economic policy focused on reassurances to local and international business, and the developmental state ideas were abandoned. Subsequent assessments of economic performance found strong path dependency effects, with the benefits of trade liberalization being realized by those firms that were already internationally competitive in 1994 (Aghion et al., 2013; Bell et al., 2018; Mondliwa et al., 2021). Industrial financing, including by development finance institutions, continued to flow towards the upstream industries (Black and Roberts, 2009).

---

[9] The Competition Act was amended in 2018 and the amendments seek to address questions of increased participation.

14.4.2 The More Things Change the More They Stay the Same: 2000–8

In the 2000s, under President Mbeki, there were strong elements of continuity from the compromises of the Government of National Unity. In effect, the political settlement reached in 1994 remained largely intact in terms of the balance of power and the institutional arrangements, albeit with some important additions. The benefits of liberalization, open markets, and macroeconomic stability continued to be proclaimed, reflecting the ascendance of free markets as the dominant policy paradigm. This was supplemented by expanded 'market friendly' incentives to encourage 'knowledge-intensive' activities and advanced manufacturing technologies (Machaka and Roberts, 2003). Higher levels of investment were expected from business in response. However, there was no understanding of the relationship between the economic structure and investment in capabilities and, instead, deindustrialization continued as downstream and diversified manufacturing performed poorly. In addition, the incentive programmes, in practice, tended to support the capital-intensive upstream industries (see Black et al., 2016; Mondliwa and Roberts, 2019). By the mid-2000s there was still no overall policy that aligned all the different interventions and there was no one agency coordinating government interventions to ensure wider benefits (Rustomjee, 2013).

Though there was a range of incentives to promote investment, exports, and technological improvements, and to support small firms, these were largely soft-touch measures targeted at the same industries that received support from the apartheid government, doing very little to change the structure of the economy. The three manufacturing and tradable sub-sectors that were specifically supported by government between 1994 and 2007 were automotive, resource-processing industries (steel, chemicals, and aluminium), and clothing and textiles. Examples of these incentives include the accelerated depreciation allowance (37E incentive), and the Strategic Industrial Projects (SIP) programme. Both incentives were made available to large capital-intensive projects, mostly in resource-related sub-sectors such as steel, ferro-alloys, aluminium, and basic chemicals (see Black and Roberts, 2009). The rationale for continuing to support upstream industries was based on opportunities for development through linkages to the downstream industries. However, there were no conditions placed on these incentives and there have been limited benefits for linked industries (Bell et al., 2018; and Chapters 3 and 4).

With the commodities boom driven by Chinese demand, coupled with domestic consumer credit extension and investment for the World Cup in 2010, the economy grew even while cheap imports on the back of the strong currency were hollowing out local manufacturing. At the same time, the need to bridge the gap between South Africa's 'two economies' meant social grants were increased along with greater spending by government and parastatals on extending basic services.

The approach to BEE reflected this attempt to straddle divergent realities as business committed to voluntary charters with weak monitoring and an absence of enforcement (Ponte et al., 2007; Mondliwa and Roberts, 2020). BEE effectively reinforced the existing economic structure and left black shareholders in debt to their white business partners and needing to ensure the flow of profits was maintained (Chapter 9). Large businesses successfully lobbied the government not to implement structural changes that would create opportunities for entrants, including black entrepreneurs, in exchange for firms creating BEE initiatives that effectively reinforced their position as gate keepers in the economy (Mondliwa and Roberts, 2020). This was despite the BEE Commission[10] having developed a detailed programme for BEE that aimed to bring empowerment and structural transformation, together with an emphasis on increased productive investment (BEE Commission, 2001; Mondliwa and Roberts, 2020). Again, big business was able to use economic resources to accommodate a small black elite.

Many of the BEE Commissioners later became beneficiaries of the ownership transfers and have become multimillionaires. This weakened the holding power of the remaining black entrepreneurs as there was now a policy in place with the objective of addressing their concerns, even if the instruments were weak. By 2015, the distribution of the value of BEE deals was largely in line with the economic structure in 1994. Mining attracted the highest share (32 per cent of the total value), followed by industrials representing 18 per cent of the total value (Theobald et al., 2015). The implication is that in relation to economic structure, the incentives of the new black elites connected to BEE were aligned with the status quo. The strategies of the emerging black elite were also to establish BEE holding companies that took minority shares in multiple existing companies to spread risk rather than deepening ownership and control and making new net investments. There are very few examples of BEE beneficiaries that have moved into diversified manufacturing activities; and those that have diversified their portfolios have tended to move into financial services.

The poor design of BEE also undermined the use of public procurement to drive diversification and productive inclusion. The application in practice meant that empowered importers could be prioritized over domestic producers. This came at the cost of domestic production and jobs.

The international listing of South African firms was taking place at the same time as the rise of the shareholder value movement, which saw the growing influence of institutional investors demanding intensive corporate restructuring to unlock larger and more rapid flows of cash to shareholders (Chapter 10). This underpinned the wide-scale corporate and industrial restructuring, which was in fact associated with a hollowing out of capabilities (Zalk, 2016). The impact of the

---

[10] The BEE Commission was established in 1998.

commodities boom and strong currency meant that imported goods became cheaper and that salaries were higher in international currency terms, further fuelling consumption but undermining companies' competitiveness.

On the labour front, much semi-skilled and unskilled labour, and many of the informally employed and unemployed, were progressively excluded. While popular protests grew, these were suppressed by policing, and social grants were substantially expanded to mitigate the short-term effects of deindustrialization (Runciman, 2017).

Overall, the development of industries in South Africa in the 1990s and early 2000s reflects path dependency, compromises, and continuities in the absence of a concerted and coordinated industrial strategy across the government to change the trajectory. Individual ministries did develop strategies that aimed to support advanced manufacturing and create employment, such as the Integrated Manufacturing Strategy (Department of Trade, Industry, and Competition, 2002) and the Advanced Manufacturing and Technology Strategy (Department of Science and Technology, 2003). However, there was little coordination between these policies to ensure wider benefits.

Towards the end of this period it became apparent that structural change towards more diversified industries was necessary to drive growth and to address the high levels of unemployment and curb increasing levels of inequality. As part of the Accelerated and Shared Growth Initiative of South Africa (ASGI-SA), which replaced the Growth, Employment, and Redistribution (GEAR) policy as the country's macroeconomic policy, the National Industrial Policy Framework (NIPF) was introduced in 2007. The NIPF identified the need to coordinate interventions and target sub-sectors for industrial development. The focus of the strategy was on diversifying the economy towards downstream labour-absorbing industries. However, the industrial policy did not reflect the prevailing distribution of power within the economy. As such, it has not been successful and is considered a project of the Department of Trade, Industry, and Competition (DTIC) rather than part of a government-wide coordinated strategy.

14.4.3 Shifts in the Political Settlement: Populism and State Capture, 2008–18

Growing popular sentiment against the Mbeki government was made evident when President Jacob Zuma won the leadership of the ANC in 2007 and effectively removed President Mbeki in 2008 (with President Motlanthe holding office for a short period). This was with the support of the Congress of South African Trade Unions (COSATU) and other groupings on the left inside the ANC. However, instead of a progressive economic policy agenda to engage with the country's development challenges, under President Zuma an increasingly clientelistic political settlement emerged. This included vertical fragmentation of control within the ANC as extractive rents were competed over from local to national levels of government and in state-owned corporations (Makhaya and Roberts, 2013; Public Protector, 2016; Bhorat et al., 2017). The message was that the market economy was rigged against the majority and that the only way to accumulate was through leveraging state influence.

For a time, public sector trade unions were kept onside by higher public wage settlements for government employees, while industrial unions fractured and ultimately left COSATU. The public wage premium increased during this period, and this, together with the expansion of public sector employment, increased the public wage bill, diverting funds away from other expenditure items such as investment in public infrastructure (Bhorat et al., 2016). This was the case even while the delivery of services by the state deteriorated and protests increased across the country (Runciman, 2017).

The impact of the political settlement of this period on industrial policy was profound, as conflictual stances were taken across government on a host of policy areas of central importance for industrialization, such as energy, mining, and procurement policies. Levers such as local procurement were employed for short-term rent capture across government. As a result, there were missed opportunities for building local capabilities in a number of areas, including machinery component manufacturing from the Transnet procurement process (Crompton and Kaziboni, 2020).[11]

The main strategy that President Zuma had used to gain leadership within the ANC was to divide the party and the Tripartite Alliance to alienate President Mbeki and his supporters.[12] Once he was in power, it became important to bring in wider interests, reflected in a larger and more fragmented Cabinet, with the number of ministries growing from twenty-six to thirty-six. This proliferation of government departments made coordination of policy almost impossible.

President Zuma and his alliances often made public announcements about the need to displace 'white monopoly capital', which was allegedly growing at the expense of the accumulation of black wealth. This narrative was used to remove ministers that were labelled 'puppets of white monopoly capital' and replace them with others, many of whom were to emerge later as having connections to the Gupta family associates linked to state capture.[13] The clientelism gained legitimacy even with the continued exclusion of the majority, and this narrative

---

[11] Transnet is the state-owned monopoly in rail, ports, and pipelines. In 2012, Transnet embarked on its largest-ever single order of 1,064 locomotives with local content requirements. However, the project was later found to be corrupt and the local-content requirements were bypassed in a number of instances.

[12] This is an alliance between the ANC (ruling political party), the Congress of South African Trade Unions (COSATU), and the South African Communist Party (SACP).

[13] The Gupta family is alleged to be at the centre of the large-scale corruption that characterized Zuma's presidency. See Bhorat et al. (2017).

became a source of holding power. It also weakened the stance of big business, which was seen as representing 'white monopoly capital'. Despite the rhetoric on 'radical economic transformation' and fighting South Africa's triple challenges of high unemployment, inequality, and poverty, there were very few interventions to trigger structural change or address real impacts of monopoly power on the economy. The most significant was the black industrialist programme, involving financing by the Industrial Development Corporation (IDC) and the DTIC, as well as public procurement, to address the challenges of access to markets, which has also had many challenges (Chapter 9).

The remaining industrial policy rents continued to flow towards established businesses. The incentive programme for the automotive industry was also updated in this period, but it continued to disproportionately benefit the multinational OEMs and there was limited upgrading through linkages to the automotive industry (Chapter 5). Import tariffs were introduced to support the struggling upstream steel industry at a significant cost to downstream industries (Rustomjee et al., 2018; and Chapter 8). Though the tariff support to AMSA came with conditionalities this time around, the design of the condition-alities undermined their effectiveness (Chapter 8). Incentives to support recovery from the 2008 financial crisis and the ensuing recession, such as the Manufacturing Competitiveness Enhancement Programme, also flowed to established firms, often financing investments that would have taken place without it (Beare et al., 2014). The programme's design, whereby firms had to finance the investment and claim back from government later, privileged firms that already had access to funding. Programmes that were targeted at the upgrading of collective capabilities for diversified industries were not prioritized for funding. In 2014, a cluster programme was developed to assist firms to overcome challenges with competitiveness. The programme, which involved financing and policy support for groups of firms seeking to collectively resolve challenges, was later shelved due to lack of funding (Beare et al., 2014).

While firms broadly maintained profit levels in this period (Driver, 2019), there was limited investment in expanded productive capacity in South Africa (Bosiu et al., 2017). When challenged on this, business argued that the low levels of investment were a result of political uncertainty associated with Zuma's presidency. However, the comparison of investment levels among comparable middle-income countries indicates the relatively lower investment levels in South Africa throughout the whole post-apartheid period (Chapter 1).

Zuma's presidency has often been framed as the 'nine wasted years'[14] or 'the corrupt years'. The implication of this position is that the removal of the 'bad apples', coupled with a return to the 'good governance' agenda that characterized

---

[14] In 2019, in a speech given at the World Economic Forum, President Ramaphosa referred to President Zuma's time in office as the 'nine wasted years'. See Haffajee, 2019.

the Mbeki presidency, would resolve South Africa's problems. It is argued strongly here that this is not the case. A point often missed in debates about this period is that South Africa's failure generally to mobilize higher levels of investment in productive industries of the economy materially contributed to the conditions that enabled the brazen clientelism, patronage, and corruption that characterized the Zuma presidency (Zalk, 2016; Mondliwa and Roberts, 2018).

14.5 The Political Economy of Structural Transformation in Middle-Income Countries: Lessons from the South African Case

The success or failure of countries to drive structural change can be understood in terms of whether the political economy dynamics, and the governing coalition of interests, support the growth of diversified manufacturing sub-sectors with higher levels of productivity (Khan and Blankenburg, 2009; Gray, 2018). This chapter has assessed the contestation of interests and the power balance that underpin South Africa's structural change dynamics. It contributes to the growing evidence of political economy analyses of structural change in middle income countries by engaging both with the conflicts at the micro level (in specific industries) and interaction with the meso and macro dynamics. So, what does the South African experience tell us about the political economy of structural change?

South Africa's political settlement has evolved but not in ways that have led to significant changes to the productive structure of the economy. Instead of the upgrading coalitions critical for successful industrialization, the coalitions have effectively been of incumbent firms with limited sharing with a small group of the black elite. This deal has meant the firms have retained their economic position and been able to internationalize. In South Africa's case, the large and lead firms are concentrated in commodities (linked to minerals), and regulated industries including telecommunications, healthcare, construction, and the financial sector. In commodities, the primary focus has been on extraction and export of minerals. This does not require substantial investments in capabilities within the economy. The rationalization of the activities of mining houses in the 1980s and 1990s meant that the non-core assets, including in mining machinery and equipment, which requires investment in technological capabilities to be competitive, were sold off to less funded domestic capitalists and international firms, implying an exit of capabilities and/or lower investments.

The regulated industries are mostly natural oligopolies, where high barriers to entry limit the levels of rivalry that would lead firms to invest in capabilities in order to increase market shares. The incumbent firms can also raise strategic barriers to entry to ensure the exclusion of other firms. The relative importance of both the commodities and the regulated industries in the economy also means that they have power to influence policies—what Zingales (2017) has termed the 'Medici vicious circle'. The economic power that comes with establishing dominant positions in markets readily translates into the capture of political power that reinforces those positions. This exemplifies economic structure as a source of holding power.

The implication is that there is no influential constituency backing structural change. The commodity sub-sectors have also been producing intermediate inputs for more diversified downstream firms. These upstream firms at times have charged exploitative prices that have undermined the competitiveness of downstream firms (Chapters 3 and 4). The vertical distribution of power within the South African value chains has typically been skewed towards the upstream input suppliers. The holding power of these upstream firms has not only been derived from dyadic relationships between the upstream and downstream firms, but also from the orientation of institutions towards the upstream sub-sectors— what Dallas et al. (2019) refer to as institutional power.

The levers which could have been used by the South African government, including energy and minerals policies, have been undermined by the fragmentation of the state. The division of responsibilities into many different departments under different ministers, particularly during the Zuma administration, meant that corporate interests could lobby them separately and make a coordinated approach unlikely. The separation from trade and industrial policy of initially technology policy in the 1990s followed by development finance and competition (from 2009) put further strain on the coordination requirements across government. Through the political settlements lens, however, what initially presented as an incoherent policy approach actually reflects an arrangement emerging from the need to keep the ruling coalition together.

In the agenda and actions of the state, the interests of workers and businesses in diversified industries have not been given importance, while the lobbying of the industries which prospered under apartheid have meant they have been able to continue to hold sway. Contests have largely been over the division of existing rents rather than how to create new rents. This has been true of the framing of BEE in terms of ownership in existing businesses. The issues of 'state capture' have also focused on existing rents.

Without crafting a new political settlement in which the interests of longer-term investment in capabilities have a prime position, it is difficult to see a different path being taken. Breaking down barriers to entry and growth is one side of such a settlement; new investment is the other.

South Africa's post-apartheid experience is an extreme version of factors facing upper middle-income countries struggling to enter high-incomes status in the context of liberalization, globalization, and high levels of inequality. Four key observations provide rich material for wider political economy debates.

First, the state is not monolithic but rather an arena where conflicts between powerful groups take place. The industry case studies in the book and the discussion above have shown how different interests are able to shape economic policymaking and regulation in their favour. In addition, the state's ability to monitor and enforce conditionalities on state-provided incentives is dependent on the balance of power.

Second, the constitutive power of international norms that are not necessarily associated with particular institutions can shape development outcomes (Dallas et al., 2019). The rationalizing of South African conglomerates, combined with the internationalization of businesses and a narrower focus on protecting profits and paying out dividends, undermined longer-term productive investments in South Africa.

Third, inequality makes politics prone to populism, understood in economic terms as personalized leadership that addresses broad but unorganized discontent. The rise of former President Zuma was in response to the growing discontent with outcomes for the majority of South Africans. The liberalization reforms have largely ensured the continuation of the economic status quo including inequality. As such, the variable relationship between political stability and economic transformation during the period of analysis has underpinned the accommodation of particular interests.

And fourth, institutional analysis alone does not explain the paths of economic transformation. Post-apartheid South Africa has developed world-class institutions, which on paper should have ensured that the transformation of the economy would be more inclusive. However, the way institutions work in practice depends on the responses of the organizations operating under these institutions (Gray, 2018). The state capture years have been indicative of how power lies outside formal institutions, with the Gupta family alleged to have used a web of informal networks that operate within and outside formal institutions to facilitate clientelism.

References

Aghion, P., J. Fedderke, P. Howitt, and N. Viegi (2013). 'Testing creative destruction in an opening economy.' *Economics of Transition* 21(3): 419–50.

Ashman, S., B. Fine, and S. Newman (2011). 'The crisis in South Africa: neoliberalism, financialization and uneven and combined development.' *Social Register* 47: 174–95.

Beare, M., P. Mondliwa, G. Robb, and S. Roberts (2014). 'Report for the plastics conversion industry strategy.' Research report prepared for the Department of Trade and Industry. Mimeo.

Behuria, P., L. Buur, and H. Gray (2017). 'Studying political settlements in Africa.' *African Affairs* 116(464): 508–25.

Bell, J., S. Goga, P. Mondliwa, and S. Roberts (2018). 'Structural transformation in South Africa: moving towards a smart, open economy for all.' CCRED Working Paper 9/2018. Johannesburg: CCRED.

BEE Commission (2001). *Black Economic Empowerment Commission Report* Johannesburg: Skotaville Press.

Bhorat, H., M. Buthelezi, I. Chipkin, S. Duma, L. Mondi, C. Peter, M. Qobo, M. Swilling, and H. Friedenstein (2017). 'Betrayal of the promise: how South Africa is being stolen.' *State Capacity Research Project* [Online]. https://pari.org.za/wp-content/uploads/2017/05/Betrayal-of-the-Promise-25052017.pdf (accessed 09 April 2021).

Bhorat, H., K. Naidoo, M. Oosthuizen, and K. Pillay. (2016). 'South Africa: demographic, employment, and wage trends.' In H. Bhorat and F. Tarp (eds), *Africa's Lions: Growth Traps and Opportunities for Six African Economies*, 229–70. Washington, DC: Brookings Institution Press.

Black, A., S. Craig, and P. Dunne (2016). 'Capital intensity, industrial policy and employment in the South African manufacturing sector.' REDI3x3 Working Paper 23. Cape Town: REDI 3X3.

Black, A. and S. Roberts (2009). 'The evolution and impact of industrial and competition policies.' In J. Aron, B. Kahn, and G. Kingdon (eds), *South African Economy Policy under Democracy*, 211–43. Oxford: Oxford University Press.

Bosiu, T., N. Nhundu, A. Paelo, M. Thosago, and T. Vilakazi (2017). 'Growth and strategies of large and leading firms-top 50 firms on the Johannesburg Stock Exchange.' CCRED Working Paper 17/2017. Johannesburg: CCRED.

Chabane, N., A. Goldstein, S. Roberts (2006). 'The changing face and strategies of big business in South Africa: more than a decade of political democracy.' *Industrial and Corporate Change* 15(3): 549–78.

Crompton, R. and L. Kaziboni (2020). 'Lost opportunities? Barriers to entry and Transnet's procurement of 1064 locomotives.' In T. Vilakazi, S. Goga, and S. Roberts (eds), *Opening the South African Economy: Barriers to Entry and Competition*, 199–214. Cape Town: HSRC Press.

Dallas, M. P., S. Ponte, and T. J. Sturgeon (2019). 'Power in global value chains.' *Review of International Political Economy* 26(4): 666–94.

Driver, C. (2019). 'Trade liberalization and South African manufacturing: Looking back with data.' WIDER Working Paper 2019/30. Helsinki: UNU-WIDER.

Gray, H. (2013). 'Industrial policy and the political settlement in Tanzania: aspects of continuity and change since independence.' *Review of African Political Economy* 40(136): 185.

Gray, H. (2018). *Turbulence and Order in Economic Development: Institutions and Economic Transformation in Tanzania and Vietnam*. Oxford: Oxford University Press.

Gray, H. (2019). 'Understanding and deploying the political settlement framework in Africa.' In N. Cheeseman, R. Abrahamsen, G. Khadiagala, P. Medie, and R. Riedl (eds), *The Oxford Encyclopedia of African Politics.*Oxford University Press. https://doi.org/10.1093/acrefore/9780190228637.013.888

Gumede, W. M. (2007). *Thabo Mbeki and the Battle for the Soul of the ANC*. London: Zed Books Ltd.

Hafajee, F. (2019). 'Ramaphosa's "nine lost years" speech impresses Old Mutual CEO at Davos'. *Fin24*:https://www.news24.com/fin24/Economy/South-Africa/ramaphosas-nine-lost-years-speech-impresses-old-mutual-ceo-at-davos-20190124 (accessed 2 November 2020).

Joffe A., D. E. Kaplan, R. Kaplinsky, and D. Lewis (1995). *Improving Manufacturing Performance: The Report of the Industrial Strategy Project*. Cape Town: University of Cape Town Press.

Khan, M. H. (2010). 'Political settlements and the governance of growth-enhancing institutions'. Research Paper Series on Governance for Growth. London: School of Oriental and African Studies, University of London. http://eprints.soas.ac.uk/9968/1/PoliticalSettlements_internet.pdf (accessed 22 February 2020).

Khan, M. H. (2018). 'Power, pacts and political settlements: a reply to Tim Kelsall.' *African Affairs* 117(469): 670–94.

Khan, M. H. and S. Blankenburg (2009) 'The political economy of industrial policy in Latin America.' In G. Dosi, M. Cimoli, and J. E. Stiglitz (eds), *Industrial Policy and Development: The Political Economy of Capabilities Accumulation*. Oxford: Oxford University Press.

Khan, M. H. and K. S. Jomo, eds (2000). *Rents, Rent-Seeking and Economic Development: Theory and Evidence in Asia*. Cambridge: Cambridge University Press.

Lee, K. (2015). 'Capability building and industrial diversification.' In Jesus Felipe (ed.), *Development and Modern Industrial Policy in Practice: Issues and Country Experience*, 70–93. Cheltenham: Edward Elgar.

Machaka, J. and S. Roberts (2003). 'The DTI's new "integrated manufacturing strategy?" Comparative industrial performance, linkages and technology.' *South African Journal of Economics* 71(4): 679–704.

Macroeconomic Research Group (1993). 'Making democracy work: a framework for macroeconomic policy in South Africa.' A report to members of the Democratic Movement of South Africa. University of Western Cape, Centre for Development Studies.

Makhaya, G. and S. Roberts (2013). 'Expectations and outcomes: considering competition and corporate power in South Africa under democracy.' *Review of African Political Economy* 40(138): 556–71.

Mondliwa, P., S. Goga, and S. Roberts (2021). 'Competition, productive capabilities and structural transformation in South Africa.' *European Journal of Development Research* (2021), DOI:10.1057/s41287-020-00349-x.

Mondliwa, P., S. Ponte, and S. Roberts (2020). 'Competition and power in global value chains.' *Competition and Change*. DOI:1024529420975154.

Mondliwa, P. and S. Roberts (2018). 'Rewriting the rules governing the South African economy: a new political settlement for industrial development.' Industrial Development Think Tank Policy Brief 10, Centre for Competition, Regulation and Economic Development.

Mondliwa, P. and S. Roberts (2019). 'From a developmental to a regulatory state? Sasol and the conundrum of continued state support.' *International Review of Applied Economics* 33(1): 11–29.

Mondliwa, P. and S. Roberts (2020). 'Black economic empowerment and barriers to entry.' In T. Vilakazi, S. Goga, and S. Roberts (eds), *Opening the South African Economy: Barriers to Entry and Competition*, 215–30. Cape Town: HSRC Press.

North, D. C., J. J. Wallis, and B. Weingast (2009). *Violence and Social Orders*. Cambridge: Cambridge University Press.

OECD (2013). 'OECD economic surveys: South Africa, Paris.' Paris: OECD Publishing.

Padayachee, V. and R. Van Niekerk (2019). *Shadow of Liberation: Contestation and Compromise in the Economic and Social Policy of the African National Congress, 1943–1996*. Johannesburg: Wits University Press.

Ponte, S., S. Roberts, and L. van Sittert (2007). '"Black economic empowerment", business and the state in South Africa.' *Development and Change* 38(5): 933–55.

Public Protector (2016). 'The state capture report.' http://www.saflii.org/images/329756472-State-of-Capture.pdf (accessed 6 June 2020).

Roberts, S. (2000). *The Internationalisation of Production, Government Policy and Industrial Development in South Africa*. Unpublished doctoral thesis, Birkbeck (University of London).

Roberts, S. (2020). 'Assessing the record of competition law enforcement in opening up the economy.' In T. Vilakazi, S. Goga, and S. Roberts (eds), *Opening the South African Economy: Barriers to Entry and Competition*, 179–98. Cape Town: HSRC Press.

Runciman, C. (2017). 'South African social movements in the neoliberal age.' In M. Paret, C. Runciman, and L. Sinwell (eds), *Southern Resistance in Critical Perspective: The Politics of Protest in South Africa's Contentious Democracy*, 36–52. Abingdon: Routledge.

Rustomjee, Z. (2013). '20 year review-economy & employment: Industrial policy.' Input Paper for South African Presidency 20 Year Review, May 2013. Mimeo.

Rustomjee, Z., L. Kaziboni, and I. Steuart (2018). 'Structural transformation along metals, machinery and equipment value chain—Developing capabilities in the metals and machinery segments.' CCRED Working Paper 7/2018. Johannesburg: CCRED.

Theobald, S., O. Tambo, P. Makuwerere, and C. Anthony (2015). 'The value of BEE Deals.' Report. Johannesburg: Intellidex.

UNCTAD (2018). 'Trade and development report.' Geneva: United Nations Conference on Trade and Development.

World Bank (2018). 'Overcoming poverty and inequality in South Africa: an assessment of drivers, constraints and opportunities.' Washington, DC: World Bank.

Zalk, N. (2016). 'Selling off the silver: The imperative for productive and jobs-rich investment: South Africa.' *New Agenda: South African Journal of Social and Economic Policy* 2016(63): 10–15.

Zingales, L. (2017). 'Towards a political theory of the firm.' *Journal of Economic Perspectives* 31(3): 113–30.

15

Towards a New Industrial Policy for Structural Transformation

Antonio Andreoni, Pamela Mondliwa, Simon Roberts,
and Fiona Tregenna

15.1 Introduction

The case of South Africa demonstrates why structural transformation is so important and yet so difficult to achieve. Moving to higher value-adding and more sophisticated, diversified economic activities is at the heart of a resilient and healthy economy which enables its citizens to realize their full potential. It involves investment in a wide range of productive capabilities for these economic activities to develop. The economic and social implications of the Covid-19 pandemic, which are still unfolding at the time of writing, make the building of a stronger, more diversified economic base even more imperative. It should also be self-evident that the structure and nature of production need to be environmentally sustainable and not exacerbate climate change.

Structural change (or the lack of it) is determined by the presence (or absence) of complex and interdependent processes of learning and investment in industrial ecosystems, specifically the development and accumulation of productive capabilities across sectors, organizations, and institutions. These processes require making the appropriate linkages among productive activities to effectively engage with technological change, notably digitalization, in order to integrate into global value chains (GVCs) in ways that support local capabilities development. In turn, the healthy development of the industrial ecosystems requires appropriate institutions and sound industrial policies as part of the country's political settlement. The political settlement is understood as the compromises reached between powerful groups in society which set the context for institutional arrangements and other policies, as well as their effectiveness and enforceability.

South Africa is an important case study of the challenges faced by middle-income countries in pursuing structural transformation. By the 1990s, it had developed strong productive capabilities in some industries, largely as a result of the support for industries deemed strategic under apartheid. The economy was rapidly opened up in the 1990s, with deep trade liberalization (Roberts, 2000;

Antonio Andreoni, Pamela Mondliwa, Simon Roberts, and Fiona Tregenna, *Towards a New Industrial Policy for Structural Transformation* In: *Structural Transformation in South Africa: The Challenges of Inclusive Industrial Development in a Middle-Income Country.* Edited by: Antonio Andreoni, Pamela Mondliwa, Simon Roberts, and Fiona Tregenna, Oxford University Press. © Oxford University Press 2021. DOI: 10.1093/oso/9780192894311.003.0015

Erten et al., 2019). However, despite industrial policies that have sought to pro-mote manufacturing, the deindustrialization process that began in the early 1980s has not been reversed, but has actually continued, as discussed in Chapter 11. And, within industry there has been a persistent bias towards heavy industry and an overall failure to diversify (Chapter 2).

The contributions to this book explore the changes over three decades in key industry groupings, locating the South African industry experience in an inter-national context. Collectively, the chapters analyse the linkages and interdependen-cies across activities, and point to the need to transcend the traditional 'manufacturing' and 'services' divide to understand the development of product-ive capabilities in industrial ecosystems. Issues of technological change, product-ive capabilities, and the digitalization of production are considered in cross-cutting chapters, along with the record on black economic empowerment, inclusion, inequality, and sustainability.

South Africa has largely missed out on the gains from international integration in the form of 'learning through exporting' in diversified manufacturing industries. Instead, there are 'islands' of export capabilities, such as in mining machinery, which have not been built upon as catalysts of wider structural transformation. For instance, while the auto sub-sector—which has been highly incentivized under successive industrial policies—stands out in terms of the value of exports, these have been limited to fully assembled vehicles and a narrow range of components (Chapter 5). Minerals, along with basic metals and basic chemicals, remained almost as important in the country's goods exports in 2019 as they did twenty-five years earlier. There are, however, a few counter-examples, led by high-value fruit exports and niches within machinery and equipment, which demonstrate a possible alternative path (see Chapters 3 and 6).

In services too, there has not been a sustained trend towards upgrading and towards stronger integration with other sectors. There has been growth in lower-value, lower-productivity services overall, including those statistically classified as 'other business services' (which include activities such as security and cleaning services, see Tregenna (2010)) and retail. While financial services and communication services have also grown in value added, they have only recorded modest increases in employment, and have not played a sufficiently developmental role in supporting the growth of productive industries (Chapters 1, 2, and 10).

South Africa's poor performance must be understood in the context of the evolving political settlement. The compromises reached in 1994 reflected, in part, the strength of established business groups. While policies such as tariff liberalization (leading to increased market competition from imports) and competition law enforcement might have constrained market power to an extent, there has been a subsequent failure to enforce industrial policy levers to ensure that rents have been productively reinvested in expansion and upgrading.

As with many other middle-income countries, in South Africa macroeconomic policy has emphasized 'stability' as part of the conditions for business confidence, which was supposed to underpin investment in the model promoted by the 'Washington Consensus' International Financial Institutions (Padayachee and Van Niekerk, 2019; Michie, 2020). Achieving this stability meant cutting the fiscal deficit and reducing inflation through higher interest rates under inflation targeting. In the first decade of the 2000s, high real interest rates coupled with natural resource earnings led to a strong, overvalued currency and hence a growing trade deficit exacerbated by burgeoning credit-fuelled consumer spending. The unsustainability of this path became glaringly obvious with the 2008 global financial crisis and the end of the commodities boom shortly thereafter.

As could be expected, the lack of fundamental distributional change—and the limited nature of trickle-down benefits—meant growing pressure to accumulate wealth by leveraging state influence. The vertical fragmentation of control within the ruling coalition of interests resulted in competition for extractive rents from local to national levels of government and in state-owned corporations (Makhaya and Roberts, 2013; Bhorat et al., 2017). In addition, a horizontal fracturing also occurred within both the labour and business constituencies. The fragmentation of government has made the development of a coherent strategy to reverse the trend, including an effective industrial policy, very difficult (see Chapter 2, and Bhorat et al., 2014 on policy coordination in South Africa).

This concluding chapter looks at the issues that have emerged in the book that can inform a necessary change in direction for middle-income countries such as South Africa. The chapter starts with a discussion of the foundations for structural transformation illuminated by the industrial ecosystems framework and the in-depth industry analyses. The key 'gaps and traps' which need to be confronted are then identified. This is followed by a focus on the key considerations for industrial policy for South Africa and other middle-income countries facing similar challenges. The chapter concludes with a call for the need to confront the implications of climate change and Covid-19 as an essential part of achieving sustainable transformation.

15.2 Key Foundations for Structural Transformation to Build Industrial Capabilities: Understanding Industrial Ecosystems and Value Chains

15.2.1 An Industrial Ecosystems Approach

An industrial strategy that seeks to influence value creation and capture dynamics to achieve structural transformation must locate firms and their performance in terms of industrial ecosystems to allow for the consideration of all the relevant factors. The industrial ecosystems perspective allows for building an inductive and context-specific understanding of the structure of 'the product space' emerging from the intersection of key sectoral value chains and different capabilities (Andreoni, 2018).

An approach to shape industrial ecosystems starts from the main units of analysis being the production capabilities, key enabling technologies, and the value chains, while taking into account the distribution of power. Within each industrial ecosystem, there are a number of value chains around which the productive activities (including manufacturing and services) are structured. Each of these value chains involves several productive organizations whose activities are made possible by their capabilities across different technology platforms.

The technology platforms integrate different types of technologies and technology systems. The increasing digitalization of the economy has dramatically reshaped these technology domains and the capabilities required by productive organizations to be competitive in the market. This means that some of these technology platforms underpin production processes of closely related industrial sub-sectors as well as different product-value segments within the same industrial sub-sector. Technologies are thus linked by a set of dynamic interlocking relationships spanning across sub-sectors and value-product segments.

Learning and capabilities development is the result of purposeful processes of trial and error, with investments in knowledge acquisition, reverse engineering, technology absorption and adaptation, and the scaling-up of production. Opportunities are not simply discovered but need to be created through interdependent relationships between firms and with public institutions in a dynamic ecosystem (see Chapter 1). The core underpinnings for these processes of learning and capabilities development require a coalition of interests which value the necessary longer-term investment in shared facilities, rather than short-term rent seeking (Khan and Blankenburg, 2009; Chang and Andreoni, 2020; and Chapters 1, 14).

15.2.2 Insights from Manufacturing Industries in South Africa

The studies of key industry groupings presented in the book reveal the importance of understanding capabilities and interdependencies on the ground, as well as how these interact with the dominant interests. They reflect an interesting mix of continuities and change.

The metals, machinery, and plastics industries exemplify the lack of structural transformation at the heart of the South African economy, as well as pointing to areas of potential. Over three decades, there have been major changes within industries. These have seen the internationalization of the industries in terms of ownership, technologies, and trade. However, the capital-intensive upstream basic industries were even slightly more—rather than less—important in

manufacturing value added in 2019 than in 1994.[1] This reflects the weak performance of diversified manufacturing industries and contrasts with the more
successful middle-income countries where manufacturing has continued to lead
in building industrial capabilities, such that countries have escaped the 'middle-
income technology trap' (Andreoni and Tregenna, 2020; and Chapter 11).

The dominant basic steel company in South Africa, now part of the largest
global steel producer ArcelorMittal, has continued to receive support, including
in the form of tariff protection. The upstream basic steel sub-sector, in which it is
the leading producer, has continued to record a large trade surplus. By comparison, the downstream fabricated metal products and machinery manufacturers
have recorded growing trade deficits and only islands of competitive capabilities,
in a similar continuity (Chapter 3). The main basic chemicals company, Sasol, has
performed well in South Africa while continuing to benefit from a favourable
regulatory dispensation in liquid fuels and natural gas, and has used the profits to
invest in less successful offshore ventures (Mondliwa and Roberts, 2019; and
Chapter 4). The downstream and diversified plastic products sub-sector has performed very poorly, with growing trade deficits (Chapter 4). Growth in downstream activities creates employment and has strong linkages to advanced
capabilities such as in design and engineering services. Yet, there have not been
effective industrial policies to leverage off the existing strong capabilities in segments of machinery production, led by that for the mining industry. This contrasts with a number of other countries where initiatives have successfully built
industrial clusters in machinery and equipment (Chapter 3).

Along with machinery, plastic products are a critical industry for adopting and
adapting to digitalization. The sub-sector brings together advances in materials
science, design, additive manufacturing (3D printing), and integration across
firms and along value chains to manufacture diverse components and final
products. The plastic products sub-sector in South Africa has performed poorly,
similar to the average for all diversified light manufacturing in the country
(Chapter 4). In other words, there has been a regression, rather than progression,
in terms of structural transformation. The reasons for this are a combination of a
failure to focus on the clusters of capabilities and domestic linkages which
the industry requires to meet the challenges of international competitiveness,
coupled with a need to address issues of direct cost competitiveness. In other
middle-income countries with dynamic industries, strong linkages with multinational corporations have been leveraged to support capabilities development
(Chapter 4).

---

[1] The share of basic metals industries (ferrous and non-ferrous) in manufacturing value added
increased from 7.0 per cent in 1994 to 7.4 per cent in 2019 and the combined share of refineries and
basic chemicals sub-sectors increased from 7.9 per cent to 13.9 per cent.

In terms of structure, the auto sub-sector in South Africa presents a contrast with the metals and plastics sub-sectors: there is a well-established downstream assembly of motor vehicles but very weak backward linkages into components production, where diversified industrial capabilities are developed (Chapter 5). Sharp reductions in protection to induce the original equipment manufacturers to focus on fewer models and increase scale did bring restructuring. A targeted strategy, the Motor Industry Development Programme (MIDP), incentivized the scaling-up and export of components. This had a measure of success in a few components, notably exports of catalytic convertors. However, the overall picture after twenty-five years of industrial policies (including the Automotive Production and Development Programme (APDP)) has revealed a relatively large assembly industry with weak linkages into components (Chapter 5). The policies remained oriented in favour of the original equipment manufacturers (OEMs) and did not meet the challenges South Africa faces of being a small market in a global industry. This compares unfavourably with some middle-income countries such as Thailand. There, the balance has been in the other direction, with much strong clusters of components manufacturers and fewer models being assembled, but in much larger volumes than in South Africa (Barnes et al., 2017).

The South African fruit industry offers an interesting and important comparison (Chapter 6). In the absence of government targeting, key industry actors have coordinated effectively along the value chain to build the industrial capabilities required to deliver high-value fruit to export markets. This is particularly evident in citrus fruits, where industry bodies are relatively well organized and have brought in more participants, including smaller producers, while adopting improved technologies for higher-value niche products. When the apartheid-era agricultural boards were abolished in 1997, citrus growers formed the South African Citrus Growers Association (CGA) to continue to promote market access, research and technical development, and knowledge transfer. This included what became known as the Citrus Academy, which focused on developing a quality learning system for the industry and on improving access to skills development for all participants. The CGA was funded by voluntary levies paid by the growers, which later became a statutory levy to fund research and market access (Chapter 6). On the back of these investments, South Africa became the second-largest exporter of citrus in the world. In contrast, in other fruits such as avocados and berries, South Africa has not performed as well as there has been less success in broader industry accumulation of cross-cutting capabilities, such as in research and technical development to meet phytosanitary requirements for export market access. A range of other countries demonstrate the potential for stronger growth that can be achieved through realizing the 'industrialization of freshness' (Cramer and Sender, 2019; Cramer and Tregenna, 2020).

Overall, there has been limited collaboration for 'learning' and building capabilities in South Africa, due in part to the entrenched power of existing industry interests, and the consumption orientation of urban middle- and upper-income earners. As a result, there has not been the investment and effort required for processes of adopting and adapting technology for capability-building across related activities in industrial ecosystems. While successful industrializers have managed processes of international integration to build domestic linkages in local clusters of deepening capabilities (Lee, 2019), this has not been the case in South Africa. Notwithstanding small islands of excellence, overall, South Africa has been stuck in a middle-income technology trap with premature deindustrialization (Andreoni and Tregenna, 2020; and Chapter 11). Far-reaching liberalization has meant the economy is highly internationalized in terms of trade, ownership of businesses, and portfolio capital flows. This has translated not into substantial sustained growth in foreign direct investment and exports, but rather a volatile currency with periods of overvaluation in resource booms. Power has remained concentrated in core businesses which are now internationalized. The country has not been able to drive an agenda for structural transformation supported by a broad coalition of interests.

The vicious circles at work in South Africa point to the possible 'traps and gaps' facing middle-income countries, which must be confronted for sustainable structural transformation.

15.3 Obstacles to Acquiring Advanced Industrial Capabilities: Traps and Gaps

The challenges facing the ongoing acquisition of advanced industrial capabilities have changed with the internationalization of business, growth of GVCs, and increased trade in intermediate goods. Intermediate goods accounted for almost half of total world merchandise trade in 2018 (UNCTAD, 2020: 12). There is a number of vicious circles in which middle-income countries can get trapped. There are also gaps in the support required for businesses which need to be filled by targeted policies and institutions for industrial development (such as supporting skills and technology).

15.3.1 The Complexities of Building Local Capabilities and Linking into GVCs for Healthy Industrial Ecosystems

Building the linkages required to keep pace with technological change has become harder for middle-income countries in the context of increased global concentration and changing patterns of the internationalization of business. When domestic industries do not move beyond producing at the relatively less technologically sophisticated levels of GVCs with low, and declining, shares of the overall value added, the economies get stuck in what Andreoni and Tregenna have called the 'middle-income technology trap' (Andreoni and Tregenna, 2020; and Chapter 11).

Countering this dynamic requires coordinated measures to shape the nature of articulation into the global economy—to deliberately build local linkages and thus achieve a measure of independence from the lead firms through stronger local ecosystems. This is at the heart of the challenges of structural transformation (Chapter 1). Participation in GVCs does not lead to upgrading and inclusive development outcomes 'unless increasing shares of value added are created and captured domestically and are fairly distributed among different social groups' (Ponte et al., 2019: 2). The initial integration into GVCs (the initial 'in' phase in Lee et al., 2018) has enabled international markets to be accessed by local producers, as the large firms governing the GVCs have relocated production to lower-cost sites around the world. While this has held the potential for learning-by-doing and upgrading of capabilities through GVC participation, the upgrading has largely not been realized in middle-income countries. There has also been ongoing dependence on the international lead firms. Instead, it has become evident that a partial de-coupling from the GVCs (an 'out' phase) is necessary if domestic production networks are to be built up; this enables the possibility of a subsequent re-integration into the GVCs, on different terms (Lee, 2019; and Chapter 13).

Examples of South Korea, Taiwan, and China demonstrate the value of the 'out' phase of local linkages for the outcomes of international integration in the 1990s and 2000s. Producers in these East Asian economies developed their own design and own brands—requiring local design, R&D, and marketing capabilities. Sadly, in these periods, South Africa, along with many countries in Latin America, failed to diversify and build capabilities. What happened instead was further international integration in the 2000s leading to a hollowing-out of industrial capabilities. This is reflected in the higher foreign value added in gross exports in South Africa and Latin American countries, compared with these East Asian countries (Chapter 13).

The exceptions in specific industries in South Africa and other middle-income countries reinforce these overall insights. For example, in mining machinery and equipment, countries such as Australia and Chile have built local production systems (Chapter 3). In agriculture, South African fresh fruit producers illustrate what can be achieved (Chapter 6). In the automotive industry, Thailand provides an example of strong backward linkages to components producers being built (Chapter 5). These are examples in which linking back from GVCs has seen the substitution of some imports of sophisticated intermediate goods with local production, thus reducing the foreign value added in gross exports.

15.3.2 Technology Traps, Digitalization, and Skills

A set of alternative measures and institutions is required to avoid a trap in which industrial capabilities are persistently undermined. And, the coalitions of interest to support them need to be built and sustained. Sophisticated and diversified industrial ecosystems involve strong horizontal technology linkages fostered by robust support for institutions for R&D, design, testing, and prototyping. Skills development alongside organizational capabilities are also priorities, which have become even more important given the technological changes under way with wide-scale digitalization (Chapter 12).

There has been a lack of coherence between technology and industrial policies in South Africa, as in many other middle-income and developing countries. In South Africa there is also a gap in effective institutions of industrial policy and skills development. The opportunities and challenges of digitalization and other dimensions of the fourth industrial revolution make bridging this gap and the capability shortfalls even more essential. Otherwise, instead of achieving the necessary catching-up, South Africa and other middle-income countries risk being left even further behind.

Digitalization involves both incremental and disruptive changes with transversal technological developments which cut across industries. There are three particular aspects of this that have already impacted on structural transformation in middle-income countries such as South Africa. The first aspect is the deployment of digital technologies to integrate production within and across firms along supply chains, involving a stepwise change in coordination efficiency. Together with the extensive adoption of sensors, this allows for real-time monitoring of product flow and quality. Second, the combination of design software, additive manufacturing, and material science dramatically reduces the time to develop new designs and to customize these to requirements. Third, advanced manufacturing, automation, and robotics are changing production and patterns of comparative advantage.

These links to root capabilities in engineering, electronics, design, and data analysis mean that investment in the appropriate skills and organizational capabilities is essential for countries and firms to benefit from the digital dividend. The cross-cutting nature of these technologies means that it is imperative to have functional institutions that support domestic horizontal linkages. These institutions can intermediate and fill gaps along the entire innovation and production value chains.

Some of this potential has been realized in South Africa, evident in a few islands of success (Chapters 3 and 12). However, the overall lack of coherence, particularly between skills development policy and industrial policy, means that firms have often 'privatized' the necessary training, which implies a bias against smaller firms as well as a reduced portability of skills between firms. There needs to be a national system for adult education and training. The industry studies and firm-level evidence point to a major gap here, notably regarding the performance of the Sector Education and Training Authorities (SETAs). Similarly, rather than contributing to shared facilities and a local ecosystem for product development and testing, successful firms have established their own in-house capabilities or drawn on the remote facilities of foreign parents. Overall, the government's technology and industrial policies have been fragmented and ineffective in ensuring a collective approach to structural transformation. The counter-examples, such as citrus (Chapter 6), reinforce the general picture.

Extensive company and industry-level evidence shows that achieving competitiveness is about understanding value chains and building clusters to address collective challenges in productive capabilities at different levels of the chain. In South Africa there have been very few cluster initiatives in the areas where structural transformation is strongly required. For instance, strategies to build downstream capabilities in the metals, machinery, and equipment industries, where South Africa already has a significant industrial base, have not been effective (Chapter 3). This is because of industrial policies being undermined by the influence of upstream firms (Chapters 8 and 14), the lack of coordination of policy levers across departments, and the inconsistency with macroeconomic policy. Furthermore, coordination with other areas, notably public procurement, has been lacking in design and especially in implementation.

The traps and gaps that have been identified here compound each other, and have transversal effects across firms. Individual decisions taken by a single actor—whether a firm or an institution of the state—can have implications for the competitiveness of entire production systems. As such, it is important that firms are not viewed in isolation, but rather as part of an industrial ecosystem of interdependent activities involving multiple heterogeneous actors which cooperate, compete, and co-evolve to create a web of complementary capabilities that supports innovation and continuous industrial renewal (Moore, 1993; Andreoni 2018).

15.3.3 The Political Economy of Structural Transformation

The ways in which industrial policy interfaces with powerful incumbents and, in turn, the way in which powerful organizations lobby different parts of the state can result in an insidious vicious circle (Amsden, 1989; Andreoni and Chang, 2019). In South Africa, the extreme levels of concentration have been a key challenge for the enforcement of industrial policy as weak reciprocal conditionalities and the lack of policy alignment have resulted in the undermining of policy tools. The consolidation of unproductive rents and powerful positions have then further undermined industrial policy effectiveness (Chapter 14). This includes changes in procurement policies in South Africa in the late 1990s that prioritized narrowly defined value for money, essentially ruling out developmental impacts (Hirsch, 2005). The corporatization of network industries further encouraged under-investment in electricity transmission and the rail network for diversified exports as these all reduced short-term profit margins even while being critical for medium-term structural transformation (Das Nair and Roberts, 2017). At the same time, preferential terms for heavy industry users of energy, rail, and ports had been locked in, reinforcing the existing industrial structure.

Another compounding factor in South Africa has been the process of the fragmentation of the state, notably under the President Zuma administrations in 2009–18, where a proliferation of different departments and agencies following a raft of different policies resulted in overall policy incoherence. This made 'state capture' for rent-seeking easier and undermined the National Industrial Policy Framework (Bhorat et al., 2017; Zalk, 2017). Reversing this fragmentation and breaking the vicious circle to enable a coordinated industrial strategy is one of the key challenges which has faced President Ramaphosa since 2018. It means confronting the power of incumbents as well as rebuilding the state.

The structural transformation required to build diversified capabilities will self-evidently only be promoted and sustained if it is backed by a sufficiently strong group of constituencies. As, by its nature, this transformation will broaden the returns over time, this raises the question about the mobilization of support for the medium-term investments to support such transformation. This support is critical given the concentrations of incumbent power which may see their positions as being under threat.

Transformations are intrinsically related to inequality and power. Countries where strong local linkages have been built and the capabilities challenges have been overcome to support more diverse and sophisticated industrial activities also tend to have relatively more equal income distributions (Palma, 2019a). Conversely, those experiencing premature deindustrialization have had increasing levels of inequality (Baymul and Sen, 2019; Palma, 2019b). However, the extreme inequality of outcomes are themselves unsustainable, as seen in South Africa with the pursuit of rent capture through the state. This grew dramatically as high levels of inequality persisted in the 2000s, along with mass unemployment, even while aggregate levels of growth increased. The economy experienced deindustrialization and a hollowing-out of capabilities with employment growth in low productivity services (Chapters 2 and 11).

The entrenched interests which are inimical to processes of structural transformation can be due to firms occupying quasi-monopoly positions where they are able to continue to extract profits from an inherited market structure with persisting barriers to the entry and growth of smaller rivals (Chapter 8). South Africa is an extreme case—with its high levels of concentration, the role of apartheid in supporting strategic firms and industries, and the legacy of this support (Buthelezi et al., 2019; Vilakazi et al., 2020; and Chapters 3, 4, 8, and 14). These businesses will naturally lobby vigorously to protect their narrow positions, even while some of the costs of a faltering development path will also fall on them. It has become evident that, in the early 1990s, some of the companies at the commanding heights of the South African economy had expected to make far-reaching concessions to support economic transformation. For example, the diversified mining conglomerate Anglo American was independently working out mechanisms for a redistributive tax, while Sasol was implementing a pricing structure designed to support downstream industries (Mondliwa and Roberts, 2019; Michie, 2020). These were not pursued when it became evident that companies would not be held to such measures.

Competition can discipline incumbents, with rivalry between firms further promoting productivity improvements as firms invest in upgrading and improving production capabilities in order to win market share. Competitive rivalry also relates to how easily new market participants can bring products and services to market including, in the South African context, the extent of meaningful participation by challenger black entrepreneurs. Conversely, the exertion of market power can contribute to inequality by facilitating a transfer from the poor to the wealthy in the form of management compensation, profits, and shareholder dividends emanating from anticompetitive conduct (Ennis et al., 2019). The South African experience demonstrates the problems of concentration and barriers to the entry and growth of smaller rivals and the over-reliance on competition law enforcement for making markets work and engaging with entrenched corporate power (Chapters 8, 9, 10, and 14). It should in fact be just one component that is integrated with other policy domains. Competition law enforcement cannot create competition in the face of barriers to entry and, working through legal mechanisms, it tends to be very slow (Roberts, 2020).

Industrial capability-building within and across firms requires a medium- to long-term financial commitment to investments. This is undermined where shareholders are focused on short-term returns and predatory value extraction practices (see Lazonick and Shin, 2020; and Chapter 10). The dramatic growth of financial services in South Africa has not been accompanied by higher levels of productive investment and instead reflects a balance of influence in favour of short-term returns (Chapter 10). This is particularly evident in the reliance on foreign portfolio and direct investment flows in the 2000s, which in turn pushed macroeconomic policy in the direction of high interest rates to continue attracting these footloose inflows. The policy stance was linked to a focus on macroeconomic 'stability' (narrowly understood as low inflation), as the central criterion for securing putative business confidence. The stance amplified the effect of the commodities boom in the 2000s as inflows strengthened the currency, making imports cheap, and fuelling consumption. Following the 2008 global financial crisis, the narrow inflation focus of monetary policy, with higher interest rates as a key tool—and even while the drivers of higher prices were decisions over administered prices—simply led to prolonged austerity and entrenched deindustrialization. A different settlement requires policies that are oriented to investment by, and in, smaller producers, entrepreneurs, and workers. It also needs to promote a variety of corporate forms of ownership, including employee-owned businesses, and mutuals (Michie, 2017).

Although not yet fully evident at the time of writing, the impact of the Covid-19 pandemic has further pointed to the need for a long-term perspective on building local capabilities; this is discussed further at the end of the chapter.

15.4 Towards a New Industrial Strategy

Five important lessons have been identified in the book from the South African experience. While there are aspects that are specific to South Africa, these have broader relevance for middle-income countries.

First, premature deindustrialization needs to be arrested and reversed, including the growth and upgrading of the manufacturing sector.

Second, the technological changes under way with the digitalization of economic activities mean that developing an industrial ecosystem of firms with effective links to public institutions is critical for increasing domestic value addition and strategic integration in international value chains.

Third, inclusive industrialization depends on achieving structural change, dismantling barriers to entry to allow a new system of accumulation to emerge. This is particularly important in South Africa, with its extraordinarily high levels of inequality, but also for middle-income countries more generally.

Fourth, structural transformation depends on a country's political settlement, specifically whether coalitions of interests that support the organization of industries for long-term investment in capabilities hold sway.

Fifth, purposive and coordinated industrial policies, as well as coordination between industrial policy and other relevant policy domains, are central to achieving these goals.

Along with other middle-income countries, South Africa needs an economy that is more dynamic, competitive, and sustainable, where innovation and productivity lead to better jobs with high wages, and where entry is supported as part of ensuring wider participation. For this to happen, there needs to be a new vision for reindustrialization under a political settlement that prioritizes long-term investment in productive capacity and rewards effort and creativity rather than incumbency. Rather than settling for piecemeal initiatives, placing re-industrialization and industrial policies at the centre of the country's development strategy requires a broad rethink.

Key considerations for an industrial strategy approach that is in support of inclusive (re)industrialization and structural transformation are set out below.

15.4.1 Inclusive Industrialization and Confronting Concentration

Manufacturing-driven structural transformation decreases inequality through learning, the creation of higher-earning jobs, and sharing in productivity improvements and linkages across the economy (Baymul and Sen, 2019). Along with high-productivity services in areas such as design and engineering, this is an important component of healthy industrial ecosystems. These should be accompanied by stronger worker protections, a system of lifelong learning and adult education, and equitable earnings in terms of race and gender, reflecting skills and employment opportunities. Such a trajectory is consistent with a diverse range of enterprises, with profits being earned from effort and creativity, and lower levels of concentration of ownership and control.

The negative implications of economic concentration, of which South Africa is an extreme case, are now well recognized (Buthelezi et al., 2019). While competition law enforcement can address the conduct of existing large firms and evaluate mergers between them, it does not create more competition and wider participation in the face of barriers to entry (Vilakazi et al., 2020). A broader competition policy that forms part of industrial policy is required (Mondliwa et al., 2021). In South Africa, the reductions in barriers to the entry and expansion of challenger businesses, especially black entrepreneurs, is a critical consideration. Industrial policy interventions can address vertical integration and be coupled with development finance to enable the investment in capabilities and learning necessary to grow efficient businesses (Chapter 9). Effective regulation for wider participation is an important aspect, especially in sectors where there are strong network effects, such as telecommunications. The analysis of barriers to entry has further highlighted the importance of access to markets for rivals. One example is a possible 'supermarkets code', where retailers commit to open up shelf space to smaller businesses, and engage in supplier development initiatives (Chisoro-Dube and Das Nair, 2020).

Black economic empowerment (BEE) is another important factor in inclusive industrialization in South Africa. BEE was adopted through a combination of policies, regulations, codes, and charters to aim for wide-scale economic inclusion of the historically disadvantaged population in ownership, management, and through skills development initiatives (Hirsch 2005; Bhorat et al., 2014; and Chapter 9). The model did not, however, fundamentally transform the concentration of ownership and control at the core of the economy (Ponte et al., 2007; Mondliwa and Roberts, 2020). Instead, through incentivizing large incumbents to bring influential black shareholders on board it has reinforced the political influence of the large companies and the financial sector (Chapters 9 and 14). While it has brought some racial diversification of the middle class and of management and ownership, and some growth of black-owned supplier firms, it has not fundamentally opened up the economy to wider participation, more effective competition, and investment by a more diverse set of businesses.

A focus on empowering participation will combine breaking down barriers to entry and opening up routes to market, together with more effective land reform, access to finance for wealth creation, and skills development (Vilakazi et al., 2020; and Chapter 9). This would also enable enterprises with diverse ownership models, such as mutuals and employee partnerships, to compete effectively and generate returns for a wider group of stakeholders (Michie, 2017; Michie and Padayachee, 2020). Only by bringing the core components of value creation together to reward effort, investment, and innovation can the economy be opened up, leading to higher levels of overall growth and development, and greater inclusion.

15.4.2 Building a Broad Coalition for Reindustrialization

South Africa's course for reindustrialization and inclusive growth needs to be based on a broad coalition which has an interest in, and which focuses on, productive investment and widening economic participation. The narrow coalition of elites which has largely determined the economic policy agenda has undermined investment and reinforced, rather than changed, the existing structure of economic power. Reindustrialization requires, among other measures, large-scale public investment to provide effective public transport and education for economic activity, alongside long-term private investment and entrepreneurship.

Current levels of poverty and inequality are unsustainable, and the youth are bearing the brunt of the alarmingly high unemployment rates. The creation of jobs and livelihoods is a priority for avoiding further unravelling of the social fabric and needs to be placed at the centre of a new social compact (Chapters 8 and 14). Though the current political settlement in South Africa has accommodated the small black middle class to an extent, the burden of what has been referred to colloquially as the 'black tax' (in which black professionals provide significant financial support to extended family) is just one reminder that things need to change more broadly. Higher earnings for a small minority of the black population is not a sustainable solution.

So what is the new political settlement that can inform the new deal to ensure that it delivers real economic transformation? A new political settlement for industrialization must speak to and mobilize previously excluded key constituencies (Chapter 14). In South Africa these include the industrial working class (represented in industrial trade unions) through effective skills upgrading and investment, productive black entrepreneurs through opening up economic opportunity (Chapter 9), and producers of high-value agricultural crops, as the experience with citrus shows is possible (Chapter 6).

Naturally, no such coalition is fixed over time and the managing of conflicting claims is a central dimension of industrial policy. There would also be points of contestation within such a coalition, such as conflict between industrial workers and capitalists over wages and other issues. Nonetheless, a coalescence of interests and, crucially, interventions, is needed to drive an agenda of reindustrialization and structural change. The settlement must speak to the aspirations of key constituencies, especially in urban areas, where the majority now live and where industrial agglomerations are built.

15.4.3 Incentivizing and Investing in Capabilities Development

The fourth industrial revolution is bringing the role of technology in moving countries forward into sharp focus. The unprecedented pace of the development and adoption of new technologies, and the systemic impact of these technologies, poses both challenges and opportunities for middle-income countries (Andreoni and Roberts, 2020; Andreoni and Tregenna, 2020; Sturgeon, 2021; and Chapters 11 and 12).

Digital technologies, in particular, tend to have a transformative impact on the existing technology platforms. Digitalization can widen the technology gap, or it can provide a bridge for countries to catch up. It means that industrial policy, combined with effective economic regulation, is more important than ever. Industrial economies have historically targeted and shaped the development of new industrial ecosystems by prioritizing certain technologies, as well as emerging sectors and related markets, in an entrepreneurial role for the state (Mazzucato, 2013; and Chapter 12).

While the apartheid government heavily supported innovation and industrial development in organizations related to its own objectives (such as military technologies), post-apartheid governments have had more broad-based innovation strategies. Technology is, however, embodied in investment, and the low level of investment in the economy means poor progress in technological upgrading. A strategy for building capabilities must bring together technology policy, investment, and industry incentives to present a coherent path for firms. It also requires rethinking the skills and training system to provide for lifelong skills development that is appropriate to the challenges of digitalization.

Incentives, technological change, skills development, and development finance therefore all need to work together, along with cluster initiatives at the local level. Cluster initiatives have a key role to play in linking skills development and shared facilities for technological capabilities such as design, testing, and prototyping. They can also support firms to pool resources, creating economies of scale and developing supply markets. Understanding how collective action can be supported for private investment in capabilities by groups of firms is central to building dynamic industrial clusters, together with effective institutions of industrial policy. In the few cases where clusters have been successful, local and provincial governments have played a leading role, given the geographical embeddedness of cluster initiatives—and they can continue to do so.

In order for government incentives and other support measures to have a wider impact on the economy, it is necessary that incentive packages are designed with robust and enforceable conditionalities so that deeper local capabilities are developed. The conditionalities need to ensure that the industrial policies do induce decisions that are consistent with the productive changes required for real transformation and are not another form of extractive rents (Chapter 14). On the contrary, conditionalities should ensure that rents are ploughed back into productive investment in support of expanded production and upgrading.

15.4.4 Understanding and Pursuing Regional Opportunities

The industrial ecosystems perspective proposes that geographical boundaries of ecosystems be defined by the value creation process and the structure and evolution of interdependencies, rather than national borders (Andreoni, 2018). The real boundaries of an ecosystem can therefore be identified by tracking the network of value-creation linkages involving organizations around and beyond national borders. In South Africa's case, this means that some of the ecosystems may span a number of countries in the Southern Africa Development Community (SADC). Industrial strategies of SADC countries would thus be more effective if they considered the interdependencies of organizations operating across borders. For example, regional value chains have been an integral component of Asia's rapid industrialization (Scholvin et al., 2019).

The SADC region has been less successful in developing regional value chains even while an industrialization strategy does exist. Partly this reflects the lack of commitment to a shared regional vision for industrial development across Southern Africa, even with the wider Southern African region being the most important market for many of South Africa's diversified products and services (Arndt and Roberts, 2018; Nkhonjera and Roberts, 2020). However, companies are integrating across the region, such as in the case of supermarkets, agroprocessing, and mining equipment supplies (Das Nair et al., 2018; Fessehaie and Rustomjee, 2018; Bosiu and Vilkazi, 2020). Yet, the regulatory and policy framework remains uncoordinated in practice. Moreover, regional value chains are crucial for resilience and building capabilities, especially in the context of climate change (Ncube, 2018; Paremoer, 2018; Bell et al., 2020).

15.4.5 The Climate Crisis and Environmentally Sustainable Industrialization

The climate crisis has urgent implications for what is manufactured as well as how it is produced. Whereas advanced economies were able to industrialize with little regard to the effects of industrialization on climate change (and should now bear the burden of responsibility), this is now an urgent problem facing all countries and economies. Developing countries need to demonstrate leadership in charting a path for structural transformation and industrialization that is consistent with a green new deal (Pollin, 2020). Given the climate change imperative, structural transformation is even more important for ensuring shifts to more sophisticated activities with scope for cumulative productivity increases at lower levels of CO_2 emissions. The alternative is competition in industries such as basic metals and basic chemicals on the basis of cheap energy and old dirty technologies. South Africa's dependence on these has led to it being one of the highest emitters of CO_2 per capita among middle-income and developing countries, although still behind oil producers and many industrialized nations.[2] More technologically advanced production can increase value added in middle-income countries, at lower levels of emissions (Avenyo and Tregenna, 2021).

South Africa has developed policies on labour standards and environmental sustainability. These have been in line with international moves to incorporate sustainability and labour protections into the various international trade rules and codes adopted by lead firms in GVCs. However, the changes driven by international lead firms have typically related to placing greater requirements on suppliers to meet standards. They have in fact reinforced the governance of value

---

[2] See https://www.wri.org/blog/2020/02/greenhouse-gas-emissions-by-country-sector, accessed 23 October 2020.

chains by lead firms in industrialized markets, placing even greater cost burdens on suppliers in developing countries like South Africa (Ponte, 2019; and Chapter 7). The centrality of industrial policy in the 'green transition' needs to tackle the power dynamic in GVCs, as advocated in this book.

South Africa and other middle-income countries therefore need to urgently shift to an industrialization path that is aligned with a green transition (Altenburg and Rodrik, 2017; Ashman et al., 2020; Montmasson-Claire, 2020; Pollin, 2020). This requires the identification of emerging opportunities, and the building or adapting of firm-level capabilities to take up those opportunities. A just green transition implies taking account of the emissions in consumption, whether locally produced or imported. Including the climate impacts into assessment of production means that re-industrializing countries can more effectively target being competitive exporters of those products where demand will increase, given the urgent changes required around the globe.

15.5 Conclusion: Policy Coordination for Reindustrialization in a Post-Covid World

At the time of writing, South Africa and the rest of the world are in the throes of the Covid-19 pandemic. Even after the medical emergency has passed, the economic consequences of the pandemic and of associated control measures are likely to endure for a long time. Like other countries, South Africa has seen widespread closures or downscaling of firms, and layoffs. The greater underlying economic fragility and the pre-existing crisis of unemployment in the country mean that the economic effects are likely to be especially dire. Part of the temporary rise in unemployment is likely to translate into an upward shift in South Africa's structural unemployment. The recovery initiative would need to address all the structural issues identified, to transform the economy.

The economic impacts of the Covid-19 pandemic have brought widespread recognition once more of the short-termism of markets and a growing consensus on the need for state leadership in the medium- to long-term vision for a more resilient economy and society. Countries with stronger and more diversified local production capacity and technological capabilities have been better placed to confront the challenges posed by Covid-19. Effective government leadership which can respond and mobilize the private sector has also clearly mattered, along with the importance of international collaboration and multilateralism (Jenny, 2020).

National leadership must now mobilize for structural transformation while international cooperation is essential in tackling the implications of climate change. As such, 'building back better' in the wake of Covid-19 will include a shift to a 'green new deal', and realize a more inclusive and equitable development path.

Post-Covid global economic restructuring also has potential opportunities for manufacturers in South Africa and other middle-income and developing countries. The shortening, and reconfiguration, of GVCs provides possible openings for import substitution, as well as the potential for repositioning countries and their businesses in GVCs with a focus on strengthening linkages in regional value chains.

The overarching analysis in this book demonstrates the importance of a holistic approach to structural transformation. It is one that embraces the challenges of building productive capabilities in the time of digitalization and that recognizes value-chain linkages and power relations in industrial ecosystems. In this framework, industrialization is integrated into overall economic planning and is based on an understanding of sectoral dynamics and opportunities, while taking the essential resources of land, water, and energy into account. It must reach and sustain a shared and binding commitment which, through shared growth and investment, will lead to a reversal of the growing inequality in wealth. Experience from other countries shows that successful industrial policy needs to be led politically from the apex of government and that lessons learnt along the way need to be incorporated in an iterative process of continuous improvement of policy design and implementation.

One aspect of this is the need for a planning function, driven from the top of the state, that can marshal institutions and policies in support of priority goals. In South Africa, this sort of planning would go well beyond the role of existing institutions such as the National Planning Commission (NPC) or the Department of Planning, Monitoring, and Evaluation (DPME). In particular, coordination between macroeconomic policy and industrial policy is critical for structural transformation. This includes managing the exchange rate to ensure exports are competitive, as has been a key pillar of the industrial policy of industrializing countries. It means a fiscal policy oriented to funding infrastructure investment and skills.

The vision of an integrated policy agenda towards structural transformation implies a re-shaping of policy functions, and the experimentation of new institutional forms. This may include repurposing government departments, agencies, and other public institutions, as well as development finance, regulatory, and competition institutions. Better coordination and integration of roles is needed around policies that relate to innovation, technology, industry, trade, development finance, and regulating markets—providing for clear leadership and coordination in areas such as skills development and in key sectors such as energy, minerals, and agriculture. This needs to be accompanied by improved institutional capacity and accountability of public institutions. Changes in policies and institutions must drive and be supported by the emergence of a new social contract that places sustainable and inclusive structural transformation at its very core.

References

Altenburg, T. and D. Rodrik (2017). 'Green industrial policy: accelerating structural change towards wealthy green economies.' In T. Altenburg and C. Assmann (eds), *Green Industrial Policy: Concepts, Policies, Country Experiences*, 2–20. Geneva and Bonn: UN Environment; German Development Institute/Deutsches Institut für Entwicklungspolitik (DIE).

Amsden, A. (1989). *Asia's Next Giant: South Korea and Late Industrialization*. New York: Oxford University Press.

Andreoni, A. (2018). 'The architecture and dynamics of industrial ecosystems.' *Cambridge Journal of Economics* 42: 1613–42.

Andreoni, A. and H.-J. Chang (2019). 'The political economy of industrial policy: structural interdependencies, policy alignment and conflict management.' *Structural Change and Economic Dynamics* 48: 136–50.

Andreoni, A. and S. Roberts (2020). 'Governing data and digital platforms in middle income countries: regulations, competition and industrial policies, with sectoral case studies from South Africa.' Oxford Pathways to Prosperity Working Paper. Oxford: Blavatnik School of Government.

Andreoni, A. and F. Tregenna (2020). 'Escaping the middle-income technology trap: a comparative analysis of industrial policies in China, Brazil and South Africa.' *Structural Change and Economic Dynamics* 54: 324–40.

Arndt, C. and S. Roberts (2018). 'Key issues in regional growth and integration in Southern Africa.' *Development Southern Africa* 35(2): 297–314.

Ashman, S., S. Newman, and F. Tregenna (2020). 'Radical perspectives on industrial policy.' In H.-J. Chang, C. Cramer, R. Kozul-Wright, and A. Oqubay (eds), *The Oxford Handbook of Industrial Policy*, 178–204. Oxford: Oxford University Press.

Avenyo, E. and F. Tregenna (2021). 'The effects of technology intensity in manufacturing on CO_2 emissions: evidence from developing countries.' Working Paper 846. Economic Research Southern Africa. Cape Town: ERSA.

Barnes, J., A. Black, and K. Techakanont (2017). 'Industrial policy, multinational strategy, and domestic capability: a comparative analysis of the development of South Africa's and Thailand's automotive industry.' *European Journal of Development Research* 29: 37–53.

Baymul, C. and K. Sen (2019). "Kuznets revisited: what do we know about the relationship between structural transformation and inequality?" *Asian Development Review* 36(1): 136–67.

Bell, J., J. Fleming, S. Roberts, and T. Vilakazi (2020). 'Maize and soybeans markets in the Southern and East African regions: the case for a regional market observatory.' CCRED Working Paper 2/2020. Johannesburg: CCRED.

Bhorat, H., A. Cassim, and A. Hirsch (2014). 'Policy co-ordination and growth traps in a middle-income setting: the case of South Africa.' WIDER Working Paper Series wp-2014-155. World Institute for Development Economic Research. Helsinki: UNU-WIDER.

Bhorat, H., M. Buthelezi, I. Chipkin, S. Duma, L. Mondi, C. Peter, M. Qobo, M. Swilling, and H. Friedenstein (2017). 'Betrayal of the promise: how South Africa is being stolen.' State Capacity Research Project. Stellenbosch: SCRP.

Bosiu, T. and T. Vilakazi (2020). 'Competition and inclusive regional economic growth in food production: barriers to entry and the role of African multinational corporations.' WIDER Working Paper 2020/88. Helsinki: UNU-WIDER.

Buthelezi, T., T. Mtani, and L. Mncube (2019). 'The extent of market concentration in South Africa's product markets.' *Journal of Antitrust Enforcement* 7(3): 352–64.

Chang, H.-J. and A. Andreoni (2020). 'Industrial policy in the 21st century.' *Development and Change* 51(2): 324–51.

Chisoro-Dube, S. and R. Das Nair (2020). 'Confronting entry barriers in South Africa's grocery retail sector.' In T. Vilakazi, S. Goga, and S. Roberts (eds), *Opening the South African Economy: Barriers to Entry, Regulation and Competition*, 57–74. Cape Town: HSRC Press.

Cramer, C. and F. Tregenna (2020). 'Heterodox approaches to industrial policy and the implications for industrial hubs.' In J. Y. Lin and A. Oqubay (eds), *The Oxford Handbook of Industrial Hubs and Economic Development* (pp. 40–63). Oxford: Oxford University Press.

Cramer, C. and J. Sender (2019). 'Oranges are not only fruit: the industrialization of freshness and the quality of growth.' In A. Noman, R. Kanbur, and J. Stiglitz (eds), *The Quality of Growth in Africa*, 209–33. New York: Columbia University Press.

Das Nair, R. and S. Roberts (2017). 'Competition and regulation interface in energy, telecommunications and transport in South Africa.' In J. Klaaren, S. Roberts, and I. Valodia (eds), *Competition Law And Economic Regulation: Addressing Market Power in Southern Africa*, 120–47. Johannesburg: Wits University Press.

Das Nair, R., S. Chisoro, and F. Ziba (2018). 'Supermarkets' procurement strategies and implications for local suppliers in South Africa, Botswana, Zambia and Zimbabwe.' *Development Southern Africa* 35(3): 334–50.

Ennis, S. F., P. Gonzaga, and C. Pike (2019). 'Inequality: a hidden cost of market power.' *Oxford Review of Economic Policy* 35(3): 518–49.

Erten, B., J. Leight, and F. Tregenna (2019). 'Trade liberalization and local labor market adjustment in South Africa.' *Journal of International Economics* 118: 448–67.

Fessehaie, J. and Z. Rustomjee (2018). 'Resource-based industrialisation in Southern Africa: domestic policies, corporate strategies and regional dynamics.' *Development Southern Africa* 35(3): 404–18.

Hirsch, A. (2005). *Season of Hope: Economic Reform under Mandela and Mbeki*. Pietermaritzburg: University of KwaZulu-Natal Press.

Jenny, F. (2020). 'Economic resilience, globalisation and market governance: facing the Covid-19 test.' *CEPR COVID Economics* 1: 64–78.

Khan, M. H. and S. Blankenburg (2009). 'The political economy of industrial policy in Latin America.' In G. Dosi, M. Cimoli, and J. E. Stiglitz, *Industrial Policy and Development: The Political Economy of Capabilities Accumulation*, 337–77. Oxford: Oxford University Press.

Lazonick, W. and J.-S. Shin (2020). *Predatory Value Extraction*. Oxford: Oxford University Press.

Lee, K., M. Szapiro, and Z. Mao (2018). 'From global value chains (GVC) to innovation systems for local value chains and knowledge creation.' *The European Journal of Development Research* 30(3): 424–41.

Lee, K. (2019). *The Art of Economic Catch-Up: Barriers, Detours and Leapfrogging in Innovation Systems*. Cambridge: Cambridge University Press.

Makhaya, G. and S. Roberts (2013). 'Expectations and outcomes – considering competition and corporate power in South Africa under democracy.' *Review of African Political Economy* 138: 556–71.

Mazzucato, M. (2013). *The Entrepreneurial State: Debunking Public vs. Private Sector Myths*. London: Anthem Press.

Michie, J. (2017). 'The importance of ownership.' In J. Michie, J. R. Blasi, and C. Borzaga (eds), *The Oxford Handbook of Mutual, Co-Operative, and Co-Owned Business*. Oxford: Oxford University Press.

Michie, J. (2020). 'Why did the ANC fail to deliver redistribution?' *International Review of Applied Economics* 34(4): 522–7.

Michie, J. and V. Padayachee (2020). 'Alternative forms of ownership and control in the global south.' *International Review of Applied Economics* 34(4): 413–22.

Mondliwa, P. and S. Roberts (2019). 'From a developmental to a regulatory state? Sasol and the conundrum of continued state support.' *International Review of Applied Economics* 33(1): 11–29.

Mondliwa, P. and S. Roberts (2020). 'Black economic empowerment and barriers to entry.' In T. Vilakazi, S. Goga, and S. Roberts (eds), *Opening the South African Economy? Barriers to Entry, Regulation and Competition*, 215–30. Cape Town: HSRC Press.

Mondliwa, P., S. Goga, and S. Roberts (2021). 'Competition, productive capabilities and structural transformation in South Africa.' *European Journal of Development Research* 33: 253–74.

Montmasson-Clair, G. (2020). 'The global climate change regime and its impacts on South Africa's trade and competitiveness: a data note on South Africa's exports.' Trade and Industrial Strategies, Pretoria.

Moore, J. F. (1993). 'Predators and prey: A new ecology of competition.' *Harvard Business Review* 71(3): 75–83.

Ncube, P. (2018). 'The southern African poultry value chain: corporate strategies, investments and agro-industrial policies.' *Development Southern Africa* 35(3): 369–87.

Nkhonjera, M. and S. Roberts (2020). 'Regional integration and industrial development in Southern Africa: Where does South Africa stand?' In D. Bradlow and E. Sidiropolous (eds), *Values, Interests and Power—South African Foreign Policy in Uncertain Times*, 140–59. Pretoria: Pretoria University Law Press.

Padayachee, V. and R. Van Niekerk (2019). *Shadow of Liberation*. Johannesburg: Wits University Press.

Palma, G. (2019a). 'Behind the seven veils of inequality: what if it's all about the struggle within one half of the population over just one half of the national income?' Development and Change Distinguished Lecture. *Development and Change* 50(5): 1133–213.

Palma, G. (2019b). 'The Chilean economy since the return to democracy in 1990: on how to get an emerging economy growing, and then sink slowly into the quicksand of a "middle-income trap".' Cambridge Working Papers in Economics (CWPE) 1991.

Paremoer, T. (2018). 'Regional value chains: exploring linkages and opportunities in the agro-processing sector across five SADC countries.' CCRED Working Paper 2/2018. Johannesburg: CCRED.

Pollin, R. (2020). 'An industrial policy framework to advance a global green new deal.' In J.-J. Chang, C. Cramer, R. Kozul-Wright, and A. Oqubay (eds), *The Oxford Handbook of Industrial Policy*, 394–428. Oxford: Oxford University Press.

Ponte, S. (2019). *Business, Power and Sustainability in a World of Global Value Chains*. London: Zed Press.

Ponte, S., S. Roberts., and L. Van Sittert (2007). '"Black economic empowerment": business and the state in South Africa.' *Development and Change* 38(5): 933–55.

Ponte, S., G. Gereffi, and G. Raj-Reichert (2019). 'Introduction.' In S. Ponte, G. Gereffi, and G. Raj-Reichert (eds), *Handbook on Global Value Chains*, 1–27. Cheltenham: Edward Elgar.

Roberts, S. (2000). 'Understanding the effects of trade policy reform: the case of South Africa.' *South African Journal of Economics* 68(4): 607–38.

Roberts, S. (2020). 'Assessing the record on competition law enforcement for opening-up the economy.' In T. Vilakazi, S. Goga, and S. Roberts (eds), *Opening the South African Economy? Barriers to Entry, Regulation and Competition*, 179–98. Cape Town: HSRC Press.

Scholvin, S., A. Black, J. Revilla Diez, and I. Turok (2019). *Value Chains in Sub-Saharan Africa*. Switzerland: Springer Nature.

Sturgeon, T. (2021). 'Upgrading strategies for the digital economy.' *Global Strategy Journal* 11(1): 34–57, published online 7 November 2019, DOI:10.1002/gsj.1364.

Tregenna, F. (2010). 'How significant is the intersectoral outsourcing of employment in South Africa?' *Industrial and Corporate Change* 19(5): 1427–57.

UNCTAD (2020). 'Key statistics and trends in international trade 2019.' Geneva: United Nations.

Vilakazi, T., S. Goga, and S. Roberts, eds (2020). *Opening the South African Economy? Barriers to Entry, Regulation and Competition*. Cape Town: HSRC Press.

Zalk, N. (2017). 'The things we lost in the fire: the political economy of post-apartheid restructuring of the South African steel and engineering sectors.' Unpublished PhD thesis, Department of Economics, School of Oriental and African Studies, University of London.

Index

Note: Tables, figures, and boxes are indicated by an italic *t*, *f*, and *b* following the page number.

3-D printing 266, 281

AARD 69
AB Inbev 320n6
Accelerated and Shared Growth Initiative of
    South Africa (ASGI-SA) 327
accountability 71, 356
Acer 290
Acerinox 56
acquisitions *see* mergers and acquisitions
additive manufacturing 266, 269, 271, 279,
    281, 345
Advanced Manufacturing and Technology
    Strategy 58, 327
affirmative action 191, 192
African Explosives and Chemical Industries
    (AECI) 40, 173
African National Congress (ANC)
    historical perspective on structural
        transformation 38, 41, 42
    Macroeconomic Research Group
        (MERG) 324
    political economy 312
    political settlement and economic
        policy 322, 327–8
agriculture sector
    capabilities development, obstacles to 344
    deregulation 322
    digitalization 263, 269, 271
    emerging perspectives on structural
        transformation 3–4
    fruit *see* fruit sector
    historical perspective on structural
        transformation 30, 34, 37, 45
    inequality and structural transformation 167
    'in-out-in' industrialization 294, 298
    and manufacturing sector, blurring of
        boundaries between 123, 124
    new industrial strategy 352
    post-Covid-19 world 356
    structural transformation 123–5
agroprocessing sector 199–200
aluminium sector 35, 55–6, 57, 325
Anglo 35, 36, 40, 41

Anglo American 56, 59, 173, 320n6, 348
Angola 60*f*, 61
apartheid era
    agricultural boards 342
    automotive sector 100
    chemical sector 171
    conglomerates 320n6
    economic stagnation 237
    end of 322–4
    food and beverages sector 316
    industrial development 109, 352
    industrial policy 172, 181
    innovation 352
    legacy 5, 109
    manufacturing sector 38, 40
    metals, machinery, and mining equipment
        sectors 53, 171
    petrochemical sector 178
    prosperous industries 331
    Sasol 93
    strategic industries 337, 348
    wine sector 153
Apple Inc. 218n2
ArcelorMittal 173, 176, 177, 320, 341
ArcelorMittal South Africa (AMSA) 35, 56,
    62–4, 173–7, 182–3, 320n8, 329
    see also Iscor
Argentina 126*f*, 148, 239
Asian financial crisis 40
asset prices, and financialization 224
asset stripping 59
Atlantis Foundries 271
Australia
    Enhanced Project By-Law Scheme
        (EPBS) 72
    fruit sector 131
    machinery and equipment sector 71, 72, 344
    wine sector 148, 149, 157
automotive components sector
    development 103–4, 105
    exports 12, 14, 114*t*
    insights from 342
    localization and transformation prospects in
        supply chain 114, 117

automotive components sector (*cont.*)
   ownership changes and supply-chain
      development 112–13
   and plastic products sector 79, 81, 84–91, 96–7
   scale of production and structural
      change 107–9
   value added 36
Automotive Incubation Centres 117
Automotive Industry Development Centre
   (AIDC), Gauteng 117
Automotive Investment Scheme (AIS) 105
Automotive Production and Development
   Programme (APDP, 2013–20) 8, 43, 90,
   100, 105–7, 112, 342
automotive sector 100–1, 117
   autonomous vehicles 270, 272
   capabilities development, obstacles to 344
   development 103–6
   digitalization 269, 270, 272
   employment 10, 316
   exports *see* exports: automotive sector
   global value-chain integration 304, 306–7
   historical perspective on structural
      transformation 36, 39, 42, 43, 45
   imports 9
   inequality and structural transformation 172
   insights from 342
   international context 101–3
   localization and transformation prospects in
      supply chain 114–17
   and metals sector, linkages between 56
   ownership changes and supply-chain
      development 111–14
   policy, incentives, and state–business
      bargaining 109–11
   political economy of structural
      transformation 315, 316, 317
   political settlement and economic
      policy 325, 329
   production profile 106*t*, 106
   scale of production and structural
      change 106–9
   telemetry 272
   value added 8, 36, 106, 110, 112, 113*f*, 316
   see also automotive components sector
Automotive Supply Chain Competitiveness
   Initiative (ASCCI) 115, 116
autonomous vehicles 270, 272

bandwidth improvements 278
banking sector
   corporate governance 225
   financialization 216, 218, 221, 224
basic chemicals sector *see* chemicals sector

basic metals sector *see* metals sector
Bell Equipment 69, 270
BerryWorld 131
beverages sector 36, 315, 316–17
Bevon 40
big data 264, 271
biotechnology 130–2
Black Business Council 194, 198
black economic empowerment (BEE) 145,
   189–90, 206–7
   automotive sector 115–16
   black industrialists scheme 200–6
   broad-based *see* broad-based black economic
      empowerment
   capabilities development, obstacles to 348
   economic power and inequality 176, 181n15
   evolution and challenges 192–200
   fruit sector 122
   historical perspective on structural
      transformation 38–44
   importance for structural
      transformation 190–2
   metals, machinery, and mining equipment
      sectors 59, 65, 66, 70
   middle-income economies comparison 5
   new industrial strategy 350, 351
   political economy of structural
      transformation 331
   political settlement and economic
      policy 322, 326
   Preferential Procurement Policy
      Framework Act 65
   steel sector 176
   wine sector 152
Black Economic Empowerment
   Commission 194, 195, 197–8, 326
black industrialists scheme (BIS) 44, 189–90,
   200–7, 329
blockchain 273
Boart Longyear 36
Bombardier Transportation South Africa 65–6
Botswana 60, 60*f*
Brazil
   agricultural sector 124
   automotive sector 101, 102, 115
   fruit sector 126*f*
   GDP trends 240–2, 241*f*
   global value-chain integration 289
   middle-income technology trap 245*t*, 245
   middle-income trap 238, 239, 240–2,
      254*t*, 256
   premature deindustrialization 251, 251*t*
   South Africa's structural transformation
      compared to 6*t*, 7

broadband penetration 137
broad-based black economic empowerment
    (BBBEE) 206, 207
    automotive sector 116
    black industrialists scheme 202, 203
    Codes of Good Practice 196
    evolution and challenges 195–8
Broad-Based Black Economic Empowerment
    Act 44, 195
Broad-Based Black Economic Empowerment
    Amendment Act 193n1, 196
Broad-Based Black Economic Empowerment
    Commission 196
Broad-Based Black Socio-Economic
    Empowerment Charter for the South
    African Mining and Minerals Industry
    (Mining Charter) 43–4, 70, 73
Business Assistance Agreement (BAA) 176

Canada 226
capabilities development 337
    agricultural sector 123–4
    automotive sector 106, 115, 117
    black economic empowerment 199, 204,
        206, 207
    digitalization 262, 273–7, 283
    emerging perspectives on structural
        transformation 5
    financialization 215, 223
    fruit sector 139, 342
    global value-chain integration 292
    holistic framework for structural
        transformation 16–18
    industrial ecosystems approach 338, 340
    inequality and structural transformation 171
    'in-out-in' industrialization 292
    manufacturing sector insights 341–3
    metals sector 61, 67–8, 71, 72, 74–5
    middle-income technology trap 244f, 244
    middle-income trap 254t, 256
    mining machinery and equipment sector 61,
        67–8, 71, 72, 74–5, 330
    new industrial strategy 350, 351, 352–3, 354
    obstacles to 343–9
    plastic products sector 79, 86–8, 90, 96
    political economy of structural
        transformation 315, 316, 317, 330
    political settlement and economic
        policy 324, 329
    post-Covid-19 world 356
    rivalry, importance of 190
    steel sector 177
    structural transformation through forward
        and backward linkages 80–1

wine sector 155–6
    see also education and training; learning
        processes
capital-account liberalization 40, 221, 319, 323
capital flight 40
carbon dioxide emissions 18, 354–5
car sector see automotive sector
cartels 62–3, 176
casualization of labour 39
Caterpillar 69
cell-phone connectivity 137
Centre for Competition, Regulation, and
        Economic Development (CCRED) 122
chemicals sector
    climate crisis 354
    economic power and inequality 166,
        172–4, 177–83
    exports 81, 166, 338
    financialization 219
    global value-chain integration 304
    historical perspective on structural
        transformation 35
    imports 9
    industrial policy 92, 96
    insights from 341
    investment 14
    Lall classification 13
    performance 82t, 83–4
    political economy of structural
        transformation 315, 316
    political settlement and economic policy 325
    state 63
    structural change dynamics 81–5
    value added 7, 9, 81, 341n1
Chile
    agricultural sector 124
    fruit sector 122, 125–7, 126f, 127f, 128f, 138
    high-income status 239
    machinery and equipment sector 71, 72, 344
    natural resources 306
    wine sector 148
China
    automotive sector 102
    commodities boom 325
    exports to South African black
        industrialists 205
    fruit imports 128–9
    GDP trends 240–2, 241f
    geopolitical tensions 304
    global value-chain integration 291, 304,
        306, 307
    'in-out-in' industrialization 298, 299–301,
        300f, 301t, 344
    late industrialization and poverty reduction 2

China (*cont.*)
  machinery and equipment sector 57, 69, 306
  middle-income technology trap 245*t*,
    245, 246
  middle-income trap 238, 240–2, 254*t*, 256
  plastic products moulding machinery 87
  premature deindustrialization 251, 251*t*
  Sasol 226
  South Africa's structural transformation
    compared to 7
  steel sector 176
  wine sector 149
China North Rail Rolling Stock South Africa
    (Pty) Ltd (CNR) 65–6
China South Rail Zhuzhou Electric Locomotive
    Company (CSR) 65–6
circular economy 143
Citrus Academy 342
Citrus Growers' Association (CGA) 133, 342
Citrus Research International (CRI) 133
clientelism 165, 328, 330, 332
climate change 337
  automotive sector 306
  emerging perspectives on structural
    transformation 4
  fruit sector 121, 130, 132, 133, 137, 138
  green capital accumulation 143
  holistic framework for structural
    transformation 18
  new industrial strategy 354–5
  wine sector 158
Clothing and Textile Competitiveness
    Programme (CTCP) 43
clothing, textiles, and footwear sector
  digitalization 271, 272–4
  global value-chain integration 289
  historical perspective on structural
    transformation 39, 42, 43, 45
  political settlement and economic policy 325
cloud computing 267–8
clusters 80–1, 341
  capabilities development, obstacles to 346
  'in-out-in' industrialization 293
  manufacturing sector insights 343
  new industrial strategy 353
  plastic products sector 85–6, 88, 89, 92, 96
  political settlement and economic policy 329
coal sector 94
coke sector 9, 14, 35, 82*t*, 84, 84n1
cold storage 34, 135, 139, 270–1
commodities boom 8, 13, 325, 327, 339, 349
  machinery and equipment sector 74
  steel sector 57
commodity price volatility 319
competition

automotive sector
  development 103, 104, 105, 106
  international context 102
  localization and transformation prospects
    in supply chain 115
  ownership changes and supply-chain
    development 112
  policy, incentives, and state–business
    bargaining 109, 110
  scale of production and structural
    change 107
black economic empowerment 202, 204, 205,
    206, 207
capabilities development, obstacles to 346, 348
chemicals sector 83–4, 179
digitalization 269, 270, 281, 283
economic power and inequality 179, 181
financialization 219, 221, 227
fruit sector 122
global value-chain integration 289–90,
    300, 305
importance for structural
    transformation 190–1
'in-out-in' industrialization 300
law *see* Competition Act; competition law
metals, machinery, and mining equipment
    sectors 57–9, 60, 62–3, 64, 69, 74
new industrial strategy 350, 351
New Institutional Economics 314
plastic products sector 86–8, 91, 95–6, 341
policy 20, 199, 201, 227
political economy of structural
    transformation 312, 316, 331
political settlements 323–4, 327
premature deindustrialization 247, 257
Competition Act 63, 179, 199, 281, 323–4
competition law 338
  black economic empowerment 199, 207
  capabilities development, obstacles to 348
  chemicals-to-plastics sector 179
  digitalization 281
  economic power and inequality 179,
    181, 183–4
  internationalization of key industries 171,
    173, 177
  historical perspective on structural
    transformation 39, 40
  middle-income economies comparison 5
  new industrial strategy 350
  steel sector 62–3, 177
  see also Competition Act
Competitive Supplier Development Programme
    (CSDP) 65
completely knocked down (CKD) assembly,
    automotive sector 107–8, 108*t*

Congress of South African Trade Unions
    (COSATU) 327, 328, 328n11
Constable, David 229
construction sector 263, 269
Convention for a Democratic South Africa
    (CODESA) 323
corporate social responsibility 94
corruption
    Gupta family 328n12
    historical perspective on structural
        transformation 33, 44, 45, 46
    New Institutional Economics 314
    Transnet 65–6, 328n10
    Zuma administration 44, 328n12, 329, 330
Costco 131
Council for Scientific and Industrial Research
    (CSIR) 88, 279
Covid-19
    capabilities development, obstacles to 349
    economic and social implications 337
    exchange rate and bond yield
        movements 224n6
    fruit sector 120, 135
    global value chains 304–7
    port system 135
    reindustrialization 355–6
    sustainability and resilience issues 143
credit default swaps (CDS) 215
current account 40, 224, 230
cyber-physical products 271

deindustrialization 338
    capabilities development, obstacles to 349
    financialization 220
    heterogeneity across manufacturing
        sub-sectors 17
    historical perspective on structural
        transformation 38, 41, 43, 44, 45
    inequality and structural
        transformation 167, 171
    international trends 248–51, 250f
    'inverted-U' pattern 247–8
    middle-income technology trap 246
    middle-income trap 257
    political settlement and economic
        policy 325, 327
    premature see premature deindustrialization
    reversal see reindustrialization
    structural dynamics 247
    trajectories 167
Democratic Republic of the Congo
    (DRC) 60f
Department of Agriculture 34
Department of Agriculture, Land Reform, and
    Rural Development 121, 133, 138

Department of Economic Development and
    Tourism 136
Department of Planning, Monitoring, and
    Evaluation (DPME) 356
Department of Public Enterprises 65
Department of Science and Technology 133
Department of Trade, Industry, and
    Competition (DTIC)
    black economic empowerment 195,
        201–6, 329
    economic power and inequality 180
    fruit sector 122
    historical perspective on structural
        transformation 43
    metals, machinery, and mining equipment
        sectors 58
    National Industrial Policy Framework 327
    plastic products sector 92–3
    Preferential Procurement Policy
        Framework Act 65
Department of Water and Sanitation 132, 136, 137
dependency theory 4
derivatives 215
'developmental state' nomenclature 42
development finance institutions (DFIs) 199,
    202, 203, 206
development policy 280
digitalization 21, 261–2, 282–3, 337
    business models 267–8
    capabilities and digital skills 262, 273–7,
        283, 345
    emerging perspectives on structural
        transformation 3, 4
    fruit sector 130, 134–5
    global value chains 268
    historical perspective on structural
        transformation 37
    holistic framework for structural
        transformation 17–18
    industrial ecosystems approach 340, 349
    industrial policy 277–83, 282f
    infrastructure 274, 276, 277, 278
    manufacturing sector insights 341
    metals, machinery, and mining equipment
        sectors 67–8, 74
    new industrial strategy 352–3
    opportunities and challenges 268–74
    policy and governance framework
        277–82
    post-Covid-19 world 356
    transversal technologies 262–6
    see also fourth industrial revolution;
        information and communication
        technology
distribution sector 219

dividends
  capabilities development, obstacles to 348
  financialization 213, 217, 220, 228, 232
    signs of 222, 223f, 225
  historical perspective on structural
    transformation 41
  political economy of structural
    transformation 332
domestic value added see value added
Dorbyl 36, 59
Durban Automotive Cluster (DAC) 88, 117
Duty Credit Certificate Scheme (DCCS) 39

Economic Development Department (EDD) 43
economic policy
  financialization 232
  historical perspective on structural
    transformation 38
  industrial development 322–30
  political settlements 320
  see also black economic empowerment
economic power
  inequality and structural
    transformation 165–70, 173–84
  New Institutional Economics 314
  political economy of structural
    transformation 331
  political settlements 173–80, 314, 320–1
Ecuador 126f
education and training
  automotive sector 116
  black economic empowerment 196
  digital skills 276, 278–9
  historical perspective on structural
    transformation 37
  inequality and structural transformation 168
  metals, machinery, and mining equipment
    sectors 71, 74–5
  new industrial strategy 350, 351, 353
  see also capabilities development; learning
    processes
Egypt 102
electricity
  automotive sector 115
  capabilities development, obstacles to 347
  digitalization 275
  economic power and inequality 173
  historical perspective on structural
    transformation 33, 39, 41, 44
electronic data interchange (EDI) systems 135
employment 338
  automotive sector 10, 316
  black economic empowerment 201, 202,
    205, 207
  capabilities development, obstacles to 348

chemicals and plastic products sector 81
  digitalization 261, 269, 273–4, 283
  economic power and inequality 167–8, 180–3
    internationalization of key industries 171,
      172, 176
  financialization 215, 227
  fruit sector 125, 131, 138
  historical perspective on structural
    transformation 34, 42
  manufacturing sector 9–10, 11t, 237. 341
  metals, machinery, and mining equipment
    sectors 53, 54, 57, 60, 64
  middle-income technology trap 246
  new industrial strategy 350, 351
  plastic products sector 81, 83, 90
  political settlement and economic policy 327
  premature deindustrialization 247–52, 249f,
    251t, 257
  service sector 10, 12t
  Shoprite 227
  steel sector 176
enclave effects 287
energy policy 178
energy sector
  climate crisis 354
  financialization 219, 221–2, 222f, 223f
  inequality and structural transformation 172
  political economy of structural
    transformation 331
  political settlement and economic
    policy 328
  post-Covid-19 world 356
engineering, procurement, and construction
    management (EPCM) 67, 69
engineering sector 39, 136, 139
enterprise resource planning (ERP) 265b, 280
environmental sustainability 1, 21, 337
  Covid-19 pandemic 143
  emerging perspectives on structural
    transformation 5
  green capitalism 144
  holistic framework for structural
    transformation 18–19
  new industrial strategy 354–5
  wine sector 148–9, 152–3, 156–8
Epiroc 69
Eskom 33, 44
Ethiopia 290
European Union 127, 281, 304
Evraz 35, 56
exchange rate
  historical perspective on structural
    transformation 36
  metals, machinery, and mining equipment
    sectors 59, 59f

political economy of structural
    transformation 317
risk 213, 220, 224, 230
exports
    automotive sector 9, 10, 12, 100, 117, 338
        development 103–6
        international context 101
        ownership changes and supply-chain
            development 112–13
        policy, incentives, and state–business
            bargaining 110
        scale of production and structural
            change 106–7, 108
    chemicals sector 81, 166, 338
    economic power and inequality 166, 172, 181
    failure to diversify 14–15, 14*f*
    fruit sector 120–3, 138–9, 342
        agricultural structural transformation 123–5
        constraints on structural
            transformation 135–8
        international comparison 125–7, 126*f*,
            127*f*, 128*f*
        performance 125–9
        political economy of structural
            transformation 317
        research and technology leverage 130–5
    global value-chain integration 291, 292, 299,
        300, 304, 305
    historical perspective on structural
        transformation 29, 37, 38–9, 42
    'in-out-in' industrialization 292, 299, 300
    and learning processes 338
    machinery and equipment sector 59–61, 63,
        64, 69, 74
    manufacturing sector 11*t*, 39, 343
        failure to diversify 9, 10–12, 13*f*
    metals sector 59–61, 63, 64, 69, 74, 166, 338
    middle-income economies comparison 7
    middle-income technology trap 242, 243*f*,
        243, 245
    middle-income trap 240
    minerals sector 330
    plastic products sector 81, 84, 85, 88, 90, 95
    political economy 312, 317, 318*f*, 318–19
    post-Covid-19 world 356
    premature deindustrialization 257
    service sector 10

fabricated metal products sector 53
    industrial policies, power, and
        governance 61–2
    missed opportunities for structural
        transformation 54, 56, 59–60
    performance 58*t*
    trade balance 59–60

Fairtrade wine 152, 157
fashion retail sector 271
financialization 213–14, 231–3
    capabilities development, obstacles
        to 348–9
    comparative case study analysis 226–31
    importance 214–21
    micro-level perspective 217–21
    signs of 221–5
    subordinate 217–21, 224, 230–2
    theoretical perspectives 215–17
financial services sector 16
    black economic empowerment 193,
        197, 198–9
    growth 222
    political economy 312
    value added 338
Finland 71–2
fiscal policy 43, 45, 46
flower sector 290
food and beverages sector 36, 273, 315, 316–17
food processing sector 269, 271
footwear sector *see* clothing, textiles, and
    footwear sector
Ford Motors 101, 117, 298
foreign direct investment (FDI)
    automotive sector 101, 110
    global value-chain integration 304–5
    historical perspective on structural
        transformation 40
    'in-out-in' industrialization 292, 296–8, 300
    manufacturing sector insights 343
    plastic automotive components
        sector 88, 89–90
    political economy of structural
        transformation 319*f*
foreign value added *see* value added
Fosters 149
foundries sector 56, 57
fourth industrial revolution (4IR) 1, 261
    capabilities development 274–5, 345
    holistic framework for structural
        transformation 18
    metals, machinery, and mining equipment
        sectors 53
    middle-income technology trap 244
    new industrial strategy 352
    plastic automotive components sector 86, 87
    premature deindustrialization 257
    see also digitalization; information and
        communication technology
Foxconn International Holdings
    (FIH) 218n2
France 148–9, 152, 225
Fresh Produce Exporters Forum 133

fruit sector 120–3, 138–9
  agricultural structural transformation 123–5
  capabilities development, obstacles
      to 344, 346
  constraints on structural transformation 135–8
  digitalization 273
  export markets 127–9, 129f, 338
  global value-chain integration 290
  historical perspective on structural
      transformation 37
  insights from 342
  new industrial strategy 352
  performance 125–9
  political economy of structural
      transformation 315, 316, 317
  research and technology leverage 130–5
full manufacturing stage, automotive
      sector 108t, 108–9
furniture sector 289

Gamtoos Irrigation Board 136–7
General Agreement on Tariffs and Trade
      (GATT) 103
General Electric South Africa Technologies 65–6
General Export Incentive Scheme 92
General Motors 101
Germany 149, 157
Global Engineering Capability Index 136
global financial crisis 339
  capabilities development, obstacles to 349
  financialization 215, 222
  historical perspective on structural
      transformation 35, 43
  metals, machinery, and mining equipment
      sectors 57, 60
  political settlement and economic policy 329
  steel sector 175
  wine sector 149
globalization 216, 293
global value chains (GVCs) 1
  automotive sector 117
  capabilities development, obstacles to 343–5
  digitalization 268, 272, 273, 277
  emerging perspectives on structural
      transformation 3, 4
  environmental sustainability 354–5
  financialization 216, 218, 219, 226
  fruit sector 124–5, 130, 138
  governance 80
  green capitalism 143–4
  integration 286–9, 337
    challenges for upgrading 289–92
    global patterns of sectoral value
        addition 301–4

'in-out-in' industrialization 292–300
  rethinking 304–7
machinery and equipment sector 69
middle-income technology trap 242–4
middle-income trap 254t
plastic automotive components sector 85,
      86, 96–7
post-Covid-19 world 356
power dynamics 19–20
premature deindustrialization 246–7, 257
'smile' curve 19, 290
sustainability and capital accumulation 145–7
wine sector 147–58
Government of National Unity 322–5
grading equipment, fruit sector 134
Greece 239
green capital accumulation 143–4, 147–58
green industrialization 18
green transition 354–5
gross fixed capital formation (GFCF)
  agricultural sector 34
  historical perspective on structural
      transformation 33–4, 35
  manufacturing sector 11t, 34, 35
Growth, Employment, and Redistribution
      (GEAR) policy 38–9, 327
Gupta family 177, 328, 332

Haygrove 131
heavy industries
  historical perspective on structural
      transformation 36–7, 39, 40, 44
  internationalization 172
  see also Sasol
Highveld Steel and Vanadium 56, 173, 174
holding power 170, 315, 322, 324, 331
Hong Kong 129, 213, 225
horticulture sector 37
Hungary 239, 296–8
Hyundai Motors 298

Imperial Crown Trading (ICT) 176–7
import–export complementation 103, 112
imports
  automotive sector 9, 100
    development 103–6
    international context 101
    ownership changes and supply-chain
        development 112–13
    scale of production and structural
        change 109
  capabilities development, obstacles to 349
  chemicals sector 9
  economic power and inequality 172, 181

global value-chain integration 291–2, 295, 300
  historical perspective on structural transformation 37, 38
  'in-out-in' industrialization 295, 300
  machinery and equipment sector 56, 57, 59–61, 60f, 70, 74
  manufacturing sector 9, 11t
  metals sector 9, 56, 57, 59–61, 60f, 70, 74
  plastic products sector 84, 90, 95
  political economy of structural transformation 317–18, 318f
  political settlement and economic policy 323, 325, 327
  post-Covid-19 world 356
  see also tariffs
inclusiveness 1
  economic power and inequality 184
  emerging perspectives on structural transformation 5
  importance for structural transformation 190–2
  industrialization 349, 350–1
  see also black economic empowerment
Income Tax Act 61n2
India 69, 102, 205, 226, 281
indigenization policies 191
Industrial Development Corporation (IDC)
  black industrialists scheme 202, 329
  digitalization 280
  Global Player Fund 61n2
  historical perspective on structural transformation 39, 42, 43
  investment support programmes 61n2
  Iscor 62
  plastic products sector 92
  Scaw Metals acquired by 56
Industrial Development Think Tank (IDTT) 122
industrial ecosystems 339–40
  capabilities development, obstacles to 338, 343–5, 346
  digitalization 277
  global value-chain integration 291n2
  inclusive industrialization 350
  investment 337
  new industrial strategy 349, 353
  post-Covid-19 world 356
industrial internet of things (IIoT) 264
industrialization 1–2
  agricultural sector 124
  apartheid era 38
  automotive sector 101, 110
  climate crisis 354–5
  digitalization 261

financialization 215, 220
  of freshness 121, 124, 130, 317, 342
  fruit sector 139
  future 304–7
  global value-chain integration 288, 291
  importance 21, 257–8
  inclusive 349, 350–1
  inequality and structural transformation 167, 171
  'in-out-in' 287, 292–301, 307, 344
  'inverted-U' pattern 247–8
  middle-income trap 257
  political economy of structural transformation 330
  political settlement and economic policy 328
  profits reinvestment 214
  Southern Africa Development Community 354
  structural dynamics 247
  'thin' 268, 287
  trajectories 167
industrial policy 337–9
  automotive sector 79, 102, 104–6, 115, 316
  black economic empowerment 191, 199, 201, 205, 207
  capabilities development, obstacles to 343–9
  digitalization 277–83, 282f
  economic power and inequality 176, 181, 183
  emerging perspectives on structural transformation 4, 5
  evolution 323, 327, 328, 329
  financialization 220, 221, 223, 227
  global value-chain integration 305, 306
  green 18
  historical perspective on structural transformation 39, 42–6
  holistic framework for structural transformation 18, 20, 21
  key role 21
  manufacturing sector
    failure to diversify 12, 13
    insights 340–3
  metals, machinery, and mining equipment sectors 58, 62–3, 66, 73–5
  middle-income economies comparison 5
  middle-income trap 252–6, 254t, 257–8
  new strategy 349–55
  open economy 9
  plastic products sector 84, 89–93, 96–7
  political economy of structural transformation 320–1, 331
  post-Covid-19 world 355–6
  premature deindustrialization 238
  structural transformation through forward and backward linkages 81

Industrial Policy Action Plans (IPAPs) 5, 42, 91, 202, 205
Industrial Strategic Project (ISP) 323
inequality 15
  barriers to entry and market power 191
  black economic empowerment 193
  capabilities development, obstacles to 347–8
  digitalization 262
  financialization 221
  historical perspective on structural transformation 41
  inclusive industrialization 349, 350
  new industrial strategy 351
  New Institutional Economics 314
  political economy 312, 332
  political settlement and economic policy 327, 329
  post-Covid-19 world 356
  and structural transformation 165–8, 180–4
    internationalization of key industries 170–3
    political settlements 173–80
information and communication technology (ICT)
  agricultural exports 124
  fruit sector 121, 137, 139
  'in-out-in' industrialization 299
  metals, machinery, and mining equipment sectors 53
  value added 338
  see also digitalization
innovation
  agricultural sector 124
  capabilities development, obstacles to 345, 346
  digitalization 261, 262, 267–8, 271, 272–3
  financial resources 214–15
  fruit sector 122, 130, 133, 134–5
  global value-chain integration 293, 306
  green capital accumulation 143
  inequality and structural transformation 168
  'in-out-in' industrialization 293
  middle-income technology trap 244
  middle-income trap 254t, 256
  mining machinery and equipment sector 73
  new industrial strategy 350, 351
  non-financial corporations 214
  open 267
  plastic products sector 86, 88, 95
  post-Covid-19 world 356
  premature deindustrialization 247
  wine sector 155, 157
  see also research and development

'in-out-in' industrialization 287, 292–301, 307, 344
Institute for International Finance 225
institutional economics 4
institutional investors 220, 224, 230
Integrated Manufacturing Strategy 58, 327
Integrated Production of Wine (IPW) scheme 156
intellectual property rights (IPRs)
  fruit sector 131, 132, 138
  'in-out-in' industrialization 298
interest rate risk 213, 220, 224
internationalization
  capabilities development, obstacles to 343, 344
  financialization 224, 232
  historical perspective on structural transformation 40
  inequality and structural transformation 170–3, 181
  'in-out-in' industrialization 292–3, 298
  manufacturing sector insights 340, 343
  political economy of structural transformation 317–18, 330, 332
internet connectivity 137, 139
internet of things (IoT) 264, 271, 274
  automotive telemetry 272
  fruit sector 130
  Thai plastic automotive components sector 86
internships 279
investment
  automotive sector 100, 101, 103, 105, 107, 110, 111
  black economic empowerment 194, 200, 205, 206, 207
  Black Economic Empowerment Commission 326
  capabilities development, obstacles to 347, 348–9
  digitalization 270, 280
  economic power and inequality 182, 184
  fruit sector 121, 122, 130, 131, 342
  historical perspective on structural transformation 29, 30–5, 37, 38, 41–5
  industrial ecosystems 337
  'in-out-in' industrialization 294
  manufacturing sector
    failure to diversify 13–14
    insights 343
  metals, machinery, and mining equipment sectors 56, 57, 58, 63, 66
  middle-income economies comparison 7

middle-income technology trap 246
new industrial strategy 350, 351, 353
plastic products sector 83, 92, 95
political economy of structural
    transformation 312, 330, 332
political settlement and economic policy 313,
    324–5, 328, 329, 330
post-Covid-19 world 356
profitability without *see* financialization
state support programmes 61
steel sector 182
structural regression 317
water infrastructure 136, 137
wine sector 149, 158
see also foreign direct investment
iron sector 9, 35, 57, 58*t*, 59
irrigation 132–3, 137
Iscor 35, 56, 62, 172, 173, 176, 320
    see also ArcelorMittal South Africa
Isle of Man 230
Isuzu 109n6
Italy 148–9, 152, 291n2

Japan
    mining equipment sector 306
    and Thai plastic automotive components
        sector 87, 88, 89, 90, 96
job losses
    automotive sector 316
    financialization signs 221
    historical perspective on structural
        transformation 34, 36, 41, 43, 45
    see also unemployment
Johannesburg Stock Exchange (JSE)
    black economic empowerment 196
    black ownership 40
    corporate governance 225
    dividends and share buybacks 41
    expansion 5–7
    financialization 225, 227
    political economy of structural
        transformation 319*f*, 319–20
    Shoprite 227
joint ventures
    automotive sector 103, 111, 117
    plastic automotive components sector 87, 90
    wine sector 155

Katlego Sitrus 273
Keys, Derek 323
King codes 225
Komatsu 69
Kouga Dam 132, 136–7

Kumba Iron Ore 35, 176n11, 177, 320n8
Kwatani 69

labour market *see* employment
Lall classification 13
land reform 34
learning processes 337
    agricultural sector 124
    black industrialists scheme 204
    and exporting 338
    financial resources 215
    fruit sector 342
    global value-chain integration 288, 290, 294
    holistic framework for structural
        transformation 16–18
    industrial ecosystems approach 340
    'in-out-in' industrialization 294
    manufacturing sector insights 341–3
    metals, machinery, and mining equipment
        sectors 53
    new industrial strategy 350
    wine sector 155
    see also capabilities development; education
        and training
leather sector 290
Lesotho 113
Liebenberg, Chris 323
liquid fuels sector 194–5
living standards 16, 237
LNM 62
local content 923
    automotive sector 8, 100, 272
        development 103, 105, 106
        international context 101, 102
        localization and transformation prospects
            in supply chain 114–15
        ownership changes and supply-chain
            development 112, 114*t*
        scale of production and structural
            change 107–9
    historical perspective on structural
        transformation 44
    metals, machinery, and mining equipment
        sectors 65–6, 69–72, 74
    plastic automotive components sector 89, 90
    Zuma administration 44
local production systems (LPS) 293–4, 317
London Stock Exchange (LSE) 40, 41

machinery and equipment sector 53–4,
        66–7, 73–5
    agriculture 124
    capabilities development, obstacles to 346

machinery and equipment sector (*cont.*)
  economic power and inequality 166,
    172–7, 181–3
  employment 10
  exports 10, 14, 338
  global value-chain integration 304
  industrial policies, power, and
    governance 61–2
  insights from 340, 341
  missed opportunities for structural
    transformation 54–61
  missing ecosystem ingredients 71–3
  performance 58*t*
  political economy of structural
    transformation 315, 317
  power asymmetries 68–71
  South Africa compared to other countries
    60–1, 60*f*
  technological capabilities and digitalization
    67–8
  trade balance 59–60, 59*f*
  value added 36
machine tools sector 300
macroeconomic policy
  capabilities development, obstacles to 346, 349
  evolution 324–5, 327
  financialization 221
  historical perspective on structural
    transformation 41, 42, 43
  middle-income trap 256
  post-Covid-19 world 356
  stability 338–9
Main Supply agreement 178
Malaysia
  affirmative action policies 191, 192
  automotive sector 102
  GDP trends 240–2, 241*f*
  machinery and equipment exports 14
  middle-income technology trap 245*t*,
    245, 246
  middle-income trap 238, 239, 240–2,
    254*t*, 256
  premature deindustrialization 251, 251*t*
  Sasol 226
  South Africa's structural transformation
    compared to 6*t*, 7
Mandela administration (1994–99) 322–4
Mandela Mining Precinct,
  Johannesburg 72–3, 74, 279
Manufacturing Competitiveness Enhancement
  Programme 329
Manufacturing, Engineering, and Related
  Services Authority (MERSETA) 71

manufacturing execution systems (MES) 265*b*,
  266, 280
manufacturing sector
  and agriculture sector, blurring of boundaries
    between 123, 124
  black industrialists scheme 200–7
  climate crisis 354
  deindustrialization 338
  digitalization 267–8, 277
    transversal technologies 263, 263*t*,
      265–6, 265*b*
  economic power and inequality 165–7,
    171–2, 180, 180
  emerging perspectives on structural
    transformation 3–4
  failure to diversify 7–14, 13*f*, 35–7
  financialization 219, 221
  global value-chain integration 290, 304
  heavy industry's dominance 36–7
  historical perspective on structural
    transformation 28, 29, 30, 33–9, 41–5
  'in-out-in' industrialization 294, 295*f*, 295–6,
    297*f*, 299
  insights from 340–3
  middle-income economies comparison 7
  middle-income technology trap 238,
    242, 245–6
  middle-income trap 240
  'missing middle' phenomenon 290
  performance data 9–10, 11*t*
  political economy of structural
    transformation 312, 318–19, 330
  political settlement and economic policy 325
  and service sector, relationship between 10
  state support 61
  value added 7–9, 8*f*
  see also deindustrialization; industrialization;
    premature deindustrialization;
    reindustrialization
marketing
  fruit sector 317
  'in-out-in' industrialization 292
  metals, machinery, and mining equipment
    sectors 59
  wine sector 148, 152*t*, 153–6, 158
Mauritius 230
Mbeki administration (1999–2008) 42, 194,
  322, 325–7
mergers and acquisitions (MAs) 87, 324
metals sector 53–4, 73–5
  and automotive sector, linkages between 56
  capabilities development, obstacles to 346
  climate crisis 354

economic power and inequality 166,
   172–7, 181–3
exports 60–61, 63, 64, 69, 74, 166, 338
historical perspective on structural
   transformation 35
imports 9
industrial policies, power, and
   governance 9, 61–4
insights from 340, 341
investment 14
Lall classification 13
missed opportunities for structural
   transformation 54–61
performance 58t
political economy of structural
   transformation 315, 316
trade balance 59–60, 59f
value added 7–8, 9, 53, 57, 59, 60, 341n1
see also aluminium sector; iron sector;
   non-ferrous metals sector; steel sector
Methold 193
Metropolitan Life 193
Mexico
   agricultural sector 124
   automotive sector 101, 316
   fruit sector 122, 125, 126f, 127f, 127, 128f
   'in-out-in' industrialization 296
   middle-income trap 239
microeconomic policy 42, 45
middle-class aspirations 5
middle-income countries (MICs)
   digitalization 269, 277–82
   financialization 215, 217–21, 226
   global value-chain integration 296,
      301–4, 303f
   holistic framework for structural
      transformation 16
   'in-out-in' industrialization 296
   political economy of structural
      transformation 330–2
   South Africa's structural transformation
      compared to 6t, 7, 29
middle-income technology trap 237–8, 242–6,
   341, 343
   capabilities development, obstacles
      to 344, 345
   industrial policy 252, 256
   premature deindustrialization 247
middle-income trap 237–42, 256–8
   GDP trends 240–2, 241f
   industrial policy 252–6, 254t, 257–8
   'in-out-in' industrialization 294, 298
   size of businesses 292

Millennium Development Goals (MDGs) 2
Mineral and Petroleum Resources Development
   Act 176n11
minerals and energy complex (MEC) 78, 221n3
   financialization 221, 222, 223
   global value-chain integration 304
minerals sector
   digitalization 269, 271
   economic power and inequality 171, 172
   exports 338
   political economy of structural
      transformation 318, 330, 331
   post-Covid-19 world 356
Mining Charter 43–4, 70, 73
Mining Equipment Manufacturers of South
   Africa (MEMSA) 72
mining machinery and equipment sector 53–4,
   66–7, 73–5
   capabilities development, obstacles to 344
   digitalization 271, 273, 280
   exports 14, 338
   global value-chain integration 289, 306, 307
   industrial policies, power, and
      governance 61–2
   missed opportunities for structural
      transformation 54–61
   missing ecosystem ingredients 71–3
   political economy of structural
      transformation 319, 330
   power asymmetries 68–71
   technological capabilities and
      digitalization 67–8
   trade balance 59–60, 59f
Mining Phakisa initiative 72
mining sector
   apartheid legacy 5
   black economic empowerment 194–5, 197
   digitalization 263, 269
   economic power and inequality 172
   financialization 219, 221–2, 222f, 223f
   global value-chain integration 294, 304
   historical perspective on structural
      transformation 34, 43–4, 45
   'in-out-in' industrialization 294
   insights from 341
   licences 63, 70
   machinery and equipment see mining
      machinery and equipment sector
   political economy of structural
      transformation 315, 330
   political settlement and economic
      policy 326, 328
'missing middle' phenomenon 290

Mitsubishi 298
Mittal, Lakshmi 62
Mittal Steel 62, 63
mobile-phone connectivity 137
modularity 267
Mondi 40
monetary policy
    capabilities development, obstacles to 349
    historical perspective on structural
        transformation 43, 45, 46
    political settlement 324
Motlanthe administration (2008–09) 322, 327
Motor Industry Development Programme
        (MIDP) 100, 103–5, 107–8, 112–13, 342
    historical perspective on structural
        transformation 39
    plastic automotive components sector 90
    value added 8
motor vehicle sector *see* automotive sector
Mozambique
    machinery and equipment sector 60*f*
    natural gas provision to Sasol 9, 35, 173
        179, 226
multinational corporations (MNCs)
    automotive sector 100–1, 117
        development 103, 104–5
        international context 101–3
        localization and transformation prospects
            in supply chain 114
        ownership changes and supply-chain
            development 111–12
        policy, incentives, and state–business
            bargaining 109–11
        scale of production and structural
            change 107
    capabilities development 341
    digitalization 268, 269, 272, 281, 283
    financialization 216, 226
    food and beverages sector 317
    global value chains 19, 292, 306
    metals, machinery, and mining equipment
        sectors 59, 67
    plastic automotive components sector 86–7,
        89–90, 96
    wine sector 148
    see also transnational corporations
Multotec 68, 69

Namibia 60, 60*f*
Naspers 319
National Association of Automobile Manufacturers
    of South Africa (NAAMSA) 116
National Association of Automotive Component
    and Allied Manufacturers
    (NAACAM) 103

National Development Plan 33
National Industrial Participation Programme 65
National Industrial Policy Framework
        (NIPF) 42, 43, 202, 327
    capabilities development, obstacles to 347
    plastic automotive components sector 91, 92
National Party 322
National Planning Commission (NPC) 356
National Policy Framework 5
National Treasury 43
National Union of Metalworkers of South Africa
        (NUMSA) 176–7
natural resources, and global value
        chains 305–7
Netherlands 127, 157
New Africa Investments Limited 193
New Institutional Economics (NIE) 314
New York Stock Exchange 94, 226
New Zealand 148
Nissan 109n6
non-ferrous metals sector 9, 35, 55, 57, 58*t*, 59
non-financial corporations (NFCs),
        financialization 213, 232
    comparative case study analysis 226–31
    micro-level perspective 217–21
    signs of 221, 224
    theoretical perspectives 216

October, Lionel 201
offshore listings 40
offshoring 19
OK Bazaars 227
on-farm production technologies, fruit
        sector 130, 132–3
open innovation 267
original equipment manufacturers (OEMs)
    automotive sector 316, 329, 342
        plastic components 86, 87, 90
    Competitive Supplier Development
        Programme 65n6
    digitalization 275
    global value-chain integration 288–9,
        292, 298
    'in-out-in' industrialization 292, 298
    metals, machinery, and mining equipment
        sectors 56, 65–6, 68–75
outsourcing 19, 34, 39
own brand manufacturing (OBM) 288–9,
        292, 298
own design manufacturing (ODM) 288–9, 292

packaging sector 84, 85, 92
Perishable Produce Export Control Board
        (PPECB) 137
Perodua 102

Peru
  agricultural sector 124
  fruit exports 122, 125, 126f, 126–7, 127f, 128f
petrochemicals sector 82–3, 83f, 172, 194–5
PetroSA 95
phytosanitary standards, fruit sector 129, 130,
    133, 134, 138, 342
plastic products sector 78–9, 80, 96–7
  backward linkages to polymers 81–4, 91–6
  economic power and inequality 172
  employment 10
  forward linkages to automotive sector 36,
    81, 84–91
  industrial policy 9
  insights from 340, 341
  performance 94f, 95
  political economy of structural
    transformation 315–16
  structural change dynamics 81–5
Plastics Institute of Thailand (PITH) 86, 88
Plastics SA 88
platforms, digital 267, 272, 275, 280–1
political economy 312–13
  automotive sector 109–10
  economic power and inequality 168, 183
  emerging perspectives on structural
    transformation 4, 5
  financialization 220, 231, 233
  global patterns of sectoral value addition 302
  global value-chain integration 291
  historical perspective on structural
    transformation 29
  holistic framework for structural
    transformation 20–21
  industry experiences in South Africa 315–22
  lessons from South African case 330–2
  plastic automotive components
    sector 90, 91, 96
  of structural transformation 346–9
  see also political settlements
political settlements 337, 338
  black economic empowerment 192
  economic power and inequality 169–70,
    173–80, 184
  financialization 223
  global value-chain integration 291
  historical perspective on structural
    transformation 28
  holistic framework for structural
    transformation 20–21
  industrial development 313–15, 320–30
  new industrial strategy 349, 351–2
polymers sector 79, 81–4, 91–6, 179
polypropylene sector 179
populism 165, 324, 327, 332

Portnet 42
ports system 44
  agricultural exports 124
  automotive sector 115
  capabilities development, obstacles to 347
  fruit sector 121, 135–6, 139
Portugal 148
Post-Harvest Innovation Programme 133
post-harvest production technologies 130, 134
poultry sector 36
poverty
  capabilities development, obstacles to 348
  financialization 221
  industrialization 2
  inequality and structural
    transformation 170–1
  new industrial strategy 351
  political settlement and economic
    policy 329
Prasa 44
Preferential Procurement Policy Framework Act
    (PPPFA, 2000) 65
premature deindustrialization 1, 13, 246–51,
    253t, 343
  arrest and reversal 256, 257, 349
  capabilities development, obstacles to 347
  digitalization 262
  emerging perspectives on structural
    transformation 4
  financialization 221
  global value-chain integration 296
  identifying 251–2
  middle-income economies comparison 5
  middle-income trap 237–8, 240, 257
  political economy of structural
    transformation 312, 318
  see also reindustrialization
privatization 39, 42, 174, 220, 322
  Iscor 56, 172, 173, 320n8
  Sasol 172, 226
  Telkom 137
  training 346
product lifecycle management (PLM) 265b
product-space analysis 14
profitability
  capabilities development, obstacles to 348
  economic power and inequality 181
  fruit sector 131, 134
  historical perspective on structural
    transformation 29–30, 31t, 33–4, 39,
    40, 44–5
  and industrialization 214
  new industrial strategy 350
  political economy of structural
    transformation 319, 332

profitability (*cont.*)
  political settlement and economic policy 329
  Sasol 94
  wine sector 157
  without investment *see* financialization
property prices 224
Proton 102
public procurement
  black economic empowerment 196, 326
  capabilities development, obstacles
      to 346, 347
  historical perspective on structural
      transformation 28, 41, 43
  metals, machinery, and mining equipment
      sectors 59, 61, 62, 64–6
  political settlement and economic
      policy 328, 329

Qatar 226

radio frequency identification (RFID) 273
rail system
  automotive sector 115
  capabilities development, obstacles to 347
  historical perspective on structural
      transformation 44
  Transnet 65–6
Ramaphosa administration (2018–) 45, 322, 347
Reconstruction and Development Programme
      (RDP) 39
refined petroleum products sector 9, 14, 35,
      172, 341n1
  performance 82t, 84, 84n1
regional opportunities 353–4
regional value chains *see* value chains
reindustrialization 41, 258
  digitalization 269, 283
  economic power and inequality 184
  importance 21
  new industrial strategy 349, 350, 351–2
  in a post-Covid-19 world 355–6
Rembrandt 36, 320n6
Remgro 36, 40, 320n6
rents
  automotive sector 102
  capabilities development, obstacles to 347
  chemicals-to-plastics sector 178, 182, 183
  economic power and inequality 171
  financialization 219, 220, 223, 226, 232
  global value chains 146
  historical perspective on structural
      transformation 28–9, 41, 44, 46
  metals, machinery, and equipment sector 66,
      73, 182, 183

new industrial strategy 353
political economy of structural
      transformation 320, 321, 331
political settlement and economic policy 313,
      314, 315, 328, 329
steel sector 174–5, 176, 177
research and development (RD)
  automotive sector 100, 102, 103, 111
  capabilities development, obstacles to 345
  digitalization 279–80
  fruit sector 121, 130, 133, 134, 138
  inequality and structural
      transformation 168, 176
  'in-out-in' industrialization 292
  middle-income technology trap 245t, 245, 256
  mining machinery and equipment
      sector 70, 72
  plastic automotive components
      sector 86, 87, 88
  steel sector 176
  see also innovation
Research for Citrus Exports programme 133
Reserve Bank 323
reshoring 19
residual claimant theories of the firm 217
retail sector 219, 338
  supplier development programmes 200
  see also supermarket sector
Richemont 320n6
robotics 269, 273, 275, 345
Romania 296–8
Russia 176

SABMiller 319, 320n6
Safripol 83, 95, 179
Saldanha Steel 62, 63
Sandvik 69
sanitary and phytosanitary standards, fruit
      sector 129, 130, 133, 134, 138, 342
Sanlam 193
Sasol 9, 79, 83, 92–6, 348
  economic power and inequality 173, 174,
      178–9, 182, 183
  financialization 213, 226–7, 228–31, 229f, 232
  historical perspective on structural
      transformation 35
  insights from 341
  investment 14
  political economy of structural
      transformation 316
  privatization 172
Saudi Arabia 239
Scaw Metals 36, 56, 173, 174, 175
sectoral value addition, global patterns of 301–4

Sector Education and Training Authorities
  (SETAs) 71, 346
service sector 338
  economic power and inequality 167, 171, 180–1
  emerging perspectives on structural
    transformation 3–4
  employment 10, 12t
  historical perspective on structural
    transformation 34, 37
  and manufacturing sector, relationship
    between 10
  middle-income technology trap 246
  middle-income trap 258
  political economy 312
  value added 10, 12t
shareholder value maximization (SVM)
  ideology 216–17, 224, 225, 232, 326
share repurchases 41, 213, 217, 220, 225, 232
  comparative case study analysis 228, 231
Shoprite 213, 226, 227–31, 229f, 232
Slovakia 110
social sustainability 144
sorting technologies, fruit sector 134
South Africa Foundation 36
South African Auto Masterplan (SAAM) 90–1,
  100n1, 105, 109, 115, 117, 272
South African Berries Association 133
South African Breweries (SAB) 40
South African Capital Equipment Export
  Council (SACEEC) 58–9
South African Communist Party (SACP) 328n11
South African Research Chairs Initiative
  (SARChI) in Industrial Development,
  University of Johannesburg 122
Southern African Development Community
  (SADC) 60f, 61, 353–4
South Korea
  automotive sector 102
  global value-chain integration 286, 289, 291,
    292, 307
  'in-out-in' industrialization 293, 294, 298–9,
    299f, 300–1, 344
  late industrialization 2
Spain 120, 138, 148, 149
Special Economic Zones, China 300
Stals, Chris 323
state-owned corporations (SOCs)
  black industrialists scheme 202
  Competitive Supplier Development
    Programme 65n6
  corporate governance 225
  financialization 220
  historical perspective on structural
    transformation 39, 41–5

steel sector 73
  economic power and inequality 172,
    174–7, 182
  financialization 219
  global value-chain integration 293
  historical perspective on structural
    transformation 35, 39
  imports 9
  industrial policies, power, and
    governance 61–4
  insights from 341
  missed opportunities for structural
    transformation 55–6, 57, 59
  performance 58t
  political economy of structural
    transformation 320
  political settlement and economic
    policy 174–7, 325
  trade balance 59
  value added 9
stock market
  capitalization 213, 222f
  expansion 5–7, 20
  financialization 224, 225, 228
  see also Johannesburg Stock Exchange
Strategic Industrial Projects (SIP) 325
Strategic Investment Programme (SIP) 92
structural change 28–30, 44–6
  investment and manufacturing
    profitability 30–7
  phases and processes 37–44
structural regression 317–20
structural transformation 1–2, 20
  emerging perspectives 2–5
  exports, failure to diversify 14–16, 15f
  forward and backward linkages 79–81
  foundations 339–43
  holistic framework 16–21
  manufacturing sector, failure to
    diversify 7–14
  middle-income economies comparison 5–7
sugar sector 36
supermarket sector 36, 350
  Shoprite 213, 226, 227–31, 229f, 232
sustainable development
  automotive sector 110, 114, 306
  capital accumulation in global value
    chains 145–7
  emerging perspectives on structural
    transformation 5
  fruit sector 121
  new industrial strategy 350
  see also environmental sustainability
Sustainable Development Goals (SDGs) 2, 145

Taiwan
  electronics sector 290
  global value-chain integration 286, 290,
    292, 294
  'in-out-in' industrialization 294, 344
Tanzania 7, 60f, 61
tariffs 12, 38–9, 41
  automotive sector 101, 103, 104, 107
  digital transactions 281
  economic power and inequality 175, 181
  food and beverages sector 36
  liberalization 338
  metals, machinery, and mining equipment
    sectors 64, 71, 73, 74
  plastic products sector 315–16
  political settlement and economic policy 329
  steel sector 175, 341
taxation
  digital technology policy 279, 281
  financialization 225
  inequality and structural transformation 173
  manufacturing sector 61n2
  metals sector 63
  mining machinery and equipment sector 72
  plastic products sector 92
tax havens 230
technical and vocational education and training
    see education and training
technological change 337
  agricultural sector 123
  automotive sector 100, 106, 107, 111, 112,
    115, 117
  black industrialists scheme 205
  capabilities development, obstacles
    to 343, 345
  economic power and inequality 168, 181
  emerging perspectives on structural
    transformation 4, 5
  financialization 215
  fruit sector 121, 122, 130–4, 139
  global value-chain integration 288,
    293–4, 305–6
  green capital accumulation 143
  historical perspective on structural
    transformation 37
  holistic framework for structural
    transformation 18–19
  industrial ecosystem 349
  'in-out-in' industrialization 293–4
  metals, machinery, and mining equipment
    sectors 53, 56, 58, 67, 75
  middle-income trap 254t, 256, 257, 258
    see also middle-income technology trap
  new industrial strategy 352–3
  plastic products sector 79, 86–8, 89

political settlements 313
post-Covid-19 world 356
premature deindustrialization 247
rivalry, importance of 190
structural transformation through forward
    and backward linkages 80–1
  see also digitalization; fourth industrial
    revolution
technology infrastructure 86–7
technology policy 331
telecommunications see information and
    communication technology
Telkom 137
textiles sector see clothing, textiles, and
    footwear sector
Thai Automotive Masterplan 89
Thailand
  automotive sector 101, 105, 115, 316, 342
  capabilities development 341
  machinery and equipment exports 14
  plastic automotive components
    sector 85–90, 96
  plastic products sector 36
  South Africa's structural transformation
    compared to 6t, 7
'thin industrialization 268, 287
Toyota 88
Trade and Industrial Policy Strategies
    (TIPS) 122, 122n4
trade fairs 59
trade liberalization 9, 12, 337
  automotive sector 101
  chemicals sector 83
  diversification 13
  financialization 224, 232
  historical perspective on structural
    transformation 34, 36, 38–9
  inequality and structural
    transformation 170–3
  manufacturing sector insights 343
  middle-income economies comparison 5
  political economy of structural
    transformation 317–18, 321, 332
  political settlement 322, 324–5
trade policy
  automotive sector 105
  digitalization 281
  financialization 220
  historical perspective on structural
    transformation 43, 46
  metals, machinery, and mining equipment
    sectors 71, 74
trade unions 322, 328, 352
training see education and training
transition stage, automotive sector 108t, 108

transnational corporations (TNCs)
economic power and inequality 181
global value-chain integration 289, 291, 296-8
'in-out-in' industrialization 296-8
political economy of structural
transformation 319-20
steel sector 62
see also multinational corporations
Transnet 42, 44, 65-6, 136, 328
transparency
digitalization 273
financialization 223
fruit sector 130
New Institutional Economics 314
transversal technologies 262-6, 345
data flow across 264f
key features 263t
Tripartite Alliance 328
Turkey 6t, 101, 102, 115

unemployment 16
capabilities development, obstacles to 347
Covid-19 pandemic 355
digitalization 262
financialization signs 221
fruit sector 121
historical perspective on structural
transformation 36-7, 41
new industrial strategy 351
political economy of structural
transformation 312, 322
political settlement and economic
policy 327, 329
see also job losses
United Exports 131
United Kingdom
Economic and Social Research Council
(ESRC), Global Challenges Research
Fund 122
financialization 225, 228, 230
fruit imports 127
Isle of Man tax haven 230
share repurchases 225
wine sector 148, 149, 155, 157
United Nations (UN)
Millennium Development Goals 2
Sustainable Development Goals 2, 145
United States
'Digital 2 Dozen' 274
exports to South African black
industrialists 205
Federal Reserve 220
financialization 217, 218, 220, 225, 228
fruit sector 131
geopolitical tensions 304

high-tech TNCs in Mexico 296
machine tools sector 300
middle-income countries' GDP trends relative
to 240-2, 241f
mining machinery and equipment
sector 69, 306
Sasol investments 229, 230
share repurchases 225
wine sector 148-9, 157
upper-middle income countries, South Africa's
structural transformation compared
to 6t, 7
Uruguay 239
Uzbekistan 226

value added 338
automotive sector 8, 36, 106, 110, 112,
113f, 316
black industrialists scheme 205
capabilities development, obstacles to 344-5
chemicals sector 7, 9, 81, 341n1
digitalization 273
food and beverage sector 316
global patterns of sectoral value
addition 301-4
global value chains 287, 291, 305-7
'in-out-in' industrialization 292-6, 298,
299, 301
'smile' curve 19, 290
historical perspective on structural
transformation 34, 35
inequality and structural transformation 171
machinery and equipment sector 53,
57, 59, 60
manufacturing sector 11t, 14, 35, 36, 341
failure to diversify 7-10, 8f
metals sector 7-8, 9, 53, 57, 59, 60, 341n1
middle-income economies comparison 7
middle-income technology trap 242, 243f
middle-income trap 258
new industrial strategy 349, 353, 354
plastic products sector 83, 91
political economy 312
premature deindustrialization 247, 257
service sector 12t
'thin industrialization' 268
value chains
automotive sector 100-1, 104, 107, 115
black economic empowerment 194-5,
197-200
capabilities development, obstacles
to 345, 346
chemicals sector 81, 166, 181
digitalization 263, 265, 269-74, 277-8,
280, 282

value chains (*cont.*)
  economic power and inequality 166, 176,
    177–8, 179, 181, 184
  financialization 214, 219–20, 226, 231, 232
  fruit sector 130, 131, 342
  global *see* global value chains
  governance 80
  industrial ecosystems approach 339–40
  liquid fuels and petroleum sector 194–5
  machinery and equipment sector 54–7, 55*f*,
    61, 64, 68, 74
  manufacturing sector insights 341
  metals sector 54–7, 55*f*, 61, 64, 68, 74,
    166, 181
  middle-income trap 256
  mining sector 194–5
  new industrial strategy 349, 354–5
  petrochemical 82–3, 83*f*, 94, 177–8, 179
  plastic products sector 81, 85–6, 88, 91, 94–7
  political economy of structural
    transformation 315–16, 331
  post-Covid-19 world 356
  power dynamics 19
  premature deindustrialization 257
  Shoprite 231
  steel sector 176, 177
  wine sector 144, 152–8
vocational training *see* education and vocational
    training
Volume Assembly Allowance (VAA) 106

wages
  economic power and inequality 175, 180–1
  global value-chain integration 291–4
  historical perspective on structural
    transformation 36

'in-out-in' industrialization 292–4
  new industrial strategy 350
  political settlement and economic
    policy 327, 328
  steel sector 175
Washington Consensus 221, 339
water resources
  agricultural exports 124
  fruit sector 121, 132–3, 136–7, 139
Wine and Agricultural Ethical Trade Association
    (WIETA) 152
wine sector
  economic and environmental
    upgrading 147–58, 154*t*
  green capital accumulation 144, 158
  political economy of structural
    transformation 316
  top marketers 152*t*
  top wine-consuming countries 151*t*
  top wine-producing countries 150*t*
women employees 205
World Bank 225
World Cup (2010) 41, 325
World Trade Organization (WTO) 39, 104, 281

youth employment 205

Zambia 60, 60*f*
Zimbabwe 60*f*, 61
Zondo Commission of Inquiry into State
    Capture 65–6
Zuma administration (2009–2018) 322, 327–30,
    331, 332, 347
  black economic empowerment 197
  corruption 44, 328n12, 329, 330
  state capture process 177